TURKEY UNVEILED

TURKEY UNVEILED

ATATÜRK AND AFTER

Nicole and Hugh Pope

JOHN MURRAY
Albemarle Street, London

The poem *Byzantium* by Sidney Wade, excerpted on p. 339, first appeared in the *New England Review*, Spring 1996

First published in 1997
by John Murray (Publishers) Ltd.,
50 Albemarle Street, London W1X 4BD

The moral right of the authors has been asserted

A catalogue record for this book is available from the British Library

ISBN 0 7195 5653 8

Typeset in Postscript Baskerville by
Rowland Phototypesetting Ltd.,
Bury St Edmunds, Suffolk
Printed and bound in Great Britain by
The University Press, Cambridge

For Vanessa and Amanda

Contents

Illustrations

The authors and publisher would like to thank the following for permission to reproduce illustrations: 1, Topkapı Palace Museum; 2, Turkish Ministry of Culture; 8, Patrick Pope; 9, Landroos; 10, *Cumhuriyet* newspaper; 11, 12, Reuters; 13, Riza Ezer; 14, *Turkish Daily News*; 15, 18, Fatih Saribas; 21, Sipa Press; 23, 25, Ara Güler; 6, 24, George Simpson. Plates 3, 4, 5, 7, 16, 17, 19, 20 and 22 were taken by Hugh Pope.

Acknowledgements

TURKEY IS A country of such fertile complexity that we have seen almost any theory about its politics and society sincerely argued and apparently conclusively proven. Each passing year throws up new areas of controversy, making it clear that no one person or institution can claim to know everything about this ancient land. Not surprisingly, even Turkey's most senior leaders and officials often appear to be caught off guard by events.

Over our nine years of reporting about Turkey, our understanding of the country has above all been broadened by the explanations of our Turkish friends and colleagues, and by government officials when they escape the bombast of formal statements. We have also benefited enormously from the informal help of correspondents for Turkish newspapers in the provinces, who, despite the depth of their knowledge of local affairs, have rarely had an opportunity to express this expertise in print.

A list of all the people to whom we are indebted would be very long, but we would like to express our particular thanks to Professor Asaf Savaş Akat, Şahin Alpay, Murat Belge, Yiğit Bener, Mehmet Ali Birand, Hasan Cemal, Ilnur Çevik, Professor Selim Deringil, Professor Nilüfer Göle, Semih Idiz, former minister Kamran Inan, Elif Kaban, Neyyir Kalaycıoğlu, Professor Çağlar Keyder, Merih Kılıçaslan, Dr Kemal Kirişçi, Sami Kohen, Fehmi Koru, Dr Gün Kut, Bishop Meşrob Mutafyan, Ambassador Özdem Sanberk, Fatih Sarıbaş, Ayşe Sarıoğlu, Ambassador Murat Sungar, and Professor Binnaz Toprak. Ertuğrul Pirinççioğlu and his team at *Milliyet* newspaper's Diyarbakır bureau offered a haven of hospitality and wisdom. The unfailing nerve of one particular Diyarbakır driver and his calm management of volatile armed men at checkpoints also saved us from moments of danger.

This book might have gone unwritten but for the enthusiasm and encouragement of Kathleen and Peter Hopkirk, and of our editor, Gail Pirkis. We would also like to thank others for their help and comments: John Ash, Jim Bodgener, Janet Douglas, Caroline and Andrew Finkel, Dolores and John Freely, Thomas Goltz, Dr Tony Greenwood and the staff of the American Research

Institute in Turkey, William Hale, Renée Hirschon, Philip Remler, Philip Robins, Jonathan Rugman and, most of all, Maurice Pope. Dr Lucienne Thys-Şenocak of Koç University offered invaluable advice. Without Harvey Morris and Charles Richards, former editors at the *Independent*, as well as William D. Montalbano of the *Los Angeles Times*, much of the reporting might not have been done. Patrick Pope was a sterling travelling companion to the remotest destinations and selfless in his photographic assistance. Our thanks also to Howard Davies, whose sharp eyes did much to focus our text. Of course any judgements and mistakes remain our own.

To Virginia Brown Keyder we owe a debt of gratitude for the many cups of coffee and visits that kept our morale high. Our daughters Vanessa and Amanda showed exemplary patience. And the enterprise would have been all but impossible without the constant help and presence of Şerafettin and Hayriye Doğan.

Lastly we would like to pay tribute to the inspiration of the late Jean-Pierre Thieck, a passionate orientalist without whose guidance and unfailing enthusiasm Hugh might never have come to the Middle East, and who passed to Nicole the flame he carried in reporting for *Le Monde*. We still miss him greatly.

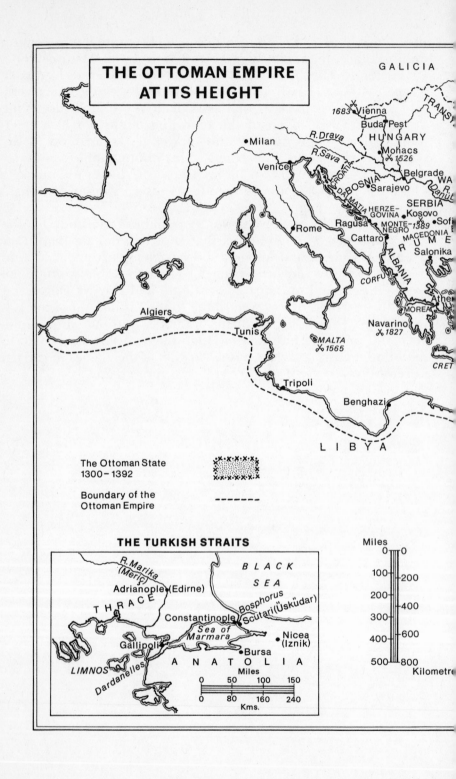

THE OTTOMAN EMPIRE AT ITS HEIGHT

GALICIA

TRANS

1683 •Vienna

Buda Pest

HUNGARY

•Milan

R.Drava

R.Sava

Mohacs
× 1526

Venice

CROATIA

Belgrade

WA

Danut

•Milan

BOSNIA

Sarajevo

SERBIA

DALMATIA

HERZE-
GOVINA   Kosovo

Rome

Ragusa   MONTE- 1389   •Sof
NEGRO

Cattaro   MACEDONIA

R
U
M
E

Salonika

ALBANIA

CORFU

Athe

MOREA

Algiers

Navarino
× 1827

Tunis

×MALTA
× 1565

CRET

Tripoli

Benghazi

L I B Y A

The Ottoman State
1300–1392

Boundary of the
Ottoman Empire

THE TURKISH STRAITS

R. Marika
(Meriç)

Adrianople (Edirne)

B L A C K
S E A

T H R A C E

Bosphorus

Constantinople   Scutari(Üsküdar)

Sea of
Marmara

Nicea
(Iznik)

Gallipoli

•Bursa

LIMNOS

A N A T O L I A

Dardanelles

Miles
0   50   100   150

0   80   160   240
Kms.

Miles
0   0

100   200

200   400

300   600

400

500   800
Kilometre

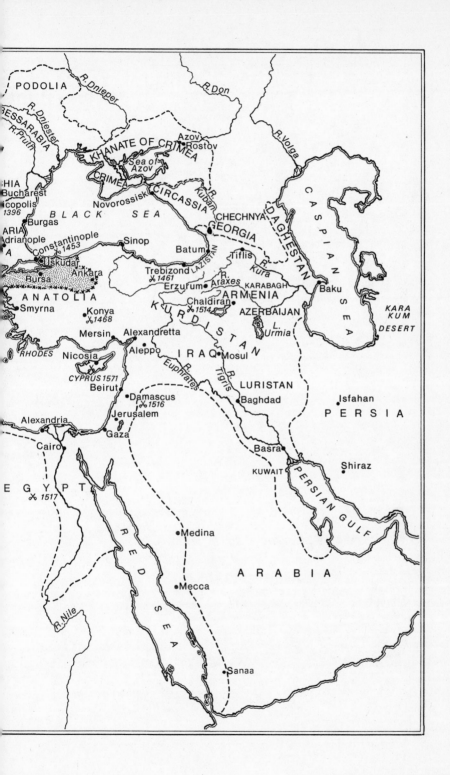

PODOLIA

R.Dnieper

BESSARABIA
R.Dniester
R.Pruth

R.Don

Azov
Rostov

KHANATE OF CRIMEA

Sea of
Azov

R.Volga

CRIMEA

CIRCASSIA

Novorossisk

C A S P I A N   S E A

CHIA
Bucharest
icopolis
1396

B L A C K   S E A

Burgas

CHECHNYA
GEORGIA

DAGHESTAN

ARIA
drianople
A

Constantinople
1453
Uskudar

Sinop

Batum

Tiflis
R.
Kura

KARA
KUM
DESERT

Ankara

Trebizond
1461

LAZISTAN

Baku

Bursa

ANATOLIA

Erzurum

R.
Araxes

KARABAGH

Smyrna

Konya
1468

Chaldiran
1514

ARMENIA

AZERBAIJAN

K U R D I S T A N

L.
Urmia

Mersin

Alexandretta

RHODES

Nicosia

Aleppo

I R A Q

Mosul

CYPRUS 1571

Beirut

Euphrates

R.
Tigris

LURISTAN

Damascus
1516

Baghdad

Isfahan

P E R S I A

Alexandria

Jerusalem

Cairo

Gaza

Basra

Shiraz

KUWAIT

E G Y P T
1517

PERSIAN GULF

Medina

R E D   S E A

A R A B I A

Mecca

R.Nile

Sanaa

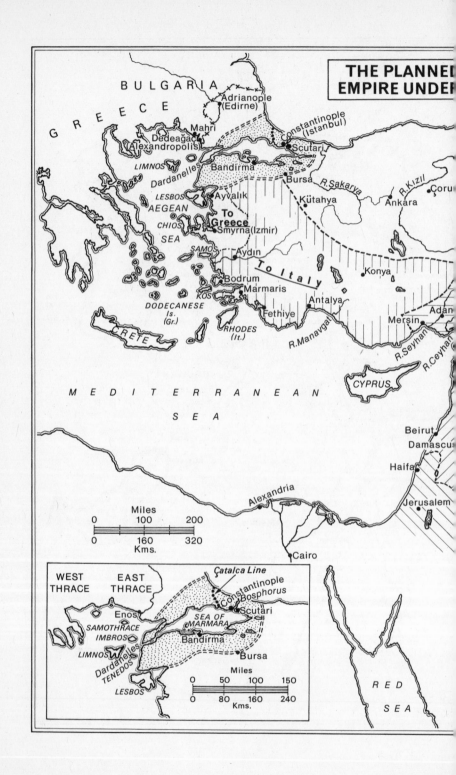

THE PLANNED
EMPIRE UNDER

BULGARIA

GREECE

Adrianople
(Edirne)

Mahri
Dedeağacı
(Alexandropolis)

Constantinople
(Istanbul)

Scutari

LIMNOS
Dardanelles

Bandirma

Bursa

R.Sakarya

R.Kizil

Çoru

LESBOS
AEGEAN

Ayvalık

Kütahya

Ankara

Ş

CHIOS
SEA

To
Greece

Smyrna(Izmir)

SAMOS

Aydın

To Italy

Konya

Bodrum
Marmaris

Antalya

Adan

DODECANESE
Is.
(Gr.)

KOS

Fethiye

Mersin

CRETE

RHODES
(It.)

R.Manavgat

R.Seyhan

R.Ceyhan

MEDITERRANEAN

SEA

CYPRUS

Beirut

Damascu

Haifa

Alexandria

Jerusalem

Miles
0   100   200
0   160   320
Kms.

Cairo

WEST
THRACE

EAST
THRACE

Çatalca Line

Constantinople
Bosphorus
Scutari

Enos

SAMOTHRACE
IMBROS

SEA OF
MARMARA

LIMNOS
Dardanelles
TENEDOS

Bandirma

Bursa

LESBOS

Miles
0   50   100   150
0   80   160   240
Kms.

RED

SEA

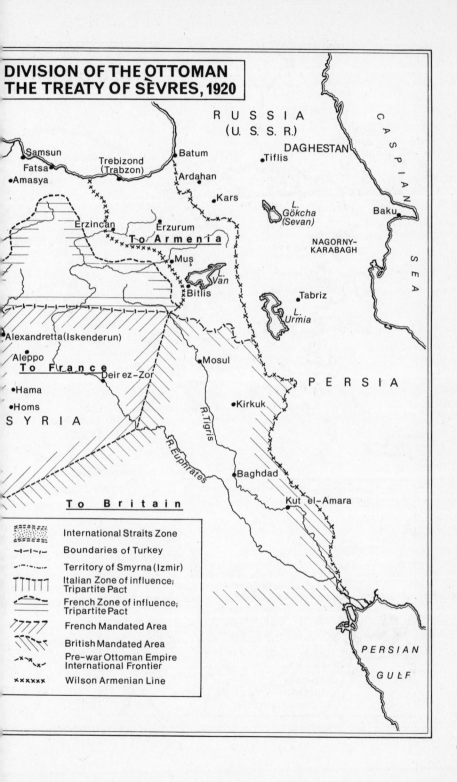

DIVISION OF THE OTTOMAN
THE TREATY OF SÈVRES, 1920

R U S S I A
(U. S. S. R.)

DAGHESTAN

C A S P I A N   S E A

Samsun
Fatsa
Amasya
Trebizond
(Trabzon)
Batum
Ardahan
Kars
Tiflis

L.
Gökcha
(Sevan)

Baku

Erzincan
Erzurum
To Armenia
Muş
Van
Bitlis

NAGORNY-
KARABAGH

Tabriz

L.
Urmia

Alexandretta (Iskenderun)
Aleppo
To France
Deir ez-Zor
Hama
Homs
S Y R I A

Mosul

P E R S I A

Kirkuk

R. Tigris

R. Euphrates

To Britain

Baghdad

Kut el-Amara

P E R S I A N
G U L F

International Straits Zone	
Boundaries of Turkey	
Territory of Smyrna (Izmir)	
Italian Zone of influence; Tripartite Pact	
French Zone of influence; Tripartite Pact	
French Mandated Area	
British Mandated Area	
Pre-war Ottoman Empire International Frontier	
Wilson Armenian Line	

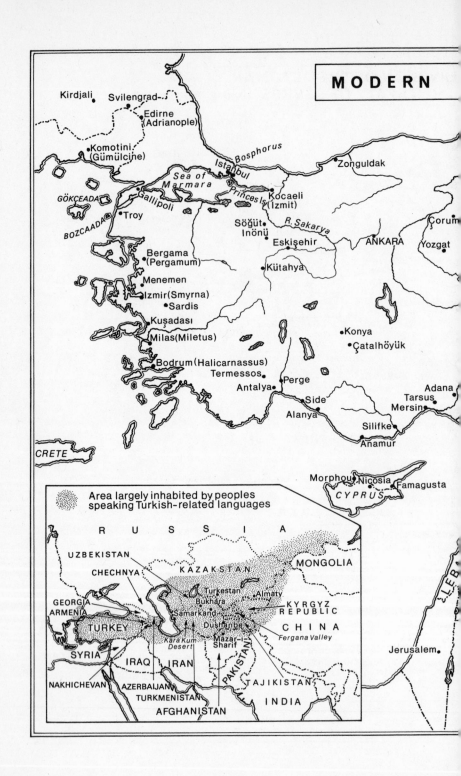

MODERN

Kirdjali · Svilengrad
Edirne
(Adrianople)
Komotini
(Gümülcine)
Bosphorus
İstanbul · Zonguldak
Sea of Marmara
GÖKÇEADA
Gallipoli · Princes Is. · Kocaeli (İzmit)
· Troy
BOZCAADA
Söğüt · *R. Sakarya* · Çorum
İnönü
Eskişehir · ANKARA · Yozgat
Bergama
(Pergamum)
Kütahya
Menemen
İzmir(Smyrna)
· Sardis
Kuşadası · Konya
Milas(Miletus) · Çatalhöyük
Bodrum(Halicarnassus)
Termessos · Adana
Antalya · Perge · Tarsus
Side · Mersin
Alanya · Silifke
Anamur
CRETE
Morphou · Nicosia · Famagusta
CYPRUS

Area largely inhabited by peoples speaking Turkish-related languages

R U S S I A

UZBEKISTAN
CHECHNYA
KAZAKSTAN · MONGOLIA
Turkestan · Almaty
GEORGIA · Bukhara · KYRGYZ
ARMENIA · Samarkand · REPUBLIC
TURKEY · Dushanbe · C H I N A
Kara Kum · Mazar-i- · *Fergana Valley*
Desert · Sharif
SYRIA · IRAQ · IRAN · Jerusalem
· TAJIKISTAN
NAKHICHEVAN · AZERBAIJAN · I N D I A
TURKMENISTAN
AFGHANISTAN
LEB

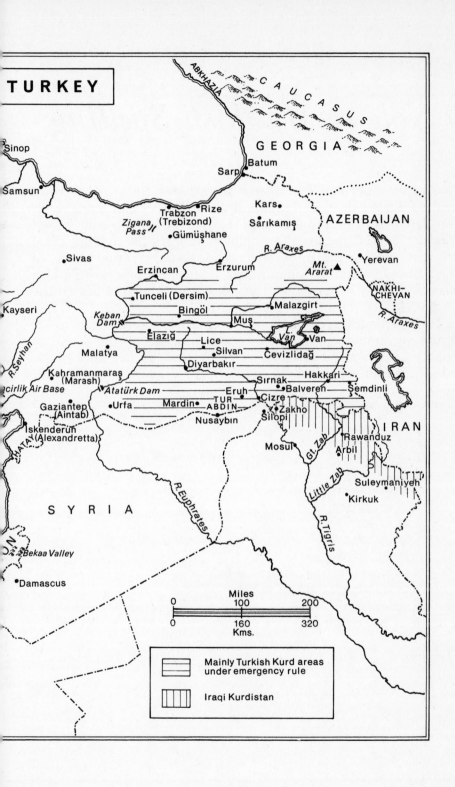

TURKEY

Sinop

Samsun

CAUCASUS

GEORGIA

ABKHAZIA

Batum

Sarp

Trabzon
(Trebizond)   Rize

Zigana
Pass

Gümüşhane

Kars

Sarıkamış

AZERBAIJAN

R. Araxes

Yerevan

Sivas

Erzincan

Erzurum

Mt.
Ararat

NAKHI-
CHEVAN

R. Araxes

Kayseri

Tunceli (Dersim)

Keban
Dam

Bingöl

Elazığ

Lice

Malatya

Silvan

Diyarbakır

Kahramanmaraş
(Marash)

çirlik Air Base

Atatürk Dam

Gaziantep
(Aintab)

İskenderun
(Alexandretta)

HATAY

Urfa

Malazgirt

Muş

Van

Çevizlidağ

Şırnak

Eruh

Mardin

TUR
ABDIN

Nusaybın

Cizre

Silopi

Hakkari

Balveren   Şemdinli

Zakho

Mosul

Gt. Zab

Rawanduz

Arbil

IRAN

Little Zab

SYRIA

R. Euphrates

R. Tigris

Süleymaniyeh

Kirkuk

Bekaa Valley

Damascus

Miles
100   200
0
0   160   320
Kms.

Mainly Turkish Kurd areas
under emergency rule

Iraqi Kurdistan

Note on Turkish Spelling

Like other aspects of Turkey that appear Western but have roots in the East, the modern Turkish alphabet looks Latin but is partly translated from the Arabic script that preceded it. We have used modern Turkish spellings throughout, and beg the indulgence of scholars used to the more traditional Arabic transliterations of the names of Ottoman sultans. Like many contemporary Turkish writers, we have dropped the caps on *â*, *î* and *û* that indicated the Ottoman usage of a written Arabic vowel.

Turkish names can look intimidating to newcomers, particularly until one remembers that a '*c*' is pronounced '*dj*' (the sound of the third letter in the outgoing Arabic alphabet). But most of the twenty-nine letters sound the same as in English and every Turkish word is pronounced exactly as it is written. We hope the following outline of usages will ease the reader's path.

c as in 'janissary'
ç as in '*church*', e.g. Çiller is pronounced 'CHILL-er'
g hard g: 'galatasaray'
ğ soft g: as in 'nei*gh*bour'
ı as in 'do*z*en'
i as in 'p*i*n'
j as in 'plea*s*ure'
o as in 'h*o*rde'
ö as in '*u*rge', e.g. 'd*ö*ner kebab'
ş as in '*sh*oe', e.g. '*şiş* kebab'
u as in 'p*u*t'
ü as in French 't*u*'

The letters *q*, *w* and *x* are not used for spelling Turkish words.

Introduction

Turkey, patriarchal in its naïve and smiling
simplicity, would amaze our benighted
romantics; it would astonish many among us
who have lost their Christian faith, but have
preserved their anti-Muslim prejudice.

Claude Farrère, 1925

WE STILL FIND it hard to pin down precisely when we fell in
love with Turkey. Perhaps it was through our young children,
when the first moustachioed and apparently fierce Turk's face
melted into an open and loving smile at the sight of a small baby.
Or maybe it was being offered a loan by an unknown taxi-driver
after finding we had no money at the end of a long ride. Or
perhaps it was during a visit to the set of Turkey's best-known,
most hilarious and most compassionate troupe of comedians.

On that day the tragedies of Turkish life came full circle with
comic art as we left the company's production building amid the
mud, diesel fumes and concrete of a Dickensian suburb of Istanbul. An old man was sitting in wait and appealed for help from
the group's comic hero. 'You know how to dress up so well,' the
old man said, slowly peeling bandages off his head to reveal a
horrible cavity where doctors had just cut out the middle of his
face. 'Could you possibly spare me a nose?'

Still wearing his baggy Ottoman costume from the set, the com-
edian, suddenly serious, called for his make-up box. Without a
trace of impatience or condescension, he offered the old man
hooked noses, long noses and pimply noses to try on. Then he
said gently: 'Take whichever one you like, but don't you think you
need something a little more permanent?'

Compassion, humour and a sense of the tragic are not qualities generally attributed to Turkey in the West. Indeed, our own first impressions of the country nearly crushed us. Driving in from Istanbul's low-lying concrete airport, the air was dark and pungent with yellow-grey lignite smog, and the winter morning seemed barely to have dawned. A sullen sky pressed down all around us. From the rain-spattered windows of our clumsy Turkish-built taxi it seemed we were edging through a tunnel of thick traffic into a miserable underworld. It was a place where one could also imagine the bleak, feudal fatalism of Yılmaz Güney's film *Yol*, or the outrageous brutality of Alan Parker's film *Midnight Express*.

But in time our hearts were won over, not just by the people, but also by sweeping skylines of domes and minarets, by the calming patterns of Iznik pottery and by hours of soft padding through carpet bazaars. We also felt a sense of achievement, a stubborn pride in hard-won victories over the bureaucracy or in the purchase of arcane pieces of household equipment. We also felt a sense of discovery as our understanding of the Turkish language cleared. Nothing in Turkey was quite as it seemed at first, and indeed was sometimes almost deliberately disguised.

We also learned not to force on Turkey any easy categorization: European, Western, Eastern, Islamic, fascistic, anarchic, whatever. It has something of all these elements, of course. But Turkey is in a category all its own. One reason for the West's difficulty in coming to grips with the country is that Turkey was never colonized and has never truly shared its history with one of the great European cultures. Nor has it been respectably grand, rich or independent enough in modern history to have attracted much literary, diplomatic or historic attention. Seen from Britain, for instance, Turkey has been either a minor wartime enemy, a poor cousin to oil-rich Iran and Arab states or simply a less powerful attraction than Persia, for whom Britons inherited a strategic fascination from the Indian Raj.

Impressions of Turkey almost always depend on the point from which the visitor approaches it. A visitor to Istanbul from Western Europe may see a poor copy of an East European city, which, despite its Westernizing airs, turns out to be run on frustratingly oriental lines. We had come from years of experience in the east, from Beirut, Tehran, and Baghdad: to us, Istanbul looked nearly as sophisticated as a Western European city. Turkish society, perhaps because of its lack of easy oil money, or the deep, long traditions of its state, also seemed to be built on a more solid and pluralistic foundation than those further east. We liked what the Turks had kept of their Muslim, eastern heritage – a heritage the Turks themselves were increasingly appreciating in the 1990s – but were glad of what they had learned from the West.

We also came to appreciate a country which, compared to the mature economies of Europe, is still involved in an amazing adventure of change. Turkey's present-day economy is commonly compared to that of Spain twenty years ago; in some places it has caught up, yet in others it feels as if one is being given a privileged glimpse of what life might have been like in nineteenth-century London. We learned to overcome our own cultural and political prejudices about the Turks, which, although not realizing it at the time, we had brought with us as part of the baggage of our Western education. We hope this book will help to overcome some of the ideas about the country that go unchallenged in the West, prejudicing the sporadic and often marginal attention that the outside world generally affords to Turkey.

But while trying to judge Turkey on its own merits, we have striven to keep our own critical faculties intact. Turkey's many contradictions make it the homeland of the absurd. When trudging through a mountain landscape in a remote corner of southeastern Turkey, a Turkish corporal, going miles out of his way to help two strangers on a rain-lashed night, replied to a question about his job with the proud announcement that he was in charge of his unit's torture section. As he detailed his duties, it was hard to know whether to laugh or cry.

We have not flinched at reporting those aspects of Turkish life which overlap with the rougher practices of their Middle Eastern neighbours; nor have we focused only upon them. The republican establishment in Ankara is much at fault for encouraging nationalist prejudice among the Turks, for failing to educate the population properly, for often preferring force to democracy and for decades deliberately isolating their country. The easy excuses for totalitarian behaviour and police brutality during the Cold War era are no longer accepted by Western partners nor, increasingly, by ordinary Turks themselves. Over the years improved communications have changed the Turks, relieving them of some of their suspicion of outsiders and allowing them to integrate more naturally with the outside world.

Turkey is no longer the poor, self-contained, predominantly peasant community in the back garden of Europe that it was thought to be even as recently as the early 1980s. The opening up of borders, and a new zest for commerce inside Turkey itself, has transformed this once economically unimportant outpost on NATO's south-easternmost flank. The end of the Cold War has brought back to Turkey's financial centre, Istanbul, much of the geographic and commercial importance that it enjoyed before the First World War, a position that had made it the centre of empires for more than sixteen centuries.

In the 1990s the people of Turkey have also embraced a revolution in mentality symbolized by the rule of the late Turkish President Turgut Özal. By an unpredictable and often uncontrolled process, civil society has started to overtake the old statist structures of the republican establishment. Whereas in the early 1980s one black-and-white state television channel aired programmes for a few hours each night, by the mid-1990s there were fifteen national television stations and hundreds of local ones. Everywhere the frontiers of public debate were being pushed forward on issues long taboo, such as Kurdish nationalism and the position of Islam.

Daily life has changed out of all recognition, as has the infrastructure of the cities. When we arrived, Istanbul was still using the same two nominally five-star hotels that had been in use for the past two decades. Ten years later, there are more than two dozen luxury hotels. Supermarkets have sprung up everywhere, while new shops and restaurants open daily. Tens of thousands of new cellphones are registered each week. Groups of single men still frequent the *birahane* beerhouses, those with no work to do still sit in *çayhane* teahouses chatting, playing cards and back-gammon. But new cafés have become focal points for the younger generation, and indeed for women who otherwise have no meeting-place of their own. Ethnic, social and economic divisions have become more marked, but the expanding economy has provided hope and kept communal frictions down. The fact that the majority of poor people own their small *gecekondu* homes, often run up in a night on the outskirts of big cities – gradually transforming them into *apartkondu* concrete apartment blocks – has ensured that even among the poor, most people feel they have a stake in society.

Old *Istanbullu* people resent the invasion of Anatolian peasants that has caused their city to expand almost to breaking point and diluted its original families to a tenth of the city's population. Previously known for its leafy streets, wooden houses and cosmopolitan sophistication – though never the ideal cleanliness with which nostalgia has invested it – Istanbul like other Turkish cities is now ringed by a sea of grey, unfinished apartment blocks thrown up in a fantastic jumble of confusion. The newcomers have gradually been transformed into an urban lower middle class, and, modernized by the new pro-Islamic Welfare Party, have gone on to take over the mayor's office and even to acquire a stake in national government.

We were inspired to write this book by a wish to hand on something of the rich complexity of the Turkey we know, a Turkey much worthier of interest than might be expected from the narrow diet of news reports about Kurdish clashes, human rights violations and economic crises usually fed to the general reader. We attempt not to justify these events, but to go beyond them to examine a country still grappling with a proud but traumatic history. It is a mistake to dismiss the Turks as unfeeling or brutal, as our mailbag shows that people often do. Time and again it has been proved that if we are to encourage change for the better, then Western sermonizing has little impact compared with that of true Western involvement.

The Turkish population, prey to successive military coups, is slowly learning to speak up. Turkey is talking in many new voices, be they Kurdish, Laz, Alevi, secular or Islamist. Corruption in the state and society, once carefully hidden, is now being exposed for what it is. The danger zone of coups, terrorism and organized crime has not been passed. There are still dark, sometimes murderous elements at work who believe in imposing their ideologies on the country by force. But the mosaic of Turkish society as a whole is rapidly emerging in new and brighter colours as its people move out of the drab uniformity forced on them by the heirs of Mustafa Kemal Atatürk.

1

Tangled Roots

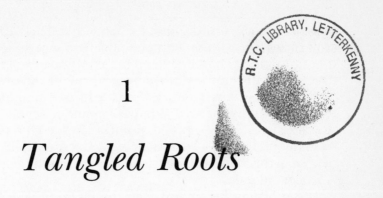

Galloping from farthest Asia
like a mare's head reaching for the Mediterranean
    this country is ours.

Wrists drenched in blood, teeth clenched, feet bare
and soil smooth as a silken carpet
    this hell, this paradise is ours.

                    Nazim Hikmet (1902–63)

EVERY SCHOOL-DAY morning a nearly identical ceremony takes place the length and breadth of Turkey. Children line up in school-yards from the gentle Thracian border with Greece to the steep mountains stacked up against the Iraqi frontier. In the massive concrete sprawl of Istanbul, in whitewashed Mediterranean villages, in the harsh towns of the Anatolian plateau and in hamlets hidden in the lush rain forests of the Black Sea coast, the voices of teachers rise above the excited chatter. When silence has been imposed, morning assembly gets under way, usually with the aid of a scratchy amplifier. Though not officially religious, the ceremony which ensues is part of a ritual indoctrination in the ideology of the Turkish republic founded in 1923 by Mustafa Kemal Atatürk.

'I am a Turk! I am honest! I am industrious!' the children shout in proud unison, whatever part their ancestors may have played in Turkey's jumbled mosaic of ethnic groups, religions and migrations. The slogans are various, but the message is the same for the young would-be citizens of modern Turkey. 'O Great Atatürk, I vow that I will march unhesitatingly along the road you opened, towards the goal you showed!'

Frowning down from an altar-like plinth is a black or gilded bust of Atatürk himself, the 'Father of the Turks'. His expression symbolizes something between loving concern and implacable determination. The same deep-furrowed brow will follow the children through their lives: from omnipresent pictures in finely cut 1920s business suits, from cast-bronze horses in military splendour, from eerie copies of his death mask moulded seamlessly onto walls. Atatürk's arm is often raised, pointing to the glittering future that so many of Turkey's leaders have pledged to their long-suffering people, a future that has never arrived in quite the shape in which it was promised.

The morning ceremony over, the children who have so loudly proclaimed their Turkish identity chase each other noisily up to their classrooms. Most have no reason to challenge the way they are educated as Turks and know no other way to start the day. They pass slogans pinned to the wall such as 'A Book is a Friend Who Will Never Cheat Me'. Indeed, school textbooks tell few outright lies. Even so, as they progress through their history lessons, Turkish students are drilled in a picture of their national origins and of the world around them that is quite different to that taught to a Christian child in Europe or even to their fellow Muslims of the Middle East.

These school history books of the Turkish republic are no idle creation. They are the direct descendants of four intimidating tomes produced by the Ministry of Education in 1932. Pretty colour pictures are now permitted, but the words are little changed. Rote learning is still the rule, and the line between reality and legend is sometimes blurred.

The Turks are taught that at the dawn of history their ancestors, led by a mythical grey she-wolf, started migrating outwards from the heart of Central Asia as the numbers of their people swelled and droughts dried the traditional grazing lands on the steppe. Some of them, they are told, even crossed the Bering Strait into the Americas, presumably becoming the American Indians. In his later, more deluded years, Atatürk himself adopted a bizarre creed known as the 'Sun Theory', which depicts the Turks as the mother race of all mankind.

'You're not really an American, you're a Turk,' Atatürk told a doubtless astonished American journalist one day in the Ankara Palas hotel. 'The Turks,' he added for good measure, 'discovered America fifty years before Christopher Columbus.' The proof of this assertion, he told the journalist, was that the Turks and Caicos Islands in the Caribbean had obviously been named by Turks, especially since their capital was called Grand Turk.[1] (The islands are in fact named after a fez-shaped cactus.) Atatürk might have been less amused to find that the only Ottoman Turks known to have reached the New World were a boatload of prisoners dumped in the American South who still call themselves the *Melunjans,* or 'cursed souls'.

Setting aside such far-fetched claims, the fact is that peoples speaking more than eighteen languages related to Turkish still inhabit not only Central Asia but also such eastern Siberian territories as Yakutia. The Mongols are ethnic cousins of the Turks. Even the Turkish, Korean and Japanese languages have strange similarities, sharing a grammatical syntax that makes it easy for Turks and Japanese to learn each other's tongues.

However, the main migrational thrust of the early Turks, which lasted broadly for a thousand years from the middle of the first millennium AD, was westwards. They and their flocks settled in many parts of south-west Asia. But their strongest hold, and ultimate place of refuge, was the great peninsula that became modern Turkey. Also known as Anatolia or Asia Minor, it is a territory the size of Britain and France combined, with 5,500 kilometres of coastline bounded by the waters of the Mediterranean, the Aegean, the Marmara and the Black Sea.

Almost all the people of this land, Turkish textbooks are quick to assert, are descended from these incoming waves of nomadic Central Asian tribes. This thesis is disputed outside Turkey. But until the 1990s, few were allowed to challenge what this meant for millions of Turkish citizens who knew perfectly well that they were not ethnically Turkish and who at home spoke Kurdish, Arabic, Laz (a dialect of Georgian) or any of a dozen other minor languages. Few had any choice but to learn the official republican history of the Turks.

The origin of the word *Turk* is obscure. It seems to have been written down for the first time in Chinese chronicles in the sixth century AD as *T'u-küe,* to describe pastoralists known for their iron-working skills. According to Western scholars, the earlier invaders of China known to the Chinese as *Hsiung-Nu* were also probably Turks, and it was to keep out such 'uncooked barbarians' that the Great Wall of China was built. It is also thought that the word *Turk* probably had a meaning close to 'strength': Turkish textbooks like the sound of that. 'The name Turk describes and symbolizes our race and nation,' they say, 'and our history is the best proof that this meaning is correct.'[2]

Strangely, given the central place of ethnic Turkishness in republican ideology – the 'heroic race' of the national anthem sung by the schoolchildren – the study of the ancient Turks by modern Turks is still in its infancy, perhaps because the subject is surprisingly unfashionable and funds are scarce. For Turks, too, there is also the fear of discovering facts that do not fit the official republican theory, as evidenced at a rare meeting on the subject of the origins of the Turks held in 1995. 'It was not so long ago,' one Turkish expert at that conference began, with a nervous smile, 'that even talking about the possibility of different Turkish peoples would have landed us all in gaol.'

Such worries had made it hard for the French institute organizing the conference even to find a venue. It was forced to settle on a little lecture theatre in the Press Museum on Janissary Street in the heart of old Istanbul. The motley group of those attending made the usual deferential references to their subject, praising each others' efforts and then flatly contradicting them: bear-like Russian archaeologists displayed new finds from deepest Central Asia, Turkish linguists presented elaborate interpretations of inscriptions and suave French historians kept the peace. The presence of a bookish Hungarian reminded those present that Turcology originally arose from his own country's nineteenth-century search for its roots in the Turks' weak ethnic link to both Hungarians and Finns. There was even an ageing American intelligence officer who, having spent the Second World War in Ankara listening to the grandiose ideas of his Turkish republican friends, had gone on to teach himself to read the ancient Chinese chronicles to find out if any of their claims about Atatürk's 'Sun Theory' could possibly be true. He was still searching for an answer.

Republican Turkey nominates the Scythians in 1,000 BC as 'the first great state that can be called Turkish', but the international scholars gathered in the Press Museum could only agree that the first Turkish-speaking tribes had probably coalesced by the first century AD. Further back than that they could not go, as the written history of the Turks loses itself in scratchy runes carved on bones, sticks and stones. One Turkish expert told of how in his search for an inscription he was reduced to feeling blindly with his fingers round the back of a statue in Ulan Bator museum in Mongolia. Sheets of syllabic decodings were passed from hand to hand to show that the first words written in Turkish on a buried goblet may have been: 'My elder brother, this hearth is for you. Stranger, fall down on your knees. And the tribe will have nourishment.' Or perhaps it meant something quite different. Nobody could be sure.

These early Turkic peoples quickly covered themselves with military glory. In the sixth century A D, as one great khan conquered the capital of China, Turkic 'White Huns' were ravaging the northwest of the Indian subcontinent. At the same time in the west, Europe was making contact in the hills of Champagne with the man whom Turkish schoolbooks describe as the first all-Turkish hero: Atilla, known in the West as Attila the Hun.

Attila has made an indelibly bad impression on the Western psyche, whose histories portray him as a barbarian who helped break the armies of Rome. Western commentators dwell on details such as his lair in the Wallachian forests (modern Romania); a wooden citadel in which he dined off plates of gold, attended by a barbarian horde in ratskin tunics and goatskin leggings.

Turkish schoolchildren, however, learn their history from the other side of the battle lines. Attila juggled his alliances as 'an extremely gifted diplomat', teachers are told to say. In tones similar to those used as Turkey aspires to full membership of the European Union, texts note that Attila 'did not count the Romans as enemies, but waited for them to accept him'. From the Turkish point of view, the conquering Turkic tribes from the east civilized and improved the primitive peoples they found on the eastern marches of Europe. The hardships of the steppes had made the Turks quick, sharp-eyed, hard-working and disciplined. Above all, their military vocation was supreme.

'The Turks are undoubtedly the people who gave the art of soldiering the highest place among the civilizations of the world . . . man and woman, every Turk was always ready for war,' teachers declaim. Any pupils in doubt about the continued importance of the army can meditate upon the fact that the first set of quotations in their textbooks is supplied by courtesy of the publications department of the Turkish military Chief of the General Staff.

Given this background, children are taught to take pride in an ancestry that can hold its own among other civilizations; in a language that is one of the 'oldest and best' in the world, and in a descent that marks them out as a single, unified Turkish people. They are not told of one of the important lessons of meetings like that at the Press Museum, that 'Turks' are almost impossible to define ethnically at an early date, or indeed at any other time. The ethnic mixing of Turkic blood in Asia started early and is still far from over.

Even so, it is hard to reject completely all the parallels that

Turkish republican ideologues have sought to draw with the Central Asian past. Among the big Black Sea noses, the curly Mediterranean tresses and the tall Balkan blondes, there are still large numbers of Turks who boast the short, stocky frame and high cheek-bones of the steppes.

Turkish mothers still refer to their sons as 'my lion', a parental endearment used in the first historical records written in Turkish, engraved on a Central Asian memorial stone in about AD 730. The ancient Turkish honorific for their rulers, *beg*, has been in uninterrupted use ever since. It now serves, in its form 'bey', as an honorific meaning 'mister'. The word for an army platoon is still a *manga*, the basic unit of ten men in a Turkic-Mongol horde; and the word 'horde' itself derives from *ordu*, the name still used for the modern Turkish army. Even the horse-tails used to denote rank in the Ottoman empire still hang in plumes from tall poles outside the tomb of Tamerlane in Samarkand.

Whatever the rest of the world may think, the impression made on Turkish schoolchildren is indelible: 'our ancestors' were a great people with a glorious history. One wall of the imposing entrance hall to the Turkish military museum honours Tamerlane, Attila and other Hun dynasties by casting their names in concrete together with those of other, later governments. Modern Turkey, according to the republic's official ideology, has carved a lonely path as 'the last independent Turkish state'.

This remained more or less true until the break-up of the Soviet Union in 1991, which gave birth to five more independent Turkic countries: Azerbaijan, Turkmenistan, Uzbekistan, Kazakstan and the Kyrgyz Republic. But the sixteen predecessor states remembered on the museum wall still huddle in a protective circle of stars around the proud single star that represents Atatürk's republic at the centre of Turkey's red-and-gold presidential seal.

Despite the enthusiasm of the republican ideologues for Turkifying the past, the Turkish republic is arguably the first state to be founded on a purely Turkish ethnic ideal. The early states founded by the Turks as they moved westwards tended to have mixed local populations of Persians, Kurds, Arabs and others. Indeed because Western scholarship has traditionally emphasized the place of these dynasties in the Islamic world, it is often not realized that some of their leaders were Turkish.

The Turks' gradual take-over of the Islamic world started early as they moved away from the shamanism of their forefathers: a religion of nature worship, especially of fire, water and air, through the agency of shamans or divinely inspired holy men. The presence of Turks in the Middle East is first recorded in AD 674, only forty-two years after the death of the prophet Muhammad, when 2,000 Turkish archers are said to have been in the service of the governor of Basra. The power of the Turkish *mamluks*, or slave-soldiers, grew as the early Islamic Arab aristocrats came to depend more and more on these mercenaries to control their subject populations. In AD 833, the caliph al-Mu'tasim, who had a Turkish passion for his army – his mother was a Turk – stepped up the hiring of Turkish mounted archers from his base in Mesopotamia (modern Iraq). Under the first of his sons to succeed him, two Turks were appointed generals. In AD 861, the Turkish Mamluks rose up and killed al-Mu'tasim's second son and heir, the caliph al-Mutawakkil, and became the military arbiters of Islamic courts from Cairo to Baghdad. In the sixteenth century the Ottoman Turks seized the caliphate itself.

Medieval Islamic history is henceforth peppered with names that in varying degrees can be represented as Turkish. The building of India's fabulous Taj Mahal was ordered by the Turkic-speaking Mogul ruler Shah Jahan, while Isfahan's prized Friday Mosque was commissioned by the Seljuks, a Turkish dynasty that ruled Iran and Anatolia. The Turks, like the Arabs, are usually associated with Sunni Islam, the mainstream branch of the religion that limits the role of the priesthood and adheres strictly to the orthodox traditions of the prophet Muhammad. But Turkic speakers or their Mongol cousins supplied most of the rulers of Iran for nearly nine hundred years until 1925 including the illustrious Safavid dynasty. The Safavids laid the foundations of Iran's most beautiful cities and its state religion, Shia Islam, a minority sect that affords a greater role to the clergy and which supported the family of the Prophet against the Sunnis in a civil war that broke out shortly after Muhammad's death. Perhaps a fifth of Iran's current population are Shia Muslim Azeris who speak a kindred language to Turkish.

At this early period, the Turks did not create sophisticated court cultures in their own language: such a culture only came with the rise of the Ottoman empire. Mahmud of Ghazna (*c.* 971–*c.* 1031), for instance, a Turkic ruler based in today's Afghanistan, funded one of Islam's most brilliant courts with booty won in his raids on India. But the arts he patronized were Iranian – among them Firdausi's *Shahnameh*, the great work of Persian epic poetry.[3] The Turks still suffer from a sense of cultural inferiority. Even in today's

highly nationalistic Turkish republic, the élite universities are
expressly set up to teach in English, not Turkish.

The illustrious Seljuk dynasty of Konya acted with similar ambivalence towards their Turkish origins, even though they were the
first to cause Anatolia to be called 'Turkey' by the likes of Chaucer.
Seljuk courts ruled today's Iran, Mesopotamia and Anatolia from
the mid-eleventh until the mid-thirteenth centuries. Lovely high-
arched stone bridges, caravanserais and fine mosques with conical
domes survive across Anatolia, attesting to their greatness and
sense of style. But their courts spoke Persian and their rule led to
the spread of literary Persian, not literary Turkish, which barely
existed. Jalal ud-Din Rumi (1207–73), the celebrated Turkish
poet and mystic who founded the religious brotherhood of the
Mevlevis, known in the West as the whirling dervishes, and whose
twenty-first grandson died in 1996 in Istanbul, wrote mainly in
Persian.

If the high Arabic and Persian cultures of medieval Islam gave
the Turks a civilization, in return the Turks bore the sword and
shield of the Muslims. But at times this military genius was nearly
the undoing of Islam. Turkic nomads fresh out of Central Asia
made up the bulk of the hordes of Mongol leader Genghis Khan
and his sons, whose campaigns in the mid-thirteenth century laid
waste the brilliant cities and carefully tended irrigation systems of
the Middle East. These peoples were an even stronger component
of the armies of the vicious half-Turkish, half-Mongol Tamerlane,
who swept as far east as the Aegean Sea in the first years of the
fifteenth century. Like Genghis Khan, their shock tactics wiped
out the population of any city that did not immediately surrender.
The Middle East was sent reeling into a dark age from which
Muslim cultural and intellectual life has never fully recovered.

For this reason, perhaps, Turkish schoolchildren are presented
with an ambiguous image of the Mongols, as if they were somewhat
unsavoury relatives. The greatest pure Mongol leader, Genghis
Khan, is not included in the official Turkish pantheon, whilst
the half-Turkish Tamerlane is. Even so, one of modern Turkey's
most popular early rock groups chose the name 'The Mongols';
and as many Turkish mothers chase after little boys called Cengiz
(Genghis) as do after those named Timur or Atilla.

In the course of these upheavals in the Islamic Middle East,
wave after wave of Turkic nomads continued to move from east
to west in search of grazing and booty. By the middle of the
eleventh century, they were probing the edge of today's Anatolia,
the western marches of the Byzantine empire. Based in Constanti-

nople, the present Istanbul, the Byzantines were the orthodox Christian heirs of the eastern half of the Roman empire. The memory of this first contact is kept alive today by the Turkish word for an ethnic Greek: a *Rum*, literally, a Roman.

The advancing Turkic nomads were somewhat unruly outriders for the Seljuks – settled Turks whose princes then held sway over much of the Middle East. The Seljuks had to decide whether to follow these raiders or risk losing out on the possible benefits of booty, new territorial conquests and the blessings of a holy war against the Christian infidels. On the other side, the Byzantines also had to confront the invaders. The Seljuk and Byzantine armies clashed at Malazgirt (Manzikert) north of Lake Van in 1071, an action still commemorated at the battlefield each year as one of the turning points in Turkish history. The Byzantines suffered a humiliating defeat and their emperor, Romanus Diogenes, was led captive to the Seljuk king Alparslan's tent. 'What would you have done had you captured me?' Alparslan asked the Byzantine emperor. 'I would have cut off your head,' the Byzantine replied. The honest answer so impressed the king that he spared Romanus's life; but from then on, the high central plateaux of Anatolia were open to settlement by the land-hungry Turkic tribes and their flocks.

These Turks were mostly from the ethnic branch known as Türkmen, or Turcomans, and their arrival in the land that was to become modern Turkey is the basis of one of the most controversial and insecure doctrines maintained by the republic: that Anatolia was, to all intents and purposes, always Turkish. As one textbook has it,

> Türkmen groups flowed into Anatolia and settled there, welcomed by the people who were unhappy with the old Byzantine administration, which certainly never represented this country. They mixed with the people of Anatolia. Very soon it was completely Turkified. Of course they did not find Anatolia empty. But its population was very small. A new Anatolian Turkish civilization was born.

This official version has the grace to mention that 'the Europeans never accepted this'. In fact, Western historians estimate that by the end of the Türkmen migrations in the thirteenth century, only a small proportion of the population of Anatolia was ethnically Turkish.[4] As we shall see in the next chapters, non-Turkish populations remained predominant in most towns until the turn of the twentieth century.

Nevertheless, much of the culture of modern Turkey grew out of what was grafted onto the Anatolian stock by the new conquerors. The Christian populations gradually dwindled as a result of Ottoman taxation and other discriminatory practices, conversions to Islam, migrations to the West and terrible massacres. Even under the republic, the state targeted the substantial minorities left in Istanbul with a crippling wealth tax in the 1940s, and had a hand in stirring up street riots in 1955 which sounded the death knell for the Greek community in the city its ancestors had founded.

Presented with this reading of their history, it is not surprising that Turkish schoolchildren today, even were they to doubt the official version of events, have little cause to question the extent and history of the Turkish-Muslim identity being preached to them. The non-Muslim minorities who have inhabited their country are a vacuum in their minds. That does not mean, of course, that these minorities have left no trace.

Most Turks have to wait until they reach university before they hear anything about those who inhabited Anatolia prior to the arrival of the first Turkish outriders. Those peoples who pose an ideological challenge to the Turkish republic – Greeks, Armenians or Kurds – get short historical shrift. It is as if Turks have been given a puzzle with several parts missing, but which is said to be whole. Small wonder that Turkish versions of history sometimes look oddly as though the pieces have been forced into place.

Anatolia is extraordinarily rich in ancient peoples. It bears some of the world's earliest traces of civilization. Like the architectural jumble of Istanbul, where buildings have been piling up on top of each other for millennia, the ethnic and historical origins of Turkey's peoples are inextricably intertwined.

A drive along the old Fertile Crescent just north of the border with modern Syria reveals settlements where people still live in conical mud huts that seem to date back to the dawn of history. Further east it is possible to find stone-built villages perched on an accumulation of ancient mounds whose Syriac Christian people speak a kind of Aramaic, the language of Jesus Christ. Such hillocks are treasure troves of history – and not infrequently of gold and silver too, as many a Turkish farmer with a plough or metal detector has discovered – where archaeologists are pushing back the limits of our knowledge of man's earliest development.

The biggest and best-known such site is Çatalhöyük, a late Stone

Age mound on the great plain near Konya discovered in the fifties by the charismatic British archaeologist James Mellaart, whose finds can be marvelled at in Ankara's Museum of Anatolian Cultures. Wall paintings illustrate hunters and bulls, showing how close the culture of the world's first known town of 10,000 inhabitants was to that of neolithic cave-dwellers; and show-cases display mirrors of volcanic glass whose polish remains undimmed from the time when these first townspeople reflected on their own image.

A new 25-year excavation programme has now started at Çatal-höyük that will include a look at the DNA structure of the bones buried under the floor of these houses nine thousand years ago. The findings should help to answer the question of where these first townspeople came from, and also perhaps of their relation to the local Turkish villagers of the present day, now performing the inevitable archaeological donkey work of carrying away the hods of earth.

A living link has already been suggested. The Turkish carpet expert Belkis Balpınar believes that some of the patterns on carpets and kilims that decorate the homes of families all over the world can be traced back to forms and ideas seen on the walls and in the artefacts of sites like Çatalhöyük. The idea is far from satisfactorily proven. But it is tempting to believe her theory when looking at the most common design of all, the hooked diamond shape known to Turkish women weavers as *eli belinde* or 'hands-on-hips': a design that instantly calls to mind the ancient clay statuettes of the fleshy, hands-on-hips Anatolian mother goddess.

Succeeding the inhabitants of Çatalhöyük came wave after wave of different peoples who made Anatolia their home. The austere-looking Hittites left formidable stone lions guarding their great fortresses, and their possible Central Asian origin is seized on by republican ideologues seeking to prove that the Turks have an ancient claim to Anatolia. Assyrian traders bequeathed storehouses full of order-books written in their wedge-shaped cuneiform script. The mystery of Troy is still being carefully sifted by a powerful international team of archaeologists on a small hill overlooking the entrance to the Dardanelles. Phrygian and Lydian rock tombs litter the tourist trail along the Mediterranean, while the imposing temples and theatres of Ephesus still radiate the strength of the Roman empire. Alexander the Great, Xenophon, Darius and Xerxes all passed through with their armies, as did Roman legions sent against the Parthians. As early as the first century AD, the Greek geographer Strabo admitted being perplexed by 'the confusion which has existed among the nations of this district'.

Successive civilizations left behind pockets of their cultures everywhere. The coastal trading colonies and cities became predominantly Greek-speaking. The Armenians coalesced as a distinct national group in eastern Anatolia. Xenophon mentioned the *Kurduchoi*, probably Kurds, in the south-eastern mountains. All these peoples were to be gathered under the rule of Byzantium by the Roman emperor Constantine, who in AD 330 chose this settlement at the crossroads of Europe and Asia as his capital, and renamed it after himself Constantinople. At first it was the capital of the whole Roman empire, but in AD 395 the empire split and thereafter the Latin west went its own way. For over a millennium the Byzantines ruled their own Greek-dominated empire, and Constantinople, the new Rome, was for most of that time the largest city in Europe and the envy of the Western world.

Steadily, however, Byzantium's borders came under attack. An Arab expeditionary force briefly threatened Constantinople as early as the seventh century, although they left little trace other than the alleged grave of one of the companions of the prophet Muhammad who fell there. He is known in Turkish as Eyüp, and his tile-clad tomb is now the holiest shrine in the city. The Byzantines had to fight off the Sassanids of Iran, lost much of Anatolia to the Seljuks and finally lost Constantinople to the Ottoman Turks, who slowly throttled their empire until it finally fell in 1453. Turkish textbooks today admire the mosaics, laws and even armies of the Byzantine empire, but treat it disdainfully as a somewhat degenerate state. Their country's large and continuing cultural debt to the Byzantines is seldom publicly acknowledged.

Few Turks realize that the names of nearly all their major cities are versions of Hellenistic originals. Ankara was Angora, Izmir was Smyrna, Sivas was Sebasteia, Kayseri was Caesarea and Konya was Iconium. The Turkish name for Constantinople, Istanbul, is simply a corruption of the Greek for 'up to town', *eis ton polis*. A scrub-down in the hammam may seem the ultimate Turkish experience, but the institution is in fact the linear descendant of the Greco-Roman bath-house. And it was Armenian architects who designed many of the grand Ottoman palaces and even mosques that have become poster portraits for attracting tourists to modern Turkish Istanbul. The projecting upper storeys of houses now thought of as typically Turkish were so common in Byzantine times that the emperors – like today's municipalities – had to make special laws to keep buildings apart.

The thousands of domed mosques springing up like mushrooms

all over the Turkish urban landscape still echo the dome of the Emperor Justinian's great sixth-century Christian basilica, Haghia Sophia in Istanbul. Even when today's Islamist radicals stage noisy demonstrations attempting to force the republican authorities to restore Haghia Sophia to its Ottoman position as the country's principal mosque – Atatürk turned it into a museum as part of his secularization campaign in 1934 – they still shout for *Ayasofya*.

This tangled history lives on in mosques like Zeyrek, the echoing former monastery church of Christ Pantocrator. The great ship-wreck of a building is now set amid a crumbling quarter of grubby concrete apartment buildings and collapsing wooden houses. One house has even been broken open to reveal in its basement ancient steps leading down to an old, disused Byzantine water fountain. Under the towering arches of the nave itself, Muslims still pray before marble-clad Byzantine apses and a minbar built of old pieces of Byzantine masonry. Its rough-and-ready appearance makes it seem as if the conquest of Byzantium had only just hap-pened, and as if the ghosts of the monks cannot be far away.

But if Anatolia's non-Muslim inhabitants of the past are now little more than spirits and memories, Atatürk and his republicans were making a mistake if they thought that all Muslims would accept membership of a Turkish ethno-religious monolith. Today different Muslim groups are increasingly determined to have their individual identities recognized. Kurds now constitute a fifth of the population. Several million people count themselves as Alevis, a heterodox sect from the Anatolian heartlands that mixes ancient Turkish shamanist customs with Shia Islam. Speakers of Arabic, Azeri and Laz are plentiful, and more than ever ready to speak up about their origins.

Trips to the provinces always turn up a surprise. High in the rain forest of the Black Sea coast can be seen the lovely faces of the girls of the Hemşin valley. They chatter away in a dialect that can only descend from Armenian, although their people found it advantageous to become staunch Muslims to escape the ethnic massacres of the First World War. A similar surprise was the dis-covery in the 1980s that one cabinet minister spoke fluent Greek. His family came from a mountain village that had once been part of the independent Greek kingdom of Trebizond but whose descendants had also converted to Islam.

All in all, though Turkey sees itself as an ethno-cultural unit, it turns out to be an extraordinary repository of the many peoples who have lived, taken refuge or simply passed through here. One recent study by the University of Tübingen has counted the relics of fifty identifiable ethnic and religious sub-groups still present in the country. For much of the republican era, the question of ethnic origin seemed an anachronistic irrelevance to the modernizers. But as the republic's ideological grip has slackened, nationalisms of all kinds have emerged. Some Kurds go so far as to demand a separate state. And descendants of Chechen and Abkhaz refugees from the Russian take-over of the Caucasus a century ago have shown themselves ready to hijack ships and planes to draw attention to their national cause. More than 200 young men even returned to the Caucasus to pick up the fight where their great-grandfathers left off.

Like the Chechens, Abkhaz, Bosnians or Albanians, many of these groups are descended from Muslim refugees who converged on Anatolia as the Ottoman empire contracted. Others came from further afield. For decades, Isa Yusuf Alptekin, a tall and dignified leader of the ethnic Turkic Uygurs of Western China, who had represented his countrymen at the Chinese parliament in Beijing before the Second World War, held court in an anonymous block of flats overlooking the railway line once used by the Orient Express. And for years the flame of the Golden Horde was kept alive in a dingy apartment on the Asian side of Istanbul. Here, amid grainy photographs of stern-faced Tartars and stacks of age-ing magazines publicizing their forgotten cause, sat the last living representative of the last independent parliament of the Khanate of Crimea.

All are proud of their separate origins. But none of them can quite compete with the court still maintained by the best-known living descendant of the greatest Turkish dynasty, the house of Osman.

2

Ottoman Glory and Decline

We were defeated because of our backwardness.
To take revenge, we shall adopt the enemy's science,
Learn his skill, steal his methods.

Ziya Gökalp (1876–1924)

THE HOTEL IS called Kismet. The word means Destiny, a name chosen deliberately by the owner of this quiet retreat just outside the Aegean coastal resort town of Kuşadası. In Turkey's egalitarian republic, she is plain Hümeyra Özbaş. But to her friends and relatives she is Hümeyra Sultan, or Princess Hümeyra, one of the few descendants of the Ottoman dynasty now living on Turkish soil. Her story is a strange footnote to the six centuries during which her ancestors decided the fate of the Turks, led the world's Sunni Muslims and at their height in the sixteenth and seventeenth centuries governed what was arguably the most powerful state on earth.

Elegant, aristocratic and proudly bearing the scimitar-shaped nose of her ancestors, Princess Hümeyra has no argument with her fate. She has built her immaculate hotel on the edge of Kuşadası bay, the vulgar concrete sprawl of the tourist esplanade kept at arm's length by a causeway and thick arbours of jasmine, a row of palm trees and banks of laurel bushes. Photographs in the gleaming lobby record visits by the royal families of Europe: Princess Hümeyra has crowned herself queen of her own court. Here, sitting at her table on an outside terrace on a summer evening, the lights of the town twinkling over the swaying masts of the harbour, she can be found entertaining ageing members of her family and sometimes ambassadors, generals and grand newspaper commentators of the Turkish republic.

Time has erased early republican suspicions of the royal family's intentions and has healed the bitter wounds of the Ottoman family itself. The Turkish public, long left dimly conscious of its Ottoman past, is showing signs of a new interest. Ottoman descent once again confers social cachet in an élite dominated by new money. Glossy magazines print loving memoirs of the Ottoman era. A new generation of television sitcoms, cinema films and academic magazines have started sprouting Ottoman costumes and re-appraisals of the past. A new brand of black olives even grades its product by the ascending ranks of the Ottoman court.

Politically, too, the Ottoman era is no longer taboo. When republican leftists sprayed blood-red paint all over the first banner of the late nineteenth-century sultan Abdülhamit II to be hung in 1990s Istanbul, right-wing Islamists rushed to its defence. The moderate Islamic Welfare Party plays Ottoman military marches through megaphones at its political rallies. *Mehter* bands in rich red costumes are now common at anniversary celebrations, per-forming the characteristic Ottoman march of two steps forward, one step back. In a way, this neo-Ottomanism is the resurfacing of long-suppressed but living links to the past.

The Turkish republic is still just young enough to have been spanned by one lifetime, and the sprightly Princess Hümeyra has forgotten nothing of what her family went through. Her grand-father was Mehmet VI Vahdettin (1918–22), the thirty-sixth and last of the Ottoman sultans, the ruler who slunk out of the imperial capital on a British warship seventeen days after the sultanate was abolished on 1 November 1922. His successor to the religious leader's title of Caliph, Abdülmecit II, saw that stripped away on 3 March 1924. The remaining Ottomans were then given a day or two to leave on the Orient Express from its grand terminal in Sirkeci in Istanbul.

'I was six when we were put on that train,' Hümeyra says. 'I remember my little cousins running in the corridors, and my dear, beloved *bacı* [African nanny] at the window, crying "What am I going to do?" '

Mustafa Kemal's new republican authorities exiled the 144 members of the *hanedan* – the 'dynasty' that comprised children and grandchildren of the sultans – with £2,000 sterling each and one-year, one-way passports into exile. Some members of the palace harems were given a year to sort out their affairs, but it was hard for everyone. Royal properties were confiscated and the sale of private assets was complicated. Unused to the ways of the world, the family entrusted their affairs to dishonest lawyers, their old servants and even a dentist who became the kingpin of many of their transactions. Perhaps more destructive was the congenital bickering within this vast dynasty. Even Vahdettin and Abdülmecit II argued to the end about which of them was the true caliph.

The Ottomans had plenty of time to rue their fate. Over the ensuing years they formed and re-formed around mini-courts in Budapest, San Remo, Beirut, Nice, Cairo, Paris and even Tirana. Two princesses married into a rajah's court in India, others into the royal family of Egypt. Many were lost and directionless. Few of the women had ever worked or had even seen food prepared. They gradually sold off their jewels and the intricate medallions that carried their respective family seals. One sultan's granddaughter ended up sending her African *kalfa*, or servant, out to beg on her behalf.

Most of the male members of the dynasty had been soldiers, and only gradually began to find work, mostly as painters, porters or copiers of *levha* Arabic calligraphy. They plotted and argued about how to win back their properties, the most elusive goal being the fabled inheritance of Abdülhamit II (1876–1909), thought to total some 10,000 properties spread over a dozen countries. Most of these claims came to nothing. Money was short. Princess Hümeyra's grandfather Vahdettin died in 1926 with a clutch of unexecuted prescriptions under his pillow. His body lay in the hall of his San Remo house because his equerry had neglected to pay the debts that needed to be cleared before he could be buried. More jewellery had to be sold and money solicited from the Arab kings of Iraq and the Hijaz to send the last Ottoman sultan-caliph to his tomb.

Despite these experiences, the family, according to Princess Hümeyra, generally felt pride in Atatürk rather than anger at the sanctions and petty surveillance by consulates to which they were subjected by the new Turkish republic. But she was lucky. Since her father had fought alongside Atatürk in Turkey's war of independence, she was given special permission to return in the 1930s, two decades before the others. On one of his evenings out in Istanbul, Atatürk even unknowingly danced with the young princess at the Park Hotel.

Most Ottomans did not share her good fortune. The men – some of whom used to join Turkish cruise ships just to talk to their countrymen and to see their homeland from on deck – were only officially pardoned in 1974, in a general amnesty honouring the republic's fiftieth anniversary. By then only a few wanted to come back to Turkey and to find work, like the prince who anonymously accepted the position of a lowly clerk in the library of the palace of his forefathers, Topkapı.

Mukbile Osmanoğlu, a granddaughter of Sultan Reşat, was one of those in the family who lived for years expecting at any time to be pardoned. But even though the palace women were pardoned earlier than the men in 1952, it was hardly what Mukbile had hoped for. It took her three years of bureaucratic endeavour to organize her Turkish citizenship. Three decades later, she still remembered her humiliation at the hands of an official endowed with the new republic's ignorance of the past.

'Are you a Muslim?' the official asked. 'What was your father's and your grandfather's religion?'

'Excuse me, but look here, my man! My grandfather was Sultan Reşat. He was the padishah, the caliph!' Princess Mukbile replied.

'OK, fine,' the bureaucrat replied. 'But was he a Muslim, this Sultan Reşat?'

Princess Mukbile had a right to feel insulted. The Ottoman sultans had for centuries led the Muslim faithful. Her family's history stretched back more than 700 years. And the Ottoman state, underneath the new Kemalist terminology, and despite many of the insults thrown at it by the Kemalist ideologues, did also create a great deal of what is thought of as Turkish in the public and private life of the republic today.

Named after their first great leader, Osman, the Ottoman dynasty emerged at the end of the thirteenth century. During the later years of the Seljuk empire, the Osmanlı tribe had migrated from Central Asia to the rolling highlands around Söğüt, midway between Istanbul and Ankara. Leading from the saddle, their chiefs had settled as marcher lords on the edge of the Muslim domains, seeking booty and Islamic glory as they harried the front lines of the contracting Byzantine empire. As the strength of the Seljuks waned, sapped by the Mongol invasions of the thirteenth century, the power of such marcher lords grew, none more pro-digiously than that of the house of Osman.

The fortunes of the once-redoubtable Byzantines on the other side of the Sea of Marmara had fallen far since Constantine I founded his great city in 330 A D to act as the capital of the eastern Roman empire. Although the heir of Roman imperial tradition, the empire was largely populated by Greeks who had taken an increasingly separate path from western Christendom. The Byzantines' more mystical eastern Orthodoxy finally parted company with what became Roman Catholicism and the western tradition in the 'Great Schism' of 1054. But for much of their 1,130-year history, the Byzantines had also had to be alert for threats from the east, beating off attacks from the Sassanian Persians and the Arab armies of the newly born Islam.

Then, soon after the Byzantine empire had begun to contract under the expanding power of the Seljuks in Anatolia, the western Christians launched a treacherous attack on Byzantium in 1204 as part of the so-called Fourth Crusade. The crusader knights had been hoodwinked by the doge of Venice into looting the Orthodox capital rather than attacking the official target of Muslim-occupied Jerusalem. The 'Latins' were to occupy the city until 1261. They carried off precious icons and even the bronze horses of Haghia Sophia, which they installed above the entrance to the cathedral of St Mark in Venice. There the horses remain today, as does a profound suspicion of Catholics among all the Orthodox churches of the east.

At the time of the Ottomans' initial expansion, the Byzantine empire had shrunk to little more than Constantinople and its immediate Balkan hinterland. A separate Greek kingdom also survived around the Black Sea port of Trebizond, now known as Trabzon. The Byzantine emperors were gradually forced to co-operate with their up-and-coming neighbours: their need for military assistance led to the first invitation to the Ottomans to cross the Dardanelles Strait into the Balkans in the 1340s; the emperor even gave his daughter's hand in marriage to the Ottoman leader as a sign of gratitude. The Ottomans were to stay in Europe for more than five centuries, ruling the whole Balkan peninsula and, at the height of their power in the seventeenth century, twice threatening the gates of Vienna. Like the Arab caliphs, the Byzantines were to pay heavily for their reliance on Turkish military strength.

Despite setbacks, such as defeat during the invasion of Anatolia by Tamerlane in 1402, the Ottomans gradually imposed their rule over the feuding Turkish princedoms of Anatolia. Constantinople itself had never fully recovered from the Latin invasion. As the Ottomans grew stronger in the fifteenth century, they won the right to ban improvements to the city's defences, to install a Turkish quarter and even to tax the emperor's orchards. Relations were surprisingly civil, extending to polite requests to permit hunting parties and mutual exchanges of presents. But in the end the Byzantines were little more than Ottoman vassals.

The final blow came in 1453. The Ottoman Sultan Mehmet II 'The Conqueror' (1451–81), believing that he was now strong enough to take Constantinople, sent his troops to surround the walls of the city. They cast and brought up the greatest siege cannons the world had ever seen: the biggest surviving example is now in the Tower of London, but others can be seen at the castle of Rumelihisar, whose circular towers, built in just four months by Ottoman generals, still stand guard over the Bosphorus. The besieging forces bypassed the Byzantine sea defences of chains laid across the entrance to the Golden Horn by dragging their ships overland into the sea inlet. The Ottoman forces however broke through at a gate in the land walls. Nearby, a five-centuries-old cannon ball remains lodged in the crumbling but still hugely impressive Byzantine walls of the city.

Mehmet the Conqueror went on to double the size of his empire in the course of eighteen major military campaigns – conquests which make him a Turkish hero even today, a man after whom bridges are still named and statues cast. His successors added to Ottoman domains. Within sixty years, Sultan Selim I (1512–20) had completed the unification of Anatolia, dealing decisively with rivalry from the new Turkish-speaking Safavid dynasty, which had reunited Iran as a political entity for the first time since the pre-Muslim Sassanids, and crushing Anatolian rebels inspired by the Safavids' Shia Muslim missionaries – a brutal campaign that earned him the title Selim the Grim. He settled the south-eastern border with Iran at the battle of Chaldiran in 1514. Before he died in 1520, Selim had conquered the mountains of Kurdistan, captured Jerusalem, defeated the Mamluk rulers of Egypt, captured the nominal caliph and proclaimed himself protector of the Muslim holy cities of Mecca and Medina.

These conquests opened up a golden era symbolized by the figure of Süleyman the Magnificent (1520–66). Architects such as Sinan built the superb imperial mosques that still grace the Istanbul skyline, their interiors dancing with the red tulips and blue tendrils of the best Iznik ceramics. Western visitors spoke in awed tones of the glories they saw, and European ambassadors allowed palace officials to take them firmly by the arm as they advanced towards the sultan, forcing them to bow at every third step.

But Ottoman history was to prove that conquest was one thing, integration another, as the centrifugal forces of the twentieth century were to show. The descendants of those inspired by the Safavid missionaries never forgave Selim or the Sunni Muslims for the suppression of their faith. They survived as the Alevis, whose heterodox Shia culture lived on in secretive village ceremonies that blossomed in the 1990s as a distinct new identity for millions of people in Turkey.

Nor, when Ottoman statecraft ran out of steam, would the Kurds accept Turkish rule as a legitimate state of affairs, any more than did other non-Turks of the empire. The ethnic fuse for many a twentieth-century Balkan conflict was lit in the fourteenth century when Türkmen settlers were sent into the Balkans. The Serbs, for one, never forgot or forgave their great defeat at Kosovo in 1389. Not everything, it seemed, could be won by force of arms.

Even so, the battered shell of Byzantine Constantinople was slowly transformed into Ottoman Istanbul, a process Mehmet the Conqueror called a change 'from lesser wars to the mightiest war'. Turkish Muslims were reluctant to move to the newly conquered Byzantine cities like Salonika or Trebizond (Trabzon); nearly a century after the capture of Trabzon in 1461, for instance, only four per cent of the population was Muslim.[1] Many bureaucratic practices of the Byzantine empire were carried through to the new regime: many taxes remained the same and for a long time Greek remained one of the principal languages of the administration. Mehmet issued a decree requesting the Jews of Constantinople to stay on, whilst Jews fleeing from Christian persecution in Spain in 1492 were invited to settle in the empire. Non-Muslim minorities including Greeks and Armenians made up half of the city's population until the fall of the Ottoman empire. Visitors filled pages of their accounts of the city describing the huge diversity of peoples and national dress that could be seen crossing the Golden Horn every day.

Like all new conquerors, Mehmet II wanted a catalogue of his new empire. The project resulted in something like the Domesday Book drawn up by the Normans in Britain. These registers, known as *Defter-e Hakani*, listed tax revenues and their intended distribution, right down to levies on animals that the pious Muslims could not bear to name because Islam considered them unclean: the *resm-i canavar*, or 'monster tax', for Christian pigs. The study of such primary sources of information on the Ottoman empire is still in its infancy, or, as one historian has put it, like a 'blind man attempting to describe an elephant based on individual gropings of separate parts of its body'.[2] The imperial archives constitute one of the last frontiers of historical research, covering as they do the seminal history of the more than thirty countries which developed from lands conquered by the Ottomans. Most Ottoman history in the West is still written from the reports of foreign observers and diplomatic histories, just as most of the pictorial record of the Ottoman empire is derived from engravings and paintings by Western visitors.

For decades the archives have been jealously guarded by the Turkish republican authorities. Most are still housed in the area of Istanbul known as *Babıali* or the Sublime Porte, the name by which the Ottoman administration became known after the grand gate with deep flowing eaves that still leads to the former offices of the Grand Vizier. Once it took months, if not years, for researchers to gain access to an estimated 100 million documents, stacked everywhere from wooden trunks to back rooms in old school buildings. Most of the Ottoman archives are now kept in two main collections, those of Topkapı palace and those now known as the prime minister's archive. Suspicions of foreign intentions are still rife and the atmosphere in the reading rooms has a Byzantine complexity of its own. Weeks of work can be saved if a researcher is trusted enough to be given a word of advice by white-haired Turkish scholars who have spent decades sifting through volumes of documents whose contents or value, even when indexed, can rarely be accurately predicted. The sense of secrecy is by no means new. To ensure the exclusivity of their craft, imperial accountants also developed a fiendishly difficult script that requires years of practice to read.

But leafing through the parchment tomes, the efficiency of the early Ottoman empire cannot be doubted. Neat line after calligraphic line recorded each and every inhabitant – 'Ibrahim son of Omar, tall with a big moustache' – and how much tax he should pay. But after the first century of effort, scribes started merely copying previous entries. The arteries of the empire hardened. The history of conquest ended in 1683 when Ottoman troops were beaten back from their second siege of the gates of Vienna. From that time on, the empire was on the defensive.

This moment of world power remains strong in the folk memory of the most republican-minded Turks as well as those who hanker after what they see as a glorious Islamic past. Republican textbooks talk freely of the Ottoman armies as 'us'. The Turkish leader Kenan Evren, then chief of the general staff, who in his own mind at least had just saved his countrymen from the political and economic chaos of the 1970s by ordering the 1980 military coup, recorded how he felt stung by criticism from a Council of Europe delegation in January 1982.

'I was very uncomfortable with the attitude of our European friends and felt relieved when they left the room,' the military ruler and future president of Turkey wrote.[3] 'I was upset that one or two people from the tiny European countries that had seen Turkey as the sick man [of Ottoman times] could speak out and take sanctions against us. Did the great Turkish nation that once ruled and brought justice to three continents deserve this?'

The Turks still agonize over the causes of Ottoman decline, partly because the problems of the later Ottoman empire often mirror those of the Turkish republic. The issues seem very familiar: the struggle by pro-Islamic conservatives against Western-inspired reform, the meddling of foreign powers, conflicts with minority groups, hostile neighbours, muddled financial management. A brilliant description of Constantinople and its people published in 1878 by the Italian writer Edmondo de Amicis shows how little some basic things have changed.

'We see this people in the crisis of transformation,' de Amicis wrote.[4]

> The progress of the reformers, the resistance of the old Turks, the uncertainty of the great mass that hesitates between the two extremes, all the phases of the fight between the new Turkey and the old can be seen in the clothes. The old inflexible Turk still wears the turban, the kaftan and the yellow morocco leather shoes ... the reformed Turk wears a long black coat buttoned up to the chin and trousers, with the only sign that he is Turkish being the fez. The turbaned Turk still believes [in heaven and hell] and goes home before nightfall ... the reformer laughs in the face of the Prophet, has himself photographed, speaks French and spends his evening at the theatre.

This profusion of cultures should have added up to a vibrant, cosmopolitan force, but by the late nineteenth century the Ottoman state was no longer managing to represent all parts of the empire, let alone project power. Government finances were in a shambles, its armies stumbled from defeat to defeat and its representatives were always kept on the doorstep of European politics. Two centuries before de Amicis made his observations, Ottoman imperial adviser Mustafa Koçi Bey had already spotted several causes of decline from the glorious years of Süleyman the Magnificent. Writing in 1631, he noted that sultans had withdrawn from direct contact with public affairs, the power of the Grand Vizier was fading, political faction was increasing and corruption spreading. Slightly later, the chronicler Mustafa Naima Efendi worried about the effect on the state budget of paying salaries to people who no longer worked, while noting the impossibility of coping with the political reaction were such people to be thrown into the street.

Contemporary Turkey lives with precisely the same dilemmas. It too shares the Ottoman problems of the short-term appointment of unqualified officials, an unfair and wasteful tax system, and regular debasement of the currency (nowadays simply done by printing more money). The Ottomans had also lost taxes and trade as the traditional overland 'silk roads' through the Middle East and Central Asia to the riches of India and China were circumvented by the development of sea trading routes around Africa by pioneering Portuguese merchantmen, a development that a little-known Ottoman naval expedition of seventy-eight ships to western India in 1538 failed to prevent. Small wonder that when the Soviet Union collapsed in the 1990s, modern Turkey jumped at the chance of winning back at least part of this trade to their regional crossroads.

A unique problem weakening the Ottoman dynasty was also the perennial issue of the succession. The early Ottomans had a peculiarly stressful system. Sons of the sultan were sent off to the provinces to learn how to rule, but once the successor was on the throne, he was expected to kill off his brothers and their male children to head off the threat to the empire of civil war between disputing claimants. Later sultans merely put their relatives in palace apartments known as the *kafes,* or cage, which was no training in the ways of the world. Right to the end, an unwanted sultan like Murat V could spend most of his adult life cooped up in a palace by Abdülhamit II.

Compounding the problem of the succession was the issue of the Janissaries. Introduced in the fourteenth century as a permanent element in an army otherwise formed by feudal levies, they were composed first of Christian captives from the conquests in the Balkans; later they included boys from Christian families taken as tribute in a levy known as the *devşirme.* For two centuries their discipline drove all before them, but from the sixteenth century their ranks began to be diluted. Although theoretically slaves of the sultan, the privileges and status of this élite were so attractive that Muslim fathers started pressing for their sons to be allowed in. By 1700, the *devşirme* was no longer necessary. From being the terror of Europe, the Janissaries became the terror of the Ottoman government, constantly intervening in politics and stirring up insurrections in the capital.

The first sultan to challenge them in 1622 was paraded in the streets of Istanbul and put to death. The next to try was Selim III (1789–1807), stung by Ottoman defeats on the battlefield, mainly against Russia, but soon threatened also by revolts in Greece, Egypt and Albania. He installed an alternative force, the Nizam-i Cedit (New Order troops), both to strengthen the army and to secure a new power base. The imposing stone barracks built for the New Order troops still stands on the Asian side of Istanbul, dominating the south-eastern entrance to the Bosphorus like a great upside-down billiard table. But the effort was doomed. Powerful factions in the Janissaries 'overturned their cauldrons' and revolted. Selim was forced to disband his new unit and was killed in Topkapı palace by Janissaries just as a pro-reform general, Bayraktar Pasha, was marching from the Balkans to his aid.

Sultan Mahmut II (1809–39) was next into the breach and appointed Bayraktar Pasha as his Grand Vizier. The Janissaries however attacked the general at his home, where he fought to the last bullet before blowing himself up with the powder magazine in his basement. Mahmut II had to wait until 1826 before he outwitted and broke the Janissaries, opening up with grapeshot as they marched on his New Order troops. All that survives of the Janissaries now are street names and a few martial traditions like the police clubbing of demonstrators in Istanbul and military interventions for better pay or ideological purity. Their sacred standards now rest in the central Anatolian shrine of Hacı Bektaş, the mystic saint whose still-popular Bektaşi sect remains an enigmatic compound of Sunni Islam, Shia hero-worship and even a few Christian traditions – a faint echo of the Janissaries' origins among the *devşirme* boys of the Balkans.

Even before the power of the Janissaries had been broken, Ottoman sultans had started to look to alternative means to strengthen the state. Apart from his attempt to found the New Order troops, Sultan Selim III had already become the first Ottoman ruler to take the West, specifically France, as a model. He communicated directly with the French king from his gilded 'cage'. His accession coincided with the French Revolution in 1789, an event that shocked Ottoman consciousness with Napoleon's invasion of Mamluk Egypt in 1798–9 and his programme of administrative reforms there. After the Janissaries had been disbanded in 1826, Sultan Mahmut II invited more foreign military advisers, abandoned the turban for the fez, started to organize the civil service along Western lines and introduced schools and printing presses. This train of reforms eventually achieved their true Jacobin potential with the revolution of Mustafa Kemal Atatürk more than a century later.

The reform movement started in earnest a few months after the death of Sultan Mahmut II. A great reforming minister, Mustafa Reşit Pasha, returned from leading an embassy to London and drew up a grand reforming decree for the new sultan Abdülmecit I (1839–61). In November 1839 foreign ambassadors were summoned to hear the formal declaration of Turkey's good intentions in Gülhane, the park that still lies under the walls of Topkapı palace. The Gülhane Rescript ushered in the era that came to be known as the *tanzimat*, or reorganization, promising security of life and property, fair trials, a remodelled administration and equality before the law for all Ottoman citizens.

For a while, the Ottomans succeeded in arousing sympathy in Europe: the army performed better, and Christians were permitted to rise higher in the administration. The Ottoman empire fought on the side of Britain and France against Russia in the Crimean War of 1854–6, which won it brief if superficial admission to the Concert of Europe. This club of European courts had been designed to keep the peace on the Continent after the Congress of Vienna in 1815; but, as with Turkey and today's European Union, the Ottoman empire was usually an object of, rather than a partner in, their discussions of the Eastern Question. The Crimean War also brought the Ottomans their first experience of foreign borrowing, although the money was often frittered away on building ornate palaces such as those that still grace the Bosphorus coastline. Nevertheless, the *tanzimat* reform process was regularly reaffirmed, culminating in a French-style constitution and parliament designed by another reforming minister, Mithat Pasha, and promulgated shortly after the accession of Sultan Abdülhamit II (1876–1909).

Russian ambitions for access to the Mediterranean were not satisfied, however. Only the protection of the *status quo* by European powers such as Britain saved the Ottomans, who began to look increasingly like a desperate balloonist casting away bits of the empire like ballast, or, as Tsar Nicholas I had put it, the 'sick man of Europe'. After the 1878 Congress of Berlin, Romania and Serbia became independent, Cyprus was leased to Britain, Tunisia was signed over to France and three north-eastern provinces were surrendered to Russia. In February 1878, unable to brook criticism of his conduct of the war, Abdülhamit II dissolved parliament. Already in 1873, the government had been forced to repudiate its debts, lacking the means to pay back the interest amid the world recession. In 1881, the Ottoman empire was forced to undergo the humiliation of signing away responsibility for a great part of the economy to a foreign debt administration.

Frustrated at his inability to suppress revolts and defend Ottoman territory, Abdülhamit II gradually concentrated all power in his informer-obsessed palace. He adopted a pan-Islamic banner under which he aimed to unite the increasingly restive Arab, Kurdish and other Muslim ethnic groups of the empire. The more Westernizing currents of 'Young Ottoman' thought represented in the 1877 parliament went underground, gradually turning into a movement of revolutionary societies. Some believed in a pan-Turkish solution, reaching into Central Asia, and another, eventually victorious group, in the solution of saving the Anatolian heartland of Turkey for a new Turkish homeland.

A group of exiles in Paris formed the Committee of Union and Progress from a combination of these political currents, including at times those of Christian nationalist groups. The young officers, students and nationalist officials became known as the 'Young Turks', and were particularly active in the ferment of multi-ethnic Macedonia, likely to be the next province of the empire to spin out of central Ottoman control. Determined to save the empire from partition, they rose up in the Young Turk revolution of 1908, led by names to become both famous and notorious in Turkey's future history: Enver, Cemal, Talaat, and, at this stage in a subsidiary role, Mustafa Kemal.

Sultan Abdülhamit was unnerved, and restored the constitution. A brief Indian summer of the Ottoman empire ensued, with genuine scenes of brotherhood between the various ethnic and religious communities. Elections brought to power a parliament comprising 147 Turks, 60 Arabs, 27 Albanians, 26 Greeks, 14 Armenians, 10 Slavs and two Jews. This constitutional period was derailed by a pro-Islamic counter-revolution in April 1909, but set back on course by army intervention and the deposing of Abdülhamit. Yet the disintegration of the empire continued. Italy took Rhodes and today's Libya in a short war in 1911–12. Greece, Bulgaria and Serbia defeated Turkey in a joint offensive to expand their territory in 1912, only marginally checked by Ottoman successes in a Second Balkan War the next year. Four-fifths of the remaining Ottoman territory in the Balkans had been given up, Istanbul had filled with tens of thousands of refugees and the best agricultural lands of the Ottoman empire had been lost.

By fits and starts, the power of the Young Turk Committee of Union and Progress grew. It had pushed through an election victory in 1912, but could not keep hold of the government. In January 1913, hearing that the hard-defended city of Edirne (Adrianople) west of Istanbul was about to be negotiated away to the Bulgarians, the Young Turks decided to act. They rode up to the Sublime Porte, shot the minister of war and took effective control in the country from then until the Allied forces of occupation arrived in the city in 1918.

The outbreak of the First World War in 1914 forced the Young Turk regime to choose sides. Initially, conflict among the Europeans allowed the Turks to revoke the hated capitulations by which foreigners and many Christians had enjoyed foreign-protected trading privileges over Muslims. But a weak group favouring neutrality in the war was outmanoeuvred by Enver Pasha and his pro-German faction.

The Allies had already brushed aside Ottoman overtures for an alliance, while Kaiser Wilhelm had shown every sign of friendship and support. The Ottoman empire could not realistically join Britain in alliance with its old enemy Russia, and a defeat of Russia by Germany could offer advantages. Then Britain's Winston Churchill confiscated two Ottoman warships being built in Britain with money raised by public subscription throughout the Ottoman empire. Turkish opinion was outraged, and by November 1914, the Ottomans had joined Germany and Austria-Hungary in their war with Russia, France and Britain.

Seizing the moment, Germany sent two warships to replace those confiscated by the British, and soon the Ottoman fleet set sail against the Russians in the Black Sea. But then came a series of disasters for the Ottoman empire. An impetuous drive east by Enver Pasha in December 1914 to block the Russians advancing from the Caucasus – and to fulfil his pan-Turkish dream of liberating the Turkic east from Russian control and uniting it with Anatolian Turkey – led to the annihilation during a battle through the mountains of a Turkish army of nearly 100,000 men, many of whom froze to death in Sarıkamış east of Erzurum, well short of the Caucasus. Russian forces soon conquered the eastern half of Anatolia and reached as far south as Rawanduz in Iraqi Kurdistan, only faltering in 1917 on the outbreak of the Bolshevik Revolution and the collapse of the old regime. The Arab provinces rebelled under the leadership of British officers like T.E. Lawrence. By 1918, the holy cities of Mecca and Medina as well as Palestine, Syria and Iraq were virtually lost to Ottoman rule.

The Ottomans had not lost all their martial qualities. The Turks briefly outfought British expeditionary forces in Mesopotamia, capturing a British general in Kut. The defence of the Dardanelles and Gallipoli against the British-led Allied assault of April 1915 was an amazing feat. Whole units were wiped out as Mustafa Kemal, in command of one flank of the Turkish force, told his troops, 'I do not order you to advance. I order you to die.' By January 1916 the poorly led Allies, despite their overwhelming naval strength, had been forced to evacuate.

But General Liman von Sanders, head of the German military mission to the Ottomans, has left a graphic account of a Turkish army whose troops were few, pitiful, poverty-stricken and louse-infested. On inspections of hospitals he spoke of a terrible stench, of a virtual absence of treatment and of the dying being locked up in utility rooms to keep them out of sight. When he noted the lack of footwear among the soldiers he was inspecting, he discovered that entire sets of uniforms were being circulated ahead of his visits to give the impression that the troops were properly equipped. 'Not a single barracks had a bath-house,' he complained.[5]

Despite their victory at Gallipoli, the Ottomans could not escape their fate. The six-centuries-old empire that had led the Islamic world and had controlled much of the Black Sea and the eastern Mediterranean was to disintegrate in a bloody finale. The old order collapsed, but the Turks and Muslims were not the only victims. Also devastated were those people whom the European powers had encouraged to rebel in order to weaken and divide the empire, but whom, when the time came, they abandoned: the Greeks and the Armenians.

3

Turkey for the Turks

When we find God in his paradise, offering comfort,
Let us swear we will refuse, saying,
No, we choose hell. You made us know it well.
Keep your paradise for the Turks.

Vahan Tekeyan, Armenian poet, 1917

IN THE HARD, rocky highlands of Tur Abdin lives the only original Christian rural community now left in mainland Anatolia.
East of the old stone town of Mardin and just north of the border
with Syria, Tur Abdin is what the Syriac Christians call their ancient
heartland. Their Aramaic-speaking ancestors split from the Greek-
speaking Orthodox Church during the theological disputes that
racked it in the fifth century AD over the question of the divinity
of Christ. Perhaps a few hundred villagers now remain. Most are
old or are merely caretakers, waiting to see if they can sell up the
family property and salvage some of the value of their stony fields.
As the villages empty one by one, the last, centuries-old, thick-
walled churches are being shut down by stooping priests. Their
silver-bound Bibles, often medieval manuscripts dated according
to a calendar that starts with the birth of Alexander the Great, are
handed into monastery archives, probably never to be used by a
parish again.

A bell-shaped belfry marks one such village, a bumpy few
minutes down a side road of earth and stones that kicks up a fine,
hazy dust in the summer heat. Like all villages in Anatolia, the
houses seem to have gathered in a protective huddle against the
outside world. Of 110 families a decade before, just ten were left
in the mid-1990s. The bitterness was tangible.

'Whenever people want someone to kick, they lash out at us,'
says one householder, waiting in his sparsely furnished room to

sell hundreds of acres belonging to long-gone members of his family. 'Nobody will buy our land. Muslim villagers around us reckon it'll be theirs for free pretty soon, so why spend the money?'

The Syriacs have never been a big community in Anatolia, and have never challenged Turkish rule. Perhaps that is why they were spared the worst during the Armenian massacres between 1890 and 1918, and were not included in the wrenching transfer of ethnic minorities between Greece and Turkey in 1923. Their culture survived the great republican push, started in the 1920s, to assimilate everybody into a new Turkish identity. But they met their fate after 1984 in the ravages of the war between Kurdish rebels and the increasingly pro-Islamic Turkish security forces. Soon all that will be left of what twelve centuries ago were 300 flourishing churches are two isolated, fortress-like monasteries, Mar Gabriel and Deir Zafaran. Their black-cowled monks are cynical about the present and pessimistic about the future as they cluster around wooden stoves to fend off the freezing cold of another winter. The ordinary villagers feel there is no place for them any more, no anchor to help them resist the temptation to join relatives prospering in Sweden or elsewhere in the West.

The Turks were not always at daggers drawn with their Christian neighbours in the Balkans and Anatolia. The Eastern or Greek Orthodox of Byzantine times could at times openly express a preference for the rule of the turbaned Turk over that of the mitre of Papal Rome. But their relations with Western Catholic Christians never truly recovered from the Crusades, a period that was to last intermittently for five centuries from 1095. The Knights of St John were at war with the Turks over Malta as late as 1565 – an epic engagement that halted the south-eastern expansion of the Ottoman empire. And the spirit of Christian-Muslim hostility that dominated the Crusades still underpins many attitudes today.

Rather than a noble enterprise led by chivalrous knights to secure pilgrim routes interrupted by Seljuk advances, the Crusades have been shown by historians to have been often brutal campaigns barely worthy of the name of religion. Whipped to peaks of fervour by Pope Urban II and his successors, the first crusaders did more to inflame Muslim fanaticism than to defeat it. They broke in on the Near East like Goths at a time when Islamic civilization was characterized by tolerance and an intellectual achievement higher than that of Europe. And instead of uniting the Orthodox and Catholic branches of Christianity, as intended, the crusaders did much to make permanent the Great Schism of 1054, after which the Roman Catholic and Greek Orthodox churches went their separate ways. They attacked Orthodox Christian, Muslim and Jewish communities alike, and, in one amazing case, were said to have cooked and eaten the inhabitants of a village that had the misfortune to lie in their path.

'I've always thought the Crusades were basically a barbarian invasion ... unfortunately their idea of God's work was rather destructive and not frightfully civilized,' the historian Steven Runciman has said. The knights and their followers were 'utterly boorish when faced with a civilization they did not understand'.[1]

Nine centuries after the First Crusade carved its way through Seljuk domains in Anatolia, many an act of Western injustice, real or imagined, is still presented to modern Turks as the work of the 'crusader mentality'. When the European Football Association annulled a notable Turkish soccer victory in 1989, for instance, the front page of the daily newspaper *Milliyet* was filled with a cartoon of scowling Christian knights-in-armour charging with great red crosses on their shields. For Europe, meanwhile, the deportations, expulsions and massacres of Slavs in the Balkans and of Greek and Armenian Christians in Anatolia during the dying decades of the Ottoman empire have long been sufficient proof that it is the Turks who are the barbarians. The language of nineteenth-century European criticism of the Ottomans often looks very similar to that employed by the West today when denouncing Turkish abuses of human rights and their treatment of ethnic Kurds.

As Christian states, especially Russia, grew more powerful from the late eighteenth century on, they began to swallow up those outlying provinces of the Ottoman empire in Europe in which Christians were the majority. The Christians in these provinces were eager to win political freedom to satisfy a growing feeling of superiority, having absorbed European scientific and commercial advances more quickly than the Muslim Turks, who tended not to learn European languages and to see their empire as a self-sufficient universe. The pattern was usually one of local Christian rebellion, followed by Ottoman suppression, European outrage, demands for 'reform' and finally a diplomatic settlement that invariably involved Ottoman loss of sovereignty or territory.

For much of the period, Armenian and Greek traders and craftsmen prospered greatly under Ottoman rule. Even the Greek war of independence did not have an immediate effect on ordinary Greek villagers in Anatolia. But the nationalist movements gaining

ground on the periphery began to affect even the heartlands of
the empire as Greeks and Armenians sought more political autonomy to accompany their growing religious and commercial freedoms. One word still has a powerful political resonance in Turkey
today, that of 'capitulations': the granting of exemption from Ottoman law awarded by the Porte from 1536 onwards, first to the
French, then to all foreign merchants operating in the empire, and
finally becoming an extraterritorial right claimed by all Christian
subjects of the sultan. This loss of Muslim control culminated in
1881 when, following an Ottoman failure to pay its debts, foreign
powers imposed a Public Debt Administration that took over
the management of most Ottoman state revenues. Coupled with
the growing ambition of foreign powers to act as protectors for the
Christians of the empire, and the Christians' readiness to claim
this as a right, the feeling grew that Christians were no longer
subjects of the same state.

Identified as the 'sick man of Europe' by Tsar Nicholas I in
1844, the Ottoman empire had continued to enjoy the support of
the European powers for a variety of selfish reasons: out of jealousy
lest a rival power acquire more concessions or territory; out of
greed, in order to preserve valued trading rights, or simply out of
fear that bonds would not be repaid. At the same time, however,
Europeans encouraged Christian subjects of the sultan either to
secede or to demand separate and greater rights for themselves.
As a result of European pressure, a new Imperial Rescript in 1856,
building on the reforming Gülhane Rescript of 1839, whose imple-
mentation had lagged considerably behind its promises, accorded
Christians further rights to enter the administration and army,
previously a purely Muslim preserve.

But when, following the Young Turk revolution of 1908, a constitution was finally introduced that offered everyone the same rights
of citizenship, the Turks found the Christian minorities unwilling
to give up their old privileges: indeed their members of parliament
stalled parliamentary work in order to win more concessions. This
reinforced a Turkish impression that pressure for reform was
simply a ruse concealing the separatist ambitions of non-Muslim
or non-Turkish subjects, often supported by foreign powers. The
same suspicion lives on today, part of the reason why European
and American pressure on Turkey for a political solution to the
Kurdish problem meets such stiff resistance. A deeper fear grew
that European protection of the Christians was making Turks
second-class citizens in their own state, and that there would soon
be a European attempt to oust the Turks themselves from parts

of Anatolia – a fear well justified in view of the Allied plan to
partition Turkey in the unratified Treaty of Sèvres of 1922. Russia
is generally blamed for backing nationalist Armenians in an
attempt to split up Anatolia, having successfully exploited similar
policies in the Balkans. Sultan Abdülhamit II (1876–1909) articulated Turkish feelings:

> By taking Greece and Romania, [the Great Powers] cut off the feet
> of the Turkish state. By taking Bulgaria, Serbia and Egypt they cut off
> our hands. Now by stirring up trouble among the Armenians they are
> getting close to our vital organs and want to cut out our intestines.
> This is the beginning of mass destruction. We must defend ourselves
> at all costs.

Nowadays official presentation of the Armenian problem by the
Turks is much less frank. Modern textbooks make no mention of
the fact that the Armenians had a distinct national identity in parts
of eastern Turkey for more than two millennia, a single script in
use for fifteen centuries and a brilliant medieval religious art of
carved reliefs upon stone churches.

The first serious clashes with Armenian nationalists flared up in
Anatolia in 1890–6. Officially, between 5,000 Muslims and 13,000–
20,000 Armenians died, but the numbers are hard to pin down.
Foreign and Armenian estimates of Armenian dead range from
40,000 to 300,000. In Europe, these clashes were usually presented
as outrageous massacres perpetrated by Ottoman Turks against
Christians. As far as the Ottomans and some foreign embassies
were concerned, however, they were felt in large part to be caused
by agitators determined to attract European support for their goal
of independence.[2]

The atmosphere was explosive, with Armenian agitation
matched by the provocations of the irregular tribal cavalry newly
recruited by the Ottomans from among the Kurds. These Cossack-
like units, known as the *Hamidiye* regiments, were named after
their increasingly paranoid patron in Istanbul, Sultan Abdülhamit
II, and bore a strong resemblance to the system of 'Village Guards'
used by today's Turkish republic against Kurdish separatist rebels.
The Porte's paranoia about European involvement was hardly surprising. It was European mediators who negotiated the end of a
bloody uprising in 1895 in the rebellious district of Zeytun – a
craggy eyrie near today's Kahramanmaraş in eastern Turkey – and
to a devastating attack on the Ottoman Bank in Istanbul. After
both uprisings, the Ottoman authorities could only watch as the

Armenian revolutionaries sailed safely back to Europe on European ships.

The advent of the First World War lifted the curtain on the final act of the Armenian tragedy. The Young Turk Committee of Union and Progress, whose power had been growing since their revolution of 1908, did not have the means to cure the empire's accumulated ills. Defeated in their efforts to build on the revival of inter-faith friendship in 1908 and to restore Ottoman rule in the empire, the Young Turk leaders changed tack and adopted a Turkish ideology that ultimately had no place for minorities such as the Armenians and Greeks.

Over the Russian border in Trans-Caucasia, Armenian militia, including the Dashnaks, were also busy organizing against the Young Turks. The head of the Armenian Church in the Russian Trans-Caucasus pledged loyalty to St Petersburg on behalf of Russian Armenians and assured the tsar of the 'unfailing sympathy' of the Armenians under Ottoman rule. Ottoman soldiers of Armenian origin started to desert in large numbers to the Russian side. The Ottoman general staff in February 1915 ordered its units to disarm Armenians and to remove them from any work in command centres. Many were forced into work battalions. Bands of Armenians took to the hills, sniping at military movements, cutting telegraph lines, supplying enemy ships and harassing Ottoman outposts.

The situation faced by the empire in the spring of 1915 was dire. An Allied fleet was bombarding the Dardanelles in the west. Most of the expeditionary force under Enver Pasha had frozen to death at Sarıkamış in December 1914, leaving the Ottoman east wide open to a drive forward by the Russians, who were secretly suggesting to the British that the Armenian partisans be armed. To the south, fighting had started near the Suez Canal and the Arabs were soon to rebel. Governors of central and eastern provinces of Anatolia cabled reports of movements by thousands of Armenians in readiness to attack Ottoman forces in the rear.

Fearing the loss of the Anatolian heartland, the Ottoman general staff ordered garrisons to crush 'in the strictest fashion' any local revolts but, in peaceful areas, 'to avoid any act that might be seen as oppression or terrorizing the population'. By April 1915, Armenian militia had barricaded themselves into their quarter in the eastern town of Van in open revolt against the oppression of the governor, Cevdet Bey, a brother-in-law of Enver Pasha. They kept Ottoman forces at bay for weeks, long enough to be able to hand the keys of the city to the advancing Russians. Turkish scholars have studied the original documents and published versions of what happened next, but Turkish schoolbooks do not dwell on the subject. Subsequent events on the Ottoman eastern front, so important in the formation of European and American attitudes to Turkey, earn at most a few dozen lines. The grim tone of the half-told story in a leading textbook leaves it open to many interpretations:

> The Russians used the Armenians as a cat's paw. Thinking they would achieve independence, they attacked their innocent Turkish neighbours. The Armenian 'committees' massacred tens of thousands of Turkish men, women and children. This made it hard to wage war on the Russians. So the Ottoman state decided in 1915 forcibly to deport the Armenians from the battlefields to Syria. This was the right decision. During the migration some of the Armenians lost their lives due to weather conditions and insecurity . . . the *Turkish Nation* [original emphasis] is certainly not responsible for what happened during the Armenian migration. Thousands of Armenians arrived in Syria and there lived on under the protection of the Turkish state.[3]

To Turkish schoolchildren, and other visitors to Turkish 'museums of barbarity' in the east, the impression is given that the massacres were committed solely by Armenians on Turks. Those Turks who know that massacres of Armenians occurred are left to conclude that since the 'Turkish Nation' was not at fault, the Kurdish tribes must have been to blame. The truth is not so reassuring.

On 24 April 1915, the day before the Allied landings near Gallipoli, the Ottoman government signalled its formal intention to take action. On that day, commemorated by the Armenians as the anniversary of what they term a genocide, the ministry of the interior ordered all Armenian 'committees' closed down and their leaders detained; officially, 2,345 Armenians were arrested including politicians, writers and many who had seen themselves as loyal to the Ottoman state. The deportations, officially ordered by the cabinet on 30 May, had probably started even before this time. Coded telegrams from the interior ministry specified that the Armenians could take with them only what they could carry. The safety of the refugee columns was to be assured.

Never can the wishful orders of a Turkish government have been so adrift from the reality of what happened. The horrors inflicted on the Armenians are some of the worst of any war. Men were separated from their women and children and massacred.

Rivers clogged up with bodies. Kurdish tribesmen looted the columns of survivors and carried off marriageable girls slung over their saddles. Of columns of up to 20,000 refugees, sometimes only one or two hundred survived. Even grandmothers were stripped of their clothes and left to stumble on naked. One or two heroic legends of resistance were born, notably that of the Armenians of Musa Dağ, who were saved from a mountaintop siege near Alexandretta (modern Iskenderun) by the ships of an Allied fleet. The suffering of the other miserable survivors was not over when they reached camps in the blistering heat of Deir ez-Zor, a river town on the Euphrates in the northern Syrian desert. Bones from the mass graves of massacred Armenians can still be dug out of river banks nearby.

As in 1890–6, numbers have assumed a symbolic importance. The most comprehensive Turkish official history calculates the number of Armenian dead in the war as 300,000. It gives evidence to show that most were killed in combat, by epidemics or by the winter cold.[4] This is not unlikely. When French occupying troops evacuated the Anatolian town of Marash in 1920, half of the 5,000 Armenians who left with them died of cold and hunger. Of more than 580,000 Ottoman soldiers known to have died in the First World War, well over half died of disease.[5] But 300,000 dead is the lowest possible estimate. One independent Turkish historian prefers the figure of 800,000 Armenian dead calculated by the Ottoman War Crimes Tribunal set up by the Allies after the First World War.[6] Armenian historians, however, allege that 1.5 million Armenians died: that is, practically the entire Armenian population of Anatolia.

Nobody seems to know how many Turkish and Kurdish Muslims were slaughtered by the Armenian militia. Some Turkish and Kurdish historians have estimated that between 30,000 and 40,000 Muslim civilians were massacred during the war. Other sources are partial and vague. To add to this confusion of numbers, it is not uncommon in Muslim villages in eastern Turkey to find, with a little prompting, that some people's grandparents were Armenian.

Vengeful Turkish and other Muslim refugees from the crumbling empire seized Armenian shops and homes. Armenian churches were dismantled or turned into mosques. The splendid Akdamar church on an island in Lake Van is an empty shell that features silently in tourist posters; the large, empty Armenian church in Diyarbakır does not. Built of the city's grey volcanic stone, its windows are bricked up, its churchyard overgrown, its congregation long gone and its gate opened suspiciously with the tug of a string by a guard who refuses to leave his shack.

Republican Turkey still defends the actions of the Ottomans. The Armenians, it is pointed out, were seen as traitors, often fighting for Russia rather than the Ottoman empire; their acts of sabotage behind the front lines would have merited instant execution in any European country at the time. It is noted, too, that the blitz of London, the fire-bombing of German cities and the atom bombs unleashed on Japan took no account of collateral civilian deaths.

The republic's sense of insecurity also shows through in the official treatment of the 80,000 Armenians left in Turkey, most of whom live in Istanbul. Their seminaries, like those of the Greeks, have been closed since 1971. Large amounts of paperwork are needed simply to get permission to repaint a church. Turkish newspapers cook up stories, later propagated by police posters, that the Armenians as a people are in league with Kurdish rebels in the south-east. A special department of the foreign ministry deals alike with Armenian and Kurdish problems behind a door of thick steel worthy of a bank vault.

Small wonder, perhaps, that the head of the Armenian Church in Turkey likes a nip of cognac with his morning coffee. Younger priests – there are not even enough left to man the thirty-four Armenian churches still open in Istanbul – have a harder time swallowing their anger at Turkish denial of the massacres and the web of petty restrictions that surround their lives. But Patriarch Karekin II tries to look forward as he receives his summer guests on the balcony of his modest residence on one of the Princes' Islands in the Sea of Marmara, half an hour by ferry from Istanbul.

'It's a ticklish question,' the patriarch says. 'There has still been no open statement by the government. On television, people now admit in debates that there were three million Armenians who can't all have simply disappeared. But it wasn't the fault of the Turkey of today. It's a secondary matter. You have to look to the future.'

The past, however, refuses to be put to rest. Following a double assassination in 1973, Turkish diplomats lived in fear of attacks by a new organization, the Secret Army for the Liberation of Armenia (ASALA). In all, thirty diplomats – including wives, children, drivers and guards – were killed in the ten years to 1984. Many innocent bystanders were also killed in attacks like those at Orly airport in France and Esenboğa airport in Ankara. ASALA was apparently broken after its leaders were killed in the course of the 1982 Israeli invasion of Lebanon. But it succeeded in entrenching Turkey's natural tendency towards a siege mentality. A whole generation of Turkish diplomats learned to live with flak jackets hanging behind their office doors. ASALA also came close to provoking revenge attacks on the remaining Armenians in Turkey.[7]

The question of whether the Ottomans actually ordered a genocide is still debated. By forced sales of Armenian property, Ottoman government documents show that it was clearly intended to cut the Armenians' links with their past homes. Any remaining parentless Armenian women under 20 and orphan boys under 10 were required to be adopted by local Muslim families. Time and again, the official orders are clear: no Armenians were to remain, first in the border areas, then in the main towns and other districts of Anatolia. In the end, even those who converted to Islam to save themselves were ordered out. The massacres that occurred may often seem local, but the pattern is repeated so often as to seem organized. Fingers have been pointed at the secret Teşkilat-i Mahsusa or Special Organization set up within the inner sanctum of the Young Turk Committee of Union and Progress. It is hard to escape the conclusion that there was some central involvement.[8]

Talaat Pasha, the Young Turk leader who was interior minister during the massacres and Grand Vizier from 1917, admitted to a degree of blame in a speech to his party congress on 1 November 1918:

> Many tragic events occurred during the transfer. But none of these happened as the result of an order by the Sublime Porte ... During a war that is about the life or death of a country, we could show no indulgence to those who endangered the security of the army ... many innocent people were undeniably sacrificed.

The speech was made shortly before the Young Turk leaders fled Turkey, and two weeks before the victorious Allied fleet anchored in the Bosphorus. Talaat knew that the Allies had vowed to bring to justice the perpetrators of the Armenian massacres. The Ottoman War Crimes Tribunal heard evidence that relevant documents had been burned by the Young Turk leaders, whilst many orders had been given verbally. The new government in Istanbul quickly promised to allow Armenians to return to their old homes and, under Allied supervision, to reverse any forced adoptions. Some minimal restitution was reported. But there was too much bad blood to allow any thorough reconciliation with

the Armenian people. Most Armenian survivors migrated to the
wealthier, safer West. In 1919, the War Crimes Tribunal condemned Talaat to death along with other fugitive leaders Enver,
Cevat and Nazim. In the case of Talaat and Cevat, Armenian
assassins got to them first.

Another ancient Christian community of the Ottoman empire,
the Greeks, did not last much longer than the Armenians. Their
fate was sealed in 1919–22 when the government in Athens, with
the moral support of the Allies, and primarily Britain, ordered the
invasion of the Aegean provinces of the helpless Ottoman empire.
While Allied troops occupied the capital, Istanbul, the Greek mainland army marched on the Turkish nationalist resistance and its
administration which had made its centre at Ankara. After three
years of bitter fighting, commemorated by Turkey as its War of
Independence, Turkish forces led by Mustafa Kemal broke the
Greek army and forced it to flee. The peace negotiations at Lausanne in 1923, supervised by the Great Powers, stipulated the
exchange of all the Greeks left in Anatolia with the mainly Turkish
Muslims in Greece. The only exceptions were to be the Greeks of
Istanbul and the Muslims and Turks of north-eastern Greece, a
region known to the Turks as Western Thrace.
   Historians cannot say whether the gradual eviction of the great
majority of Armenians, Greeks and other Christians between 1890
and 1923 was accidental or a premeditated attempt to make Anatolia into a 'Turkey for the Turks', a phrase which is still the
masthead motto of the nationalist newspaper *Hürriyet.* The Turks
often say, with justification, that they were provoked, and Talaat's
speech in 1918 is as close as any senior Turkish official has come
to an apology for the excesses. Armenian leaders, likewise, seldom
admit to any fault.
   The continued vengefulness in the Armenian diaspora and
among Turkish radicals makes the process of overcoming the
mutual suspicions between the newly independent republic of
Armenia and Turkey a slow business fraught with pitfalls. Turkey's
fears are somewhat allayed by the fact that nobody talks seriously
any more of attaching its eastern provinces to Armenia (although
these are now populated by Kurds with claims of their own).
Former Soviet Armenians also show a readiness to bury the past.
   Moves to break the taboo in Turkey were started in the late
1980s by Prime Minister Turgut Özal, who suggested that since
modern Turkey was not responsible for the events of the Ottoman

era, the debate should be left in the hands of the historians. In 1989, the cabinet ordered the opening-up of new sections of the Ottoman archives beyond the old and not very innocent-sounding cut-off date: May 1915. His action – along with grave threats from Turkey regarding the damage likely to be caused to Turkish-US relations – may have helped defeat the Armenian diaspora's last significant attempt, in 1989–90, to win the US Senate's official recognition of the massacres as 'genocide'. This liberalization of access to the archives has been of great value to researchers, but documents are still vetted and as yet no surprising new evidence has been published on the Armenian question. Only one or two foreign researchers have even bothered to look.

The baton, however, was taken up by a major Turkish publishing house in 1992, when it decided to publish the first frank assessment of the massacres by a Turk. 'We want to talk about it,' the publisher noted in a preface. 'The taboo is the same in Turkish and Armenian society. It is treachery to say anything other than that the fault is on the other side.'

In his book *The Turkish National Identity and the Armenian Problem*, Taner Akçam, a political exile in Germany at the time, said he preferred the Turkish word *kırım*, or 'deliberate slaughter', to the modern word 'genocide'. He also pointed to differences between the Turkish action and the genocide inflicted by Nazi Germany on the Jews. The Ottoman administration, for instance, had no ideology of racial purity, whatever the beliefs of the Young Turk leaders in the cabinet. He also pointed out that in Germany ordinary people have usually pleaded ignorance of the Jewish holocaust, while the state has admitted collective guilt. In Turkey, many older Turks know full well what happened to the Armenians and will privately admit it; it is the state which denies it.

In conclusion, Akçam maintains that republican Turkey must attempt to make some amends for the wrongs of the past. He laments that Turkish official histories show no trace of regret for the deaths of so many Armenians, whether or not these deaths were, as the official account has it, unintentional. He also fears that the republican state is applying a similar logic to the Kurds. 'It is not right to use others' crimes to mask our own,' he writes. 'Trying to show we were right is only trying to justify our barbarism . . . and can be a preparation for greater massacres.'

Even small gestures of regret and conciliation can have remarkable effects, as was apparent when the first non-Communist prime minister of Bulgaria, Philip Dimitrov, came to visit Turkey. He must have expected a rough ride after three decades in which

ruthless policies of assimilation in Bulgaria had forced hundreds
of thousands of ethnic Turks to migrate to Turkey.

'What will you do about all the Bulgarians forced to leave their
homes, to change their names and even to leave their country?'
Dimitrov was asked at a press conference by a Bulgarian immigrant, now a Turkish journalist working on a nationalist newspaper. The reporter spat out the words in the fluent Bulgarian
he had learned in his youth.

Dimitrov met the issue head on.

'You're right,' he said. 'I apologize in the name of Bulgaria.
This was not our fault, but the fault of the Communists. And I
add that any of our citizens who wish to come back may do so
and will receive all possible help from the state.'

A silence descended on the press conference. The journalist sat
down again. There was nothing left to say. It was as if a huge
burden had been lifted from everyone's shoulders. Relations
began to normalize; Bulgarian Turkish families went to and fro
across the border and a Bulgarian Turkish political party began
to play an important role in Bulgarian politics. Until the old Communists returned to power in 1994 and stirred up Bulgaria's
internal ethnic conflicts once more, the subject was hardly ever
mentioned again.

There is one other unexorcized ghost of the Armenian massacres
that may help explain why the Turkish republic is so reluctant to
discuss the question openly.

Many of those indicted by the Ottoman War Crimes Tribunal
were Special Organization operatives and also members of the
gangs that became the kernel of Turkish resistance to the Greek
invasion of 1919. Some were to rise high in the new republican
order. Topal Osman, an early chief of Mustafa Kemal's presidential
guard, was also wanted for his role in Armenian massacres in the
Black Sea area. The 1950s president of Turkey, Celal Bayar, was
in charge of Special Organization affairs in the Aegean port of
Izmir at the time of harassment of ethnic Greeks. And the sultan's
government in 1919 – possibly for political motives of its own,
since the Grand Vizier asked the British to carry out the arrests –
tried to have Mustafa Kemal and other leaders of the nationalist
movement hunted down for alleged involvement in the massacres.

One of the first decisions of the new nationalist parliament was
to give an amnesty to all those wanted for the massacres by the
Ottoman tribunal. This leniency may be one reason why the

nationalist cause was favoured by the Muslim traders of Anatolia, who had taken over Armenian shops and businesses at fire-sale prices, if at any cost at all. Republican Turkey's most successful businessman, Vehbi Koç, got his start in the vacuum left by the minorities who had dominated trade and business in pre-republican Ankara, although Koç always made a point of underlining in respectful terms how much he had learned from the non-Muslim merchants who were his first employers.

Early Kurdish solidarity with Atatürk's nationalists may also be explained by a shared sense of guilt in regard to the massacres and a shared hostility to the Allies' initial wish to create a US-protected Armenia in the First World War peace settlement. Anti-Christian attitudes have recurred disturbingly in the republic. As President Süleyman Demirel was to state baldly in 1995: 'We are all – barring non-Muslims – owners of this land.'

A living symbol of the scars left by this past is the headquarters of the newspaper *Cumhuriyet* (The Republic), the standard-bearer of Atatürk's revolution, which was assigned to an empty house in Istanbul formerly owned by an Armenian merchant and later used as the headquarters of the Committee of Union and Progress. *Cumhuriyet* has since built itself concrete offices in the garden at the back. But the decaying old wooden mansion overlooks it still, a silent reminder of one of the foundations on which the republic was built.

Few people spend much time thinking about the origins of the old building. If the Turkish republic does not dwell on the eviction of the country's ancient Christian inhabitants, it does spend great energy in educating its people in that other key product of the dying years of the Ottoman empire: the sense of Turkish identity formed around the hero of the Turkish War of Independence, Mustafa Kemal Atatürk.

4

Atatürk, Immortal Leader

Mustafa Kemal Pasha will have a pedestal in
the heart of every true Turk, even among
those who have been irretrievably wronged by
him.

Halide Edib (1884–1964)

IT WAS A grey November morning in 1994. Traffic was speeding
along an eight-lane ring road near Istanbul when a policeman
threw himself into the midst of the cars, trucks and inter-city buses,
his arms waving dramatically, his silver whistle squealing. Vehicles
screeched to a halt all round him. Miraculously, no one was hurt.
Drivers started to clamber out and, one by one, to stand to attention beside their vehicles. Air raid sirens began to howl in the
distance. It was 10 November, the anniversary of Mustafa Kemal
Atatürk's death, commemorated all over the country at precisely
9.05 a.m. The policeman's suicidal gesture was meant to keep alive
the memory of the Immortal Leader, the Father of the Turks.

The standard-bearers of Atatürk's revolution – the military, the
police, the civil servants – take the duty of preserving his legacy
seriously. Even in private, ordinary people stand stiffly in front of
their television sets. Time has done little to dilute the Turks'
reverence for the founder of the republic.

Most towns in Turkey have their Atatürk museums where
belongings of the late statesman are proudly displayed: silk
pyjamas, beautifully crafted shoes to fit his thin and elegant feet,
and suits cut by the best Armenian and Greek tailors of the day.
The son of one of his intimates even boasts of preserving the
butt of the great leader's last cigarette. Dominating the country's
capital, Ankara, is a large temple-like monument, a latter-day Acro-
polis built in honour of the country's saviour. The cabinets of new

governments, newly appointed army officers, civil servants and schoolchildren on patriotic outings all come to pay their respects in front of the impressive marble sarcophagus in the mausoleum.

In many ways, Atatürk has not yet relinquished the hold he had on his nation when he was alive. Frozen in time, his life and achievements have become the stuff of legend. The house where he was born in the Macedonian port of Salonika is preserved as part of the Turkish consulate in modern Thessaloniki in Greece, a shrine and place of pilgrimage. Mustafa Kemal is now a demigod whose every important utterance, and many that are not, must be learnt by heart by schoolchildren. Indeed, critics of his fiercely statist and secularist policies claim that the republican establishment has turned Kemalism into a form of religion. It is illegal for anyone else to use the surname he chose for himself in 1934, Atatürk, 'Father of the Turks'. Several other laws protect his memory, and public displays of disrespect are punishable by gaol sentences. Such is his appeal more than half a century after his death that groups of ageing intellectuals can be seen in shops peering at newly discovered and rather blurred photographs of their hero, chatting with all the excitement of teenagers exchanging football cards.

Atatürk's republic adopted the Western calendar, including the Christian concept of AD and BC. Recent Turkish history, however, is often presented to the public as neatly divided into the pre-Atatürk and the post-Atatürk republican era. Apart from a few great moments, such as the conquest of Istanbul in 1453, old-fashioned Kemalists view the Ottoman and Islamic past as a dark age. To outsiders republican Turkey, and especially the nationalistic Committee of Union and Progress, may seem to be very much the child of the Ottoman empire. But for true Kemalist believers, Atatürk's revolution heralds an age of enlightenment and the new, modern Turkey.

Atatürk was indeed a visionary statesman. He burst on the scene at a time when the Turks had lost faith in themselves, after the Ottoman 'sick man of Europe' had crumbled and collapsed. He was as complex as Turkey is today, full of contradictions, pulled in various directions, yet never losing sight of his ultimate goal: to unite the Turks and to create a modern state. He succeeded in imposing drastic reforms, but never completely set the heart of his country at rest. He led Turkey on the path of Westernization, but left it stranded half-way to full democratization because, deep down, he was not a democrat. He imposed a secular state, yet never won over those entrenched in their Islamic beliefs. In his eventful life are reflected the contradictions that still beset Turkey in the 1990s, the pull between East and West, the comfort of tradition disturbed by the necessity for change, an awe of the achievements of Christian technology and culture held in check by a strong attachment to the Muslim faith.

Few people watching General Mustafa Kemal disembark from the steamer *Bandırma* in the Black Sea port of Samsun on 19 May 1919 would have guessed that his discreet arrival would mark a turning point in the country's history. So momentous were the events of the following weeks that the day is now a national public holiday. In Samsun, the great leader himself, in the form of a statue, annually repeats his historic landing, brought ashore in the arms of local stalwarts struggling through the waves.

Kemal had left Constantinople with official orders to end the harassment of restive Christian minorities in the Black Sea region by Turkish nationalist gangs. It was a dying gesture from the dispirited Ottoman capital, its every action vetted by Allied proconsuls. Weary and humiliated by their defeat in the First World War, the Turks were being forced to pay the price for having taken Germany's side. Allied forces had occupied their city and were preparing to divide up the country between them.

The writer Halide Edib pointed to the deep sense of injustice felt by the Turks when they saw the renewed privileges granted by the Western forces to Christian minorities. The pettiness started at street level: Christian women, for example, were allowed to travel first class with second-class tickets on the ferries that crisscrossed the Bosphorus.[1] A rumour, strongly believed, had it that a Christian thief pursued by the Ottoman police could throw his passport on the ground, step on it with one toe and thus claim the protection of all-powerful foreign embassies.

By the time Kemal arrived in Samsun, nationalist groups had already started to rebel against the Western occupation and indeed against their own weak sultan who had allowed the empire to sink to such depths. But mystery still shrouds the reasons behind Kemal's appointment as the powerful Inspector of the Ninth Army. Admittedly, as the popular hero of the Gallipoli campaign, the man who had defeated the Allies' attempts to enter the Dardanelles, he had the necessary military credentials. He was a known rival of the disgraced Enver Pasha, but a nationalist nevertheless. Luckily for the future republican cause, Kemal's name meant nothing special to the British occupation authorities in Istanbul, who could have blocked his appointment.[2] Most believe his posting was the result of behind-the-scenes machinations by influential sympathizers of the fledgeling nationalist movement. Some are also convinced that there was complicity at the highest level. Mustafa Kemal had been aide-de-camp to the sultan when Mehmet VI Vahdettin (1918–22) was heir to the imperial throne. They had travelled to Europe together and the outspoken officer had not hidden his views.

It is therefore possible that the sultan, who was too frightened and helpless to work openly against the Allies, had implicitly given his blessing to Kemal's plans, or had hedged his bets by supporting both his prime minister and the rebellious officer. The sovereign's words to the man himself on the eve of his departure for the Black Sea were suitably ambiguous. 'Pasha [general], you have served the state well till now. But I want you to forget all this. The service you are about to perform is possibly greater than any you have yet performed. You may be able to save the state.'

Among those who believe that Vahdettin had given his implicit backing to Kemal is Hümeyra Özbaş, the granddaughter of the last Ottoman sultan.[3] As she recalls in a childhood anecdote, Vahdettin, though driven from the country when Mustafa Kemal abolished the sultanate, still respected the republic's new leader. The children of the imperial family, then in exile in San Remo, were playing in the garden, Hümeyra among them, and chanting a popular revolutionary song that included the words 'Long live Mustafa Kemal'. A servant, frightened that the deposed sultan would hear them, reworded the couplets to say 'Death to Mustafa Kemal'. A few minutes later, a furious Vahdettin emerged on the balcony and berated the terrified children for their lack of reverence. 'Mustafa Kemal is a Turkish general. He is my general. I will not allow any insult to a Turkish soldier.'

The truth may never be known. What is certain, however, is that Atatürk alone cannot be credited with starting the resistance to the foreign invaders. Few remember this now, but one who does is Cemal Kutay, an elderly gentleman living in an old wooden *konak* on the Asian side of Istanbul surrounded by yellowing pictures, disintegrating furniture and boxes overflowing with notes from the 127 books he has written on the subject of Atatürk. An acrid smell of burned paper lingers in musty corners of his ageing house, the relic of a tragic fire that spread to his archives from the house next door. The blaze was the result of an almost symbolic act of vandalism against history, but one typical of twentieth-century Istanbul. His neighbour had started the fire and razed to the ground the old wooden house next door in order to build one of the characterless modern concrete apartment blocks of the republican era.

One of Kutay's proudest achievements was to open a museum in Sakarya, site of the most important battle of the Turkish republic's war of independence, to 'remember the unknown heroes'.[4] As a young journalist on the official newspaper *Hakimiyet-i Milli* from 1928 until Atatürk's death in 1938, Cemal Kutay got to know Mustafa Kemal well. Unlike many today who see Atatürk as a supernatural being who rose above human failings, Kutay remembers and admires the man he was, a man who sometimes made mistakes and who, 'unlike Jeanne d'Arc and other heroes of epic tales', could not possibly have founded the republic of Turkey on his own.

'Five men started the liberation struggle: Ali Fuat Cebesoy, Kazım Karabekir, Mustafa Kemal, Rauf Orbay, Refet Bele,' the 85-year-old writer declared. When Kemal arrived in Samsun, he had with him only thirty-nine men, hardly a powerful force. The real troops in Anatolia were under the command of Ali Fuat, who had brought together the remains of his 20th Army Corps, and Kazım Karabekir, who had regrouped the 15th Army Corps in the eastern province of Erzurum.

This fledgeling liberation movement then received an unexpected and electrifying shock. The ambitious Greek government in Athens, strongly encouraged by the British, decided to act on its claim to the Aegean coast, where the Greek minority's history dated back to the colonists of ancient Greece. On 15 May 1919, just as Atatürk was leaving Constantinople for Samsun, a Greek expeditionary force landed in Smyrna, the jewel and principal port of the Aegean coast now known as Izmir. At the same time, the threat that the Great Powers might plan to impose a separate Armenian state in the eastern provinces of Anatolia fuelled resistance in the east, and fired the hungry and humiliated Turks into action against the foreigners now attacking from all sides.

In Samsun, Kemal defiantly joined the ranks of the rebels. When Britain demanded his immediate recall, he trekked up the mountain passes inland to the arid Anatolian plateau. There he spent the summer of 1919 trying to impose his leadership on the various strands of rebellion.

A first congress of the eastern nationalists was held in Erzurum on 23 July 1919, followed in September by a meeting in Sivas. Kemal, who had resigned his army commission, was elected the president of the Society for the Defence of Rights, which framed a set of principles for the resistance movement. In this 'National Pact' were two crucial tenets: total rejection of any foreign intervention either in the form of a mandate or protectorate and the indivisibility of the state within its national frontiers. Having on 12 September severed all their ties with the capital, the resistance sent telegrams demanding the loyalty of all civil and military authorities in Anatolia to the structure they had created.

The pressure of the growing nationalist movement caused the collapse of the Constantinople government on 2 October. A new assembly was formed that was still loyal to the sultan but espoused many of the patriotic principles dear to Kemal. Several of his nationalist friends, uncomfortable with the legal limbo in which they found themselves in Anatolia, decided to join this new parliament, which opened its doors on 12 January 1920. They made overtures to Kemal, who refused to join them and settled in Ankara instead.

As it turned out, he was right to stay away. On 16 March, the British staged a mini-coup, made official the foreign occupation of Constantinople and arrested many nationalist deputies who were sent into exile in Malta. Others, forewarned, managed to escape and returned to Ankara where Kemal was waiting for them. To escape detection, the writer Halide Edib and her husband Dr Adnan had to travel across the Bosphorus disguised as a provincial imam and his peasant wife. Using the odd password 'Jesus has sent us', they were let through by guards into the grounds of the grand Özbekler Tekkesi, a wooden kiosk belonging to a Muslim brotherhood on the Asian side of the city. There they met up with fellow nationalists also on their way to Ankara to fight the war of liberation.

Sultan Vahdettin had chosen not to resist the Allies. On 10 August 1920 his representatives signed the Treaty of Sèvres, a document that amounted to a death sentence served on the Ottoman empire. Under this accord, national territory was to be parcelled out to create an independent Armenian republic in the east and an autonomous Kurdish region in the south-east. The rest of the country was divided between the French, Italians and Greeks. The Straits and Constantinople were to be demilitarized and placed under international control (see pp. xiv–xv).

The Treaty of Sèvres, never ratified or implemented, is still deeply embedded in the Turkish memory. Its provisions spelled out the Western powers' ambition to coop the Turks up in a small, rough and poor northern canton in Anatolia. Sèvres is still a rallying cry for suspicious nationalists who believe the Europeans have never given up their plans to partition modern Turkey. This secret agenda, in their eyes, explains why Europeans back the Kurds in their demands for greater rights and the Armenians in their calls for an official Turkish apology for the atrocities committed between 1890 and 1918.

At the time, the treaty only served to strengthen the resolve of the nationalists. Realizing after the British take-over of the Ottoman capital that no help was to be expected from their own weak government, they had opened a break-away Turkish National Assembly in the dusty provincial town of Ankara on 23 April 1920. To house this historic gathering, the nationalists had requisitioned an unfinished building on a barren hill overlooking the vast and empty Anatolian plain. The deputies were a colourful mix of civil servants, religious leaders in their turbans, dervishes in felt hats, landowners, journalists, and tribal chiefs wearing cummerbunds and baggy trousers. Pictures hanging in the building, now a museum squeezed between two major avenues in the middle of the bustling capital, show them all sitting on wooden school benches in the modest hall dominated by a tribune from which Mustafa Kemal, elected chairman the next day, gave a rousing speech: 'It is known to all that the seat of the Caliphate and Government is under temporary occupation by foreign forces and that our independence is greatly restricted. Submitting to these conditions would mean national acceptance of a slavery proposed to us by foreign powers.'

Turkey now had a budding alternative state, but its territory was still under occupation. The troops mustering in Anatolia to fight the invading Greeks bore little resemblance to the disciplined Ottoman armies that once made the reputation of the warrior Turks. Fighting alongside the tattered remnants of the army were many irregulars, often little better than bandits and outlaws. Some of them, however, became legendary. At one stage, Çerkez Ethem (Ethem the Circassian), a giant of a man who could shoot while standing bare-back on his galloping horse, saved the capital in 1920 from the advancing Greek troops; but not before panicky residents, including parliamentarians, had already packed their bags ready for a speedy evacuation.

This confusion was made worse by the fact that on 11 April 1920, the religious leaders in Constantinople, hoping to sway the bulk of the conservative Anatolian population against the rebels, had issued a *fetva* for *jihad*, an Islamic edict declaring holy war against the nationalist resistance. To make its point, the government also sentenced Mustafa Kemal and his comrades to death *in absentia*. As a result, while the Greek armies were fast advancing against them and the British were landing troops to take control of the Sea of Marmara and the Straits, the nationalists' meagre troops found themselves harried by small-scale counter-revolts loyal to the sultan. Clashes also continued on the Caucasus front with Russian and Armenian forces.

In September, the nationalist army managed nevertheless to repel an Armenian offensive in the eastern part of the country and retook several provinces that had been lost to the Russians. The Greek army proved harder to dislodge. Twice repulsed at Inönü by Ismet Pasha – Mustafa Kemal's long-time companion, who later took the surname Inönü, even though his role in the battles is controversial – the Greeks broke through to take the city of Eskişehir on 21 July 1921. The loss of this key rail junction just 220 kilometres west of Ankara marked the lowest ebb of the nationalists' fortunes.

The rural population was largely passive. The suffering during the Great War had left it with little desire to fight on. In some places, Turkish troops would advance through Muslim villages already hung with Greek flags in anticipation of Athens' victory. The journalist Falih Rıfkı Atay, who lived on the Princes' Islands near Istanbul where members of minorities such as the Greeks had their summer residences, complained that he had to endure 'drunken processions with barrel organs playing Greek marches outside Turkish houses till morning. All the local Greeks wore infuriating smiles . . . Even the most ardent nationalists began to lose faith.'[5]

Kemal ordered his troops to withdraw and dig in at the Sakarya river. The Greeks launched a new offensive on 14 August 1921. After a fierce battle of many weeks' duration under a searing sun, the Turks, on the verge of exhaustion, successfully forced the Greeks to retreat. The tide had finally turned in their favour, a trend that was noticed abroad as well. On 21 October, the French government distanced itself from the Allies by signing the Ankara agreement with the Turks, a separate peace treaty that implicitly recognized the nationalist government.

The final Turkish offensive was launched on 26 August 1922. By 9 September, a victorious Mustafa Kemal was able to enter Smyrna (Izmir) at the head of a long convoy, applauded by the Turkish population, but feared by the Greeks and Armenians who were desperately trying to escape by sea. The Turkish celebrations were short-lived. A huge fire broke out a few days later in the Christian quarters. Much of the city was razed to the ground.

The origins of the fire, clearly started deliberately, are still hotly debated. For the Greeks the burning of Smyrna, with its images of women and children drowning as they tried to swim to Allied warships standing offshore, is the outstanding symbol of the catastrophe that ended two millennia of Greek civilization in Anatolia. But the Turks can point to the many other Anatolian towns ravaged by the retreating Greek army. A French journalist who had covered the war of independence arrived in Smyrna shortly after the flames had died down and was shocked by the wanton destruction of one of the foremost trading cities of the world. 'The first defeat of the nationalists had been this enormous fire,' she wrote. 'Within forty-eight hours, it had destroyed the only hope of immediate economic recovery. For this reason, when I heard people accusing the winners themselves of having provoked it to get rid of the Greeks and Armenians who still lived in the city, I could only shrug off the absurdity of such talk. One had to know the Turkish leaders very little indeed to attribute to them so generously a taste for unnecessary suicide.'[6] Falih Rıfkı Atay however believes a spiteful Turkish officer may have been responsible. 'At the time it was said that Armenian arsonists were responsible. But was this so? There were many who assigned a part in it to Nureddin Pasha, commander of the First Army, a man whom Kemal had long disliked . . .'[7]

Turkish dead in the war of independence numbered some 10,000 men in the fighting and 22,000 from disease.[8] Greek dead and wounded were estimated at around 100,000 men. Anatolia had been freed, and the war had forced the Western Allies to accept the Ankara government. With the signature of the Treaty of Lausanne, on 24 July 1923, the world officially recognized the country that the Turkish nationalists had built for themselves on the ruins of the Ottoman empire.

A major task awaited the Turks, who formally declared themselves a republic on 29 October 1923: they now had a recognized territory, albeit ravaged by war, and their country, the Republic of Turkey, had a name. But they had yet to build a real nation. Atatürk's revolution was only beginning.

To understand the dramatic changes Turkey has undergone over the past seven decades – and those it has failed to implement – it is worth remembering that the young republic started virtually from scratch. By 1923, the country had been laid waste. The war-torn towns of Anatolia were full of confused Muslim refugees from decades of wars, the human remnants of the demoralized rump of the Ottoman empire. The Armenians and Greeks who had been the backbone of city life had gone. Everything had to be rebuilt, above all a new identity. So, for these people, Atatürk and the young republicans consciously created a new concept of the 'Turk'.

Originally, this 'Turk' was not a narrowly racist idea but a broad term for anybody who chose to become a citizen of the new republic. In this they were following the prescriptions of the Young Turk ideologue Ziya Gökalp, himself probably partly Kurdish, who held that upbringing was more significant than ethnic origin. He also recommended that priority be given to securing the nation-state within its borders.

The Turks badly needed to regain a sense of pride in their identity both at home and abroad. Little of Europe's early admiration of Ottoman military prowess survived into the years of Turkish decline. Antagonism to them was – and often still is – a natural state of affairs in Europe. Views were highly coloured by folk memories of Muslim hordes at the gates of Vienna, reinforced by centuries of hostile opinions voiced by people whose only knowledge of the Turks was of their brutal and unsuccessful attempts to shore up their crumbling empire. Voltaire condemned them as enemies of the arts and gaolers of women, and accused them of usurping and laying waste the ruins of Greek antiquity. The tar of European opprobrium, however, only began to stick after the Turkish suppression of a pan-Slavic revolt that spread to Bulgaria from Serbia in 1876, during which Turkish irregulars known as *başıbozuk* (crazy heads) carried out the brutal massacre of some 15,000 men, women and children. The events inspired British politician William Gladstone, in relative obscurity at the time, to write a hugely popular leaflet attacking the pro-Turkish policies of his rival Benjamin Disraeli, the prime minister of the day. *The Bulgarian Horrors and the Question of the East* sold 200,000 copies within a month. Liberal opinion has never quite recovered and still looks askance at the Turks even today.

Prime Minister Lloyd George described the Turks in 1914 as 'a human cancer, a creeping agony in the flesh of the lands which they misgoverned'.[9] For the French historian André Mandelstam, writing on the fate of the Ottoman empire in 1917, the Turkish people had 'done nothing to justify their existence from the point of view of civilization. It is a people that has borne no fruit. Its historic mission was to destroy, and destruction needs no soul.'[10]

The *New York Tribune* took up the baton in 1919, telling its readers that 'the Turks have always been a parasite and a stench in the nostrils of civilization.'[11] Amid a flood of pamphlets after the First World War calling for the outright expulsion of the Turks from Anatolia, a former American ambassador to Berlin suggested that the Turks could be dealt with by adopting the US system of park-like reservations such as were used for the American Indians.[12] This explicitly racist view of the Turks persists in various forms. The British historian Robert Blake felt able to dismiss the Ottoman state in 1992 as 'a regime whose tyranny was mitigated only by corruption and incompetence'. Alan Parker's powerful film *Midnight Express* fixed a prejudice that somehow all Turks were corrupt, sadistic and dangerous. The theme is still heard among the current generation of travel writers, who can unthinkingly dismiss modern Istanbul and its 12 million people as a 'cultural desert'.

Even for the Ottomans, the word 'Turk' had derogatory connotations, being associated particularly with the peasant 'Turk', and one of the nationalists' first tasks was to redefine and broaden the concept. 'The Turks are those people of Turkey who founded the Turkish republic' was an early definition drawn up by Atatürk.[13] Within a few years, however, Turkishness had acquired an ethnic tinge. The line between geography and race soon became blurred. After all, the racial model was in fashion in Europe, so Turkishness became the thing.

Ironically, Turkish nationalism grew partly as the result of confrontation with the early nationalistic Christian states of the Balkans. Among the young officers of the Ottoman army like Mustafa Kemal, the successful struggle of the Balkan states seemed to offer a way forward to creating a new Turkish national state in Anatolia. It is no coincidence that the Young Turk movement began in the ferment of Macedonia or that those Turks who were the most nationalistic were those who had been evicted from their centuries-old Balkan homes.

A Turkish national state was harder to build in practice than in theory. Until the Great War, most trade and crafts had been controlled by the Christian minorities. The exchange of population with Greece left the Turks destitute, for barely 5 per cent of businesses had been in their hands. Peasants and even provincial governors begged for Greek and Armenian tradesmen to be allowed back into the country. 'I do not think any backward Anatolian town nowadays is as primitive as Ankara was then. We had a table made, for eating and writing. No two of its legs were of the same length. All the civilized life of Ankara had gone with the

Armenians and Greeks. We were going to have to rebuild the city and indeed the whole country, from the foundations to the roof,' commented journalist Falih Rıfkı Atay.[14] Carpenters were needed to manufacture wheels for horse carts and tinners to tin copper pots to prevent the population from being poisoned. New crafts had to be learnt, a whole economy to be built up.

Mustafa Kemal set about doing this. With his military victory at Sakarya he had overcome his rivals and become the undisputed commander of the nationalist troops. But although Turks today take for granted the admiration their forefathers felt for the revolutionary leader, at the time he still faced stiff political opposition, and not just among those nostalgic for the sultanate.

The new national assembly was restive. The official version of events usually portrays his opponents as 'reactionaries' unwilling to face modernization. But many, among them some of Kemal's closest collaborators, simply objected to the dictatorial tendencies of the leader. It was a trait that Atatürk himself did not deny. 'I am dictating democracy to my people,' he told one visiting American journalist. Mustafa Kemal was admired, sometimes venerated but not always liked by his contemporaries. Convinced that he was always right, he did not hesitate to impose his will by force rather than seek compromise. Any criticism was perceived as treachery and few were spared the lash of his sharp tongue.

Halide Edib, a dedicated nationalist who became the only woman officer in the war of independence, had doubts about him even before joining his struggle. 'He was a man of extraordinary intelligence and cunning, as well as of abnormal ambition,' she recalled. These misgivings were confirmed by her close working relationship with Kemal. 'What an astounding man! Is he just some elemental force in a catastrophic form? Is there anything human about him at all? And how can this cyclone ever come to rest when the nation has reached its goal?'[15] Like many other early revolutionaries, she fell foul of the great leader and was forced to leave the country.

Mustafa Kemal's main asset was his tremendous energy, but his working methods exhausted most of those who came close to him. He would gather his friends around his table in the evenings for lengthy brainstorming sessions that often turned into night-long drinking bouts during which he would speak at length about his ideas. No one dared leave his table before the signal was given. Kemal would then sleep for most of the morning and only get up at midday for a meal of rice and beans, while humbler beings had to get on with their daily life.

Today, Turkey attributes everything that is deemed modern in the state to Kemal. His radical reforms are well known: he abolished the caliphate and declared Turkey a secular republic (1923), the reform his followers today are most thankful for; he forbade the fez and any attire remotely connected to Islam in favour of the hat and the Western suit (1925); he replaced Islamic law by the Swiss civil code and Mussolini's penal code (1926); he introduced the Latin alphabet (1928) while launching a country-wide literacy campaign; and he forced everybody to take a surname (1934). Then, exhausted by the strains of office, fast living, heavy drinking and womanizing, he died of cirrhosis of the liver in 1938. By the end, the day-to-day running of the state did not interest him. He was a man who painted the large brush-strokes and left the finer points of government to men he trusted and who were, in any case, under his control.

A Westernizing trend had in fact started in the Ottoman empire long before this blue-eyed leader from Macedonia arrived on the scene. Arguably such reforms could have been implemented gradually, with a less traumatic effect on the population. But Kemal was impatient, keen to impose his vision of the new Turkey. When he commissioned proposals to introduce the Latin alphabet, his assistants came up with plans that foresaw a transition period of five to fifteen years. Atatürk would have none of it: it would have to be done immediately. He personally introduced the new alphabet to an astonished population at a public fête near the Topkapı palace in 1928. With a few strokes of his pen, this conservative and religious country, which was 80 per cent rural – as it had been in the fifteenth century when Mehmet II conquered the rump of the Byzantine empire – was ordered to become a modern Western state.

In the same spirit, Mustafa Kemal decreed that modern Western music was good for his people. This was taken to heart by Ismet Inönü, Atatürk's right-hand man and Turkey's second president, who described to his son Erdal[16] how he 'discovered' classical music when on a military campaign in Yemen, shortly before the First World War. The officers had found an old gramophone and a pile of records left behind by a French construction company. Looking for something to enliven the long evenings, they decided to try them. 'We put on one record; it was an opera song. We did not understand anything; we stopped it. We tried another one, a symphony; we found it very noisy, we stopped it too and gave up playing the gramophone,' Ismet Pasha explained. But entertainment was sadly lacking in Yemen and the officers kept trying. 'I don't know over how many evenings, listening for a while, then leaving it, we slowly got used to it and began to understand and like this music. I thus learned that only by getting people to listen to Western music often could we make them like it.'

Ismet Pasha was true to his policy. Later, as head of state, he even took cello lessons and would go regularly to concerts. In the provinces, local authorities would organize European-style balls. Local bureaucrats would have to waltz stiffly around the floor in couples to the sound of Western instruments. But their hearts were often not in it. In the same way, Kemal himself only showed signs of emotion when he sang the folk-songs of his native Rumelia, the Balkan or lost European 'wing' of the Ottoman empire where he was born.

Even today, when Turks get together to drink a few glasses of *rakı* or 'lion's milk', they will still join spontaneously in a Turkish folk dance to the sound of drums, or slowly sing together the melancholy, long-drawn-out ballads of their ancestors. Suppressed as unWestern by the early republicans, the highly strung tones of Turkish classical music are again in fashion and its dinner-jacketed specialists claim a serious niche on cultural-minded state television programmes.

Amongst the younger generation, Western and Eastern cultures have also to some extent fused. The synthesis is in constant transition: whereas before 1990 Turkish pop music was dominated by underground *arabesk* ballads of despair, with Western influences grafted on to a Middle Eastern base, a new generation of musicians is now having greater success with a more upbeat music using Western rhythms with Turkish overtones.

Thanks to Atatürk, Turkish women proudly boast of having won legal equality long before many of their Western sisters. But at the same time as introducing these reforms, Atatürk also disbanded those feminist groups that had been agitating for greater rights in the last years of the Ottoman empire. The women's movement never quite recovered from not having had to fight for its rights.

Kemal himself was no great feminist. 'He was never Western in his understanding of women ... He was extremely jealous, his inclination was towards the harem. But intellectually he believed that women should be free and equal to men.'[17] A well-known womanizer, he was briefly tamed by Latife, a sophisticated, French-educated girl he met when he entered Smyrna in 1922. When she refused his advances, surprising a man not used to being rebuffed, he abruptly chose to marry her. 'No sooner had he arrived [in Smyrna, from Ankara], than he went straight to her house: "That's it. We are getting married." Seeing her frozen to the spot, speechless, he added rapidly: "Right now, with no ceremony, without telling anybody." She managed to defer it a few hours. The next day, they went out together and stopped the first imam they met on their way; Mustafa Kemal gave his name and rank, and demanded that the marriage vows be pronounced. The imam, astounded, could not understand. He had to be urged on repeatedly before he could complete the office.'[18]

The union soon turned sour. The intelligent and ambitious Latife wanted to share the burdens of her husband's life. Basically a soldier, a rough man educated in military schools, Kemal perhaps felt exposed by her education and the manners she had learned while living in Paris. His Western ways had been acquired largely from intensive reading, with the help of friends who had lived abroad and a stint as a military attaché in Bulgaria. Marriage did not change his ways, and he went on drinking until the small hours with his friends, while she would tap the floor angrily upstairs, causing him intense embarrassment. Two years and four months after they were married, he decided on divorce with the same fixity of purpose that had led him to marry her. Enough was enough. Women's rights did not impede his decision: without even consulting Latife, he drew up a divorce decree, signed it and had it approved by parliament. There was no appeal. The marriage was over.

Atatürk acted out his desire to mould people's thoughts by adopting a number of children. His sexual appetites and fast living would certainly not make him the ideal adoptive parent in the eye of today's social services. Some indeed claim he had close relationships with some of his daughters, especially Afet who, aged 18, became 'a surrogate wife' after Latife's departure.[19] But he did give his children the education he hoped all Turks would one day receive, sending them to universities abroad. Sabiha became a well-known airforce pilot at a time when few women were allowed into military forces in Europe, Afet became a history professor and Sabriye a judge.

More important perhaps than its cultural flaws are the structural defects of Atatürk's republican state. The repression, the intense national paranoia, the shortcomings of its democracy and the over-reliance on the army can all be traced back to the foundation of the republic, and indeed to the later years of the Ottoman empire.

Atatürk spoke for a Western system but his autocratic tendencies and his vanity required that he be sole leader of a hierarchical state. Furthermore, founded by army officers, the new state naturally had militaristic tendencies. As a result the Turkish republic, although a parliamentary democracy, never really developed the concept of teamwork central to party politics. In the 1990s, most of the political parties present on the Turkish scene are dominated by leaders who make key decisions virtually alone. The lack of compromise and co-operation among politicians, even within a party, accounts in large part for the continuing sense of crisis and gridlock in politics.

Instead of choosing parties for their ideas and principles, Turks elect leaders, somehow always in search of someone with the stature of a second Atatürk. When a deputy disagrees with his party leader, he breaks off and starts a new political formation, much as an argument in a Turkish or Kurdish village may lead to the breakaway of a sub-clan and the setting up of a new hamlet further up the valley. Like cells multiplying, the single party of the republic's early years and its conservative rival set up in 1946 – the Republican People's Party and the Democrat Party – are the ancestors of most of the twelve parties that competed in the 1995 elections.

Rather than improving on the incomplete Kemalist revolution, however, Atatürk's successors froze the picture when he died: the Turkey he had delivered was taken to be a finished product. Any change from then on was portrayed as straying from the path laid down by the *ebedi şef,* or Immortal Leader.

The early republicans set out with a genuine sense of mission to civilize the ignorant Anatolian masses, but met serious difficulties. In his classic novel *Yaban* (Stranger), published in 1932, Yakup Kadri Karaosmanoğlu describes the disappointment of an officer wounded in the war of independence and taken in to convalesce by Anatolian villagers. They are exhausted by war and unable or unwilling to share the hero's enthusiasm for Mustafa Kemal and his plans for a new Turkey. 'As the days go by I understand better: the Turkish *aydın,* the enlightened Turk, in this wide and desolate world that he calls his Turkish country, is indeed a very lonely man,' he wrote despairingly. 'Is there a deep chasm between the literate class and the villagers in every country? I do not know. But between a child of Istanbul and an Anatolian peasant there is a difference greater than that between a London Englishman and an Indian of the Punjab.'

As the early revolutionaries turned into a well-entrenched élite, they no longer made efforts to reach out and bridge the gap that separated them from the ill-educated peasant population. Instead they developed a patronizing attitude that resulted in the creation of a state 'for the people, despite the people'.

This patronizing attitude still prevails and is often used to justify anti-democratic moves. Dissent is dealt with harshly. Leftists and especially Kurds bear the brunt of the state's inflexibility. Torture, summary arrests and disappearances are common occurrences. This again is no surprising deviation from Atatürk's model: his own attitude to criticism was equally harsh. In 1925, using his fight against religious backwardness as a pretext, he cracked down with virulence on the Kurdish-Islamic uprising led by Sheikh Said in the eastern part of the country. Dozens of leaders were hanged, thousands of people deported.

The worst excesses of the early republic took place in 1926. A plot was uncovered in Izmir to assassinate Atatürk. A few genuine suspects were arrested and confessions extracted. But at the same time Kemal seized the opportunity to purge all those who had complained of his dictatorial style. He ordered the arrest of men who had earlier been his closest allies and companions: Arif, his friend and aide-de-camp for years, Kazım Karabekir, Refet Bele, Ali Fuat Cebesoy, early heroes of the liberation struggle, were all dragged in front of independence tribunals 'that struck terror in the hearts of many Turks . . . the era resembled the reign of the guillotine during the French Revolution'. Popular feeling for the great generals forced the courts to acquit Kazım, Refet and Ali Fuat, who had never conspired against Kemal. But others equally innocent, including the loyal Arif, were hanged. While this gruesome sentence was carried out, Mustafa Kemal gathered foreign diplomats for a dazzling ball at the presidential palace on Çankaya hill above Ankara. The total number of victims of the purge is not known but hundreds are believed to have been summarily tried and executed until the tribunals, having completed their grisly mission, were dissolved.

These terrible events were of course not out of tune with their times. The wind of democracy was not sweeping through Europe. Atatürk was a contemporary of Mussolini and Hitler. The ends justified the means.

There are still powerful forces in Turkey today who hold the cumbersome procedures of court justice in contempt; the attitude affects not only the many 'mafias' who operate outside the law but organs of the state as well. Courthouses still freeze for lack of fuel in winter, judges are poorly paid, witnesses are easily intimidated, fines are made ridiculous by inflation, laws are rarely reformed and, with courts sitting only once every few months, trials can take years to complete. Just as the independence tribunals became to some extent a state within a state, summary executions or torture of Kurdish nationalists or leftist militants are carried out today by unknown assailants believed to be linked to the security forces. Police raids on militant safehouses usually end in what look remarkably like extrajudicial executions.

With Atatürk as an example, today's Turkish leaders have felt few inhibitions in adopting arbitrary rule, at least until the advent of the summary and equally unaccountable 'justice' meted out on national live television. The Kurds' modest demands for cultural rights are still silenced by the same ruthless methods used in the 1920s, even though ignoring these demands has only provided short-term relief. Revolts have flared up throughout the history of the republic and will continue to do so until the government can move ahead of the popular will and capture its imagination with bold and innovative steps.

Atatürk twice toyed with the idea of allowing opposition as a safety-valve in the country. But the Progressive Republican Party founded in November 1924 threatened his own authority and was closed down in June the next year. For the second attempt, he thought it more prudent to choose his old friend Fethi Okyar to start a party which would operate under his instructions. Even Kemal's sister Makbule was recruited as a member. But the runaway success of the experiment frightened him and challenged his need for absolute control. Ninety-three days later, the party was closed down. It was not until 1946 that Turkey made another attempt at multi-party democracy.

Officialdom never admits it, but the Turks today are still struggling to digest the heavy burden of Atatürk's legacy, from the idealized public image to the rougher reality. Like any politician, Atatürk said many things at many times, so the cult of Kemalism can be interpreted to suit almost any purpose.

What is a pure Kemalist in the 1990s? 'He is above all secular, he wants to banish religion, he believes in progress, he worships reason. But he cannot accept rational criticism,' believes newspaper editor Şahin Alpay.

Few imagine that Atatürk was an Islamic fundamentalist. But this was what one 15-year-old Turkish boy who ended up in gaol for carving a hammer and sickle on his school desk was told by the Islamist prison *hoca* or teacher in the late 1980s, despite evidence that Atatürk had nothing but contempt for religious feelings. (According to his biographer Jacques Benoist-Méchin, in moments of anger, Atatürk described Islam as 'the absurd theology of an immoral Bedouin', a 'putrefied corpse that poisons our life'.) Extreme right-wing nationalists argue that with his insistence on the Turks' Central Asian origins, Mustafa Kemal was an advocate of pan-Turkism. In the eyes of leftists, however, he had a socialist vision of the world, since he gave control of the lion's share of the economy to the state. Even the Bolsheviks were fooled. Although Atatürk was first and foremost a Turkish nationalist, the young Communist government in Moscow gave him gold for years in the belief that he would turn out to be an ally and a Turkish Lenin.

The cult of Atatürk pervades all aspects of Turkish life. When the army intervenes in politics as they did in 1960, 1971 and 1980, or when the security forces crack down on activists, they do so in the declared belief that they are carrying out what Atatürk would have wanted. Their desire to preserve intact an ideology that was tailored to the 1920s leads to their lagging behind a society that is moving towards more openness, more freedom or indeed towards a newly restructured form of Islam. As Mehmet Altan, member of a revisionist movement for a 'second republic', said in his newspaper column in 1994, 'Kemalism is dead, but nobody knows how to dispose of the corpse.'

As Kemalism – whatever it is – gradually loses its grip on society and Islam-based ideologies raise their heads, the panicky old guard see no alternative but to repeat again and again the slogans coined by Atatürk. School curricula, already saturated with propaganda, have increased the Kemalist dose. So afraid are the Turks that opening the debate will cause the collapse of the whole structure that they prefer to stop their ears to calls for progress and modernity. Paradoxically, by doing so, they are going against the Westernizing trend advocated by Kemal.

The *Halaskar Gazi* (Saviour and Warrior) of the Turks, the man who had founded the secular Turkish republic, finally closed his eyes on 10 November 1938 in the splendour of the Dolmabahçe palace built by the Ottomans he had ousted. His death had a profound impact on the population and is still vividly remembered by many key players on the political scene. Bülent Ecevit, who was to lead Atatürk's Republican People's Party in the seventies, was among the thousands of schoolchildren who filed into the palace to pay their respects to Kemal's mortal remains. Alparslan Türkeş, later spokesman for the 1960 coup, was among the military cadets in the guard of honour around the coffin. Another cadet, 1980 coup leader Kenan Evren, marched in front of the gun-carriage on the first stage of its last journey by ship and train to Ankara.

Once there, it spoke volumes about the state of mind of his successors that they did not know what to do with their dead leader.[20] For years, he lay in state in the Museum of Anatolian Civilizations as Turkey's new rulers tried to decide what to make of his legacy.

5

Walking the Tightrope

He who has burned his lips on boiling milk
will blow on yoghurt.

Turkish proverb

SITTING AT THE terrace of a water-side café or fish restaurant
by the Bosphorus, tourists and local inhabitants alike can engage
in a favourite activity, boatwatching. On any day, within the space
of a few hours, a fascinating variety of craft slip past, be they rusty
freighters, small fishing-boats, long and throbbing oil tankers or
sleek and gleaming cruise liners.

This famous waterway in its idyllic setting of gentle hills, rapidly
losing its orchards and forests of pink-blossomed Judas trees to
ever bigger housing developments, is not only an asset for tour
operators and real-estate promoters. As Turkey has had countless
opportunities to find out over the past two hundred years, the
Bosphorus is of major strategic importance. The only sea passage
out of the Black Sea, it has been the central issue of many disputes
and even a cause for war.

Although the status of the Turkish Straits – connecting the Black
Sea to the Aegean and the Mediterranean through the Bosphorus,
the inland Marmara Sea and the Dardanelles – has been regulated
since 1936 by the Montreux Convention, the question of free
passage is still topical. Often the majestic large vessels on the
Bosphorus break their silence with desperate horn calls as fog
or intense traffic makes navigation hazardous on the notoriously
difficult and winding waterway. But when in 1994 Turkey introduced new regulations to improve safety, for the ships themselves
and for the 12 million *Istanbullus* living on the shores of the Bosphorus, the Turkish government faced Russian protests that the
new rules contravened the principle of 'free passage'.

Such a reaction was hardly surprising. Russia, a landmass with no direct access to warm waters, has always begrudged Turkey its sovereignty over the Straits. Since the late eighteenth century, when the Russians and the Turks first fought for control of the Bosphorus, the threat of a Russian take-over of this strategic area has always been foremost among the preoccupations of Turkey's diplomats. This was particularly true in the years before, during and after the Second World War, when a determination to maintain sovereignty over the Straits became one of the guiding factors of Turkey's cautious foreign policy.

As Atatürk's health began to deteriorate in the mid-thirties, clouds were gathering in the European skies. Turkey, only just recovering from its traumatic birth, was forced to take stock of its position. The phrase 'Peace at home, peace in the world' coined by the country's founder to signal Turkey's desire to retreat within its borders, while building up its new nation in isolation from the outside world, began to ring hollow. Whether it liked it or not, Turkey was forced out of its shell by the growing threat of a European war.

The safety of the Straits, a strategic asset that could also be a vulnerable flashpoint, was among the first items considered by Turkish leaders. At the Lausanne Conference in 1923, the powers at the table, although taking into account some of Turkey's needs, had decided to place the Straits under the control of an international commission. Furthermore, the whole area of the Bosphorus and Dardanelles was to be demilitarized, including the Gallipoli peninsula, for which the Allies had fought and lost at great cost in human lives a battle that they had hoped would give them control of the waterway.

At the time, the new Turkish state, relieved to be granted international recognition of its borders, had not greatly protested. Over a decade later, however, as tension began to rise again in Europe, the Turks felt the time had come to regain control. The most immediate threat was posed by Italy's attempts to commandeer the Mediterranean. A diplomatic note was therefore sent, inviting the signatory powers to a conference. This took place in the Swiss city of Montreux between 22 June and 20 July 1936 and ended satisfactorily for Turkey with the signing of the Montreux Convention, still in force today. The Straits Commission was abolished and Turkey regained full sovereignty over the waterway, although it had to guarantee free passage at any time to commercial vessels and allow for naval ships to transit under certain conditions. To ensure regional security, Turkey was also authorized to re-militarize the areas around the waterway.

Control of the Straits, however, did not mean that Turkey was ready for the war that was shortly to break out in Europe. Its economy was still in disarray and the military equipment at the disposal of its army was insufficient for the proper defence of the country.

Furthermore, when the war started, Turkey was still mourning the recent death of Atatürk and still unsure of his successor, Ismet Inönü, the man who inherited the burden of steering the country through the war years. Inönü, a long-established figure on the political scene, well known as Mustafa Kemal's companion and prime minister, had little of his predecessor's charisma and did not command the same respect. He was chosen despite the fact that he had fallen out with Atatürk shortly before his death.

Those who knew Ismet Pasha as a young officer in the early years of the independence struggle often described him as a gentle person, with a sharp sense of humour. Trusted by Atatürk, he often acted as a counterweight and checked some of the leader's worst excesses. The writer Halide Edib, in her memoirs of the war of independence, recalled an incident when Inönü argued for sparing the life of two men who had been captured by the nationalists, whereas Atatürk believed that to show mercy was a sign of weakness. Inönü won the argument, but by the time Atatürk had granted a reprieve, it was too late. Both had been executed.[1]

There are conflicting reports of Inönü's performance on the battlefield during the war of independence. He took his last name from the site of battle in which the army under his command won a decisive victory against the Greeks; but some historians question the importance of the battle and indeed of Inönü's role in it. During the 1950s, when the Democrat Party of his hated rival Adnan Menderes was in power, Inönü's name was erased from schoolbooks and monuments.

Although described as shy and sensitive in reports by his Ottoman contemporaries, Inönü turned out to be something of a martinet when he came to power as second President of the Turkish republic. Stepping into Atatürk's shoes was no easy task, but he set about it in a highly authoritarian manner. He assumed the title of 'National Leader' and had himself elected permanent head of the Republican People's Party which, given the one-party system in place at the time, meant he could keep the top slot in the country indefinitely.

His lack of warmth and personal appeal made him the butt of constant criticism, which he suppressed with an iron hand. Using the war as a pretext, he cracked down on the press. The conflict also allowed him to conduct all discussions on foreign policy behind the closed doors of his party's parliamentary offices, rather than on the open floor of the Grand National Assembly. But, whatever his faults, Ismet Pasha is generally credited with having kept Turkey out of the Second World War, no mean feat given the intense pressure exerted on Turkey from all sides.

As a military man, Inönü was well aware of the poor state of his army, which badly needed new, modernized equipment. By the time German troops had advanced through Greece and Bulgaria, foreign diplomats calculated that it would take them a mere forty-eight hours to conquer Istanbul. Kenan Evren, who was to lead the military coup on 12 September 1980, was at the time posted as a young officer near the Greek border. He describes in his memoirs the sorry state of the exhausted soldiers who were meant to protect the country from the might of the German armoured columns. The Turks were sleeping in dugouts and were equipped with artillery drawn by horses so hungry they would eat the paint off walls. The single truck in his unit was used by the commander to evacuate his personal effects.[2]

It was mainly in order to obtain arms and equipment that Turkey agreed in 1942 to send 45,000 tons of chrome to the Krupps armament factories in Germany, much to the Allies' annoyance. But the British were aware of Turkey's needs. By themselves supplying them with military equipment, they hoped to bring Turkey decisively on to their side. A Foreign Office memorandum of late 1940 reported that 'the Turkish army is very short of rifles and has asked us to supply 150,000'; failure to comply, it stressed, would have a negative psychological effect.[3] Although equipment was sent, it was never enough to satisfy the Turks.

To gain time for his country, Ismet Inönü sometimes resorted to methods which had served him well when negotiating on Turkey's behalf at Lausanne in 1922 and 1923, deploying his very real deafness to drive his diplomatic opponents to distraction. When those talks hit on difficult subjects on which Inönü was determined not to give way, he would stubbornly profess himself unable to hear and force the Allies to go over the same points time and again. It was such a 'dialogue of the deaf' that had led to the adjournment of the conference in 1922, as well as winning Turkey several points in the subsequent round of talks that ended with a signed settlement in 1923.

Similar tactics were used during the Second World War. Although Inönü himself, now President, was rarely involved directly in talks with Germany or the Allies, his diplomats – mainly the influential Numan Menemencioğlu, foreign minister from August 1942 to June 1944 – displayed a 'diplomatic deafness' in their relations with both sides. Turkey was playing for time and would often talk at cross purposes, impose new conditions and drag its feet in the hope of delaying the moment when a real decision was needed. This attitude led one of the participants at the Cairo summit in 1943 to remark that the Turkish delegation 'wore hearing devices so perfectly tuned to one another that they all went out of order at the same instant whenever mention was made of the possibility of Turkey's entering the war'.[4]

The Allies – in particular the British – felt that Turkey should make a clear choice between the two camps. The Turks however viewed the situation differently. Having fought the Germans' battle in the Great War, and having paid a heavy price for their defeat, they were not prepared to fight solely to please the West. Instead, Turkey took out insurance policies by signing a series of treaties with the various parties to the war.

With Moscow, Turkey already had a Friendship and Non-Aggression Treaty, signed in 1925, that was still valid. Their close connection was rattled by the surprise Nazi-Soviet Pact concluded in August 1939, but the Turks tried to maintain good relations with their historic enemies.

To the treaty with Moscow, Ismet Inönü then added a double alliance with Britain and France in 1939 that pledged assistance 'in the event of an act of aggression by a European Power leading to war in the Mediterranean area'. But he was careful not to jeopardize relations with the Russians; under pressure from Moscow, he added a clause stating that Turkey could not be compelled to act with the Allies if such an action might involve their taking up arms against the USSR. Heavily reliant on German trade in the pre-war years, Turkey could not afford to break its ties with Berlin either. In 1941, a Friendship and Non-Aggression Treaty with Germany was added to the long list of pacts, thus balancing Turkey's diplomatic links with all the main belligerents.

As the war progressed and the Soviet Union joined the Allied camp, Turkish leaders increasingly perceived their country as being sandwiched between two threats. At first, the split between Germany and the Soviet Union had served their interests: faced with the combined forces of the two giants, they had felt very uncomfortable. In fact, Erdal Inönü recalled his father's tremendous relief when he and his brother Ömer, accompanied by an aide-de-camp, woke the president to tell him that Germany had invaded the Soviet Union. 'My father opened his eyes. Seeing us and his aide-de-camp in front of him, "What is it?" he asked. Ömer started to explain: "Süreyya Bey has called from Ankara. The Germans have invaded Russia . . ." ' The two young boys witnessed their father's extraordinary reaction. 'He started to smile. Then moments later he burst out laughing; on he went for minutes on end, unable to contain himself . . . Obviously my father wasn't laughing because a new war had started. What cheered him up and turned his relief into laughter was the fact that the potential dangers that had been weighing on his mind and been the cause of constant anxiety to him over the past months, had all of a sudden lifted and vanished.'[5]

This relief was short-lived. As Moscow gained influence among the Allies, the Turks foresaw the post-war danger of an increasingly demanding Russia, while at the same time fearing the lethal power of the Axis forces. The concept of a new world order, to be constructed on foundations laid down by Churchill and Stalin, was worrying to the Turks. As the Italian ambassador to Ankara, Ottavio de Peppo, put it in 1942, 'the Turkish idea is that the last German soldier should fall upon the last Russian corpse.'[6]

While it seemed likely that Germany would win, some Turkish newspaper commentators urged the government to join in on Hitler's side; President Inönü always privately opposed the idea, eventually feeling strong enough to gaol a pro-Nazi right-wing group in 1944. Although Ankara gradually leaned closer to the British as the war progressed, Turkish officials remained determined not to upset the Germans, who, having conquered most of the Balkans, continued to pose a very real threat. Nor were the Turks impressed by promises of assistance in case of an attack coming from Europe. The Allies, it was clear, already had their hands full. A bungled Allied attack on Rhodes in 1943 only reinforced the Turks' cautious attitude. Whenever their diplomats made concessions to the Allies, they made parallel moves to reassure the Germans of their friendship. The reverse was equally true.

Throughout the war, the Turks were intensely suspicious of Moscow's ultimate aims. It took the British and the Americans years to realize that Russia had designs on Turkey and the Straits, and indeed on the whole Balkans. When this notion finally found

an echo in Washington, it marked the little-known beginning of
what grew into the Cold War between the US and the Soviet
Union.

As the war progressed, increasing pressure was brought to bear
on Turkey to choose sides. To make matters worse, the economic
situation within the country was deteriorating. Little versed in
economic theory, Turkey's authoritarian leaders imposed statist
policies heavily dependent on central planning and investment
and offering no incentive to private enterprise. Two decades
earlier at Lausanne, Sir William Tyrell, a British delegate, had
already spotted this weakness in the nascent Turkish nation when
he confided to a French journalist: 'The Turks are remarkable
soldiers, but I couldn't say the same from an economic point of
view. In that field, they fall very far short.'

For the ordinary Turk, although the country was not at war, life
became increasingly difficult. The state kept increasing taxation
to finance the cost of permanent mobilization. In 1943, Inönü
introduced a controversial 'wealth tax', a form of state racket-
eering that found a particularly easy target in the vulnerable
religious minorities – Jews, Greeks and Armenians – who were
bled dry by the authorities' astronomical demands. Resentment
was building up in the population, but Inönü, with a firm hand,
ensured that dissent was crushed.

From the outside, the Allies were also applying pressure.
From 1942 on, Churchill in particular became increasingly frustrated by his inability to extract a Turkish pledge to enter the war.
Although he had persuaded Roosevelt to let him approach the
Turks about such a move, the Americans were less than enthusi-
astic. Operation 'Overlord' – the landing in Normandy – was then
on the drawing board as their top priority. They feared that action
in the Mediterranean would risk diverting resources from this
project.

Turkey was facing a dilemma. The Germans threatened to bomb
Istanbul and other cities if Ankara entered the war, yet the Turks
worried that if they did not, they would have no say in the post-war
reshuffling of geo-political cards that was being discussed between
Churchill, Stalin and, to a lesser extent, Roosevelt. When the three
leaders met for dinner during the Tehran Summit in November
1943, Churchill aired the view that 'a large land mass' like the
USSR 'deserved access to warm water ports'. Such statements
confirmed the Turks' fear that the carpet would be pulled from
under their feet to the benefit of the Soviet Union if they did not
make an active contribution to the conflict.

The Turks had never categorically refused to join the conflict, having so far simply temporized whenever approached by the Allies. At the Cairo Summit in 1943, where he met Allied leaders, President Inönü reluctantly agreed 'in principle' to enter the war, but set a number of conditions – a joint plan of action between the Allies and Turkey, and the provision of further military equipment – which ensured that Turkey would not need to commit itself at once.

By 1944, however, the Turks' ambivalent position was no longer tenable. Under pressure, Ankara suspended its shipments of chrome to Germany in April. Two months later, tension rose between the Allies and the Turks regarding the passage through the Straits of German warships. To placate the Allies, Inönü sacrificed his foreign minister Numan Menemencioğlu, perceived – wrongly by most accounts – as being pro-German. A few weeks after his resignation, Turkey broke off diplomatic relations with Berlin. It finally entered the war as a symbolic gesture on 21 February 1945, by which time the conflict was virtually over. This late involvement ensured that Turkey could claim a place among the founding members of the United Nations.

For six years, Turkish diplomats had played a masterly game of hide-and-seek that they called 'active neutrality', with the Germans on one side and the Allies on the other. To some Europeans, this waiting game, this endless dithering, was proof that Turkey did not deserve to be accepted as a full member of the Western alliance. After all, it had not played a full part in the war. But others acknowledged more realistically that Turkey's engagement in the war, at a time when she was weak and exposed, would have had disastrous consequences. The Turkish leaders, they realized, had acted in the best interests of their nation.

While the politicians and diplomats negotiated, others in the early years of the war had been involved behind the scenes in intrigues and machinations intended to influence the course of the conflict by less official means. Neutral Istanbul, located at a strategic crossroads, became a capital for spies of all provenances who would plot, collect information and spread disinformation through large networks of agents. The setting was perfect. Always a cosmopolitan city, Istanbul now swarmed with refugees of all nationalities. Among them were more than 200 German academics – Jews or opponents of the Nazi regime – some of whom stayed on to educate a new generation of Turkish professors and scientists.

The Park Hotel in Istanbul's Ayazpaşa district, overlooked by the imposing German consulate, had once been Atatürk's favourite watering hole. It no longer exists today, but during the war the Park Hotel was at the height of its prestige. The leathery atmosphere of its bar provided the background for the meetings of shady characters – pro-Ally or pro-Axis – who would often drink side by side. Secrets were bought and sold over large quantities of food and drink. One of the popular night-club songs of the period, 'Boo boo, baby, I'm a spy', was even written by an agent.

Among the most famous cloak and dagger episodes that took place in Turkey at this time was the 'Cicero' affair. Of Balkan origin, 'Cicero' worked by day as valet to the British ambassador in Ankara. By night he photographed the documents that the diplomat carelessly took home from the office and sold them on to the Germans. This successful trade, which enabled the Axis powers to get privileged information on movements of troops and supplies, lasted for eight weeks before a mole in Germany finally alerted the British to the danger.[7]

Turkey's policy of active neutrality meant that its leaders often had to walk a diplomatic tightrope between the various players. This was never more apparent than during receptions at the Çankaya presidential palace where diplomats from the various belligerent powers were forced into unwelcome contact. They usually resolved the situation by retreating with their friends to different rooms of the palace. The Turkish security forces struggled to keep track of all this activity on their soil. Occasionally they would act against flagrant agitation, once raiding the Germans' elegant Teutonia Club, then suspected of being a Nazi meeting-place. But on the whole, the Turks watched nervously from the side-lines.

The assassination attempt against Franz von Papen, the German ambassador in Turkey, tested Turkey's diplomatic high-wire act to the limit. Von Papen was no ordinary diplomat. For a brief period German chancellor, he saw himself as a successor to Adolf Hitler. The high profile of this diplomat underlined the importance Germany attached to its relations with Turkey and its need to draw Ankara into the Axis camp. When he narrowly escaped being shot while walking with his wife in an alley off Ankara's Atatürk Boulevard on 24 February 1942, the Turks were obliged to come up rapidly with suspects. The assailant could furnish no clue: his controllers had given him what they said was a smoke-bomb to help him escape, but it turned out to be a real bomb that killed him instead. Legend has it that von Papen's only comment was: 'Damn it, my best suit.'[8]

In quick succession the Turks arrested two Soviet diplomats as well as two Turks of Balkan origin, who were all convicted of complicity in the murder attempt. Although they produced little convincing proof at the trial, the Turks had obtained confirmation of their suspicions from secret sources, one of whom was the former Czechoslovak ambassador. The Russians had approached him for help, thinking that his hatred of the Germans occupying his country would prompt him to act against von Papen. When he refused, he feared the Soviets' retribution and sought help from the Turkish authorities. Another informant was the Soviet press attaché who, although having nothing to do with the attack himself, feared being made a scapegoat for the botched attempt.[9]

With this bizarre episode, the Soviets had apparently hoped to sour relations between Turkey and Germany, thus forcing Ankara to join the Allies. This fiasco only served to confirm Turkey's suspicions of Moscow's intentions and the means it was prepared to use to reach its ends. As the war went on and Stalin's influence grew, Turkey became increasingly uneasy, remembering the long history of conflict and rivalry with its powerful northern neighbour. The two countries had fought no less than ten wars between 1676 and 1878 and their borders had moved back and forth several times, mostly in Moscow's favour.

Paradoxically, Russia had been the first foreign power to lend Ankara a hand at the birth of the republic, Lenin sending Mustafa Kemal money and moral support for his Turkish revolution. When Turkey's first five-year plan was issued (1934–9), the Soviets, presumably encouraged by the statist policies imposed by the Turkish leaders, lent Ankara 8 million dollars worth of gold, interest-free.[10] Despite this gesture of friendship, the underlying rivalry between the two countries continued. Indeed, it is still alive today, belied at a superficial level by the successful trade relationship that has operated in the 1980s and 1990s.

When Moscow's White House was shelled in August 1991, in the coup attempt against Mikhail Gorbachev that later brought Boris Yeltsin to power, Turkish contractors were hired to rebuild it. When the rebuilding of the Chechen capital Grozny was put out to tender, a Turkish company won the contract. Whole areas of the old city in Istanbul have been taken over by traders from the former Eastern Bloc, who shuttle back and forth, bringing into Turkey dollars or tradeable flotsam salvaged from the Soviet empire, returning home with bulky sacks of denim jeans and fake crystal chandeliers. A whole terminal at Istanbul's Atatürk airport is now used for flights to the ex-Soviet Union. Traders loaded with the produce of their shopping spree – up to 500 kilos' worth per passenger – pile into airliners that have sometimes had their seats removed to accommodate more cargo. At its height in the mid-1990s, this semi-legal trade was said to be worth 6 billion dollars. More than 30,000 Turkish workers are also employed in all corners of Russia, building airports, hospitals and housing estates.

Towns along the Black Sea coast became prosperous, welcoming thousands of visitors from the ex-Soviet Union every day. At 'Russian bazaars' almost anything could be bought: deep-sea diving equipment, Red Army surgical kits, watches, cheap plastic toys. Above all, the Black Sea coast area has become famous for the flesh trade with the arrival of thousands of 'Natashas', the Turkish term for Russian prostitutes. The invasion of Natashas certainly pleased the local men at first, but it had the local women up in arms and eventually helped persuade the townsfolk of Rize to elect a fire-breathing Islamic mayor.

Prostitution aside, there is clearly plenty of room for commercial co-operation between Turkey and Russia, but diplomatic tensions between the two countries are never far from the surface. The war between Armenia and Azerbaijan and the Chechen crisis have only served to heighten the mistrust that these two countries harbour for each other. Some Russian nationalists, such as the flamboyant and controversial Vladimir Zhirinovsky, still hanker after a 'push for the south' that will leave 'everyone speaking Russian, from Constantinople to Kabul, to the shores of the Indian Ocean . . .' If, in the process, 'the whole Turkish nation perished', he asserted, 'no harm would come to the world'.

As early as 1922, when Ismet İnönü was arguing his newly independent country's case in Lausanne, Russia was already seen as a potential threat by the Turks. In the eyes of the Allies, however, Turkey's new regime and the Soviet Union were part of a single front, to which they tried to oppose a Balkan union. The Soviets had been the first to recognize the new Turkey, and, despite Atatürk's repression of Communists in his country, the centralizing statist ideology of the nascent state, as we have seen, raised Moscow's hopes of winning Turkey over in the end.

İnönü, however, knew the Russians had not forgotten their ambition to control the Turkish Straits. To French journalist Berthe George-Gaulis, he admitted in 1922:

Your Balkan bloc shows us the dangers of the future. Constantinople and Thrace are not the main question. Anatolia and its Asian dependencies are the most vital matters. Our alliances are there. They will conflict, and they are conflicting already, with Russia which will one day unite with England against us. We must outwit this manoeuvre and play for time. We must above all salvage our position in Asia, and our links with the Muslim world.[11]

These words were prophetic. While the Soviets and the British were not in conflict with Turkey during the Second World War, Churchill played into Russia's hand by allowing them to state their demands, by casually giving Stalin details of Turkey's defences over the dinner table at the Kremlin, and by suggesting that Moscow might secure a degree of access to the warm-water lifeline of the Straits.

The crunch came once the war had ended. First, the Soviets cancelled the Treaty of Friendship and Non-Aggression that had linked the two countries since 1925. The Soviet price for a new pact was high and unacceptable to Turkey: they demanded nothing less than the return of the border provinces of Kars and Ardahan, which had been ceded to Turkey in 1921, the right to have bases on the Straits and a revision of the Montreux agreement. The Turks felt increasingly vulnerable as rumours spread of troop movements in Bulgaria. The authorities in Ankara tried to attract the attention of Britain and the US to the Soviet danger.

At Potsdam, in July and August 1945, Churchill still felt enough sympathy for Russia to describe it as 'a giant with his nostrils pinched by the narrow exits from the Baltic and the Black Sea'. But both the British and the Americans were becoming suspicious of Soviet power. President Harry Truman agreed in principle with a revision of the Montreux rules, but none of the changes he had in mind included Soviet bases on the Straits. By the end of 1945, the belief had grown in diplomatic circles that the Soviets were trying to turn Turkey into one of their satellites, as they had done with other Balkan countries. One of the more colourful and eccentric inhabitants of the Park Hotel, George Earle III, who had been posted to Istanbul after a stint as US ambassador in Bulgaria, had written to Truman's predecessor President Roosevelt, who was a personal friend, to warn him that

the most important and most difficult problem you will have to face in post-war Europe will be Russia. This country, today probably the

most popular in America and England, thirty days after the cessation
of hostilities, will be the most unpopular, due not to [Communism]
but to Russian imperialism.[12]

Similar words were to be heard on the lips of American diplomats
after the collapse of the Soviet Union, as they struggled to defend
the Turkic and other states of the Caucasus and Central Asia from
the still overbearing demands of Moscow.

Fearing a Soviet military intervention after the war, the Turks
kept their army fully mobilized. By March 1946 when the Soviets
invaded Iranian Azerbaijan, confirming the worst fears in the
region, even Churchill, once Stalin's closest ally, had seen the
light. 'From Stettin in the Baltic to Trieste in the Adriatic, an iron
curtain has descended across the continent,' he said during a
speech in America in March 1946. 'Turkey and Persia are both
profoundly alarmed and disturbed at the claims which are being
made upon them and at the pressure being exerted by the Moscow
government.'[13]

The attack on Azerbaijan proved a turning point. As the sun
was setting on the British empire, it fell to the United States to
take on the task of policing the area. Whatever hesitations the
Americans still harboured were brushed aside in the following
months as the administration developed what became known as
the 'Truman Doctrine', a decision to 'support free people who
are resisting attempted subjugation by armed minorities or by
outside pressures'. Turkey was described as 'essential for the
preservation of order in the Middle East' and both Greece and
Turkey were promised help by the US administration. In August
1946, a US memorandum acknowledged that Moscow's objective
was to control Turkey and that, once this goal was attained, it
would be difficult to prevent it from controlling the whole Near
and Middle East. Free access to the Straits was of vital importance
to the Americans. Another memo by the American Joint Chiefs
of Staff declared Turkey, for this reason, to be 'the most important military factor in the Eastern Mediterranean and the Middle
East'.

As the Americans defined their policy towards Moscow, the
Turks felt vindicated. Their misgivings about Soviet intentions
were proved correct. The shift in policy was to affect more than
just Turkey: what was to be known as the Cold War, the latent
conflict that dominated the world for more than four decades, had
just started. But for Turkey itself, the Truman Doctrine marked the
beginning of a privileged relationship with the United States that

still conditions its foreign policy today. This link was also the defining feature of the rule of the man soon to take power in Turkey, Adnan Menderes.

6

A New Beginning

A man in politics has only two shirts: one for
feasting, the other for his shroud.

Ottoman proverb

A PAGODA-LIKE MONUMENT, looking rather out of place, stands
in the middle of a spaghetti junction on the ever expanding network of motorways that ring Istanbul. Few people find their way
to visiting it. Inaugurated with great pomp by Turgut Özal in
1990, this mausoleum is a belated tribute to former prime minister
Adnan Menderes, who led Turkey's first experiment in democracy
and liberal economics in the 1950s but paid a heavy price for his
failings. He was hanged, with two of his ministers, after the coup
that deposed him in 1960.

Although their origins were very different – Adnan Menderes
was a wealthy landowner from the Aegean region of Aydın, Turgut
Özal the son of a bank manager from the eastern town of Malatya
– the two men played a similar role in Turkish politics. Menderes
had been elected in a landslide election in May 1950 that marked
the end of twenty-seven years of one-party rule. Özal arrived at
the helm of the country after three years of military dictatorship.
Both, advocating a free economy, shared a distaste for state controls. The side effects of the rapid development they encouraged
– high inflation, huge budget deficits and foreign debts – have
marred their achievements.

When the bones of Adnan Menderes and his two ministers
were disinterred from the prison island of Yassıada in a somewhat
morbid ceremony attended by the families and the press, to be
transferred to their new and grander resting-place, Özal was in
his way passing on a message to his opponents that the killing of

the prime minister, a frequent fate of grand viziers in Ottoman times, would not intimidate him. Not all of Özal's motives were noble. He was also looking to seize the advantage from Süleyman Demirel in the struggle for dominance of the conservative heartland once led by Adnan Menderes.

As is often the case in Turkey, where the protest vote is a dominant factor in any elections, the tidal wave that had brought Menderes and his Democrat Party to power in 1950 was as much a reaction against a quarter-century of tight rule by a bureaucratic élite as a vote for specific new policies. The total control that Ismet Inönü had exerted over the country during the war years was increasingly resented by the people. His line may not have been very different from that drawn earlier by Atatürk, but whereas Mustafa Kemal was admired as the saviour of the country, even if the people did not always approve of his policies, 'in the hands of lesser men than himself, his authoritarian and paternalistic mode of government degenerated into something nearer to dictatorship as the word is commonly understood'.[1]

By the end of the war, the wind of democracy was beginning to blow in Turkey's direction. Even Inönü felt it was time to start loosening the reins and discussing reform. Why did this man, who had assumed an almost dictatorial role, suddenly decide to release his grip? A combination of factors probably convinced him that times were changing. Not least among these was the new relationship Turkey was developing with the United States, a link Ankara hoped would be of strategic and financial benefit to the country. Through the Truman Doctrine, the Americans had already pledged military assistance to Turkey, and the Marshall Plan for reconstruction in Europe held the promise of further funds. Turkey, having failed to pay its military dues during the conflict, may have felt the need to be on its best behaviour. The same need to impress later prompted Prime Minister Adnan Menderes to send a total of 25,000 troops to Korea to join the UN war effort. As was witnessed again in 1995, when improvement in human rights and commercial laws became a condition for access to the European Customs Union, pressure from the international community combined with the carrot of financial aid served to persuade reluctant Turkish politicians to approve long-delayed reforms.

The new post-war climate helped bring about the birth in 1946 of the Democrat Party, founded by Adnan Menderes and other politicians who had left the Republican People's Party (known in Turkish as the Cumhuriyetçi Halk Partisi or CHP), mostly expelled in the course of 1945 as a result of their vocal demands for reform. Inönü may have thought he would experiment with controlled opposition, as Atatürk had tried in 1930, but it soon became obvious that the Democrat Party, as the only alternative to Inönü's CHP, was attracting a lot of support. Inönü rushed into early general elections in 1946 in the hope of stemming the flow, but his rivals nevertheless succeeded in returning sixty-one deputies to parliament, a substantial achievement considering that their party was only six months old and that there were strong rumours of foul play during the elections.

The four years that followed were difficult for both parties. Trying to gain the high ground, the two sides hurled acrimonious accusations at each other. As president, Inönü hesitated over which path to follow. At first, he chose a hard-line premier, Recep Peker, but by July 1947 the tension on the political scene was such that the head of state felt the need to intervene. He held consultations with Prime Minister Peker and the leader of the opposition, Adnan Menderes, to try and restore calm. Rising to the occasion, Inönü showed himself the statesman and announced publicly that as president he was non-partisan and above party politics. By distancing himself from the CHP, Inönü triggered a government crisis that led to the departure of the prime minister, who was replaced by the more liberal Hasan Şaka.

The CHP was not the only political party that was finding it difficult to define its line in the new climate of post-war Europe. The Democrats also suffered from internal disputes. By the end of the 1940s its parliamentary group had shrunk by half through the defection of dissenters, some of whom founded the more nationalist and religiously inclined National Party in 1948.

Despite the difficulties confronting it in Ankara, the Democrat Party was gaining rapid support in the countryside, building a lasting network of supporters in rural areas that survived the 1960 coup and went on to strengthen its successors, the Justice Party and the True Path Party.

Economically, many Turks were suffering from the inflation that had developed during the war years, when the government had to bear the cost of troop mobilization and the purchase of military equipment. In rural areas, people's main experience of the state had been of tax collection and heavy-handed rule. 'Everybody had problems with the police. Until 1946, there was not a peasant, not a villager who had not been beaten up by the police,' explains Turkey's most famous novelist Yaşar Kemal, whose lifelong commitment to socialism started at that period. 'If one villager could not pay his road tax, or the taxes on his fields, the whole village would be punished. It had become a tradition.'[2]

The poor villagers or independent peasants surviving on small-holdings were joined among the DP's supporters – or perhaps rather as opponents of the CHP – by the rich landowners who felt threatened by a land reform law introduced by Inönü in 1945 which promised to nationalize estates larger than 500 *dönüm* (123.5 acres) and to distribute state land to poor peasants.

The CHP was also viewed with suspicion by a budding private sector, even though it had begun to relax its statist policies. The infamous wealth tax, introduced during the war, had hit mainly the merchants from the religious minorities. They were sent into internal exile and had properties confiscated if they failed to pay astronomical levies, which were often ten times greater than those demanded of Muslims. But the tax had also destroyed Muslim businesses. Bolstered by the power of their growing wealth, the new commercial class was no longer willing to submit to the domination of the bureaucrats.

Until the Democrats' victory, the country had been dominated not just by the army but by an élitist and tyrannical bureaucracy whose rule went back to the latter days of the Ottoman empire. Its position had not been challenged by Kemalist Turkey mainly because Atatürk himself believed that this élite had a role to perform, leading and training the masses who, in the 1920s, were still largely uneducated and living in rural areas. But whereas Atatürk expected his bureaucrats to act as educators spreading the message of Westernization, 'for the bureaucratic intelligentsia the élitism in Ataturkist thought was not a means but an end'.[3]

The attitude of disdain of the educated classes and the state towards the 'little people' is still evident, several decades after the DP's success served the bureaucracy its first notice. In the early 1990s, a delegation from a short-lived Foreign Press Association paid a courtesy visit to the then governor of Istanbul province, Hayri Kozakçıoğlu. This took place a few days after Turkish television journalists had been dragged in front of a military court for a documentary on conscientious objectors that had offended the army. 'Don't worry,' Mr Kozakçıoğlu said. 'You can write what you want, because your articles are published abroad. But you must understand,' he added, 'that our people in Turkey are not equipped to cope with certain ideas. This is the reason why we have to impose limits.'

This unwillingness to take popular feelings into account has largely contributed to the rise in the 1990s of the Islamists who,

alone among political parties, are willing to canvass at grass roots
level and pay attention to the voters' grievances, or at least pretend
to.

A large number of Turks found the patronizing attitude of the
establishment particularly difficult to swallow in the late 1940s.
The Kemalist reforms had done little to improve their lot, but had
stripped them of their religion by imposing secularism, a move
resented by ordinary people who could not understand why their
age-old traditions – which could hardly be described as fundamentalist, in a country where Islam has traditionally assumed a
very pragmatic form – were summarily dismissed as obscurantist
superstition.

Feeling the heat, the CHP pushed through a number of reforms
to placate the population. Inönü relinquished his right for life
to leadership of the party, and abolished the title of National
Leader he had awarded himself. Religious instruction, eradicated
from the school curriculum in the secularist drive, was reintroduced, albeit as an option. Martial law, which had been extended
since the war years, was finally lifted in 1947 and workers' unions
were allowed. But it was too late.

Inextricably linked to the state in the eyes of the voters – Inönü
had made local governors head of the party branches – the CHP
did not stand a chance when the population was finally allowed
to choose its leaders.

In May 1950, an overwhelming 90 per cent of the population
turned up to cast its vote in general elections. The Democrat Party
won 408 seats in parliament, while their rival, the CHP, was left
with only 69 deputies. Inönü conceded defeat and stepped down
from the presidency. Celal Bayar, who had been prime minister
briefly under Atatürk, was elected on 27 May to replace him.

The army felt unsure of what action to take. 'It was rumoured
that the army chiefs went to the then president Inönü to offer to
intervene, and that he refused,' recalls General Kenan Evren, who
was to lead the 1980 coup. 'Nuri Yarmut [the new chief of staff]
... collected all the officers in a garden behind the General
Staff headquarters and told them that the country had gone
over to a democratic system; they were to carry on with their
jobs and not to interfere in politics. Basically most of the officer
corps, especially the younger officers, were pleased with the result.
Those unhappy were mostly the elderly and those with strong links
to the past.'

With the army's implicit blessing, Turkey enthusiastically
entered a new era under the leadership of Prime Minister Mend-

eres. The bureaucracy took its revenge in 1960 when, joined by the academic world, it backed the coup that overthrew the Democrat Party and killed the once popular leader. Officialdom, however, never fully recovered its prestige nor its grip on the population. The 1950 election proved to be only the first blow dealt by the Turkish people to the machinery of the state. Four decades later, the bureaucracy is still struggling to retain its hold but, financially and ideologically bankrupt, it is fighting a losing battle.

It is symptomatic of the change that whereas in the 1920s members of parliament would often resign to seek bureaucratic positions,[4] which guaranteed them a comfortable living as state employees for the rest of their days, in the 1995 general elections a reverse trend was observed. Now dozens of bureaucrats – police chiefs, treasury administrators, central bank officials – regularly leave their once prestigious positions to run as candidates for various political parties.

For a while after 1950, the Democrats seemed to fulfil the dreams of their voters. New roads and schools were built. The electricity network was extended to provide power for the countryside, which until then had been largely overlooked. Steady investment in infrastructure – transport, communications, agricultural equipment – led to a rise in production of both agricultural and industrial goods. State land was distributed to the poorest among the landless peasants and American foreign aid was used to purchase thousands of tractors. Villagers, attracted by the prospect of work in new factories, began now to leave the countryside and erected the first *gecekondu*, the shanty towns literally 'built by night' on the outskirts of the big cities – although it was only in the sixties and seventies that urbanization became a dominant trend. At last, ordinary Turks were beginning to see the benefits of the desire for modernization that had fuelled the more high-minded revolutionaries of the 1920s.

The ambitious Democrats were keen to integrate this more developed Turkey with the Western world. Moving away from Atatürk's cautious foreign policy, they edged closer to the Americans. In 1950, they applied for membership of NATO. Their determination to be accepted, combined with the bravery of Turkish troops in Korea and the concern in Western military circles for regional stability, finally bore fruit. Turkey was accepted as a member of NATO in 1952.

Turkey's neighbour Greece also joined the alliance. Until the problem of Cyprus raised its ugly head, relations between the two countries were amicable. But in 1955, an unfortunate incident drastically changed the trend. The Greeks, the Turks and the British were having talks in London about the future of the island. The Turkish press, in typical fashion, was whipping up nationalist sentiment. The government, feeling the need for popular support, planned a limited demonstration against Greek claims to the island. When a bomb exploded near the Turkish consulate in Thessaloniki, located alongside the house where Atatürk was born, Turkish feelings, already at boiling point, exploded. On 6 and 7 September, mobs attacked shops and houses owned by non-Muslims, wreaking havoc in several areas of Istanbul. A witness remembered standing ankle-deep in broken glass in Istiklal Street, the heart of Istanbul's shopping district. Another foreigner was woken up on the Asian side of the old Ottoman city by the noise of an approaching crowd. Armed with long sticks, the mob systematically destroyed the shops in his neighbourhood. He thought of calling the police, but then noticed that policemen were standing by at the entrance to the street, where municipal buses were parked. Having completed the destruction of all the shops belonging to non-Muslims, the demonstrators got back into the buses that had brought them and went on to finish their job elsewhere.

Tens of thousands of Greeks left the country never to return. To this day, many derelict houses are slowly decaying, unclaimed by the Greek owners who fled with the title deeds or by their descendants. Only in the 1980s was a law introduced by Turgut Özal allowing some Greek families to claim their inheritance and repatriate the money.

These incidents cast a shadow over Turkey's international reputation. But Turkey's developing friendship with the United States survived, and from his new allies Menderes obtained assistance and loans that helped finance his development projects. In exchange, the Americans obtained extensive basing rights that were the subject of much debate in later years. Many Turks felt their leaders had given too much away without adequate reward and the deal was renegotiated in the seventies.

Membership of NATO shook the old-fashioned Turkish army to its foundations. 'Suitcases of books and [NATO] documents started to arrive. Messages came asking for replies. Then our translations of the original message would arrive, but the translators did not know proper English. You needed another translator to translate them.'[5] Younger, better trained officers, who spoke English or were trained engineers, were taken abroad for training in other NATO countries. Modern equipment was shipped in as part of military assistance and educated young officers suddenly assumed a more prominent role than their rank allowed. Yet, opportunities for promotion were rare in the hierarchical Turkish army. 'Because there had been no war, there had been a multiplication of high-ranking officers. The way was blocked to the younger generation.'[6] The discontent in the lower ranks caused by this situation contributed to the 1960 coup, which was not only an intervention against the government of the day but also a coup within the army itself, a rebellion of younger officers against their more hidebound superiors.

The military, traditionally a privileged class, were losing buying power to the growing inflation rate as well. Regular contact through NATO allowed them to measure the gulf that separated them from their Western colleagues. Their worst indignity was to be known in Ankara bars as *gazozcular*, or those who could only afford soft drinks. Adding insult to injury, the defence minister once kept the chief of general staff waiting for fifteen minutes in his anteroom, a terrible crime in the eyes of the proud army.[7] Such slights would come to count heavily against the government.

The economic situation worsened. Obsessed by the need to sustain a high growth rate, Menderes liberally printed money to fuel it. Like Özal after him, this led to crippling inflation that eventually forced him to heed the calls of the international community and to impose a stability package recommended by the IMF in 1958.

More worrying still was the increasing polarization of the political scene. Ismet Inönü had stepped down after his defeat, but the resentment that built up in his CHP made relations between the two parties even more tense than they had been in the late 1940s: 'neither the DP nor the CHP knew how to oppose responsibly or accept opposition fairly.'[8] The venomous climate in Ankara poisoned the atmosphere in the country as a whole. Party politics have changed little since then. Constructive opposition is still unknown, as demonstrated in recent years by the rivalry between Süleyman Demirel's True Path Party – a direct descendant of the Democrat Party – and the Motherland Party, founded by Turgut Özal after the 1980 coup. The ideology of these two parties is virtually identical, yet, instead of supporting each other's push for much-needed reforms, they have consistently opposed any idea introduced by the rival party. At times, they have even gone against their own policies, as in the Motherland's absurd opposition to

Customs Union with Europe in 1995, even though the party, seeking full integration with the West, had itself applied for full membership of the European Union in 1987.

The Democrats, with a strong majority in parliament, were able to some extent to overcome these political obstacles. But opposition to their policies was steadily mounting. Staunch Kemalists in the bureaucracy felt their principles were being undermined by reforms aimed at pleasing the pious Muslim constituency of the DP. Religious *imam hatip* schools were allowed to open for the training of Muslim prayer leaders. Now virtually a parallel education system, they are still the object of much controversy in the 1990s. The Arabic call to prayer was brought back to replace its Turkish equivalent, which had never been fully accepted by the population, and attempts at imposing a Turkish translation of the Koran were abandoned. The fasting month of Ramadan, one of the customs that modernist Turks had been happy to abandon, was again celebrated throughout the country.

Faced with a restive phalanx of intellectuals in the universities and in the bureaucracy who were rapidly turning into CHP supporters, Prime Minister Menderes resorted to the repressive methods used by his predecessor. In 1953, a law was passed that allowed the government to 'retire' without appeal judges, professors, or any officials who had reached the age of 60 or had served twenty-five years. This was a shocking development for a bureaucracy that had always been protected by special laws precluding interference by politicians. More and more irritable, Menderes also decided to muzzle the press with new laws that led to the arrest of several journalists, including Metin Toker, Ismet Inönü's son-in-law, and the suspension of five newspapers in 1955. That same year, the secretary-general of the CHP was arrested for 'insulting the government' in a public speech.

Most of these measures did not directly affect the man in the street. Rural areas, bought off with populist policies of agricultural subsidies and cheap credits, still supported the Democrats. Menderes' miraculous escape in 1959, when he survived a plane crash near Gatwick that killed fifteen people, further convinced the traditional-minded that God was on his side. Over the decade, the gap between the party in power and its republican rival narrowed somewhat, but the DP nevertheless maintained a healthy lead over the CHP in elections that were held in 1952 and 1957, and might even have won again if elections had been held in 1960.

Under pressure, Menderes became increasingly paranoid. Instead of calling early elections that could have saved him, he

carried on with his policy of wholesale repression. His rival Ismet
Inönü, touring the country, was twice attacked by mobs. In April
1960, the Democrats established a committee to investigate the
activities of their rival, the CHP, putting at its head the most
zealous of their deputies. The committee immediately imposed
strict limits on political activities and banned the press from
reporting their investigations. These outrageous laws provoked
a fierce reaction among intellectuals, leading to violent student
demonstrations that were brutally checked by the police.

By early May Menderes felt time was running out. In the lobby
of Istanbul's equivalent of the Cavalry Club, in Taksim Square,
under a portrait of a fierce-looking Atatürk, Mükerrem Sarol, an
elderly gentleman who was a Democrat Party state minister at the
time, remembered a conversation he had with his prime minister
ten days before his fall.[9] 'No one who has been *sadrazam* [an old
word for prime minister] for ten years can expect to be deposed
in the normal way,' Menderes had said. 'He either has to be exiled
or killed.'

7

The Army Shows Its Hand

In Turkey, we have no oil or heavy industry.
But we have something much stronger than
that: military discipline.

Admiral Vural Beyazıt, 1996

IN A LONG face marked by deep creases, his thin mouth cuts a
sharp line. Alparslan Türkeş, the leader of the extreme-right
National Action Party, may look like an old crocodile but at nearly
80 he is still an active player in the power game. Politicians rarely
retire in Turkey, unless they are forced out. Türkeş is a man who
preferred to do the forcing.

The length of his political life is not out of the ordinary. Others
who, like him, first emerged in the sixties, are still in the public
eye today: Süleyman Demirel as President of the Republic, Bülent
Ecevit as leader of the Democratic Left Party. Some of them rose
painstakingly through the ranks of political organizations, others
appeared more suddenly on the political stage. But Alparslan Türkeş's arrival was among the most dramatic. Most Turks old enough
to remember have vivid memories of the day he burst into national
politics.

In the early morning of 27 May 1960, Colonel Türkeş's deep
gravelly voice punctured the silence on the radio, delivering a
shocking message. At 3 a.m. that night a group of young officers
had staged a coup and had overthrown the government of Prime
Minister Adnan Menderes. Within a few hours, the rebellious
officers had the capital under control. Democrat Party ministers
and MPs – men who for the past decade had held power – were
rounded up all over town and unceremoniously forced into open
trucks as zealous cadets hurled insults at them.

The junta, as yet unidentified, only encountered two slight difficulties. At Çankaya, the President's residence, Celal Bayar refused
to surrender, arguing that he had been elected by popular will
and would not be removed. He even pulled out a gun, with the
intention of shooting himself, and had to be disarmed.

Prime Minister Menderes was out of town while the tanks closed
in on strategic points of the capital. In Eskişehir, where he had
been to give a speech, he was woken up at the crack of dawn
with news of the coup. Taking his escort with him, including
Finance Minister Polatkan, he tried to flee by car, but their convoy
was spotted from the air by jets. On arrival in Kutahya, he was
detained. Nervously smoking cigarette after cigarette, the prime
minister was then taken back to Eskişehir sitting on oil drums in
an uncomfortable airforce plane normally used by parachutists.
Worse was to come.

The intervention was welcomed by many urban Turks who
poured into the streets after hearing the announcement on the
radio, braving the curfew to share their happiness. The enthusiasm
was such that members of the army were allowed to travel
free on buses for three days in Istanbul and Ankara. The city
élites in particular felt the coup had rescued the country from
the clutches of the Democrat Party and put it back on the rails
of Kemalism. In the countryside, the response was more muted.
There, tears were even shed for Adnan Menderes whose populist
style, contrasting sharply with the distant and rather superior
attitude of his predecessors, had won the hearts of the rural
population.

Having succeeded in overthrowing the government, the organizers of the coup soon realized that they were totally unprepared
for the huge task of running the country. Not only had there been
no forward planning, but the members of the junta had widely
differing views on what to do next. 'There was no discipline in
this coup,' admits Alparslan Türkeş.[1]

The official leader of the National Unity Committee (NUC)
formed by the army was the highest ranking officer among them,
General Cemal Gürsel, but the coup was in fact concerted by
colonels and junior officers. 'There was a need to introduce young
blood, to modernize the army. The young officers were talking
about it all the time,' explains Türkeş. General Gürsel had been
brought in to give legitimacy to an intervention that had violated
not only the principles of democracy but also the strict hierarchical
code of the army. Issuing an official list of the coup organizers
was the first hurdle: too many people wanted to be on it. After

much squabbling, an agreement was reached to publish the names of thirty-eight officers who went to make up the NUC.

For the next step, that of providing a new framework for the political system, the junta enlisted the help of prominent academics. University faculty members and students had led the opposition to the Democrat Party in recent years and were therefore perceived as being sympathetic to the coup's aims. Carefully selected professors were hurriedly gathered in Ankara to be told they were now part of a 'constitutional assembly' that would have to come up with a new government and a political system capable of preventing the vindictive excesses that had plagued the Menderes era.

Some of the officers, having successfully rid the country of unwanted politicians, felt their mission was then complete. They wanted early elections and a rapid return of power to the civilians. But this view was not shared by some of the most prominent professors who, ironically, begged the military to stay on. A faction of the NUC, led by Colonel Türkeş, also wanted the military to take a more interventionist approach and rule the country directly for a while. 'We said, "let's make a party of national unity. The Democrat Party is finished. Let's take over its supporters and stage elections," ' says Türkeş.

The 'democrats' in the NUC – although the term was almost a dirty word in those days – were now in danger of losing control. Successfully moving to regain the upper hand, they staged a palace coup within the group. On 13 November 1960, the NUC was dissolved and re-formed, minus fourteen of its members including Colonel Türkeş, who were briefly detained before being sent, in the best tradition of Ottoman-style exile, to 'diplomatic posts' abroad.

For a while it looked as if democratic principles would win the day. The more open-minded academics had also had the upper hand in their dispute with authoritarian-minded colleagues and produced the most liberal constitution Turkey has ever known. The document guaranteed extensive rights, including religious freedom, to the Turkish people. The press was to be free, labour unions were recognized and a bicameral national assembly provided the necessary safeguards against abuse of power by one political party.

Despite these encouraging developments, tensions persisted. The debate had, by then, moved on to the fate of the former Democrat Party members. Again, the more lenient NUC members were inclined simply to send them into exile and start a fresh page in Turkish affairs. Unfortunately, those who were determined to see them punished won the argument.

Four hundred prisoners were taken to Yassıada, a small island in the Marmara Sea, within sight of Istanbul, where a special tribunal was set up for them. There was no proper attempt to try the ex-DP members fairly. The ground had been prepared with a smear campaign in the press, accusing them of a variety of heinous crimes, including the killing of students whose mass graves were alleged to have been found. Despite the authorities' efforts – which included dragging the prisoners out of bed in the middle of the night for photo sessions that showed them engaged in leisurely activities – many Turks felt sorry for the fallen politicians, who were kept incommunicado in prison, and were allowed to see their families only twice during the entire period of their detention. In September Celal Bayar, using his belt, tried to commit suicide in his cell. He was found with a purple face and blood pouring out of his ears, but recovered to face trial.

For eleven months, starting on 14 October 1960, 'Yassıada Hour' on the radio had the Turkish population glued to their wireless sets listening to the highlights of each day's sessions. In many ways, the trial was a farce. There were 592 defendants in nineteen separate cases. Some of the charges were downright absurd: Celal Bayar was convicted of having ordered Ankara zoo to buy a dog given to him by the Afghan king, whilst Menderes was acquitted of having killed a love child he was alleged to have had with an opera singer. Refik Koraltan, the speaker of parliament, was convicted of illegally bringing into the country a German girl as a private nurse. Other accusations were more serious. The main defendants – Menderes, Bayar, and their ministers – were accused of violating the constitution and were held directly responsible for incidents such as the anti-Greek riots of 1955 and the firing on students by police.

Menderes and Bayar sat side by side for months without talking to each other. In an effort to embarrass the new regime, Menderes' lawyer tried to bring to the attention of the jury a letter General Gürsel had written to the prime minister shortly before his downfall, humbly putting his name forward to replace the then President Bayar. But Menderes, depressed and defeated, stood up and asked for the motion, which might have saved him, to be withdrawn.

After a trial lasting a total of 1,033 hours, fifteen defendants were sentenced to death. They were moved to nearby Imralı island where as a contingency some eighty graves had already been dug even before the verdict was pronounced. Messages started pouring in from all over the world – from Queen Elizabeth, from President Kennedy, from Charles de Gaulle – asking for their lives to be spared. Ismet Inönü himself visited the members of the NUC to intercede in favour of his former rivals, but to no avail. In an all-night session, the NUC decided to approve three executions and commute the remaining sentences to life imprisonment. Although the rule that prevented prisoners over 65 years old from being executed had been lifted before the trial – with Bayar in mind – the NUC felt uncomfortable about sending an elderly man to be executed and his sentence was commuted. Ironically, Bayar, who was sent to Kayseri prison, lived for another twenty-six years and died, aged 103, in 1987.

Foreign Minister Zorlu and Finance Minister Polatkan were sent to the gallows immediately after the NUC had reached their decision. In the case of Menderes, there was a last-minute complication. The former prime minister had carefully saved the sleeping pills he was given over the weeks and took them all in one go, hoping to be spared the indignity of a death by hanging. He was found at the last minute and was sent to the hospital to have his stomach pumped. His son, Aydın, whose political career was cut short by a car accident in 1996 that left him paraplegic, remembered trying to get news of his father's health. 'One of the most difficult things in the world is to be given news of the health of someone condemned to die. If they get better there should be hope, but it is often then that they may be sent to their death,' he recalled.[2] Barely recovered, dressed in the white shirt of the condemned that he had so often talked of, Adnan Menderes, who a decade earlier had been elected prime minister as the shining white hope of a democratic Turkey, staggered to the gallows between two guards on 17 September 1961.

With the former Democrat Party leadership out of the way and the hard-line faction in the NUC ousted, Turkey could finally return to a semblance of normal life. The NUC members were to retire from active politics and take their place in the newly created Senate. The military interlude, which had culminated in the death of three once-popular politicians, was about to end, or so most people thought. In fact, the 1960 coup was only the first of three successful army interventions and the military presence was to be felt for decades to come. This was hardly a new trend: during Ottoman times, five sultans and forty-three grand viziers had been garrotted in military uprisings.[3]

Within a week of Menderes' execution, the first post-coup electoral campaign got under way. The Democrat Party's electorate was now divided, with three parties claiming the legacy of the defunct organization and its conservative, pro-Islamic politics. Inönü felt confident of a comfortable victory for his CHP, now emerging as the party of the secularist republicans, with support from the heterodox Alevi community and others who made up a group generally thought of as Kemalists: intellectuals, proponents of state-led economic development and above all supporters of Kemal Atatürk's Westernizing reforms. But the extent of popular support for the old Democrat Party line was once again vividly demonstrated when the Justice Party – the Adalet Partisi or AP, its principal successor – came within a hair's breadth of Ismet Inönü's Republicans, winning nearly 35 per cent of the vote, against the CHP's 36 per cent.

The stunning results stirred new unrest in the army. Its leaders even considered staging another intervention, but Inönü let it be known he would not support it. The military still preserved some respect for the old pasha and a compromise was found. The political parties were forced to sign an agreement with the NUC, promising not to grant an amnesty to the imprisoned DP members and not to reinstate some 4,171 officers, including 235 generals, who had been purged after the 1960 coup. Only when these conditions were laid out and accepted did the army allow Inönü, whose party had not captured a majority in the parliament, to set up Turkey's first coalition, an unwieldy partnership of the Republican People's Party and the new Justice Party.

The NUC had also wanted its leader, Cemal Gürsel, elected as president. The Justice Party had its own candidate, an academic from Istanbul who, while the army was laying down the law to the politicians, was on his way to Ankara. A military reception committee intercepted him when he arrived in the capital and pressed him to withdraw his candidacy. The arguments must have been forceful. Professor Başgil not only agreed to pull out, but left the country in a hurry.[4]

The army leadership was now satisfied, although it still kept a close eye on the politicians. But among younger officers, frustrations were again beginning to build up. What had the coup achieved? The same people were back in power under a different name.

The activist faction was led by an officer named Talat Aydemir, commander of the military academy in Ankara. A believer in enforced reforms, Aydemir, though not a member of the NUC, had been among those officers agitating for the 1960 coup. He felt there was a lot of unfinished business still to accomplish and made no secret of his feelings. Prime Minister Inönü, in true military style, decided to confront the problem head on and staged an official visit to the military school. The atmosphere he detected there convinced him at once that Aydemir was dangerous and he resolved to have him transferred.

Before this could be done, Aydemir and his cadets launched their 'Saviour Patriots' Offensive' on 22 February 1962. Their tanks surrounded the parliament and the army headquarters with surprising ease and the rebels nearly succeeded in capturing the whole capital. Prime Minister Inönü, informed of the crisis, called for a meeting of the cabinet, the chiefs of staff and the party leaders at the presidential palace. While all the country's leaders were gathered at Çankaya, the commander of the presidential guard decided to throw in his lot with Aydemir. The fight seemed over.

It would be easy to depict Talat Aydemir and other leaders of army coups as power-hungry individuals seeking an opportunity to grab the reins of government. In most cases, however, they are acting out a sometimes misguided concern for their country's future and adhering to a strict code of honour. This was certainly the case with Aydemir, who would probably have succeeded in his intervention, had he not decided to free the political leaders surrounded by his followers at Çankaya. 'Let them go, I have no quarrel with them,' he said.

This proved to be his downfall. The politicians and the military rushed to the radio station where they recorded messages to the nation. They then organized a counter-offensive. Lengthy bargaining ensued with Colonel Aydemir who, in the end, agreed to give himself up, provided he was not prosecuted. Inönü forced him to retire from the army but kept his word and let him go free.

Aydemir, now a civilian, had not abandoned his project. He tried to take power again a year later, on 20 May 1963. This time, blood was spilled: eight people were killed and the country's leaders were less inclined to be lenient. An entire generation of cadets was expelled from the military academy; some were sent to prison. Talat Aydemir and a major were executed.

As later events were to prove, Aydemir's death did not resolve the conflict between those who believe that society should be trusted to follow its own inclinations and eventually to find new balances, and the 'reformists', who believe that a firm guiding hand, imposing reforms from the top, is the only way to progress.

For the time being, the civilians were given a chance, but the political front was hardly stable. The fragile coalition set up between Inönü's CHP and the new Justice Party, the successor of its old rival the Democrat Party, rapidly showed signs of strain. When Inönü extended his prime ministerial pardon to Colonel Aydemir after his first coup attempt in 1962, the Justice Party brought up the delicate subject of a similar amnesty for former Democrat Party members, 450 of whom were still languishing in Kayseri gaol. The tension in parliament rapidly reached breaking point. Ismet Pasha was forced to resign, but was immediately asked to form the next government. This time he chose other bedfellows and joined up with two smaller right-wing parties.

But the question of the amnesty was never far from the agenda in those days. When in March 1963, Celal Bayar, then 80 years old and ill, was released from Kayseri, thousands of supporters poured into the streets to welcome him to Ankara. Then opponents of the Democrat Party joined in and the thunderous reception turned into an uncontrollable riot. The Justice Party headquarters was attacked, and Bayar was re-arrested that same night.

Local elections at the end of 1963 showed the Justice Party in the ascendant – polling 45 per cent against 37 per cent for the CHP – while the two minority right-wing partners in the coalition were losing votes. They believed this erosion was due to their alliance with the Republicans who were forever linked in the voters' mind with strong statism and with the military coup. While Inönü was in America attending John F. Kennedy's funeral, his coalition partners abruptly pulled out of the government, forcing him to rush back to Ankara.

Ismet Pasha formed yet another government, a minority one this time, but the old warrior was running out of time and options. It was becoming clear that his career had run its course. His final government did not last long. An injection of young blood was needed in Turkish politics.

The first new leader to emerge on the political scene in the 1960s came from the Justice Party, not from Inönü's Republican People's Party. As is often the case in Turkey's shallow party politics, the man was, to a large extent, an outsider. Having started life as a shepherd-boy in the province of Isparta, Süleyman Demirel rose through the republican educational system to become an engineer in charge of dam-building in Menderes' administration. He had joined the Justice Party, toyed briefly with politics, but later decided to try the private sector instead. He taught engineering and worked on construction projects, representing an American engineering company in Turkey, which was then helping to build the campus of Ankara's Middle East Technical University (METU). By the time the Justice Party leader – General Ragıp Gümüşpala, who had been forcibly 'retired' after the coup – died on 6 June 1964, Süleyman Demirel was a prosperous man. Yet, when party officials approached him for the leadership of the Justice Party he hardly hesitated.

When he was elected, the Justice Party was still in opposition; but not for long. Early in 1965, Inönü was defeated on a budget motion and he decided to bow out of government. Demirel, who had never been elected to public office, could then have become prime minister, but he preferred to let a senator of his party take the driving seat – joining forces with other conservative parties – until the elections that were to be held a few months later. In the October 1965 elections his star rose further as the Justice Party crushed the CHP by taking 53 per cent of the vote. Aged 40, Süleyman Demirel, the village boy made good, was now prime minister.

The election results confirmed the worst nightmares of the interventionists in the army. Not only were the successors of the Democrat Party in power, thus cancelling the effect of the 1960 coup, but for the first time an avowedly socialist party, the Turkish Labour Party, had entered parliament with fourteen deputies and 3 per cent of the vote. Talat Aydemir must have turned in his grave. Clearly, the elections showed that civilians could not be trusted with politics.

One of Demirel's first actions was to tackle the inevitable question of an amnesty, which brought him immediately into sharp disagreement with the military, who still opposed the release of the ex-Democrats. In the end a compromise solution was found. Talat Aydemir's partners in the failed coup attempts had their sentences reduced while the former Democrat Party members were released, but the ban on their political activities was maintained.

Demirel needed all the enthusiasm of his supporters to succeed in the difficult task of governing Turkey. There was plenty of work to be done. The economy was at a standstill, his party parliamentary group was unruly – a feature that still plagues his successors three decades later – and the Cyprus question was overshadowing all other diplomatic issues.

Cyprus had emerged as a major problem when Greek Cypriots killed scores of Turkish Cypriots in the so-called 'bloody Christmas' of 1963, a watershed in the conflict. Turkish nationalists wanted the military to intervene to protect their Turkish cousins on the island. Inönü, weighing the risks involved, had almost decided on this step when US President Lyndon Johnson sent a strongly worded letter warning him off in no uncertain terms. The Turks changed their mind about a military operation in Cyprus, but the incident was felt like a slap in the face and cast a shadow over Turkish-American relations for years.

In society as a whole, the age-old rift between the state establishment and the majority of the population was becoming ever more pronounced and developing under different guises. The traditional divide between religion and secularism and modernists and conservatives was now assuming a left–right aspect as well. Atatürk's old party drifted further to the left, under the influence of the young journalist and poet, Bülent Ecevit. A former university student of Sanskrit who had dropped out, he had joined Inönü's first cabinet after the coup as labour minister – a job particularly important at a time when workers were starting to organize, using the rights newly conferred on them by the liberal constitution. Ecevit persuaded Ismet Pasha that a more left-wing position would boost the party in confronting its right-wing and conservative rival, Demirel's Justice Party.

For a while, Turkey ran almost smoothly. Demirel earned one of his nicknames, 'Süleyman the Builder', with various large projects such as the Keban Dam and the spectacular Bosphorus Bridge that linked Europe and Asia in Istanbul. The economy started to grow steadily and rapidly.

But Turkey, now more open to the world, was directly affected by global trends. As the student movement grew stronger with the approach of 1968, university campuses became virtually liberated zones. At first, student demonstrations were no more than the usual peaceful expression of the political aspirations of the young. Among leftist students was a handsome young man, who used – so some say – to ride a white horse through the campus of METU. Aged only 21, the charismatic Deniz Gezmiş emerged as a natural leader and soon became a symbol of student unrest.

The right-wing Republican Peasants' National Party, headed by ex-NUC member, Alparslan Türkeş, who had staged his return as a civilian politician, started organizing summer camps where students were trained in the art of urban guerrilla warfare. Many leftist students also received training, sometimes abroad, in Palestinian camps.

By the end of the 1960s the situation on campuses had dramatically worsened. Leftist and rightist students were now armed. Who was initially to blame remains a subject of dispute. The end result, however, was plain for all to see. Confrontations led to bloody clashes between rival groups and with the police that fuelled a cycle of protest marches and further violence.

With both sides raising the stakes, the situation rapidly spun out of control. Anti-American feeling aroused by the Johnson letter was expressed in violent student demonstrations when the US Sixth Fleet paid a visit to Turkey. Left- and right-wing factions – the latter joined by religious fundamentalists who proclaimed the fighting a *jihad* or 'holy war' – both opposed the Americans for different reasons, and found a pretext to spar with each other. 'Our path is that of the revolution / Come, brother, come / Our motherland is full of yankees / Hit, brother, hit' was taken up as a slogan of the left. The Islamic right also urged its demonstrators to 'hit' out but in their case, it was 'for Allah'. Two people were killed and more than a hundred wounded when the two groups clashed, using clubs and iron bars, stones and Molotov cocktails.

With demonstrations, marches, clashes, Demirel's government had run into serious trouble. On top of that, the army was restless once again. Demirel thought he had bought the goodwill of the military when he had Chief of Staff Cevdet Sunay elected president to succeed Cemal Gürsel on the latter's death in 1966. In fact, as earlier in the decade, plots were being hatched by various groups in the lower echelons of the army.

The government got a taste of the army's hostility when the elderly Celal Bayar tried to have his political ban lifted in 1969. He approached Inönü, who had been not only his long-time rival but also a companion in the war of independence, and gained his support. Inönü felt it right to help an old man who had fallen on hard times. Needless to say, Demirel's party was all in favour of lifting the interdiction and a majority of the parliamentarians approved the motion. The army, however, was still determined to block Bayar's path; it succeeded in putting pressure on Demirel and Inönü and the bill was never brought before the senate.

In a deteriorating national climate, Demirel also faced internal trouble within his party. A smear campaign began, with dissidents demanding the opening of enquiries into his brother's assets. The truth of Demirel's motto, 'Whichever way you get into politics, you will leave in the same manner', was borne out when the rebellious faction in his party blocked his budget in January 1970 and caused the fall of his government, just as he had defeated Inönü a few years earlier. It was not the end of the road by a long way for Demirel who, expelling his opponents, bounced straight back with a new government. He was to lead a total of seven cabinets and become president in 1993.

Meanwhile, demonstrations were multiplying, often with dire consequences when the police moved in to stop the marches. As labour unions became more and more vocal and the economic situation worsened, the government was forced into a sharp devaluation of the lira, a move that was deeply felt by salaried public sector workers, civil servants and the military. The students, by then totally politicized, were also hardening their tone and using new methods. On 4 March 1971, four American airmen were kidnapped by leftists, who demanded the release of imprisoned demonstrators. The whole country was thrown into turmoil. Luckily, the incident ended peacefully with the release of the four Americans, but clearly unrest was reaching unacceptable levels.

Certainly the army officers who were now busy plotting to intervene thought so. They were not alone. While not quite working hand in hand with them, like-minded intellectuals were preparing the ground for a reformist government through newspaper and magazine articles.

The first serious warning for the government came on 21 November 1970 when General Muhsin Batur, head of the air force and one of many dissatisfied officers, sent a strongly worded letter to the government, mentioning the 'organizations' developing within the army. If the authorities did not act rapidly to redress the situation, the regime risked falling, his letter warned.

This time the coup organizers, determined to avoid the mistakes of their predecessors in 1960, had prepared everything down to the last detail, including a list of future cabinet ministers. Again the operation was to be kept outside the usual military chain of command, since the chief of staff seemed determined to stand by the government. The date had been set. The coup would take place on 9 March 1971. But at the last minute, as the plotters were about to act, one of their leaders got cold feet and blew the whistle on his comrades.

The intervention was thwarted, but by then Chief of Staff Memduh Tağmaç had realized that unless he acted decisively, other groups would repeat the attempt. A meeting of senior officers was called to decide an appropriate course of action. After much deliberation, it was decided that the government should be handed a warning letter and that Süleyman Demirel should be asked to step down.

When Demirel received the message, on 12 March 1971, his first reaction was to resist the pressure to leave. But then he thought better of it. If he complied, the army might not close the parliament and democracy would have a chance of regaining the upper hand. With this hope in mind, Demirel and his cabinet reluctantly signed their letter of resignation.

A civilian government of technocrats and representatives of the various parties was put together, and an ambitious package of reforms unveiled that included land redistribution and an improved education system. Initially, at least, messages of support poured in for the generals. Leftist intellectuals, in particular, who had opposed Demirel's conservative leadership and the heavy-handed methods of the police, were delighted. But radical opinion on the campuses sensed what lay in store. The military's hopes of bringing stability to the country were rapidly crushed as student demonstrations flared up again.

The army, this time firmly in the driving seat, bypassed the helpless government and imposed martial law in several provinces. Leftist and rightist organizations were closed down, newspapers seized and journalists arrested. When the Israeli consul was kidnapped by a leftist group, on 17 May 1971, the security forces took their revenge by arresting intellectuals all over the country. Within hours, hundreds of people were detained. The list reads like a who's who of Turkish political and cultural life: film-maker Yılmaz Güney, of *Yol* fame, Mehdi Zana, the Kurdish activist, Uğur Mumcu, the secular journalist who was killed by a car bomb in 1990, and many more. Some of them had welcomed the coup, but all of them were its victims.

The Israeli consul was eventually found dead and his kidnappers were arrested, but their companions continued the struggle. There were other events and further repression. One famous episode involved two British and a Canadian radar engineer who were taken hostage in the Black Sea area. The army surrounded the house where the hostage-takers and their victims were hiding out. In the shootout that followed, all but one of the eleven kidnappers and the three technicians were killed.

Deniz Gezmiş, who had been arrested in March, had nothing to do with any of these tragic events. But the army were determined to make an example. As a well-known figure and symbol of the student movement, he was to pay the price for these excesses. The young student leader and two of his friends were hanged on 6 May 1972. Turkish politics had come full circle.

In 1960, army officers, encouraged by some intellectuals, had overthrown a government and had hanged three conservative politicians. Just over a decade later, the prime minister had again fallen under pressure from the army, and this time three young leftist radicals ended their life on the gallows. Leading intellectuals were gaoled or tortured.

The military-dominated regime that ran the country after the 12 March 1971 memorandum forced through some changes. Liberal aspects of the 1961 constitution were curtailed to reflect the military's concern for state security, trade unions were repressed and a Universities Law, introduced in June 1973, reined in the sometimes wildly autonomous Turkish campuses. But the regime was too weak to impose fundamental change, enacting 'not reform, but chloroform', as one academic remarked on the new order.[5]

Political life also remained in a state of suspended animation. In one of his classic prevarications, Süleyman Demirel described himself as neither supporting nor opposing the cabinets that followed 12 March. The bickering politicians could only agree on resisting the army's first choice for president: the compromise candidate, retired admiral Fehmi Korutürk, was elected in April. The run-up to general elections in October 1973 was to prove a turning point, however. The emergence of nationalist and Islamic parties split the traditionally dominant right-wing vote that was once the monopoly of the old Democrat Party. At the same time, the bright young hope of the Turkish left, Bülent Ecevit, managed to outflank the republican old guard around the ageing Ismet Inönü. With his new thinking – 'it is necessary for us to give up claiming that only intellectuals know what is best, and to accept that the people know perfectly well where their interests lie'[6] – Ecevit managed to outdo Demirel in the October 1973 election. His CHP won 185 seats to the AP's 149.

But Ecevit still lacked a majority. Coalition negotiations dragged on for months, setting the tone for the later political disasters of the 1990s. Ecevit eventually agreed to work with Necmettin Erbakan, a charismatic, maverick newcomer whose appeal to old-fashioned small businesses and traditional Islamic conservatism had secured 48 seats for his National Salvation Party (the Milli Selamet Partisi, or MSP). A long-debated amnesty for prisoners of the military-backed regime got the coalition off to a positive, if shaky start. But before they could go further, Turkey was overwhelmed by a new eruption of the long-simmering problem of Cyprus.

8

The Cyprus Disaster

I see the Greek as an enemy, and love him as
such. The strange part is that the Greek feels
no love for me. He sees me purely as an
enemy.

Özdemir Kalpakçıoğlu, 1994

SETTLED COMFORTABLY ON his soft sofa, his colourful parrots
perched on his ample shoulders or fluttering around the warm,
sunlit room of his presidential mansion on the old Venetian walls
of Nicosia, it is easy to see why the portly leader of the Turkish
Cypriots has so little desire to change the *status quo*.

Rauf Denktaş knows his strength. He, if anybody, is the political
incarnation of the principle that Turks and Greeks, like oil and
vinegar, cannot mix: force them together as hard as you like, they
will almost always separate. Even in his youth, Denktaş was one of
the few Turkish Cypriots who went to school with Greeks, one of
the few who could speak fluent Greek. But at the privileged British
school of the colonial-era élite, even the Armenians turned out to
be better friends.

'The Greeks would not open their hearts to us. Even your best
friend would say, "What are you doing today, you dirty Turk?"'
Denktaş tells his visitors. 'Of course, we would reply in kind.'

The urbane lawyer, veteran of four decades of struggle against
the Greeks, can now afford to take a relaxed view. His people
have repeatedly voted him into the presidency of his fiefdom, the
self-declared Turkish Republic of Northern Cyprus. His backers
in mainland Turkey will never abandon him, since the Turkish
people respect him more than most Turkish politicians. And the
fact remains that in the decades following the Turkish invasion of
1974, only a handful of people have been killed. Even the deaths

in the summer of 1996 of four Greek Cypriots and a Turkish Cypriot along the Green Line dividing the island, though a reminder of the latent tensions, did not alter the picture. They were the product largely of a lethal combination of deliberate provocation on the Greek Cypriot side and a trigger-happy response on the part of Turkish Cypriots. For the most part, ethnic Turks and ethnic Greeks are no longer physically at each others' throats. Life on the sleepy Mediterranean island may not be normal, but for most of the time the United Nations troops separating the two sides have to keep holding exercises to remember that they are not on an extended holiday.

Time has done much to distance memories of the savage communal violence on Cyprus during the 1960s and the shock of the 1974 invasion. The UN-patrolled mother of all 'Green Lines' that keeps the rival communities apart has healed from an ugly wound carved through the city into a scar that has to be searched out to be seen.

The two halves of the city look very different, however. The Turkish side remains undeveloped, old-fashioned, stuck in a time-warp: isolated from international recognition and starved of investment since 1974. In some ways its small, old-fashioned houses are more charming than the rampaging, white-painted concrete of the Greek side. Its modesty compares with the gleaming new buildings that boast the Greek Cypriots' success in turning their part of the island into one of the richer corners of Europe. Even the Greek Cypriot refugees from 1974 have largely made good in enviable housing, although, as with the voluble expatriate community, comfort and wealth have done nothing but sharpen the sense of outrage at what was taken away.

Yet rich or poor, Greek or Turk, nobody sleeps entirely easy on Cyprus. Greek Cypriot commuters into Nicosia still have to drive past a bastion of the Venetian walls from which they are watched by a Turkish soldier armed with a machine-gun. The Turkish Cypriots scan their morning papers with a nagging worry in the back of their minds that, one day, the international community may succeed in forcing them back under Greek rule.

The Turks, whose 30,000 troops hold the physical advantage, want a 'confederal', separated solution; they believe anything less will swamp their 22 per cent minority of the population. But the Greeks, who have the economic and diplomatic advantage, feel no pressure to agree to anything that will allow the Turks to keep most of the 38 per cent of the island that they gained by force in 1974. The continuation of the Cyprus dispute is also useful to both Greek Cyprus and mainland Greece as a wedge to drive between Turkey and Europe, as well as a perennial store of ammunition for the vocal Greek lobby in the United States, where some two million often well-to-do Greek-Americans outnumber Turkish-Americans by at least twenty to one.

Thus it is that negotiators continue to come and go between the soft chairs in Denktaş's mansion, the Greek Cypriot presidency, Athens and Ankara. The great powers huddle together to discuss what to do and all agree that the present situation must be changed.[1] Yet invariably their initiatives fizzle out. Their main mistake is usually to believe that Cyprus, which looks temptingly easy to solve on its own, can somehow be isolated from the matrix of problems that have brought Turkey and Greece to the brink of war twice in the past decade and arguably date back to antiquity.

Greek political leaders have nearly always viewed the Turks as an invading barbarian enemy, a threat residing in the dark landmass of Anatolia that rises from the sea east of the Greek islands of the Aegean. On Cyprus the Turks even set a taunting star and crescent in whitewashed stone on the dry flanks of a mountainside north of Nicosia; it is left to the vivid imagination of the Greeks to decide what it means. The Turks, seeing Greek militarization of islands just off their coastline, have also had plenty of reasons to suspect their neighbours' intentions.

Some scholars date the competition between eastern Anatolian highlanders and the people of the Aegean-Mediterranean coast, including islands like Cyprus, far back into history. Peace only prevailed when an empire – whether Roman, Byzantine or Ottoman – managed to hold both sides at once. 'What miraculous wisdom of modern man will resolve a conflict which, starting with the Trojan wars, has already lasted three thousand years?' asked the scholar Stéphane Yerasimos.[2]

Nationalists keep alive in the Greek psyche the memory that it was Turkish raiders who snatched the Anatolian heartlands from the Greek-speaking Byzantine empire, and an Ottoman Turkish sultan who in 1453 finally captured the greatest Greek city, Constantinople. For the traditional-minded, pious Greek, the name still used by Greeks for Istanbul is a more potent symbol of Greekness than Athens itself. And along the way, after the fusion of Hellenistic civilization with Christianity, the West as a whole has tended to espouse the Greek thesis that outsiders attacking

from the east – be they Achaemenid Persians or the more recent
Turks – are necessarily barbarians.

The Turks, however, believe they showed their new subject
population good faith. After displacing the rule of the Byzantine
Greek court, Mehmet the Conqueror did little to interfere with
the Greek Orthodox Church or the dominance of Greek traders
and shopkeepers, either in the ports of Anatolia or in major towns
of the interior. Some Byzantine princely families were even initially
allowed to retain their estates. Mehmet reorganized the Greek
Orthodox into a self-governing religious *millet*, or community,
under their patriarch, as he did the Armenians and other
non-Muslim groups. In return for taxes and political loyalty, they
were then free to prosper. Some traders and bankers, such as
the 'phanariot' families – named after a once-fashionable district
alongside the Golden Horn – became fabulously rich. With their
enthusiasm for learning European languages, later Greeks acted
as privileged *dragomans*, or translators, for the court or for foreign
missions.

Even after the wrenching wars and ethnic conflicts of the nineteenth and early twentieth centuries, ordinary Greeks and Turks,
especially in village communities, preserved fond memories of
cohabitation. A study of refugees from Asia Minor in Greece
reported that

> people often mentioned how they had lived peacefully with their
> Turkish neighbours in an atmosphere of mutual respect. Older people
> were quite categorical that the disturbances and military confrontation
> which finally resulted in their flight were not the responsibility of
> ordinary Turks. This contrasted with the more chauvinistic views of
> their contemporaries among metropolitan Greeks. One must con-
> clude that enmity towards the Turks is a product of the nation-state
> of Greece, of exposure to political rhetoric reinforced by the media,
> and of an educational system which espouses a narrow nationalistic
> teaching of history. The actual victims did not express the supposed
> 'atavistic hatred' of Turks and Greeks. As the refugees said: 'It's the
> politicians and the Great Powers who bring the hatred.'[3]

Much the same could be said for the feelings of ordinary Turks
on the Aegean and Mediterranean coasts whenever politicians in
Athens and Ankara have provoked tension between the islands
and the mainland. They had no problems with the Greeks against
whom they were being set, and wished they could be left out of a
dispute that they believed was caused by outsiders.

But as European ideas of national self-determination overtook the Christians of the Ottoman empire during the nineteenth century, the Greek Orthodox élite became dissatisfied with subject status. The advances of the Greek mercantile community brought with it other ambitions. Hunger for land was frustrated by laws that prevented the transfer of Muslim-held property to Christians. The Greeks began to feel the backwardness of the Ottoman Turkish administration compared to the technology and cultural advances of Christian Europe. When the once-invincible Ottoman armies began to fall back through the Balkans in the eighteenth and nineteenth centuries, and subject Christian populations closer to Europe began to rise against them in the nationalist spirit of the age, some Greeks felt the need to stake their claim to what they saw as their historic heritage.

In this, the Greeks received encouragement from their closest Orthodox co-religionists, the Russians, who were also the most redoubtable enemies of the Turks. Tsarina Catherine the Great (1762–96) made little secret of her 'Greek Project' to restore Constantinople to the Greeks and thus further her expansionist ambitions for Russia. She pushed her military advantages by claiming and obtaining treaty rights to protect the Ottoman Greek community. And among Greek aristocrats high in the service of the tsars, as in Odessa in the early nineteenth century, the seeds of what would become the Greek war of independence were planted.

The Ottomans had confronted rebellions before, but the 1821 Greek uprising revealed the new weakness of the Ottoman state. Crushing it required the politically expensive step of calling in extra troops from the powerful, autonomous viceroy of Egypt. A stalemate had been reached when the British and French fleets intervened and sank the Ottoman and Egyptian navies at Navarino Bay in 1827. Truce negotiations had been in confused progress at the time, but the upshot of the four-hour action was a massacre: 60 of the 89 Ottoman ships were sunk and 8,000 of their sailors were killed. The allies suffered 176 dead, but lost no ships.

After further, European-backed military consolidation, Greece became independent in 1830. Its territory was originally only half what it is today. It gradually expanded, taking Thessaly from the Ottomans in 1881. Crete rebelled in 1900 and joined Greece in 1913, the same year that Athens won Epirus, Samos, Lesbos and part of Macedonia. Western Thrace was added in the settlement of 1923. Italy had also taken Rhodes and other south-east Aegean islands of the Dodecanese from the Ottomans in 1913, but passed them on to Greece in 1948.

After the First World War, overestimating Allied commitment to wartime promises enshrined in the 1920 Treaty of Sèvres, Greece launched its ill-fated invasion of the Anatolian provinces. By 1922, the Turks had retaken Izmir (Smyrna), a victory that had drastic consequences for the ancient Greek inhabitants of Anatolia. Strengthened by their military success, the new Turkish nationalist government was able to overturn the crippling provisions of Sèvres, which had never been ratified. Under the Treaty of Lausanne of 1923, the two states agreed to exchange their remaining populations, with the exception of the Greek population of Istanbul and the Turkish population of Western Thrace, the area of northeastern Greece adjacent to the new Turkish border.

The movement of people was huge, involving more than a tenth of the population of Anatolia at the time. Between 900,000 and 1.3 million Greeks were uprooted and sent to Greece.[4] Sometimes villages simply swapped land. Others built new refugee suburbs in big cities. Back in Anatolia, some places became ghost towns, like a Greek settlement now known in Turkish as Kaya, near Fethiye on the Mediterranean coast. Hundreds of stone-and-plaster houses climb up a hill of narrow roadways, hauntingly empty except for curious tourists peering at the remains of imposing churches, and, once a year, dwindling busloads of Greek pensioners who come on the old town's saint's day to mourn the end of the great Hellenic history of Asia Minor.

Between 350,000 and 500,000 Turks were transported to Turkey, most settling in big cities or on the Aegean and Mediterranean coasts. The fact of their uprooting is often unknown to their descendants, repatriation never having become the same burning issue as in Greece – perhaps because this was only one of many forced migrations in the new Turkish state. Similarly, there is little popular thought given to repossessing the territory of present-day Greece, even if the Turkish army may have remote contingency plans one day to join forces with the 100,000 or so Turks remaining in Western Thrace.

On the whole, the Turkish memory of the Greek war of independence and these territorial losses is muted; they are thought of as only one part of the complicated story of the collapse of the Ottoman empire and the growth of the Turks' own sense of national identity.

But Turkish army officers can still remember the *enosis*, or forced union, of 1913 that joined Crete to mainland Greece, with its expulsion of Muslim Turks and subsequent Hellenization of the island. They hold it up as an example of Greek perfidy and proof of the dangers that lie in wait for the ethnic Turkish community on Cyprus. And when Turkey's Islamist-nationalist fringe wants to stir up support by taking a stand against the Greeks, the Ecumenical Patriarch of the Greek or Eastern Orthodox Church is seen as the most easily available symbol of Istanbul's Greek past. Bombs are thrown into the patriarchate garden and old cemeteries desecrated. Even supposedly mainstream Islamist politicians can be heard reminding their listeners of the fate of the patriarch at the time of the 1820s rebellion, who was hanged in the gateway of the patriarchate in revenge for Greek massacres of Turks in the Morea.

In a continuing gesture of protest, the patriarchate still keeps that gate bricked up. But none of this does much to reassure the few ethnic Greeks descended from those who chose to stay in Istanbul.

Despite this turbulent history, more than 100,000 Greeks had remained in republican Istanbul, a possibility foreseen by the Lausanne Treaty of 1923. For some, it was a question of not wanting to leave their businesses, even if profits were increasingly invested in Greece or elsewhere, just as the Thracian Turks of north-eastern Greece moved their investments to Turkey. For others it was simply a case of having nowhere else to go. At first, they seemed to have made the right choice. A new start in inter-communal relations was heralded by the Ankara Treaty of Friendship of 1930 between the old rivals Mustafa Kemal and the Greek leader, Eleutherios Venizelos.

During the Second World War, however, the heavy-handed application of the wealth tax struck Greeks and all non-Muslim minorities hard; it was a calculated blow aimed at forcing commercial life into Turkish hands. Nevertheless civilized relations continued between Greece and republican Turkey, and the life of the substantial Greek community in Istanbul remained relatively untroubled. But from the mid-1950s onwards, the relationship was poisoned by cheap nationalist politics, a lack of mutual contact and distorted media coverage surrounding the gathering communal disaster on Cyprus.

The decline of the British empire had left the fate of the island unclear. Leased by the Ottoman empire to Britain in 1878 as part of the Treaty of Berlin, Cyprus had become a British crown colony in 1914. In 1954, the Greek government had raised the claim of *enosis* between Cyprus and Greece. At the same time, Turks claimed that the island should be returned to Turkish sovereignty. As negotiations continued in London, calamity struck in Istanbul in 1955 in what became known as the 'events of September', when officially directed mobs armed with rocks and staves attacked pre-selected minority targets and wrecked 3,000 buildings. Shop-keepers in the main shopping street of Istanbul can still point to chips in the stonework and gouges in the wood-panelling dating from this time. In the ensuing months tens of thousands of Greeks packed their bags and fled.

More direct government action was to come. After the 'bloody Christmas' massacres of ethnic Turkish Cypriots in December 1963, the Inönü government of the day determined to take revenge. Its resolve was hardened by a decision of the Syrian government in January 1964 to expropriate and expel 10,000 eth-nic Turkish Syrians, who now began to arrive in Turkey. The Greek Orthodox community in Istanbul became the whipping boy. On 16 March 1964, Prime Minister Ismet Inönü cancelled the 1930 treaty of friendship with Greece, an action he knew would affect the agreed residence rights of 12,000 Greek passport-holders in Istanbul. Although he put a six-month moratorium on the action, the bloodshed in Cyprus and a vicious anti-Greek campaign left him no room for manoeuvre. Prominent Greeks (and many who were not so prominent, who were sick or, in some cases, even dead) were indiscriminately denounced for anti-Turkish activities. They were given twenty-four hours to leave, allowed to take 20 kilos of baggage (not including household effects) and 22 dollars. The rest had to be out by September. The government confiscated the remainder of their property. The Turkish treasury profited to the tune of 200–500 million dollars.[5]

Of course, many of these people were married or related to Greeks who held Turkish passports. These Greeks felt obliged to leave as well, bringing the total emigration to 40,000 people. This was at a time when more than half the members of the Istanbul Chamber of Commerce were still ethnic Greek citizens of Turkey. Much of their property was left in a legal limbo. Their old wooden houses joined those abandoned by the panic-stricken Greeks who had left after the 'September events' of a decade before. To this day, some 70,000 Istanbul Greeks living in Greece keep up their Turkish passports in the hope of selling properties that are now often worth millions of dollars.

Churches and religious institutions also have always been regarded with intense suspicion by Turkish republican authorities – so much so that some Christian churchmen pine for the liberal regime of the Ottomans. In the run-down quarter of Fener, long deserted by the rich Phanariot families and now a poor and fundamentalist-inclined Muslim district, the Greek patriarchate had to wait forty-six years for permission to refurbish its premises after a fire in 1941. Similar delays held up the smallest applications for improvement or restoration in other churches, and in 1974 all Greek and Armenian seminaries for educating priests were closed. At the same time, strict republican rules dictate that the heads of the churches must be born in Turkey and be Turkish citizens.

Part of the reason for this was the equally hostile treatment by the Greek authorities of the 100,000-strong Turkish Muslim minority in Western Thrace (north-eastern Greece). Any slight to either hostage minority was often repaid in kind, a problem that hit schools particularly hard. Ethnic Greek students in Istanbul could pass the stringent exams for entrance to Turkish universities, but be barred on technicalities arising from mutual sanctions. Other technicalities forced Turkish students in Greece to use antiquated textbooks; the community refused to take up the snappy offerings of the Greek ministry of education, with their Aesop's Fables in Turkish and a liberal sprinkling of Greek flags to colour in.

Here the Lausanne Treaty, which started as such an important guarantor of Turkish-Greek peace and co-operation during the early republic, has become something of a curse. Using the pretext of the mutual guarantees, neither community has allowed itself, nor been allowed by its 'parent' country, to be absorbed into the society of its host country. They have been both trump cards and hostages in cynical diplomatic disputes that usually have nothing to do with them.

By now the small towns of Thrace, an hour west of the Turkish border, have no need of Cyprus's green line: divisions already exist in people's minds and in Greek laws about who can own what businesses where. The Turks stick to their single-storeyed, whitewashed homes in one quarter, almost unchanged from Balkan photographs of a century ago. Modern development is confined to the Greek quarters of town. Ethnic Turkish businessmen look to Istanbul and students apply to Turkish universities. The good fortune of having a European Union passport is helping a new generation to seek work in Europe. But it has done little to make them feel any more like full citizens of Greece. Athens denies their Turkish ethnicity by designating them 'Muslims', their elected representatives have been harassed by lawsuits and election rules have sometimes seemed designed to deny them national representation.

The Greeks in Istanbul were historically better educated than the Turks and indeed were the backbone of the city's élite. Even today, the heirs of Byzantium look down on the Greeks of Greece with a certain snobbery. Nevertheless, by the 1990s, only 2,500 Greeks remained in Istanbul, many of them old and poor. Those few who ran successful companies often chose to do so behind the safe screen of a Turkish- or European-sounding name. The only Greeks left in the provinces, under the terms of the Lausanne agreement, were a handful on the two Aegean islands which remain in Turkish hands, Gökçeada and Bozcaada (Imbros and Tenedos), selling thick homemade red wine in near-deserted villages clinging to the upper slopes of the barren, rocky islands. For a long time, the republic encouraged local Greeks to depart by using the islands as open prisons. Nowadays, large concrete housing estates for immigrants and people displaced by dam projects show modern Turkey's determination to complete the process of Turkification.

Quixotically, the Turkish republic has also refused to budge on the issue of the status of the patriarchate. The ecumenical patriarch is acknowledged throughout the world as the 'first among equals' of the independent Orthodox churches and their 250 million adherents; he is visited by prime ministers and ambassadors and is a potential status-enhancing jewel for Istanbul. But the Ankara government, again citing the Treaty of Lausanne, has stubbornly refused to acknowledge that the 270th holder of the office in a line stretching back to the first century AD, His All Holiness Patriarch Bartholomew I, is anything but the chief priest of a dwindling minority in Turkey. With its insistence that only a Turkish citizen can be elected, Ankara likewise drastically limits the field of choice for leader of this most ancient of churches.

Against this background, Cyprus was a terrible accident waiting to happen, a time-bomb of unfinished business between Turk and Greek, which, when it blew up in 1974, ripped the Mediterranean island apart. The military operation ordered by Prime Minister Bülent Ecevit on 20 July 1974 confronted a shocked world with the full dimensions of the crisis. It also marked the moment when a Westernizing Turkish republic showed how sharply its interests could diverge from the West's.

Ecevit took the final decision to intervene after a last, tense briefing from the military in a war command and control bunker beneath the hulking grey walls of the General Staff Headquarters in Ankara. A few days before, an ethnic Greek street leader and EOKA guerrilla called Nicos Sampson had staged a coup in Nicosia in the name of *enosis*, or union with Greece. He had the backing of the military dictatorship then ruling Greece, the junta known as the Colonels, who were keen to oust the Greek Cypriot President, Archbishop Makarios. Britain, the third guarantor of independent Cyprus, declined to do anything. Turkey was on its own.

Politically, then as now, no Turkish government could cope with the popular press headline, 'Cyprus is slipping out of our hands'. Aside from the fate of ethnic Turks on Cyprus, the Turks were alarmed by the idea that Greek territorial borders would stretch theoretically almost the whole way round their southern Mediterranean coast. Ankara also saw a chance to implement what it had sought ever since Britain initiated discussions on Cyprus in 1955, that is, segregation of the two communities.

The fuse of the conflict had of course been lit long before 1974. Cyprus had already been effectively partitioned for more than a decade. The Turkish minority lived for the most part in thirty small cantons, to which they had been confined after the elaborate independence arrangements of 1960 had broken down in December 1963 amid mutual recriminations and threatening troop movements by the Turkish army. The first UN force arrived soon afterwards. Neither side was completely innocent; while the ethnic Greeks had organized fighters from the days of the anti-British EOKA group, largely backed and armed by Greece, the Turks had their own Turkish Resistance Organization, the Türk Mükavemet Teşkilatı, known as TMT for short.

The genesis of TMT illustrated Turkey's haphazard response to events. Its formation was held up first in 1957 by a feeling that peaceful methods should be given a chance; it was then enmeshed in a mire of domestic political wrangling, and finally sidelined when the Turkish government became distracted by the 1960 coup. Arms were first sent over by wooden fishing-boats, two of which sank with their young sailors, then on a 25-ton fishing-boat that had to be scuttled when an English patrol-boat appeared on the horizon. By the time of the breakdown of the Cypriot constitution in 1963, when the TMT squads were formally ordered to attack, their membership may have numbered some 500 people, with mainland Turkish co-ordinators working under cover as bank inspectors or teachers.

One of the TMT activists, Mehmet Ali Tiremeşli, later described the atmosphere of those times. He and his fellow militants had gone to dig up the weapons sent to them by the Turks, wrapped up in beeswax to stop the soil from corroding them while they lay buried in their fields.

The Turks said we were not to use these weapons until the order came. And if we hadn't had those weapons in 1963, we would have been wiped out. Even so, we couldn't find some and others didn't work. I was a farmer, but we were carrying out three actions a day. We were hungry and penniless, but we fought on. We were not paid a thing. [After an EOKA band ambushed the car of some newly-weds, killing the bridegroom,] I jumped on my bike and cycled 6–7 kilo-metres to the nearest Greek village to kill the local EOKA leader. I waited in ambush between a house and a coffee-shop. I killed him at 20 metres. He died with the first shot. I ran up to him. He'd been hit in the heart. If he'd had a chance, maybe I'd have taken him to hospital. But as I saw he was struggling for life, I shot him twice more to put him out of his agony. In those days the English radio gave the news of murders straight away. We listened to it like a football match. When we heard of an incident, we answered it within the hour. We had to keep the retaliation going. The Turkish people had to believe they had an organization.[6]

A more sinister aspect of TMT was its efforts to make sure that the Turkish community was not tempted into co-operation with the Greeks. It decided, for instance, to force Turkish workers out of mixed trade unions and then to place advertisements in the papers with comments like 'I will always support the Turkish cause and I say our slogan should be, "segregation or death" '. At least three Turkish Cypriots were killed, apparently to intimidate others, although TMT's involvement has not been proven. Gradually, the Turks were collected together into a new all-Turk union.

If the TMT's hit-and-run raids were amateurish, neither was Turkey's full-scale intervention of 20 July 1974 a clean-cut affair. The Turks had no experience of amphibious warfare and had only just started helicopter training. The first landing was on the wrong beach and a murderous hail of machine-gun fire ripped through the Turkish ranks. Poor co-ordination then sent Turkish warplanes repeatedly strafing a Turkish destroyer, which later sank with great loss of life. Storms held up re-supply moves. But after three days, the Turks had established a broad bridgehead and accepted a United Nations cease-fire.

For the next three weeks, negotiators in Geneva tried to find a solution. As a guarantor state of the 1960 Cyprus constitution, the Turks argued that they had been justified in their invasion and demanded five cantons for the Turkish Cypriots; the Greek side rejected this. The two sides prepared for war again. Turkey's second operation in August left Turkish troops in control of the entire northern third of the island, from Famagusta to Morphou.

By the end of operations, the Turkish armed forces had lost 498 dead and the Turkish Cypriots an estimated 1,000 dead. The Greek Cypriot side lost 3,000 dead, soldiers and civilians. But, as with so many other conflicts, it is the missing that have left an open wound. The Turkish Cypriots lost 203 missing during the 1960s and about 600 missing during the invasion. The Greek Cypriots are still missing 1,619. When in 1996 Denktaş admitted the truth, that they had probably been captured and killed, it became another issue debated and condemned in Athens and the European Parliament. Nobody knows what happened to the missing Turkish Cypriots, but most Turks assume that they too are dead.

The future president Kenan Evren, head of Turkey's land forces at the time, maintains that the military always intended to hand back some of the territory captured on Cyprus in return for peace. But Ecevit's coalition partner and deputy prime minister, the pro-Islamic leader Necmettin Erbakan, was less flexible.

> That wing of the coalition [Evren has written] could not be persuaded to give up one inch of captured territory, as if 'land won with blood' could not be returned. They torpedoed all the talks. But the land taken was more than what we had decided [to keep]. These extra pieces were to be given back in the compromise. But Erbakan allowed the negotiations to fail as if he had been a warrior fighting at the front . . . and because [he] was the key, the Cyprus problem was never solved. Soldiers took the land in two days. They did their job in the best manner. But the politicians got no result in more than ten years.[7]

The same pro-Islamic Erbakan rose again to dominate Turkish politics in the latter half of the 1990s, with a new slogan that boded ill for any future settlement: 'The fact that we have not seized the whole island is concession enough.'

The most obvious piece of real estate prepared by the Turks for any future peace settlement, a strip of 100 hotels and guesthouses that the Turkish army has kept deliberately empty along the best beach in Cyprus south of Famagusta, stays exactly as it was when the tourists fled during those fateful days of July 1974.

Suitcases lie open where they were abandoned and mildewed bed-clothes remain scattered around the rooms. Behind the chained and padlocked hotel entrances, the reception desks are empty, the stacks of registration papers languishing under ever-deeper layers of dust.

The cause of segregation meanwhile continues to gather momentum. One by one, the links between the two communities have been cut. There are now different airports and different television stations. Memories of friendships have faded, as has the shared experience of British colonial values. Former ethnic Greek properties have been profitably absorbed by the new Turkish Cypriot élite. All that remains of mutual reliance is some water supplied from the Turks to the Greeks, in return for some electricity from the Greeks to the Turks. This separation may not necessarily be what everybody on the island wants, but it is now an established fact of life.

Older Turkish Cypriots – even Denktaş's chauffeur – secretly bet on Greek Cypriot race meetings, but their children, since they are no longer taught Greek, cannot even read the racing form in newspapers smuggled over from the other side. More Turkish Cypriots live off the island than on it; in their place have come mainland settlers with no interest in a solution. Officially, these newcomers number some 23,000, including 1,000 Turkish veterans of the 1974 'peace operation'. Local politician Özker Özgür believes they may comprise as many as 80,000 of the 171,000 inhabitants.

Integration is pursued with mainland Turkey. Turkish Cypriot football teams compete in Turkish leagues. Telephone and postal services pass through Turkey, as do airline routes and, increasingly, trade, after a European court decided that Turkish Cypriot validation was not good enough to qualify for tariff concessions made to European imports from Cyprus. The currency on the Turkish part of the island is now the Turkish lira.

Few youngsters try to bridge the divide. Left-wing journalist Serhat Incirli was one of the few young Turkish Cypriots who has been over to the Greek Cypriot side. He is one of the minority, mainly in the Communist Party, who believes that reunification would be best for both communities, even though he was shot through both knees by Greek Cypriot gunmen in a massacre at his school when it was being bombed by Turkish planes in 1974.

'We met the Greek Cypriots in Limassol. We tried to warn them that "if you don't make a deal with us now, soon you will have no Turkish Cypriots left to talk to",' he said.

But Incirli and his fellow journalists at a newspaper run from a portakabin outside Nicosia have little confidence that their small group can influence the majority who have flocked to support the continuation of the current 'no-solution solution' favoured by their rulers. Cypriot nationalism is unable to win the day. Few ethnic Turks want reintegration with ethnic Greeks, any more than Greek wants it with Turk.

That truth is usually left unspoken, since the Cyprus problem, sleepy though it now seems on the island itself, is an international diplomatic dispute played for high stakes in the lobbies of Washington and Brussels. Denktaş was furious at the damage done to his negotiating position in 1994 when Derviş Eroğlu, a younger nationalist leader manoeuvring for the succession, dared to articulate his rejection of a federal, integrated solution for the island.

'It destroyed everything,' Denktaş complained. 'Basically we may be very close in our evaluation of the situation. But I am not accepting his tactics of making a fool of me while federation is still on the table.'

Eroğlu was unrepentant, and spoke with the relief of a confession. 'After ten years, I have to say the truth, so that future generations can live in peace. We shouldn't be thinking of gaining time. We should have an agreement on two states. Forcing the two communities together could bring a bloodbath.'

Eroğlu, prime minister at the time, later had his view endorsed by parliament in a decision 'to take measures between the TRNC [Turkish Republic of Northern Cyprus] and Turkey commensurate with those military and defence measures taken by Greece and Greek Cypriots, by concluding agreements with Turkey on foreign affairs, defence and security . . . [and also to complete] economic integration between the two countries'.

Once again, Turkey has been left to pick up the bill. Turkey is not necessarily the country that takes the initiative on Cyprus, and the tail often wags the dog. Denktaş's decision to declare a nominal independence in 1983, for instance, took the Ankara government by surprise. Once done, however, the mainland Turks felt they had to back their kinsmen, although massive American and Western pressure dissuaded anyone, even willing friends like Pakistan and Bangladesh, from joining Ankara in recognizing the self-declared Turkish Republic of Northern Cyprus.

Mainland Turkey, in fact, is not as comfortable with the *status quo* as Denktaş. It has paid dearly for its loyalty to its ethnic kin, far beyond the $200 million a year subsidy it must pay to keep the breakaway state afloat. International sanctions against Turkey for its Cyprus invasion during the 1970s helped hamstring the Turkish economy and its access to military supplies. In the 1980s and 1990s, Turkey was still condemned as the aggressor in the Cyprus dispute, a crucial disadvantage in many of its negotiations with Europe.

The European umbrella may well be the one under which Cypriots negotiate a new way to live side by side. To a certain extent, the advent of a higher authority in Brussels has made life psychologically easier in the one place where Turks and Greeks still live together in large numbers, the green hills of Thrace in northeastern Greece. But the mainstream Turkish Cypriot leadership is against reintegration under any umbrella.

President Turgut Özal nearly rolled the boulder up to the top of the mountain in 1991, when a four-way conference on Cyprus between Turkey, Greece, Turkish Cypriots and Greek Cypriots was on the cards. But the then prime minister, the nationalist Mesut Yılmaz, influenced by hard-liners in the Turkish foreign ministry, backed out of the deal even before it was clear what position Greece would take. And even Özal would not have conceded much that the Greek side passionately demanded. 'These two groups hate each other. How are you going to marry them off? The only solution is a loose federation,' Özal said.

The United Nations marked a critical point in such thinking in April 1992, when the Security Council advocated a bi-zonal, bi-communal, federal formula of two politically equal units. When this plan got nowhere, attention switched to confidence-building measures, a possible exchange of the Turkish hotels of Famagusta for a Turkish stake in a jointly administered, reopened Nicosia International Airport. First one side, then the other undermined this initiative. US President Bill Clinton's White House, with more than half an eye on the Greek vote in an election year, announced that 1996 was to be the year in which a solution was to be found for the Cyprus question; but then, rather like the faintly absurd concept of the 'non-map map' of earlier negotiations, the resolve slipped away.

The Cyprus dispute, in short, is always useful somewhere, inside or outside the island, for the politicians, refugee leaders and hard-liners who are able to make political capital out of it on both sides of the divide, and often despite the interests of ordinary Cypriots. 'I don't believe these talks [on Cyprus] will have a result. But in order that the Turks should not be seen as the side obstructing them, we say we support their continuation,' President Evren bluntly admitted.

The Cyprus issue also served as a catalyst for Turkey to reappraise its relationship with the United States. The brusque tone of the letter from US President Johnson warning Turkey in 1963 not to use American weapons was a shock that tempted Turkey to experiment with relationships outside NATO. A rapprochement with the Soviet Union, some Turks believed, would deprive the Greek Cypriot administration of a monopoly in Moscow, and would bring aid not available from the United States. A more neutral foreign policy, Turks began to reason, might gain support from non-aligned states and the United Nations.

This Cyprus-inspired mind-set that gathered strength through the 1960s lay behind Bülent Ecevit's move, on coming to power in 1973, to instruct his foreign policy mandarins to open Turkey's doors to the Soviet Union. As the victor of Cyprus, Ecevit was also persuaded to try to cash in his chips by calling a general election. Neither initiative was to bring him much good fortune.

9

Wilderness Years

One day Nasruddin Hoca's friends asked him:
'At a funeral, where should one stand? Should
it be in front, beside or behind the coffin?'
'Anywhere,' the Hoca replied, 'just not inside
the coffin itself.'

Turkish folk-tale

UP IN THE carpeted luxury of their executive floor, the shock
must have been total. It was the morning of 9 January 1996. The
brothers Sabancı were preparing for a routine meeting in the
boardroom at the recently finished symbol of their business success, the gleaming new Sabancı Towers in Istanbul. Its security
system was supposed to be state of the art. Prior to the meeting,
the youngest brother, Özdemir Sabancı, was going through the
details of the operations of their newly opened 100,000-car-a-year
joint venture with Toyota of Japan. In the back of his mind was a
massive refinery deal soon to be completed with Amoco of the
United States. For the Sabancıs, industrialists, bankers and phil-
anthropists in the tradition of nineteenth-century Europe, the late
1990s held massive promise of further expansion, creation of jobs,
factories and profits.

Suddenly, Özdemir and his manager must have noticed that
something was amiss – their attention caught perhaps by an unusual
sound from the reception area outside, the cough of a silenced pistol as it snuffed out the life of a secretary sitting at her desk. The door
to the wood-panelled office burst open. Perhaps Özdemir Sabancı
recognized the young girl student who had appeared months before
to serve tea on the executive floor. He would have had no doubt as
to the intentions of the two youths who were now with her, guns at
the ready. They shot him and his car factory manager dead. Beside the

bodies slumped on the floor they left a flag from the latest faction of Dev Sol, the Revolutionary Left. Their protest message condemned the brutal suppression of a prison rebellion in the preceding weeks; for the Sabancıs, as for most Turks, it was a re-run of a nightmare they hoped had been forgotten.

The bloody curse of political violence bequeathed to Turkey by the 1970s had struck again, neither for the first nor the last time. It was long a doctrine of the radical left that shock tactics would destabilize the old order and open the way to the promise of a just order in the new. So it was perhaps no coincidence that when the Sabancı Centre triple murder occurred in January 1996, Turkish politics was in an uncertain power vacuum typical of the 1970s.

Amazingly, the names of the political leaders were also almost the same: the ascetic poet-nationalist Bülent Ecevit, nicknamed the *karaoğlan*, or likely lad; the pro-Islamic opportunist, Necmettin Erbakan, known as the *hoca* or teacher; the nationalist Alparslan Türkeş, *başbuğ* or commandant of the sinister right-wing Grey Wolves; and above all Süleyman Demirel, who rose from Anatolian shepherd-boy to the highest posts in the land. This consummate operator also coined the ultimate politician's motto: 'Yesterday was yesterday, today is today.' It symbolized a 1970s legacy of short-term politics above long-term national interest that still undermines Turkish progress today.

Turkey in the 1970s never had much of a chance. The decade had had a turbulent start with the machinations and state persecution of leftist intellectuals after the March 1971 military 'coup by memorandum'. By the end of the decade, thirteen weak coalition governments had swapped power amid a growing political instability that led inexorably to the more sweeping military coup of 1980. More than 5,240 people died in political violence during the decade. At least three times that number were wounded. The whole country paid an enormous price in development delayed.

Ironically, it was military success in Cyprus in 1974 that tipped the balance against the country. The intervention may have created an enduring safe haven for the Turkish Cypriots, whose population is equivalent to that of one mid-sized Turkish town. But for mainland Turkey, the Cyprus problem was to become a key ingredient in a diplomatic, economic and political disaster that cast a shadow over the rest of the decade and beyond. Far from uniting the Turks in a glow of achievement, the Cyprus adventure had within two months helped to bring down Prime Minister Ecevit's first coalition government, elected in the October 1973 election under the slogan, 'We are out to change this social order'.

Sitting at his desk more than twenty years later, his small frame dwarfed by the huge, square meeting room in the Turkish parliament, Ecevit blinked behind thick glasses as, in the typical fashion of Turkish politicians, he blamed someone else for his failures. The September 1974 downfall of his first eight-month-old administration, he said, was the fault of pro-Islamic party leader Necmettin Erbakan: 'the basic reason was our differences on Cyprus.'[1]

Ecevit's own hope that success in Cyprus would lead to electoral success was dashed when the assembly rejected his plan for early elections, the deputies reluctant as ever to risk defeat and the loss of their many privileges. Instead of gaining a parliament with a working majority, the country was plunged into a six-month-long political crisis. Ominous reports of clashes started to appear. Even when Süleyman Demirel took over in March 1975 with a right-wing 'National Front' coalition for the fourth of his governments in the 1970s, he was only voted in by a majority of four. It made little difference to the country as a whole, which was beginning to sense the difficulties ahead.

State bureaucrats had found the Turkish economy relatively easy to run during the 1960s, a period of cheap oil, plentiful farm exports and global growth. But this was to change. Price hikes by the oil-producing countries after the Arab-Israeli war of 1973 dealt a devastating blow to Turkey, which imported almost all its energy. The rapidly growing population began to leave village holdings in ever larger numbers and to move to the outskirts of cities. Added to these problems, commencing in February 1975, was an American embargo on arms and military aid that followed the Cyprus intervention; the International Monetary Fund and other institutions followed Washington's lead.

By the end of the 1970s, shop shelves had become depleted of goods. Ordinary Turks had even worked out a method of repairing the filaments in broken light bulbs. Candles were often of more use, since electricity blackouts were commonplace. Travelling between cities was hampered by fuel shortages. Heating oil was so scarce that even senior officials would receive visitors in freezing offices bundled up in their overcoats. Imports were so heavily restricted that Turgut Özal, then a senior civil servant, remembered hobbling past customs officers after a trip abroad wearing several pairs of tights for his wife Semra. Nothing seemed to go right. People feared to go out at night in big cities for fear of political violence at home, and Armenian gunmen had declared open season on Turkish diplomats and Turkish targets abroad. Even Turkish Airlines acquired a disastrous reputation as more than five of its planes crashed in Izmir, Istanbul, Isparta, Ankara and Paris, the last setting a record at the time when 345 people on board died.

'There's no oil, no foreign currency, no goods, no medicine, no raw materials, no fertilizers and no production ... we can't even close the 351 billion lira deficit by printing money. Even if we had paper, ink and a printer it would not be possible. It would be another way of saying that the state has sunk,' Demirel told an epic 11-hour meeting of the government and the military on 24 January 1980, after announcing a stringent stabilization package, an austerity plan that Turkey – and its Western backers – had once again judged vital to put the country back on course.

One sceptical military officer at the meeting retorted that there still seemed to be enough money to import books from Russia on Lenin and Marx. The bitterness was real: the armed forces were suffering too. Officers were struggling to pay spiralling rents for their housing. Whenever a rumour suggested that foreign currency had arrived at the Central Bank, someone from the general staff was ordered round to try to jump the queue. Its Second World War-vintage, American-supplied armoury was running out of spare parts. By 1977, 'the number of defective armaments we held was rising every day,' General Evren wrote. The only slight benefit of the post-1975 breach with the United States was that it forced Turkey to become more self-reliant in arms manufacturing and, when the time came to mend fences, it allowed Ankara to renegotiate the generous basing deals more or less given away by Menderes in the 1950s.

Turkey's years in the international wilderness – including a missed chance to join Greece in applying for membership of the then European Economic Community – were to last until August 1978. By this time Washington's moral indignation and Greek anger over Cyprus were outweighed by the prospect that its formerly staunch NATO ally appeared to be going down the same troubled course as its neighbour Iran, then facing the first rumblings of Islamic revolution. Turkey was to be saved once more by the double-edged sword of its 'strategic importance'.

Alarmed by a spectacular outbreak of bloodletting in the eastern Turkish town of Kahramanmaraş in 1978, the Guadeloupe Summit in January 1979 agreed to help Turkey. Within days, President

Jimmy Carter, previously severe in his dealings with Turkey, had
sent his Secretary of State back to Ankara. By the end of the year,
the OECD had rescheduled 1.5 billion dollars of Turkish debt;
after the Demirel government had pushed through the stabilization measures of 24 January, more than one billion dollars was
made available in April 1980. Despite heated differences over the
resumption of American U-2 spy plane flights over the Soviet
Union – Turkey remained embarrassed by the shooting down of
Gary Powers' flight from the Incirlik base in 1962 – a new bilateral
defence treaty reactivating a dozen US bases in Turkey was signed
in March of the same year.

Perhaps Turkey would have stumbled even without the post-
Cyprus domestic upsets and foreign embargoes. But the change
in international sentiment came too late. The turmoil in the
government had already left the field open to viciously opposed
ideologies whose street scuffles turned to gun battles that scarred
a generation. It also led to the September 1980 coup, which skewed
Turkish democratic development for years to come. The martial
law declared in Turkish Kurd and other south-eastern provinces
in 1978 continued as a 'Region of Extraordinary Situation' into
the second half of the 1990s. And extremist political groups like
the one that ordered the murder of Sabancı, leaders of the Kurdish
rebel insurgency and even the thousands of mafia gunmen of
1990s Turkey all had their roots in the political violence of the
1970s.

With its commercial bustle, hell-for-leather building and the all-
night dynamism of its big cities, Turkey in the 1990s has changed
so much that even Turks forget how hard life in Turkish cities
became as the 1970s wore on. Turkish leader Turgut Özal was to
conjure up images of straitened, violent times to great effect in
his 1980s election campaigns. But after his death in 1993, the issue
was allowed to fade. It would be generous to suppose that older
politicians feel too guilty to raise the subject. Most voters are now
simply too young to remember.

The reality was bleak indeed. As economic and international
difficulties undermined Turkish society's sense of purpose and
republican unity, divisions grew up between Sunni Muslim and
Alevi Muslim, Turks and Kurds, and, above all, between left
and right.

University campuses were the most obvious ideological battle-
ground. But government buildings, teachers' unions, police forces

and, towards the end, even army boot camps became radically divided. Supporters of each tendency would eat in different canteens or sit on opposite sides of offices. Neutrality was usually not an option in the face of armed toughs and ideologues calling for action.

These were strange times when lecture theatres in universities were built with an integrally designed police surveillance booth – police would even check that students were carving their names, and not political slogans, on the desks. A Marxist medical student remembered taking part in pitched battles with the right-wing 'idealists', and then, when he resumed his internship at the local hospital, treating those whom his side had just injured. Maoists undertook marriages arranged by their organizations. Murders of political rivals became commonplace. Kidnaps and killings of 'agents of imperialism', especially American soldiers, were head-line-snatching achievements eagerly sought by radicals. The mentality of the day could be summed up by the text of this note found at the head of a murdered ex-director of a state bank in April 1979:

The long-awaited day has come. Another enemy of the people has been eliminated. He is not the first, nor will he be the last. It has been decided to remove the physical infrastructure of the men of the monopolistic bourgeoisie ... Freedom or death, the road to revolution is that of the Cayanlar [followers of the chief ideologue of the left].

The army and the right wing were convinced that their old enemies the Russians, now in the guise of the Soviet Union, had a hand in stirring up left-wing unrest. This has neither been supported by studies in the aftermath of the Soviet collapse, nor does it seem a foregone conclusion, given Moscow's reluctance to extend credit for oil to the supposedly pro-Soviet Ecevit government. In fact, Communist agents may have been as confused as the Turkish authorities. While the more disciplined rightists restricted themselves to six or seven organizations, there were a multitude of groupings on the left agreed on little more than the principle of overthrowing the existing system to create a Marxist-Leninist state. In 1979, a left-wing newspaper serialized no less than forty-nine left-wing party manifestos, including those of a dozen Kurdish nationalist groups.[2] Often, they fought each other more fiercely than the opposition.

'There were five pro-Albanian factions alone, with about 25,000

armed militants. They used to fight among themselves for the
favour of the Albanians. When the Albanian representative came,
he couldn't believe it and quietly told one of the leaders, "there
are not so many pro-Albanians in Albania",' recalled a one-time
revolutionary. Ironically, by the 1990s he and many other former
leftists were to be found rising fast in the capitalist establishment
of Istanbul, becoming bankers, advisers to foreign institutions and
noted businessmen.

A few stalwarts rejected this path to middle-class respectability.
When the hated Romanian regime of Nicolae Ceauşescu fell in
1989, some Turks even took to the street to condemn the popular
uprising against Communism as 'reaction'. May Day shows of
strength in 1996 were still led by young radicals so entrenched in
their views that one newspaper called them leftist *tarikats*, after
the word for Islamic brotherhoods. Fidel Castro's visit met with
applauding crowds in June 1996. A bemused Daniel Cohn-Bendit,
a leader of the Paris uprising of 1968 that had so inspired the
Turkish left, visited Turkey as a Euro-MP in 1996 and felt bound to
inform his starry-eyed interlocutors that in his considered opinion,
'Marx was wrong'.[3]

That would have been a risky comment to make at the height
of the political conflicts of the 1970s, however. Then, students
and youths had to plan their paths carefully across cities to avoid
rival neighbourhoods. Leftist factions could command 60,000
armed militants and the rightists even more. The biggest leftist
newspaper hit a peak circulation of over 115,000 copies, its sales
only limited by a lack of access to newsprint.

To survive, many followed certain dress codes. The left-wingers
tended to wear longer hair, but not so long as to be considered
decadent. Green parkas with fur-trimmed hoods and corduroy
trousers were favoured. Factions could tell themselves apart by the
bushiness of their moustaches. Generally the more Stalinesque
the growth, the further to the left the faction. The right-wingers,
for their part, favoured shorter hair. Their moustaches were
trimmed to accord with the romantic image of the Central Asian
horseman, with a long flowing drop at the ends. They wore ties
and suits or blazers and some tucked their trousers into their
boots. The pro-Islamists, who in general tried to stay out of the
fighting, preferred a straighter moustache and might be distinguished by a slight bagginess around the seat of the trousers.

The left started in 1974 with many advantages. It was riding the
wave of anti-establishment events in Europe. It had a martyr, the
youthful hero Deniz Gezmiş, hanged in May 1972. Its intellectual

élite had been released in the general amnesty of May 1974. Exiles were returning from abroad. The revitalized Republican People's Party (CHP) had proved itself the biggest party in the elections of 1973. In January 1974, its new leader, the young Bülent Ecevit, took power in the first left-of-centre coalition government for a decade. The one-time translator of T.S. Eliot and Ezra Pound was pulling the CHP away from its élitist, rigid past and its affiliation to the state bureaucracy.

The leftist mainstream's hopes foundered on many rocks. From the start, Ecevit had to share power with the opportunistic, pro-Islamic Erbakan. By September, their coalition had collapsed over policy towards Cyprus. A quixotic second attempt to form a government by Ecevit's party after it had been returned ahead of the other parties in the 1977 election – but without a majority in parliament – survived only a month. The third coalition government lasted for most of 1978 and 1979 after Ecevit bought the loyalty of no less than twelve of Demirel's parliamentarians with ministerial seats. But his right-wing opponent never forgave him. 'You may have declared yourselves a government, but you will never be able to govern,' Demirel thundered. Refusing even to grace Ecevit with the dignity of his title as prime minister, he stumped up and down the country denouncing the 'head of this shameful administration'.

Demirel was not the only force ranged against the left. Some in the army were also concerned about Ecevit, who famously suggested that the greatest strategic threat to Turkey was not the Soviet Union, but its supposed NATO ally Greece. Ecevit was also full of glowing praise for the Yugoslav experiment in federal non-alignment after a visit to Belgrade. More serious was opposition in the security forces. Of 40,000 men in the police force, 19,000 were unionized: 17,000 in the rightist police union and only 2,000 in the leftist one.[4]

The leftists themselves had no doubt who was helping the right-wing *ülkücü* (idealist) street fighters. In many a clash, the 'idealists' would melt away to be replaced by police, or vice versa. This was not an inviolable rule; some police took the leftists' side. But with a hint of distaste, the later President Kenan Evren admitted that the security forces protected the rightists, believing that they were performing a patriotic duty. The vehicle used was the National Action Party, the Milliyetçi Hareket Partisi or MHP, of Alparslan Türkeş, who, unlike any of the leftist factions, also managed to spend a total of nearly two years and eight months in the 1970s as deputy prime minister in the governments of Süleyman Demirel.

A raid on Türkeş's Ankara headquarters in June 1979 turned up guns and documents that clearly implicated the rightist party in the violence. Evren, who elsewhere in his diaries called the MHP a 'wicked organization', noted that 'maybe they spilled less blood than the left, but they still shed it. The painful side of it was that the idealist organizations were directed from the MHP headquarters, as was discovered after the 12 September [1980] coup.'

The point of no return in the violence was reached on May Day, 1977. Thanks to the Ecevit government, it was the first workers' day to be celebrated as such in fifty years and tens of thousands turned out in Taksim Square, the main square of modern Istanbul. The events that followed remain the subject of debate two decades later; such demonstrations are still plagued by the triple curse of leftist in-fighting, provocation from all sides and murderous gun-fire, often from plainclothes men in the security forces. Trouble started when a Maoist group tried to force its way into the square to denounce its 'socialist-fascist character'. Shots rang out; nobody is sure from where, but accounts agree that right-wing or police sharpshooters on rooftops all around were responsible for some of the thirty-seven deaths. The ensuing stampede did the rest.

For the remainder of the decade the country lurched from clash to clash, gradually dividing not only left from right, but Turk from Kurd, Sunni Muslim from Alevi Muslim. The Alevis, with their heterodox Turkish form of Shiism, had been at odds with the Sunni Muslim Ottoman government since the fifteenth century; for this reason, they have also been the most ardent believers in the secular form of government idealized by Atatürk's republic. The political result has been that Alevis have tended to support Atatürk's party, the secular CHP. The Sunni Muslims have meanwhile gravitated towards right-wing and Islamist politics.

The first significant Sunni-Alevi clash came in September 1978 in Sivas, a town to the north of the central Anatolian plateau. Twelve people died and a thousand buildings were damaged before the army could restore order. Sivas still marks the northern edge of an area where these two main elements in the Turkish population are most evenly mixed and where inter-communal friction is at its most volatile. On the south-eastern edge of this area lies Kahramanmaraş, a proud hill town that was the first to evict French occupation troops after the First World War. All Turkey was shaken by the events that took place here in December 1978.

The precise details of what happened are still in dispute, but a contributory cause was doubtless the nature of Turkish politics in the 1970s, in which members of each government fought for ministries and patronage that could award jobs to their supporters. Under the right-wing 'National Front' government of Demirel, Erbakan and Türkeş between 1975 and 1977, Kahramanmaraş had been run mainly by the Sunni Muslim right; the situation switched in favour of the Alevis with the advent of the leftist-Islamic coalition headed by Ecevit in 1978. Feelings began to run high in the town. At issue was not just ideology, but work on roads, water-works, forestry and even postings in the police. All was ripe for an outbreak of sectarian violence triggered by an initial killing of leftist Alevis blamed on the Grey Wolves; for two days and nights, the town was plunged into an orgy of violence and terror. At least 107 people died and more than 1,000 were wounded. Babies were ripped from the bellies of pregnant mothers and dead men strung up from electricity poles: post-Second World War Turkey had never seen the like.

Motorized military units set out over the hills from Gaziantep to put down the violence in which 500 shops were burned, mostly those belonging to Alevis. Evren, then chief of the armed forces, tended to blame the right-wing MHP, as he did later when similar riots killed more than thirty people in the north Anatolian town of Çorum in May 1980. 'On the surface, it looks as if reactionary and anti-state forces acted against the state,' he noted in his diary in 1978. 'But if one looks at the details, this was an explosion of feelings that had long been brewing against a biased government.'

In thirteen provinces martial law was immediately declared, another step towards the military rule that Turkey seems unable to avoid in times of crisis. General Evren, seeking to justify the coup he was to lead, and to show how long the military delayed their action in order to give the civilians the chance to put things right, has published minutes of several of the Martial Law Co-ordination Meetings between the military and the government. They are highly revealing.

The minutes show, for instance, that although the fight for Kurdish national identity was later to be dominated by the Kurdistan Workers' Party, the Partiya Karkaren-e Kurdistan or PKK, Kurdish areas of south-eastern Turkey were already in ferment by the late 1970s. The precursors of the PKK were only the eighth of the groups listed as active. In April 1979, a report from the gendarmerie, which keeps order in Turkey's rural areas, talks of a 'growing fever on the southern borders ... leading to chaos. Only a brave officer will go into a village with less than twenty people to catch an outlaw. Our colleagues feel like a colonial army.' State authority had been undermined to the point where witnesses to political murder in the south-east had to be arrested and forced to testify; state prosecutors felt so intimidated that one case was refused by three of them. Even a resident secret policeman in the border town of Cizre reported to the country's leaders in Ankara that all the signs pointed to a classic revolution around the corner as 'the rug is being pulled from under my feet'.

The situation was little better elsewhere. Martial law commanders hesitated to use the police, seeing them as biased, but the gendarmerie conscripts were under-trained. The numbers of men were limited in both cases, and often lacked cars, fuel or mobile radios. Only seventeen of the sixty-seven provincial security directorates possessed so much as a camera. In Istanbul, there was one coastguard boat to stop the smuggled weapons flooding into Turkey, one laboratory to study ballistic evidence, in which laboratory there was just one microscope. Bullets kept as evidence were sometimes dumped, undated and unnumbered, into sacks.

Morale was sapped by the fact that carrying illegal arms and bombs was a crime under martial law only if a link to an illegal organization could be positively proved. One man caught with 1.7 million rounds of ammunition, for instance, had to be released to the slow and unintimidating mercies of the civilian courts. Even then, only one-third of more than 9,000 suspected militants arrested in 1979 were convicted, and only 103 of them were sentenced to spend more than a year in gaol.

Even when it was possible to put militants behind bars, the prison system was in chaos. A tour of inspection showed that all were burdened with double their capacity of prisoners, with more pouring in all the time. Some prisons could not pay their phone bills because of the number of intercity calls made by prisoners. In those gaols that had bars on their windows inmates were bending them open, using heat from the stoves on which they were permitted to cook and make tea. Demirel told one meeting that they had turned into 'schools for anarchy'. Prisoners lived a quasi-autonomous existence in dormitories under the direct rule of banned organizations, easily able to bribe guards or to intimidate the guards' families in order to obtain supplies of almost any goods they wanted.

The system became more organized over the years, but not necessarily in the interest of the state. In the mid-1990s, a prison director was arrested for smuggling in guns to inmates. A blood-chilling videotape was smuggled out of another gaol showing the forced confession of a member of one of the far-left organizations descended from those of the 1970s. Accusing herself of self-love by breaking and talking under police torture, she 'accepted' her guilt and her sentence. Her body was found outside the cell door the next morning, strangled by her cell-mates. By 1996, the interior minister candidly admitted that control of the gaols was in the hands of illegal organizations, not the state.[5]

In April 1980, the country's leaders focused on the gaol in Adana. The minister of justice summed up by saying that the government was responsible for everything, but could control nothing. There 1,710 inmates were squeezed into a facility built to take no more than 700 prisoners. They slept in doorways and corridors right up to the entrance. Lynchings and beatings were common. To supervise this nightmare were just forty guards and a barbed-wire fence; escapes averaged 150 per month. Small wonder that right-wing hitman Mehmet Ali Ağca was able to slip out of his Ankara gaol in 1979, having murdered Turkey's best-known newspaper editor Abdi Ipekçi, and make his way to Rome to attempt the assassination of Pope John Paul in 1981.

'We have the choice of watching them go or mowing them down with machine-guns,' the Adana martial law commander, seething with frustration, told his leaders in the capital. 'You just give the order.'

Unable to give any such order to open fire, or even to have much impact on a politician like Demirel, who openly told friends that he did not believe the military would intervene against him, the army command became increasingly restless. Aware as always of their self-appointed role as guardians of a republic that seemed to be on the road to self-destruction, the generals prepared to make their move.

In December 1978, on the same day that they decided to declare martial law following the Kahramanmaraş massacre, senior army commanders started a series of secret discussions with a meeting in the Selimiye barracks, the First Army Headquarters built for Sultan Selim III's New Order troops nearly two centuries before and which still overlooks the Bosphorus strait. It was the beginning of a process that was to lead twenty-one months later to the coup of 12 September 1980.

The generals disguised the purpose of their meeting by bringing their wives with them, and indeed, until the end, the country's feuding politicians refused to see the seriousness of the army's intentions. 'When I met politicians at cocktail parties I tried to say what we thought as clearly as possible, even warned them not to force us to carry out a coup. But they didn't take us seriously,' Evren said.

Demirel tried to argue that only fifty of Turkey's 575 *kazas*, or districts, were affected by violence. The army was unimpressed; everybody had been touched by events, even their chief of staff, General Evren, who in the early 1970s had been shocked to discover that leftist hero Deniz Gezmiş had been given sanctuary by the tenants of his Ankara flat. Later he had personally to negotiate his daughter's escape from a besieged university hostel.

Not only did the situation inside Turkey appear to be spinning out of control, but threatening events were also occurring elsewhere in the region. Within a year, the Soviet army had invaded Afghanistan, another of the Soviet Union's neighbours. And in the east, Ayatollah Khomeini, flushed with success in Iran and dreams of a pan-Islamic revolution, had announced that the government of Turkey, as well as those of Egypt and Iraq, did not 'represent the will of its people'.

When the commanders met again in the Selimiye Barracks in December 1979, however, they were not yet ready or willing to intervene directly. Instead they decided to despatch a letter to the government, warning that it had an 'inescapable obligation to work together with an Atatürkist national vision' to stop terrorism and separatism. It also criticized the sterile approach of the opposition. Unlike the memorandum of March 1971, the text contained no suggestion that the military would take power if their warning was not heeded. Although the commanders spoke to the politicians of rising pressure in the officer corps demanding such action, Demirel, for one, brushed aside the threat as one not addressed to his new minority government, his third administration since the restoration of democracy after the 1971–3 military intervention. It had swapped places with the third Ecevit government thirty-five days before, and Demirel was in no mood to give up.

'I thought of relieving the generals of their posts. But they gave no sign that they were thinking of an intervention. The president [Fahri Korutürk] did not want to get involved – I couldn't ask for his support [against the army]. I couldn't trust Ecevit at all; he could have tried to bring me into conflict with the army. The MHP was the same. And in the end, the letter came through the chain of command. That's why I had no choice but to try to gain time, and show a willingness to help where they had shown

themselves to be sensitive,' he told Turkish commentator Mehmet
Ali Birand.[6]

Playing for time, the leitmotif of Demirel's political career, was
not about to set the country straight. Ecevit also decided that the
letter was not addressed to him. Newspaper caricaturists portrayed
the letter as a joke, a ball being tossed from person to person.
Not that Ecevit had any miracle solution. As Birand was to note:
'Ecevit's charisma no longer sufficed to hold things together;
as the conductor he was reduced to the undignified position of
waving a baton while the orchestra fought over the tune it was
supposed to be playing.'

Arguments over exactly who the military was threatening were
as nothing, however, to the abdication of responsibility displayed
by the two leaders when President Korutürk's seven-year term
ended in April 1980. Demirel and Ecevit refused absolutely to
compromise over his successor. Like a broken record-player,
parliament sat through nearly a hundred rounds of voting as the
months went by and they failed to reach a decision.

Despite warnings in coded public speeches or private meetings
with individual ministers, however, the military coup that occurred
in September took a long time to mature. On one hand, the
generals disagreed on how far any intervention should go, remembering from bitter experience how hard it was to stage the subsequent return to barracks. On the other, the high command had
to spend much time watching its back, fearing that frustrated
junior officers might jump the gun. But all the time the certainty
was growing that there would have to be some sort of intervention.

'I was determined not to intervene unless forced to, because I
had seen the damage done to the armed forces from the 1960
and 1971 interventions. I wanted to wait until the knife hit the
bone. Otherwise the people might not believe in it or accept it,'
General Evren wrote in his diary in April 1980.

Evren ordered his staff to make preparations for the intervention, right down to the address he would have to give on the
radio. By May, the commanders were firmly decided to act. The
coup was set for July – just after another meeting in Europe on
Turkey's foreign debt – but had to be delayed as Demirel won a
new lease of political life and the military headed towards its sensitive annual round of promotions in August.

By July, the death toll from political violence had risen to more
than ten people a day. The Black Sea hazelnut-growing town of
Fatsa had turned into something of a self-declared left-wing republic, while the rightists had established more or less free zones in

the north Anatolian towns of Çorum and Yozgat. Already sickened by the spectacle of left–right squabbling in parliament, the commanders' resolve hardened as they watched the behaviour of Necmettin Erbakan and his pro-Islamic National Salvation Party. Erbakan refused to attend the army's Victory Day celebrations on 30 August, telling Evren cheekily that 'we are neither for Victory Day nor against it. We are part of it.' Then on 6 September, a big march in Konya led by Erbakan echoed to the chant of slogans calling for the imposition of Islamic *sharia* law, complete anathema to the army.

Evren had hung on till the last minute, keenly aware that previous army interventions had seemed to favour the left. It would not look good for the army to act against Demirel directly, despite Evren's personal distaste for Demirel's long speeches, his unprincipled changes of policy and especially his businessman brother Şevket Demirel. Evren had more time for Ecevit, but thought him over-optimistic and unable to see that under martial law certain democratic principles would inevitably be laid aside. After watching Ecevit distraught over a horse that fell during a military parade, he also came to the conclusion that he was over-excitable.

'Emotion is to be praised,' Evren wrote. 'But statesmen must leave all soft behaviour to one side and take every precaution to make the state's presence felt when there is a situation that imperils it.'

When the tanks finally rolled out of garrison compounds before dawn on 12 September 1980, softness was one mistake Evren and the generals were in no danger of making.

10

The Generals Take Charge

> You can take power with a bayonet. But you
> can't sit on it.
>
> Süleyman Demirel

ONE EUROPEAN NEWSPAPER called it the 'Coup in Velvet
Boots'. Certainly, nobody was killed in the operation that became
official at 4 a.m. on 12 September 1980. The army's fear that it
would have to fight leftists in the streets proved unfounded;
exhausted by their war, militants on both sides seemed to give up,
almost with relief, as if a referee had blown a whistle. The number
of political killings dropped dramatically. Execution of 'Operation
Flag', planned to the last detail over the preceding year, was
smooth. The army took power with practised ease.

Chief of Staff General Kenan Evren had wanted maximum surprise, ordering the plotters to use the windowless war operations
room in the bunker of his heavy grey stone headquarters in central
Ankara and to black out upper windows against the eyes of prying
reporters. But word spread soon enough through the political
élite as soldiers converged on the capital and armoured vehicles
clanked into place on street corners. Right-wing National Action
Party leader Alparslan Türkeş, who knew a thing or two about
running a coup, went straight into hiding. Prime Minister Süleyman Demirel's aide Nahit Menteşe packed a small suitcase before
going to bed. Eventually, hearing the rumours, opposition leader
Bülent Ecevit dialled the General Staff.

'There's a tank outside my house. Is there a coup going on?'
he asked.

The military at last abandoned the excuse it had circulated for
current troop movements, that of an ongoing NATO exercise.
Ecevit was told the truth; to his friends, he voiced relief that the

coup appeared to be 'within the army hierarchy'. Then his phone line went dead. Up at the prime minister's residence, Demirel's phone line also cut out. His twelve-man bodyguard surrendered their weapons without protest to a military unit. Necmettin Erbakan was also arrested. With the flick of a single switch, all Turkey's international communications were cut.

The generals met none of the resistance they had anticipated as they took over ministry buildings and key installations. Indeed some politicians, called in to act with them, congratulated them on the thoroughness of their plans. Only one general declined to co-operate, but was soon talked round when he realized that the chief of staff was in charge. At Ankara's General Directorate of Security, police chiefs welcomed the army officers with open arms and tearful cries of 'Blessed be the nation!' Evren made sure the military cadets were kept well out of events, in case, as in 1960, they should get ideas above their station. The coup commander commented without a trace of irony that 'those young children saw themselves as the lions saving the country'.

The plan met with an initial frustrating delay as the old-fashioned transmitter of Ankara radio had to be turned on and warmed up. But soon enough the Turkish army march was playing out again over the airwaves, 'Forward, O Turk, Ever Forward'. The text of Communiqué No. 1 from a newly formed all-military National Security Council set the tone for the next three years of military rule. The military had seized power, it said, based on a law that made it their duty to protect the republic. It announced the fall of the government and the dissolution of parliament. Then it declared a curfew, a ban on foreign travel and martial law throughout the country. At dawn, jeeps fanned out across major cities to fetch key bureaucrats and technicians.

Turgut Özal, the head of the State Planning Office who was soon to launch a 1980s revolution of his own, had gone back to bed after hearing about the coup. 'I thought, oh well, what can I do? What's done is done,' he told his biographer. Then a knock came at his door and he was escorted to his office, where he found a naval officer awaiting him. 'Get to work,' the commodore ordered.

The military's aim, the communiqué said, was to 'restore the authority of the state and remove the obstacles in the way of the democratic order'. Justifying its action it declared:

The state has become unworkable and constitutional organs have fallen into dissension and silence. The sterile and uncompromising positions of political parties mean they have not been able to create the necessary unity. Destructive and separatist forces ... have put the life and property of citizens in danger ... promoting reactionary and other perverted ideologies ... that have brought us to the brink of division and civil war.

According to commentator Mehmet Ali Birand, no natural friend of the army or military coups, 'almost everyone who was listening to the radio took a deep breath and said to themselves: "At last it has happened." ' Newspaper caricaturists had already been drawing pictures depicting the Turkish nation being saved as Demirel, Ecevit and Türkes drowned together in a boat at sea. The mainstream Turkish press and commentators also welcomed the coup. 'What else did our politicians expect?' asked *Hürriyet*'s main columnist, Oktay Ekşi. 'It's as inevitable as rain falling,' wrote left-wing *Cumhuriyet* columnist Uğur Mumcu. 'This is bankruptcy, the bankruptcy of the people who think they have been governing us for thirty years, and of their political thought.' Turkey's leading industrialist Vehbi Koç wrote to Evren to pledge his support, adding a word of advice suggesting that Evren should always take an afternoon nap. It was back to business as usual.

The reaction from abroad was mixed. Washington, thoroughly relieved, sent a statement of support and made sure the taps of international finance remained open. Shortly afterwards, the cover of *Time* magazine showed a paternalistic portrait of General Evren clasping a collage of the Istanbul skyline in his arms with the caption 'Holding Turkey Together'. Europe showed a more wary response, laying stress on the military's stated intention to hand back the country to civilian rule. It quickly began to voice concern about human rights, however, a concern that, thanks to the brutal repression of all dissidents during the coup and later under coup-era laws, was to grow in the following years into an inflexible doctrine in its relations with Turkey.

The three arrested party leaders and their wives – Türkeş only gave himself up two days later, after Evren had threatened him with dire penalties over the radio – were taken with their suitcases and shown off before the cameras at a military airport outside Ankara. Ecevit, always the gentleman, shook everyone's hand. They sat silently in different corners of the room. Erbakan and Türkeş were sent to one military holiday resort near Izmir, while Demirel and Ecevit, still barely on speaking terms, were taken to another near Gallipoli. Ecevit later recalled strained tea-parties with the camp commander as they were summoned to listen to military statements on television. But being at the mercy of the army did not mean they were defeated, even less reformed.

'We were not allowed to talk alone. The commander of the compound was always present,' Ecevit said. 'But we both adopted the same attitude towards our imprisonment. The commander gave us a message from Ankara that we would be released if we promised not to speak out, not to write, and not to engage in any political activities. Both of us rejected it.'

The junta believed it could mould Turkish politics and society in its own image. But this recalcitrance of Turkey's former political leaders was just a first hint that not everybody was prepared to march forward to the military's beat.

From his diaries it is clear that General Evren realized at once how hard the junta's mission was going to be. But he was not a man to be easily turned from his purpose. His critics have cast him as an ogre. Taking their cue from the barking tone of his lengthy speeches up and down the country, they hold him person- ally responsible for the torture of hundreds of thousands of sus- pects. From another perspective many of the successes, as well as the failures, of Turkey in the 1980s and 1990s are a memorial to the often underrated character of this typical Turkish army officer.

Kenan Evren was 63 years old when he issued the order for the coup to proceed. Like many members of the Kemalist republican élite, he was the child of refugees from the Balkans: his father, an inspector with the Ottoman Debt Administration, came from Macedonia, as did Atatürk. His mother's family was from Bulgaria. Like 90 per cent of the army, he was a village boy. After a tough childhood in the Aegean provinces ravaged by war with Greece, he won much-coveted places at military academies and officer- training colleges. Such schools were for an élite, but Evren remem- bers bed bugs, rats as big as cats, living in tents for months and eating dusty food full of bees, flies and beetles. He was taught to rub urine into sores on his legs as he trained for the horse-drawn artillery. Martinets ran an Ankara academy where negligence led to thirty-five dying from pneumonia; Evren nearly died as well, but was saved by his characteristic good fortune.

Evren maintains that he was committed thereafter to improving military schools and to side-lining disciplinarians. These views, however, did not make him a liberal. He thought the enforcement of capital punishment was the main reason that political violence subsided after the coup. He also told his fellow coup leaders that if any one of them were assassinated, all members of any political group behind the assassination 'inside and outside gaol' should be rounded up and immediately shot.

Nevertheless, according to his Kemalist lights he tried to be scrupulously fair – 'we are neither to the left of Atatürk, nor to his right,' he would say – and the first execution order he signed took the lives of two leftists and two rightists convicted of terrorist crimes. But he could not resist setting a Kemalist example as well, also signing execution orders for those who killed relatives in blood feuds or to 'cleanse the family honour'. A total of twenty-five executions were carried out during the coup and post-coup period, with the last being carried out in 1984, since when the death penalty has not been enforced. 'We knew from their conversations in gaols after 12 September that execution was what scared them most,' Evren wrote. 'My conscience would not allow me to accept that, simply to look good to the Council of Europe, we should refrain from executing those who killed innocent people like chickens and turned the country into a lake of blood.'

One of the discoveries that surprised him most while serving in the Korean war in the 1950s, he said, presumably echoing a general sentiment in the Turkish officer corps, was the high value that American officers placed on human life. Perhaps it was such experiences that persuaded him to introduce compensation for those killed or injured on active service. In 1980, he was at last able to reform a system under which relatives of privates killed while serving in Turkey had themselves to pay to bring their sons' bodies home. From now on, the army would shoulder the cost.

The general, who had two daughters, tried to do his bit for women's rights too. He legalized abortion. As he criss-crossed the country he argued publicly against the need for women to wear the heavy black veil. Ever tending towards the dictatorial, he harangued a set of Afghan refugees to whom he had given asylum: 'If you don't educate your women, I'll send you back to Pakistan.' Evren also seems to have been scrupulously honest, publicly counting his pennies, stopping at traffic-lights and going to great lengths in the early days of the take-over to maintain an image of legitimacy for his assumption of power. 'You've carried out a coup. You've made your own law,' one of his advisers tried to reassure him. The problem of legality was solved quickly enough. General Evren's National Security Council re-adopted the 1961 constitution, but added an article declaring that none of the Council's actions could be judged unconstitutional.

Evren's public concerns ranged wider than his predecessors'. It was he who at last permitted Turkish cultural exhibitions to travel outside the country. 'We hadn't done this for fear that if we sent our treasures abroad, they [the foreigners] would steal them. The idea was that if people wanted to get to know us, then let them come here,' he wrote. This move cleared the path for splendid later successes like the Süleyman the Magnificent exhibition. All the exhibits made it safely back home.

Even so, the general's own horizons and imagination were limited. Like many Turkish officers, the army was everything to him, from cradle to grave, from holiday camp to war. Volunteering for service in Korea in the 1950s was a career move, but also a step towards purchasing those great luxuries of the day, a refrigerator and a washing machine. He maintained the integrity of his normal life after his rise. It is not often realized that throughout the first years of the military intervention, the coup leader was sleeping in the corridor of his military villa in order not to disturb his diabetic wife Sekine after she had suffered a stroke. The daytime general often had to carry his wife to the bathroom several times a night; she died, to his great distress, in 1982.

Evren's chief political passion seems to have been reserved for what he calls the *yobazlar,* or religious bigots, an impression reinforced by a religious education that enabled him to quote the Koran freely in his speeches. 'What do those bigots understand of the nation?' he writes in his diary.

> They think that being a Muslim simply comes from putting on a fez or a turban, believing in those who cure by breathing on the sick, taking part in ceremonies in *tekkes* [dervish lodges], veiling their women and leaving them ignorant. These bigots have allowed the country to be occupied by enemies, have exploited its assets, left it ignorant, distanced us from the civilized nations, left us behind in science and technology.

Ironically, however, Evren himself is strangely obsessed with the role of the number seven in his life. His wife believed deeply in saints and portents, and superstition prevented her from cutting her toenails and fingernails on the same day. The general even reprinted in his memoirs a facsimile of a child-like drawing by his wife that she had hidden in a shoe box. It showed, he believed, that she predicted that he would one day rise to the highest post in the land.

Climbing smoothly up the military hierarchy was probably more important for his career, however, and Evren made all the right moves. As well as fighting in Korea, he had a notable success as chief of staff of the armed forces during the invasion of Cyprus. Nevertheless it was a fluke that landed him the job of chief of the general staff in 1977. Prime Minister Demirel had decided to upset the army's usual system of promotion and to refuse its recommended candidate for the post; the army's strict and complicated system of retirement came into play and suddenly Evren found himself in the job.

His methodical ways paid off, both before and during the coup. He held back until the last minute, in order to gain maximum public support. He ensured that wherever he went, he kept his fellow generals in the National Security Council close by. Learning from the chaotic example of the 1960 coup, he insisted that he alone be allowed to speak for them. When his fellow generals disagreed with him, he would go along with them and hold them together, even against his better judgement. And in the end it was Evren who managed to convert his leadership of the coup into a seven-year presidency.

The Turks have now largely forgotten the enormous popularity Evren enjoyed for setting the country straight in the early 1980s, and leftist intellectuals have never forgiven him. Since his retirement in 1989, he has lived in a heavily guarded compound of villas for former generals by the Mediterranean Sea. He has spent his old age painting, mostly landscapes, but also some fairly daring nudes. They command extraordinary prices from those in the Turkish élite who still wish to flatter and also, perhaps, to express their gratitude.

The showy civilian Turgut Özal was to take most of the international credit for building the so-called Turkish economic miracle of the 1980s. But the fact remains that the ground was cleared and guarded by Evren, the 'peasant pasha', plodding president and anti-terrorism crusader who could boast in his diary that he had kept the same formica dining table for twenty years and blandly note that watching a parade of masked terrorists in Libya was quite *enteresan*.

When Evren and his fellow generals said they did not want to repeat the mistakes of the interventions in 1960 and 1971, they did not just mean to ensure that the army chain of command stayed in line. During the long year of preparation for the coup Evren's aides had drawn up an almost architectural plan for a future Turkey as the military envisaged it. The 1961 constitution had been too liberal for Turkey, they felt; a new constitution was necessary. And that was only the start.

Originally Evren had a list of 103 aims for the coup. Of the sixty-six recorded in his diaries, a good many read like permanent desiderata for fixing the weaknesses of the Turkish system – including mundane matters like putting an end to long-winded political statements on the television news. Other aims reflect military priorities derived from the period of disorder prior to the coup – from the immediate carrying out of death sentences to compulsory attendance at lectures by students.

Evren failed in some of these goals. His greatest regret was not to have been able to create a directly elected presidency with an authority comparable to that given by the American system. He felt also that he had failed to persuade people of the therapeutic value of executions. But to a remarkable extent Evren achieved what he set out to do. He then returned the country to parliamentary rule within the time-scale that he had promised. And his new constitution, overwhelmingly approved in a 1982 referendum, laid down a severe set of parameters for the coming era.

'The 1961 constitution was too loose a garment, we slipped around in it until we came to the 12 September coup. We have to sacrifice some personal rights for the security of the community . . . we can't buy everything ready-to-wear from the West,' Evren wrote.

The perceived need to control, to avoid the disorder of the 1970s, shines through almost every article of the 1982 constitution. It orders the working of the state in every detail, setting out exactly how parliament will operate, how presidents will be elected, how soon governments have to be formed. Higher education, in particular, is firmly subordinated to officialdom. The aim of such detail was to avoid the political impasses of the past. But the constitution is also a remarkable exercise in giving with one hand and taking away with the other. 'Everyone has the right to life', for instance, but not in a series of 'self-defence' situations in which the state security forces might be at risk. This loophole was later to become a morbid mantra as police reported that yet another group of 'terrorists' lying dead in an apartment in their pyjamas had 'returned fire when called upon to surrender'.

The list of partial freedoms is long. 'No one shall be required to perform forced labour', except when ordered to do so by the government. 'Everyone has the right to freedom of residence and movement', but the government may decide to the contrary for reasons including social, economic and urban development. 'Everyone has the right to form associations without prior permission', except in a wide variety of cases. 'Everyone has the right to freedom of thought and opinion', but not, of course, if this conflicts with the preamble's vague 'determination that no protection shall be afforded to thoughts or opinions contrary to Turkish national interests'.

Those national interests, above all, are the protection of the indivisibility of the state. More than fourteen references are made specifically to this overriding goal, this 'integrity', the result of the ever-present Turkish fear of separatism or claims on its territory by Armenians, Greeks and particularly Kurds. And ethnicity and nationality are deemed to be the same thing: the great and tragic mental block of the modern Turkish state.

'Everyone bound to the Turkish state through the bond of citizenship is a Turk,' says Article 66. 'The state's language is Turkish,' says Article 3, buttressed by another article saying that Article 3 can never be changed. 'No language prohibited by law shall be used in the expression and dissemination of thought,' it goes on. The law in question prohibits the use of any language not the principal language of a state recognized by Turkey – effectively excluding Kurdish, or any of a number of minor dialects in the country.

Some articles turned out to be more often honoured in the breach. Article 24 orders that 'No one shall be allowed to exploit religion in any manner whatsoever for the purpose of personal or political influence', but political leaders are rarely prosecuted for their often flagrant abuses of religious sentiment. A noble statement of the 'security of the person' is a bitter joke in Turkey's south-east, where hundreds of Kurdish nationalists have been killed in 'mystery murders' usually blamed on the security forces. Other stated ideals are also ignored. Minors still work, developers continue to plunder coastlines and historic sites and a supposed state monopoly of television and radio has been allowed to crumble away. But the theoretical responsibilities of the government include one quirky aim: amongst all sections of society, one is singled out for the special honour of unqualified support: 'the state shall protect successful athletes.'

The constitution was largely the product of months of work by a constitutional assembly, its 160 members individually chosen by the military and provincial governors. Its chief architect was Orhan Aldıkaçti, who, as they wound up proceedings, proclaimed: 'We have built an armoured wall against those who want to split our country.' The military then had a last look. Evren maintains that he softened some elements of it, particularly reducing the number of senior state officials to be appointed directly by the president. But the military safeguarded their own interests, special status and internal laws. The coup-era generals were to stay on for another six years as a presidential council; these generals also persuaded Evren to drop the idea of an upper house in parliament because things might get 'too crowded'. Lastly, they all took out a guarantee of their own safety, inserting a special provision in the constitution that no allegation of unconstitutionality, or of criminal, financial or legal liability could be made against those who carried out the coup or implemented the junta's orders.

A key institution bequeathed to the nation by the 1982 constitution was the National Security Council, empowered to 'submit its views' on national security to the cabinet of the day. Most of Turkey's strategic decisions have been taken at these monthly meetings, held in a large, austere room under the chairmanship of the president of the republic. Its membership ensures that the government virtually never resists giving the required 'priority consideration' to NSC recommendations. Ex-officio members are the five most important ministers in the government, sitting on one side, and the five senior generals of the armed forces, sitting on the other. This provision guaranteed a leading role for the army long beyond the formal hand-over to democracy in December 1983.

After such efforts, Evren was to take no chances. During the last fifteen days leading up to the referendum on the constitution on 7 November 1982, he refused to allow anybody to speak out against it or to criticize his speeches promoting it. He also linked the vote to his personal prestige, since the same vote was to sanction his presidency for the next seven years. Heavy penalties ensured a turn-out of more than nine voters in ten. Evren was delighted with the result: 91.3 per cent of the vote favoured the constitution.

Such discipline had one valuable side-effect during the period of military control. One of Evren's most significant contributions was to bring order to the state's finances. Having been running at over 50 per cent in the late 1970s, inflation reached a high of over 100 per cent in 1980, then fell sharply. For most of the coup years consumer inflation was about 35 per cent. The balance of trade improved markedly as exports started to rise. The troubled external debt was sorted out by a major rescheduling agreement in 1982, a one-inch thick document that is in many ways a blueprint of Turkish economic policy in the 1980s.

As Evren tried to build up an image of a stable, well-managed Turkey, signs of a new trust emerged in international markets. In this he was greatly helped by Turgut Özal, whom he appointed deputy prime minister in charge of the economy at the start of the coup. Özal turned out to be a popular and seductive negotiator with Western bankers, fronting for the generals in economic matters from the coup until July 1982.

Özal was to claim that it was he who, well before the coup, had weaned the generals away from their attachment to the early republican economic model of state direction and self-sufficiency during the extensive briefings which had accompanied the stabilization measures of 24 January 1980. But somehow the later Özal never managed to implement the new, painful monetarist doctrines that he preached, while under Evren, strict fiscal housekeeping kept the country to its financial targets. It was also typical of Özal's free-wheeling style that he was forced to resign in July 1982 when a mismanaged liberalization of deposit-taking led to an interest rate war and a collapse of fringe bankers.

The military regime nevertheless enjoyed considerable success in pushing through the goals of the January 1980 stabilization programme. As inflation fell from 100 per cent a year to 35 per cent, state enterprises were allowed to raise their prices and denied automatic access to Central Bank funds: as a result, their deficits shrank from 8–9 per cent of GNP to under 2 per cent. Exports rose quickly and the economy started to bounce back. 'Our measures have begun to bear fruit,' Evren noted with satisfaction.

Strong backing from Washington was another key element in the junta's success, with the United States anxious to prove to weak-willed Latin American governments that its austerity-led IMF packages could fix inflation-ridden economies. During those years Turkey was receiving nearly one billion dollars a year of American assistance, third in the world after Israel and Egypt. Within months of the coup, new American and British credits were approved. Before a year had passed, the influential banking magazine *Euromoney* selected the then deputy prime minister Turgut Özal as 'Man of the Year' and Turkey as 'Country of the Year'.

Other important projects that would strongly influence Turkey's development were also put in place during the coup years. The extension of a Soviet natural gas pipeline from Bulgaria was agreed; the deal pioneered a vibrant trading relationship with Moscow, particularly for Turkish building contractors, and also helped fight air pollution first in Ankara and then Istanbul. The purchase of 160 F-16 front-line warplanes from the United States was also agreed, with their assembly to take place in Turkey. Tourism was encouraged with new airport terminals and yacht marinas. The grand network of dams, hydro-electric power stations and irrigation works of the South-East Anatolian Project, the Güneydoğu Anadolu Projesi or GAP, is too huge to have any one author, but the junta has as good a claim to it as any. Another milestone was passed in December 1981, when the ascetic Evren at last gave in to his prime minister's request for 10,000 dollars to import beans to make Turkish coffee, at least for the tourists: a psychological boost for a country that had given its name to a thick, sweet way of preparing coffee but whose leaders had declared it a luxury the nation could not afford. For some, Turkey seemed to be putting the misery of the 1970s behind it at last.

The coup era also marked the beginning of a preoccupation in the West, sometimes to the exclusion of all else, with Turkey's human rights record. On 1 July 1982, five countries (France, Sweden, Norway, Denmark and the Netherlands) took the unprecedented step of referring the country to the Human Rights Commission. In January 1982, the European Parliament, with just 99 of its 434 members voting, had already stopped all financial aid until the return of democracy. More than a decade and four general elections later, most aid restrictions remained in place.

It was at this time that the unrelenting sadism of Alan Parker's 1979 film *Midnight Express* about a drug-runner's experience in a Turkish gaol came to symbolize the West's worst fears and prejudices about the Turks. Along with the bleak vision of Yılmaz Güney's films like *Yol* – which won the Palme d'Or at Cannes in 1982 – Turks began to have a hard time explaining to the world that not all in their country was bad. Alan Parker now admits he got parts of *Midnight Express* wrong.[1] Güney's first-hand experience of the Turkish underworld included being gaoled for his murder of a judge. But critics had a point to make. It is clear that whatever velvet had been on the army's boots had come off fairly quickly. The regime was determined to stamp out what it saw as a form of urban terrorism that threatened to destroy the republic.

In the four years after the coup, 178,565 people were detained, 64,505 formally charged, 41,727 convicted and 326 death sentences passed. Of those sentenced, 25 were executed.[2] Newspaper reports indicated that about three-quarters of those arrested were leftists, one-sixth rightists and the rest 'separatists', that is, Kurds. Some 15,000 activists or intellectuals who fled the country were also stripped of their nationality. The security forces justified their severity with additional figures. They confiscated 638,000 hand guns, 48,000 rifles, 7,000 machine-guns, 4,000 automatic pistols and 6 million rounds of ammunition.

Mass trials of suspects continued into the early 1990s, a heavy cloud lowering on the political horizon, any original idea of justice lost in a mindless, snail-slow judicial system that hears cases for one day once every few months. Sometimes the hearings involved over one thousand people whose cases had been amalgamated into one trial and one indictment. Those detained would shout defiant slogans. Their relatives turned out to give them support. Their organizations would mutate and harden in jail. The notorious system of state security courts reinforced by the coup – each consisting of three judges from the civilian and military systems, as well as a special prosecutor – has also remained as a stick with which to impose repressive laws on any intellectuals who step out of line.

Appeals against the notorious Decree 1402 of September 1980, by which martial law commanders could summarily dismiss university professors and other civil servants, only began to be effective in the early 1990s. Under military rule, even mainstream newspapers were closed for infringing the new code of conduct; writers of books were targeted too, like the radical Yalçın Küçük, who earned a seven-and-a-half year sentence for his book entitled, appropriately enough, *For a New Kind of Republic*. Similar rules were deployed against other books and newspapers challenging the establishment thereafter, leading to the closure of a string of radical pro-Kurdish publications.

The repression was at its worst in the south-east. Gaols overflowed with prisoners. Organizations may have been crushed, but the fierce resolve of all who passed through those prisons was hardened into steel. One group came to dominate the cells and dormitories in Kurdish areas, the Kurdistan Workers' Party (PKK), whose leadership had managed to slip out of the country just before the coup. Solving one problem, the military had created another.

In their efforts to set everything right in a neo-Kemalist mould – including a much-trumpeted 'Year of Atatürk' in 1981 that has left the name *yüzyıl* (century) on many a school and park in honour of the centennial of his birth – the generals also set the stage for much that later went politically and socially wrong. Perhaps their biggest problem was dealing with the politicians who, they believed, had created the mess in the first place.

Packing off the four main political leaders of the 1970s to face each other over stiff tea-parties hosted by military holiday camp commanders was easy enough. It turned out to be more difficult to decide what to do with them next. They had refused to retire without a fight. So, after a month, the military released Demirel and Ecevit and placed them under house arrest in Ankara with orders – on pain of imprisonment – to keep quiet and to stay out of politics. Erbakan and Türkeş were held in detention for longer. Erbakan was to be sentenced to four years' imprisonment for trying to set up an Islamic state, a judgement later overturned by the supreme court; the prosecutor sought the death sentence for Türkeş for his National Action Party's involvement in political murders.

The generals were determined to create a new political system, one that would no longer be undermined by the debilitating demands of small parties holding the balance of power, that would never again have parliament voting a hundred times to elect a president, or be so impotent in the face of Islamist and Marxist threats to their secular Kemalist orthodoxy. They viewed their military intervention as a strong dose of medicine necessary to set the Turkish body politic to rights. As Ecevit quoted his mentor Ismet Inönü as saying, 'We have a democracy of fits and starts. We politicians break its rules, the army patches it up. The restoration will always fall to the army, and there will always be periods between the restorations.'

To start with, somebody had to replace Demirel as prime minister. Evren, craving legitimacy, wanted a civilian. But any candidate with political weight was automatically involved in the old networks. Having spoken to Evren, they would quietly ring up Demirel or his agents to check if they should co-operate. Things were not working out quite as the military expected.

Evren decided to postpone the civilian option. He offered the job of head of government to Haydar Saltık, his trusted former deputy and architect of the coup's preparatory plan. General Saltık declined to leave the military for the uncertain world of politics. Former Admiral Bülend Ulusu was called out of retirement and reluctantly took the job. But he refused point-blank to carry on with it into the new period of democracy.

Once the shock of the take-over had worn off, the politicians began to see the military's action as no more than the usual ten-yearly spring cleaning. It was time to calculate where their future interests lay. Few would move without their old leaders' say-so. Even in the military's hand-picked constitutional assembly, factions started to appear. This infuriated Evren, and led him to a decision that may have given short-term satisfaction but in the end was disastrously counter-productive. He suppressed all the old parties, banning a list of 723 leaders and cadres from active politics for five or ten years. He then confiscated the property of these by now well-rooted institutions of democracy.

'You're making a mistake if you think they will ever return to head a party,' Evren told one politician he suspected of talking behind his back to the old guard. But Evren was wrong. All four of the politicians banished on 12 September 1980 were back on top of the political ladder fifteen years later.

Not surprisingly, Evren soon regretted not having created his own political party, citing the model of General de Gaulle in France. 'We made a mistake,' Evren told his fellow generals. 'We've walked this sheep to market and now we are presenting the meat to somebody else.' When Henry Kissinger visited Turkey, Evren complained that he had never realized that political parties would spring up like mushrooms once the military relaxed its grip. Evren's problem lay in his determination to maintain absolute control and his failure to allow natural political growth from below. Even he seems dimly to have realized this.

'This is not like forming a brigade or an army,' Evren told a retired general who was setting up a party that looked like a front for Demirel. 'The people you will work with are not officers. It won't be like the army. You can't shout "Attention!" and line them up as you do in the army. They are such political jackals, you'll find yourself one day out of the door.'

These words turned out to be correct for the ex-general in question, and could turn out to be prophetic for the army as a whole. The junta, with the support of many Kemalist intellectuals, had written a constitution far more restrictive than the 1961 constitution it replaced. The generals' experiments in social engineering echoed their belief in military discipline and a permanent Kemalist blueprint for Turkish society. They designed their projects almost deliberately to be inflexible. Not surprisingly, one by one, these projects have collapsed. Change has usually occurred despite the system, undermining respect for state legitimacy. This has been most clearly seen in the way those pushing for greater Kurdish rights and those wishing to suppress them have both started to operate outside the law.

The two-thirds majority required to amend the 1982 constitution in the Turkish parliament has always needed something between a miracle and a national emergency to produce it; apart from the lifting of political bans by referendum in 1987, constitutional reform of any significance has only been achieved once, when certain changes were made a condition for Turkey's admission to customs union with Europe in 1995. The fractured political system that followed the coup has made it almost impossible to update with any facility the laws relating to Kurds, Islam, freedom of expression and freedom of association.

'It was a negative reaction. The military did not have confidence in the common sense of the people, so they imposed a constitution, which closed almost all the doors to active participation by the masses or organized groups in politics,' Bülent Ecevit has said. 'They prohibited the parties from co-operating with charitable and religious endowments, labour unions, associations, and so on. In doing so, the constitution prevented participatory democracy from functioning in a proper way. We are now paying the price.'[3]

Some projects simply backfired. The generals decided to reintroduce Islam into school curricula. Their intention was to teach children a state-approved version of their religion and to steal the thunder of the obscurantist *hocas* who would otherwise have a clear field with their fundamentalist vision of Islam. A secondary benefit sought by the military was to buttress popular psychology against the perceived menace of Marxism. Guarding one-third of NATO's flank against the Warsaw Pact, Turkey's leaders never saw this as a merely intellectual problem. Neither goal was achieved. In the late 1990s, Turkey is one of the few places left on the globe where Marxist-Leninist doctrines still attract passionate support among a significant body of the young. Islamic fundamentalists are also highly influential.

Perhaps Turkish society was already in the process of re-Islamification. After all, the *imam hatip* schools were growing strongly before the coup, and have continued to gain ground. Socially, they might be seen as the equivalent of church schools in the West. But for its fundamentalist adherents, Islam is also a political religion: and since the *imam hatip* schools are run by the state, this poses obvious problems. The process of placing pro-Islamic bureaucrats in the education ministry and others during governments in which Erbakan was deputy prime minister had started long before. But Kemalist intellectuals and army officers were shocked by the Turkish-Islamic synthesis that was seen to have entered the mainstream a decade later, and many blamed the coup-era generals for enabling it to happen.

Even before the end of the coup period, however, the stitching of the junta's overall plans was coming apart at the seams.

As preparations for the first general elections under the new constitution got under way, Evren decided to form two parties, one on the left and one on the right, both sympathetic to the military's views. But wanting to be seen to be playing fair, and under pressure also from the United States, Evren allowed the foundation of a third party. He did not think it had a chance of winning the 1983 general election, but even so made indirect threats to close it down right up to the last moment. This was the new Motherland Party, the Anavatan Partisi or ANAP, of Turgut Özal.

Evren had miscalculated. With the pseudo-conservative party leader Turgut Sunalp arrogantly behaving as if he was already in power, and the pseudo-leftist party under Necdet Calp making little impact, the electorate decided to take a jump into the unknown with Özal, who, unlike Evren, Sunalp and Calp, was not a former general. For a people now sick of being ordered around by the military, the final endorsement for Özal was perhaps an unfortunate speech from Evren hinting strongly that they should not vote for the newcomer. He won an overwhelming 45 per cent of the poll.

Although he had already lost any liking he had for the other politicians, Evren felt deep misgivings when Özal won, comparing it to the snub dealt to Britain's Winston Churchill after the Second World War. As he prepared to receive Özal to present him with the mandate to form the next government, he expected his former employee perhaps respectfully to kiss his hand. Özal, however, surprised him and showed how he meant to go on. Before the assembled cameras of the Turkish media, he embraced the tired general with a hearty Anatolian kiss.

11

The Özal Revolution

Live a life to make the undertaker weep at
your grave.

Arabesk song

THE COUP WAS good to Turgut Özal. Or, it can be argued, much
of the good that came of the military intervention of 1980–3 was
due to the ambitious bureaucrat the generals chose to run the
economy for them. The dynamism and contradictions of this short,
stocky, canny Anatolian character were the catalyst for much of
the breathless pace of change that revolutionized Turkey during
the 1980s and early 1990s.

Özal, now buried close to the tomb of Adnan Menderes outside
the walls of old Constantinople, often acknowledged that he was
carrying on from where Turkey's mould-breaking prime minister
of the 1950s left off. Undermining the Kemalist bastions of state
dominance of business and the media, flamboyantly popularizing
a new ideology of the market and international trade, irreverently
breaking taboos about the military, Islam and the Kurds, Turgut
Özal became Turkey's most influential political personality since
Atatürk.

Even so, like Atatürk, his untimely death in 1993 left his revolution half-finished, with notable failures in the delivery of some
fundamental reforms. The new Turkish élite, including his own
family, was found to be enriching itself with little sense of social
responsibility. The old secular state system was in tatters, but Turkey's fledgeling civil society and its emerging consumer lifestyle
would be prey to the powerful forces of religious and ethnic
extremism that competed to fill the moral gap left by the decline
of the old Kemalist republican ideology.

General Evren had no idea what sort of genie he was letting out of the bottle when he summoned Turgut Özal to his office two days after he seized power in September 1980. He wanted Özal in his coup-era cabinet for two reasons. Özal had impressed the military when as deputy prime minister he was asked by his mentor, Prime Minister Demirel, to brief them on the January 1980 stabilization package. Having the well-known and popular Özal on board would also be good for the junta's image abroad. So, Evren asked him, how about the ministry of foreign affairs? Özal, ever the gambler, held out for more. He wanted the economy. All of it.

'But that would be unconstitutional,' said one man in the room, the military's first choice for prime minister.

'The commanders are here,' Özal coolly replied. 'I'm sure they can settle it right away.'

Still cautious, Özal took the time to call Demirel, then detained far away in a military holiday camp, to see if it was all right to accept the job. Demirel declared it to be in the national interest, allowing Özal to accept the post of deputy prime minister, with an unprecedented amount of day-to-day power over the economy. For nearly two years all went well. Then Prime Minister Bülend Ulusu began to complain that his free-wheeling deputy was continually threatening to resign. 'Özal is always late for meetings, even of the cabinet. He never takes notes. He wants to be number one,' Ulusu told General Evren in February 1982.

In July, Özal's position, already undermined by a statist establishment worried by his liberalism, was made untenable by a crisis among a new generation of corner-shop deposit-takers, chiefly the famed 'Banker Kastelli', who had been encouraged by Özal's new liberal policies to enter into an interest-rate race. Some of the deposit-takers ran pyramid scams, with interest being paid out of incoming deposits. Other problems were simply mismatches in maturity as the deposit-takers invested in hard-to-sell assets like property and faced runs on their banks. Senior military men were among the many investors who had lost money. Özal quietly handed in his resignation to Ulusu.

Cautiously avoiding a farewell interview with the authoritarian Evren, Özal changed the official plates on his car, switched off the radio and sped south to the Mediterranean holiday town of Side, where he stayed for three months, plotting late into the night with his intimates. No big companies offered him a job in Istanbul, the traditional next stop for a senior bureaucrat. He was considered finished. But Özal was working on other ideas.

'Everyone stopped me on the beach and elsewhere and asked, why don't you form a political party?' he told his biographer.

Özal did not trumpet his ambitions at the time, even though rumours of his intentions were circulating in the press. First he decided to travel to the United States, where, at the insistence of a friend, he stayed on for a check-up in Houston. He had been smoking two packets of rough Samsun cigarettes a day, and his coughing fits would turn him an unnerving shade of purple. His heart had given him problems. Having received a stern report on his health, Özal sat down with his wife Semra and there and then they both decided to go on a crash diet. Within two months, he had lost 25 kilos, although he was still no lightweight, tipping the scales at 83 kg. He also lightened up the frames of his glasses. By the time he was back in Turkey in February, it was a new man who visited Evren to seek his blessing for forming a party. Evren gave him a cautious nod, confident that the military-inspired parties held all the trumps.

'The soldiers thought I wouldn't get 10 per cent of the vote. They thought my miniature party would be proof of democracy in Turkey. They made up two parties, one on the right and one on the left . . . mine was like a garnish on the menu,' Özal said.

But Özal turned out to be a political natural and support quickly grew. Prime Minister Ulusu brought him a message from Evren that he was working 'too hard'. The coup leader even called him in to ask if he wouldn't work with the arrogant retired general Turgut Sunalp, leader of the military's pseudo-conservative party, who was begging Evren to close down Özal's increasingly powerful third force. Even the British ambassador, so Özal recorded, advised him to join Sunalp, who was the early favourite to win the election.

Blocked on all sides by political bans, Demirel also began to stir uneasily in his lair. He forbade people from joining Özal and warned him to stop work on the Motherland Party, which Demirel correctly saw as a threat to his own attempt to revive his conservative Justice Party, closed down by the coup, in the form of the 'Grand Turkey Party'. In the end, Demirel asked Özal to come to see him alone. Özal declined the invitation, believing that Demirel only wanted him in order to protect his new party from closure. Evren, however, quickly banned Demirel's political stalking-horse. Anyway, Özal wanted nothing to do with the old guard, especially if they were loyal to the more powerful Demirel, with his declared agenda of vengeance against the military and their actions.

'Everyone is still fighting the old battles,' Özal said. 'We want nothing to do with these struggles. If the military stepped in, they did so with the best intentions. We saw it. We went along with them. Whether they knew what was best in the circumstances is altogether another question.'

In May 1983, Özal sent Demirel a fateful message announcing that their paths had parted. As the November elections approached, his party somehow survived the military sanctions that closed down more than a dozen other parties. By the time the generals realized how strong Özal's challenge had become to their two pseudo-parties, it was too late to turn back. The military establishment put great pressure on Evren to act: he did so, making a speech that implicitly warned people against voting for Özal. It had no effect. With more than 45 per cent of the electorate choosing Özal's new Motherland Party, it secured 211 seats in the 400-seat assembly.

Although Özal was to say later that he knew he would win all along, the news took everybody by surprise as the returns began to mount up. Özal, his wife Semra and their friends, who were driving through the night over the mountains from Istanbul to Ankara, picked up news where they could from grainy black-and-white television sets in coffee shops and crackly telephone lines. One of Özal's intimates, Güneş Taner, the tough-talking former manager of an American bank branch in Turkey, took up the story after they arrived in the capital.

'Semra said: "We've got to celebrate. Get some champagne." I called hotels, black marketeers, everyone. Eventually an American friend found me some. He sent it round with some Hershey Kiss chocolate and M&Ms,' Taner recalled a decade later, rolling a big cigar around his mouth in the garden of his luxurious villa overlooking the Bosphorus waterway.

'I opened the first bottle in the kitchen. It went all over the ceiling. Özal was really annoyed that we had opened it without him. Like a spoiled child, he went and locked himself in the bedroom. Even Semra couldn't talk him out. She sent me in. He did have a childish streak . . .'

So, having overcome all the odds, the Özal inner circle inaugurated a new era for the patient people of Turkey.

General Evren believed that Özal had won simply because the public did not know the other two ex-generals and because he had outmatched them in a pre-election debate. Columnist Hasan

Cemal thought the public wanted something soft-spoken and liberal after the brassy *bangır bangır* of Evren's militaristic speeches. Many people liked the sound of the Özal slogan that it should be 'the state for the people', not the other way round, as many Kemalists believed. Özal himself attributed his success to the way the Motherland Party supposedly unified the main currents of Turkish politics. First the Turkish public, then Turkey's foreign partners, even US President George Bush, discovered that they had fallen under the spell of a new and exciting one-man phenomenon.

Turgut Özal was not like the Turkish republican statesmen before him, most of whom were refugees or sons of refugees from the Rumeli provinces of the Ottoman empire, the rich, Westernized towns of the Balkans. Özal was an Anatolian boy, born to a well-connected family in a village in south-eastern Malatya, the apricot-farming hill country where for hundreds of years Alevi villagers, Kurdish tribes and Armenian townspeople had lived side by side. This marked his ancestry. His father's father was of mixed Turkish-Arab blood, while his father's mother was a pure-blooded Kurd. His mother's parents were from a Türkmen village by the Euphrates river.[1]

'Her father was the *kahya* [estate manager] of the minister of the interior in the time of [Sultan] Abdülhamit Han. He used to supply trusted men to Istanbul. I do the same. When I need a trusted man, I call for him from Malatya. I know which families are good and which are not,' remembers Turgut Özal's brother Korkut, a senior minister in three governments in the seventies who also introduced his older brother to politics.

Turgut was born the eldest of three boys on 13 October 1927. His father Mehmet Sıddıq had been educated for sixteen years in the Ottoman *medrese* school system to become a religious imam, or prayer leader. Sensing which way republican preferment was blowing, Mehmet became a schoolteacher and later qualified with flying colours to become a local manager of the Agriculture Bank, which until recently was still the main agency of development in rural Turkey.

The Özals moved around the country as their father headed local branches of the bank. Turgut saw the beauties of the Mediterranean coast; lived in the picturesque town of Mardin in the southeast, whose carved stone houses mark the crossroads of Syriacs, Arabs, Turks and Kurds; accompanied the family on a posting to Söğüt, the historic town where the Ottoman dynasty first sprang to prominence, and where the young Özals watched Türkmen tribespeople come each autumn to render homage to the *gazi* warriors of Ottoman times.

These moves kept him in good schools – a considerable advantage in his case, since he had damaged his arm as a child in a bad fall off a donkey, which disqualified him from the state scholarship that someone of his talents would normally have won. The accident nearly cost him his arm, but typically Özal told the doctors that if they cut it off they might as well kill him. They risked another treatment, and he recovered.

Özal seems to have been less fond of his father than his mother, a teacher and by all accounts a forceful character. According to Özal, she came under the influence of religious *hocas* in her last posting in the conservative Istanbul district of Fatih, becoming a devout follower of one of the sheiks of the Nakshibendi Muslim *tarikat*, or religious brotherhood. Özal however seems to have been eclectic in what he took from his religious education.

'I didn't learn to pray at home,' he told his biographer. 'Civil servants like my parents had become the cowboys of the revolution. I remember the Republic Day balls, the New Year's Day Balls. They made people go and dance and change partners, because "that was how they do it in the West".'

Ironically, it was contact with the real West that seems to have crystallized the Islamic consciousness of many second-generation Turks from the countryside. His brother Korkut described the process – in his case, oddly enough, among the Mormons of Utah.

'From our family we got the values of the past. Gradually, with the Kemalist revolution, different ideas started to reach us. We came to the conclusion that something was wrong with us. The Kemalist system pointed at religion as the main culprit. We were caught between the two,' he said. 'I thought I was a Muslim if I just repeated a few words. My conversion, as it were, came when I went to America. We learned that religion and progress could go together.'

Turgut and Korkut Özal had already been among the small group of dissident students who used to pray in a janitor's room among the heavy neo-classical buildings of Istanbul's Technical University. The man who introduced them to this unorthodox practice was a *hoca* expelled from the old Ottoman Darülfünun University in 1930. One of those who also joined these meetings was Necmettin Erbakan, destined to lead Turkey's pro-Islamist movement. Erbakan was two years ahead of Turgut Özal and in the same class as Süleyman Demirel, the future prime minister and president. Özal graduated in 1950, and was soon appointed as a planner to the booming and prestigious Electrical Studies Institute in Ankara. This group of technical students appears to have been a Noah's Ark of future leaders of a Turkey obsessed with progress.

'Turgut was in electrical development. I was a civil engineer. Demirel was a very close friend of ours, I worked under him for five years as his deputy. The big thing then was the Keban Dam, the pet project of all governments in those days. I was the specialist, Turgut the implementer. This brought us into close contact with politicians early on,' said Korkut Özal.

In his first job at the Electrical Studies Institute, Turgut Özal also met his second wife Semra, a secretary whom he got to know better by secretly sabotaging her typewriter and then offering to fix it for her. Short, plump and naturally intelligent like her husband, Semra was to prove both a boon and a handicap. The two of them walked hand-in-hand in public, a symbol of changing sexual codes in the Turkey of the 1980s, replacing the innocent age-old custom – till then more commonly seen – of young Turkish men walking together in the street with fingers linked. With her taste for whisky and long thin cigars, she symbolized a certain Western lifestyle and was always a fervent supporter of secular, liberal politicians in the Motherland Party. Her political importance was to grow, with some disastrous consequences for the Özal family's reputation.

Özal's own style was as personal as that of his predecessors. In Atatürk's day there were balls held on the hill in Çankaya that seem to have been a mixture of deep drunkenness, school dance formality and fear of the consequences of stepping out of line. President Inönü's evenings were regular as clockwork, as he played billiards after work, conducted sober dinner-time conversation with the great and good and then went out to the theatre, the opera or a concert. President Evren was dutifully dull after all the years spent around his old formica table; he admitted once that he could find little to say even to his daughter.

The later President Özal, for all his Muslim piety, liked to finish off a bottle of his favourite Courvoisier brandy during meetings with his intimates that went on late into the night. He loved practical jokes. He liked pencils that gave electric shocks. He adored gadgets, taking his grandchildren off to amusement arcades in the capital and then playing on the machines himself. Computers were a passion. Interviews with the president would often be conducted as Özal zapped through the channels on a huge television set, generally settling on CNN, but also, on one memorable occasion, the cartoon film *Who Framed Roger Rabbit*. For bedtime reading, cartoon stories about the cowboy Lucky Luke were likely to win over state papers.

Özal's conversation had none of Ecevit's naïve and eloquent honesty, Demirel's ungraspable fluidity or Erbakan's colourful turn of phrase. Transcripts of what he said, especially in English, sometimes seemed barely intelligible. But all who listened to him could sense exactly what he meant. And when the moment came, he could listen too. On the top floor of the army hotel that towers above the Istanbul Hilton, a look of intense concentration would cross his face during a discussion about something apparently trivial, such as the frustrations felt by Turkish students at police harassment and the laws restricting their freedom of action. Özal could then seem like a powerful force-field sucking up information – although his fellow student and rival Erbakan thought the process rather the reverse.

'Özal is always influenced by the people he is with. He is like a piece of soft iron. Whatever magnet he sees, he sticks to,' said Erbakan, summoning up another of his inexhaustible fund of metaphors. Özal's long-serving henchman Güneş Taner agreed about his powers of attraction. 'Özal was like a sponge. He would seize on whatever was novel in what you were saying, then sell it on as if it was his own. He showed us vision, gathered light and focused it like a spotlight.'

Özal did not see himself as a magnet or a sponge. He likened himself to bulls and boxers, saying he could not have survived the hurly-burly of Turkish politics otherwise. 'In Turkey, a politician should have a big heart, and an even bigger stomach to absorb the punches. Otherwise you cannot be in politics,' he said.

The bold effrontery Özal showed in raising his own and his country's profile was deployed over and over again. Back in 1988 he had not hesitated to call up George Bush to give him advice on his election campaign. During the Gulf War, Turks joked that he had become CNN's Ankara correspondent. The relationship with Bush blossomed until Bush paid him the unprecedented compliment for a Turkish leader of inviting him for a weekend at Camp David. And when foreign leaders were jostling to meet the newly elected US President Bill Clinton, Özal simply flew to the United States. When his meeting was deferred to a date after his presumed departure, Özal simply changed his schedule until he got his foot in Clinton's door.

Özal liked to live to the limit, and his recklessness could sometimes prove dangerous. If he was ready in the run-up to the Gulf

War to throw his country into battle, in private he was ready to risk his own life too. When touring the country he liked nothing better than to get behind the wheel of his latest BMW car and roar off at over 100 miles per hour, his cortege careering along behind him with sometimes fatal consequences.

'Come on, Semra. Stick on a cassette and let's have some fun,' he was once overheard to say as he closed the car door and gestured to a pile of tapes. He liked the music known as *arabesk*, the melancholy music of the newly urbanized villager in the *gecekondu* districts around Turkey's big cities whose Western style was grafted on to eastern melodies with lyrics of unbelievable despair, in which a suicidal singer, for example, might plead with his fatally ill lover not to come and grieve by his grave. Official bans on its use in state media did nothing to hurt its counter-culture popularity. Somehow, peasant or president, the abject misery of the songs did much to raise the spirits of Anatolian Turks as they struggled to keep their place on the greasy pole of Turkish society.

Özal's eating habits also raised eyebrows among the old republican élite. He was a man of enormous appetite. He could bolt down food without pausing for breath, swallowing chunks of meat almost whole. He also liked to do his most important brainstorming work through the night, sleeping only a few hours before getting up at 9 a.m. for a slow start to the day. All of this doubtless contributed to the growing health problems that would eventually cut him down before his time.

Back in 1952, however, his future already beckoned brightly. Özal's career showed early promise as he was chosen by the Electrical Studies Institute to travel for further study to the United States. On his return, he began to rise rapidly through the bureaucracy. Özal's contacts from university stood him in good stead. In 1967, he got his big break as chief of the then powerful State Planning Office in the golden years of Süleyman Demirel's first premiership. The main innovation credited to him was a system of incentives. As prime minister he would revive the idea of kick-starting the private sector. 'The planning office was like a school,' Özal said later. 'And we were powerful then. Ministers couldn't make a move without our approval.'

Özal found it wise to move to the United States after Demirel's government stumbled into the 1971 'coup by memorandum'. He landed himself a job at the World Bank as a special projects adviser in industry and mining. Nobody much noticed the tubby man with the thick black-rimmed glasses, and members of the Turkish élite would later say that his best friends seemed to be modest folk from the Washington mosque. But some remembered him well. 'In the middle of a meeting, he would bring out his prayer carpet. Nobody would pay any attention. We'd just say, oh, that's Turgut going to pray,' said John Golden, who shared a room with this emerging free marketeer who mixed his Muslim faith with a huge enthusiasm for American technological progress.

Özal came back to Turkey after two years, as the grip of the military was loosening. He worked with the big Sabancı group as their general co-ordinator – notably bringing their headquarters from Adana to Istanbul – and as the chief of an employers' union acquired a reputation for tough dealing. Then in 1979 Demirel called him back into government service to help handle the economy. Özal had also flirted with politics, campaigning as a candidate in Izmir for Necmettin Erbakan's and his brother's pro-Islamic National Salvation Party in the 1977 elections. The seat was unwinnable, but it planted a seed of ambition that he was soon to be given a chance to develop as the chief of the Motherland Party.

When setting out in politics in 1983 with his new image and briefly slimmer looks, Özal had been hard-pressed to fill his war chest and find backers for the party that would be the vehicle of his ambitions. Businessmen were betting on the retired general in charge of the military's pseudo-conservative party. And once Demirel had blacklisted Özal, nobody of substance from the old guard would join him. In the end he scraped together thirty-seven people ready to act as party-founders – basically, in his own words, 'anyone who came along'.

Özal would talk later of uniting in the Motherland Party the 'four currents' of Turkish politics, the pro-Western liberals, the Islamists, the nationalist left and the far right. But this was mostly window-dressing. The Motherland enrolled few leftists of proven stature. Liberal 'princes' brought in by Özal owed everything to him and rarely acquired much grass-roots support. Within a few years of his death in 1993, they had mostly returned to private business, or were back outside the country or in gaol.

In fact, Özal's most natural constituency lay in Turkey's dominant political conservatism, the territory of the old Democrat Party, a tendency still expressed in various parties that account for nearly two-thirds of the vote. Özal believed that all republican political parties descended from the Committee of Union and Progress, the Turkish nationalist movement that dominated the dying years of the Ottoman empire. One wing was statist and leftist, represented by Atatürk's Republican People's Party. The other was right-wing and conservative, associated historically with a line from Bayar, Menderes to Demirel. That was where he saw his real mission. His first choice of acronym for his Motherland Party (Anavatan Partisi) was, tellingly enough, the AP, the same as Demirel had used for the Justice Party (Adalet Partisi). The military did not like that echo from the past, and ordered him to change the acronym to ANAP.

In the early days, at least, there was real enthusiasm throughout the party for a broad agenda of change. But the deputies on the first Motherland ticket were almost all inexperienced in parliamentary life. Özal hardly knew them: he appointed two men to be ministers in his first cabinet whom he had not even met. With the military still in control, Özal and his newcomers were only able to win real power gradually, having to struggle each step of the way to seize the reins from President Kenan Evren and the generals. The relationship was most clearly expressed in the way he was obliged to stand well below the military chiefs in the official protocol rankings of Turkish state ceremonies.

'For the first couple of years, some ministers listened to Kenan Pasha more than to me . . . they were frightened of him, not me,' Özal said. 'It wasn't a completely civilian administration.'

To begin with, Özal himself was cautious. Even before military rule ended, he promised the generals of the National Security Council that he would never do anything to undermine them. Evren obliged Özal to change his foreign minister and vetoed Özal's wish to give a ministerial portfolio to his young favourite Adnan Kahveci. He was also able to force Özal to dismiss two politicians implicated in a smuggling scandal.

That is not to say that there were not arguments. The generals had curious beliefs, fearing, for instance, that allowing Turks to travel abroad would use up all the country's foreign currency. Özal for his part was determined that people should be allowed to leave the country more than once every three years. In fact, the last bureaucratic obstacle to foreign travel, a $100-per-exit tax, was only lifted in 1996. By then, as a result of the usual process by which Turks find loopholes in and erode unwanted laws, the government of the day was forced to admit that only one in five people was actually paying the levy any more.

Time, too, was on Özal's side. At every opportunity the prime minister ensured that civilians were placed in charge of the administration. When he discovered that the National Intelligence Service (MIT) was giving more information to President Evren than to him as prime minister, he forced through the appointment of a civilian head of his choice, at least briefly. 'The security forces behaved like a state within a state,' his wife Semra complained.

The army was in for a still bigger shock. Angry about his place on the protocol list, Özal was determined to teach a lesson to an institution that he suspected had worked out who was going to be in charge for decades ahead. In 1987, the head of the army, Necdet Öztorun, was so sure that the cabinet would not oppose the top brass's carefully laid plans for his promotion to chief of general staff that he had sent out invitations to the inaugural ceremony well before his official appointment. Only a week before he was due to take over, Özal informed Öztorun that the post was not his. The general telephoned to beg to be allowed to take the job 'just for a few months'. Özal refused.

'The military were never a real problem,' said Güneş Taner, himself the son of a general and a bull of a man who, like many privileged children of Turkey's military élite, was a civilian who felt he had nothing to fear. 'They chose the next chief of staff without telling Özal. I said, "It's a showdown. You have got to show who is boss. We don't want Öztorun." We spent a restless night after that. We feared there might be a take-over. Afterwards they did nothing. It showed we were really in charge.'

The military remained suspicious and resentful. And on no topic were they more sensitive than Özal's softness towards Islam and the Arab world, which they feared would open the door to a fundamentalism that could undermine or even destroy the secularist structure that the Kemalist republicans had been struggling to build. As columnist Hasan Cemal points out, the Özal family, following their mother's lead, were close to a leader of the Nakshibendi *tarikat* who was known to preach that 'to break the rule of the sultan you have to stand next to him.'[2]

Evren recounts with distaste how, almost as soon as Özal took power, the new prime minister asked for the Director of Religious Affairs – the tamer republican equivalent of the Ottoman Sheikholeslam – to be moved up the state protocol line. Then Özal asked for an obscure Nakshibendi sheikh to be spared his exile on a bleak Aegean island, where he had been sent, according to Evren, for acts that included encouraging his followers to drink his bathwater.

'If I'd know he was a member of that *tarikat*, I wouldn't have let him run for office,' Evren muttered in his memoirs. 'Religious fanatics are more dangerous than Communists. They want to take the country back fifteen hundred years. At least the Communists want to go forwards.'

The Motherland Party also campaigned against beer, both for its alcoholic content and also, some believed, because one brewery company's owner had supported Demirel. They sought to end the television advertising of beer and its sale in corner groceries, arguing that children were buying it after school. Such an approach might cause no comment in the United States or even Europe, but for Evren and the generals it was another sign of the Motherland Party's emerging Islamic agenda. Evren – though himself happy to take shorthand notes in the old Ottoman script – warned Özal to limit Arabic classes in schools and not to think about reintroducing Ottoman lessons. He also objected to the length of skirts of girls performing at the National Sports Day. Having found them too short and revealing before, he now found them too long.

'We either go too far, or not far enough,' Evren grumbled, and called in the pro-Islamic minister of education, Vehbi Dinçerler, for a dressing-down. In September 1985, he forced Dinçerler's resignation. Soon afterwards he summoned Özal again to tackle him on the subject of the 'reactionaries'.

'Özal said it was impossible to force Turkey back on its tracks. He always reacts like this. He is always optimistic. He never thinks that with each little concession he offers he opens the way to larger dangers,' Evren said.

Özal himself never felt any contradiction between his Western habits and his religious beliefs, although his lifestyle would have shocked an Iranian or Saudi zealot. He believed that Islam had fallen behind the West because it had not had the benefit of a renaissance that would have fostered freedom of thought. He never forced his children into religious ways. 'I see a strong belief in God as an important factor in the health of society. But this should not be a reason for being opposed to new things, or being closed to the world,' Özal said.

The clearest statement of Özal's view of Islam came in his book *Turkey and Europe.* Özal spoke for many younger Turks when he wrote:

> The Turk is aware that faith in itself does not affect secularism, does not prevent him from being rational. In everyday life, there is no difference in this respect between a European Christian and a Turkish Muslim. A synthesis has been realized between the West and Islam.

This synthesis has ended the identity crisis of the Turk. I am a believer and open to all kinds of innovations. Not having a problem of identity, I feel no need to defend my own culture, nor to attach myself to an ideology or an extremist nationalism.[3]

Like Özal's synthesis between Islam and Western ways, the economic miracle of 1980s Turkey was a hybrid beast. Its full effect in revolutionizing the way Turks lived and worked would not be felt for another decade. A people who had been conditioned by the Kemalist republicans to living on a carefully controlled cultural and economic island were cajoled by Özal onto an uncertain path of integration with the outside world. The Turks were to emerge tougher and more competitive, far more confident about their place in the world and their future prospects as a regional commercial power.

In 1983, it was a case of one step at a time as Özal once again picked up the banner of the January 1980 reform programme. Strangely for a man whose only book was called *Turkey and Europe*, one of Özal's first acts as prime minister on behalf of the economy was to push through legislation that would allow the operation of interest-free Islamic banking houses. Another measure effectively permitted Arab princes to buy coveted properties by the Bosphorus where they liked to spend their summer holidays.

If the priority seems odd, perhaps it is understandable in the context of a belief shared even by President Evren at the time that the Middle East offered the best potential for Turkey's fledgeling export industry. The military government, moreover, had left him an economy that was already heading in the right direction and whose principal regulations Özal himself had been in charge of implementing. Inflation was a manageable 31 per cent in 1983. Exports were already showing signs of improvement and diversification.

The opening to the Islamic east was for a while successful, but perhaps not where Özal would have expected. His hopes of massive investment from Saudi Arabia and the Gulf never materialized. But Turkish food exporters did great business in selling to the two belligerents in the Iran–Iraq war of 1980–8. Turkish contractors also began to work abroad in Libya. Large fleets of Turkish trucks plied between Europe and the Middle East, with Turkish truckers earning themselves an indestructible reputation. These were essential first steps. Within a decade Turkish contractors would be taking their skills first to the Soviet Union, then to several new states around the Black Sea, in Central Asia and deepest Siberia.

'Our ships had never left coastal waters before. I had to have a fierce argument with my father before we could even send a ship over the Mediterranean to Libya. Now we sail all over the world,' remembers Mehmet Aksoy, whose family, in a typical story of Turkish company growth in the 1980s, gradually built up a mid-sized merchant fleet from a family shipyard on a beach near Gallipoli.

Özal dated his conversion to free-market doctrines back to the late 1960s. His period as a World Bank official in 1971–3 opened him to American ideas. Özal's speeches and letters to Demirel show him formulating a free-market concept for Turkey. Prime Minister Demirel, Özal, who was then Demirel's deputy, and others all take credit for the incorporation of these concepts in the January 1980 stabilization measures, the first major signal of Turkey's intent to move towards a freer economy. Evren and Özal themselves compete in claiming credit for the capitalist reorganization of the economy during the coup.

In short, by the time Özal took over as prime minister in 1983, he had had time to consider and experiment with the policies he intended to introduce. On top of that he had a strong government. The trade unions, the left wing and the Kemalists were far from convinced by his free-wheeling rhetoric, but they were in no position to mount much resistance.

One of his first targets was the bureaucracy and red tape. There were some 35,000 categories of civil servant in Turkey in 1983; he reduced the number of titles to 150. Bureaucrats were forced to come back to him five times until they had succeeded in simplifying foreign currency regulations from seventy-five pages of instructions to fifteen. He knew how to pull all the ropes: the man he appointed as governor of the Central Bank, Yavuz Canevi, remembers that quite junior officials would suddenly be called to explain themselves to the new prime minister. But it was a constant battle.

'The bureaucracy started growing again, all by itself. You can't control it,' Özal lamented later, claiming that he had done well to limit the increase to 150,000 during his time in office, most of them police, teachers and imams. A total of about 1.6 million people still work as civil servants in Turkey, with another 550,000 working in state-owned industries.

As the seamy side of the Özal years emerged after his death, with many associates and even his son facing court cases for corruption, people tend to remember Özal for his legendarily smug comment on kick-backs: 'my civil servants know how to look after themselves.' But at the beginning, when politically strong, he regularly followed up allegations of corruption. When his bright young protégé Adnan Kahveci brought him a tape-recording proving that a minister had accepted a pay-off for contracting a shipment of oil, Özal took action.

'I must have listened to the tape a dozen or two dozen times. At last I called the minister to my home. I got on my exercise bicycle, sat him on a chair and I can say I forced him to confess and sign his confession. It was the first time in the multi-party period that a party in power sent one of its own to gaol,' Özal said. The minister in question was sentenced to two years' imprisonment.

Gradually, the Turkish people absorbed what Özal was trying to say. Özal's revolution sought above all a change in mentality. The nationalist military had assumed that Turkey would always be dependent on foreign aid. The economy in 1980 was on its knees. Could a country whose main exports were wheat and hazelnuts ever compete against industrialized economies? Could a country where it was a serious crime to carry a dollar bill truly create stock exchanges and foreign currency markets? Could an economy whose foreign income was dominated by American military aid and remittances from guest workers in Europe learn to stand on its own two feet? For all the official self-congratulatory bombast, these questions stood as great obstacles to the country's belief in itself, perhaps most of all in the minds of the privileged and protected élite.

'Societies that are herded like sheep can only be as successful as sheep. We tried to make people realize that the state was not an employer or a father, that people had to rely on themselves. But it is not easy. A stick-in-the-mud attitude prevails,' Özal said. 'Everything is upside-down. The best people work as inspectors, the middling ones in the executive. The state trusts neither its own officials, nor its own citizens. Everybody is frightened of making a mistake or taking responsibility.'

Frustrated with the bureaucracy at all times, he brought in a new class of contract bureaucrat, often Turks who had been successful in America, coaxed back by Özal's charms. Later it was seen that some had also lined their pockets. But others genuinely felt a national duty to help their country. At their height a core of about thirty 'princes' were in charge of key government agencies and institutions.

Özal also streamlined the decision-making mechanism, loosening the grip of the old ministry of finance and concentrating power in the hands of the prime minister's office and a new interagency Money and Credit Board. Although this sometimes allowed Özal to cut too many corners, in the long term it enabled economic management to work more efficiently.

On his visits to the United States, Özal liked to go window-shopping not just for people but to see what was new. He wanted to communicate his consumer hunger to his people, while Evren, representing the caution of the old system, believed money spent on new imports was wasted. When Özal's first set of import regulations took the revolutionary step of publishing a list only of what was banned, not what was permitted, Evren muttered, 'I thought this dangerous. They will start to import all sorts of extravagances.'

But Özal went further, lifting quotas on imports as well. He was convinced, rightly, that freer trade would force Turkish businessmen to improve their products, and that the sight of fancy foreign goods on previously monotonous shop shelves would encourage the Turkish people to work harder to earn more money to buy them. He also seemed to believe that the increasingly common sight of rich people in expensive four-wheel-drive vehicles in Istanbul would encourage the rest to greater efforts. 'I like rich people,' he once commented in his famously tactless way.

And, during his first governments, none had more money and power than Özal and his men. Based on his early planning experience, he believed in the lure of incentives, whether encouraging Turkish businessmen to produce for export in the 1980s or to explore new markets in Central Asia in the 1990s. Manufacturers were allowed to import raw materials duty-free, and an export insurance scheme was introduced. Municipal borrowing soared for huge new projects. The system was abused but it worked, successfully blazing trails along which important numbers of businesses would later follow.

In some respects, Özal's reforms were merely bringing legal order to what was being done already by the black market. Özal was keenly aware of this. President Evren would complain that he was giving licences to deal in foreign exchange to well-known black-marketeers, but for Özal, this was all part of changing the rules so that everybody could participate. With the money he won for the state by eliminating the black market in cigarettes, for instance, Özal reckoned he financed the building of 150,000 housing units a year. But he also believed that it was the angered cigarette-smuggling mafia that was behind the attempt to assassinate him in 1988.

Another of the mechanisms that Özal quickly learned to manipulate was the power of the state to set prices. If at first this

1. Where the Wild Things Are: curious mediaeval *Siyah Qalam* ink drawings are the first art form linked to the Turks, but, like the Turks themselves, their origins are lost in the obscurity of the Central Asian steppe

2. Martial Spirit: the backbone of Turkish states has always been the military. Most successful were the Ottomans, seen here in battle order as they march to conquer the greatest empire of their day

3. A Nation of Immigrants: the Bulgarian Turks pictured here fleeing to Turkey in 1989 were only the latest actors in a century-long movement of Turks and other Muslims. As the Ottoman Empire split into more than 30 countries, most fell back to a new homeland in Anatolia

4. Ghost Town: the once bustling ethnic Greek town of Karmylassos near the Mediterranean resort of Ölüdeniz is now known in Turkish as Kaya, a mute witness to the wrenching exchange of populations and massacres that emptied Anatolia of most Christian minorities between 1890 and 1924

5. Last Rites: a Syriac priest reads from a hand-written Bible in a stone church dating back to the first centuries of Christianity. Syriacs near Mardin in south-eastern Turkey were the last Christian community to cling to their ancestral lands, but conflict and the lure of the West meant few remained by the 1990s

6. Grease Wrestlers: this ancient Turkish sport is as popular at folk festivals today
as when first recorded more than 700 years ago. Still played as it was portrayed
by Ottoman miniaturists, the winner is he who turns his opponent's belly up
to the sky. The slipperiness and the reaching inside leather trousers have bred
many a metaphor for Turkish politics

7. Polo with Javelins: one of the few living links with the Turks' Central Asian past is the game of *cirit*. Individual riders from two teams of horsemen charge up a football-pitch sized field by turn, aiming to strike one of their opponents with the throw of a blunt wooden spear and then to escape a similar fate while heading back to their own lines: the bravado of the players is as important as their skill

8. Father of the Turks: republican founder Mustafa Kemal Atatürk has
dominated the lives of three generations of Turkish schoolchildren.
Few remember the days when a similar absolute allegiance was pledged
to the sultan-caliphs who preceded him

9. Tightrope Walker: the second president of the republic, Ismet Inönü, kept Turkey out of the Second World War. Feigning diplomatic deafness or pitting competing nations against each other, he was a master of Turkey's favourite tactic at moments of weakness: playing for time

10. Shooting Star: populist Aegean landowner Adnan Menderes surged to power in Turkey's first free elections in 1950, but repression and corruption in later years prompted an army-led coup in 1960. His 1961 execution echoed the fate of many a grand vizier garotted before him

11. Süleyman the Survivor: seven times prime minister, ousted by two military interventions, Süleyman Demirel rose from shepherd boy to president of the republic. The conservative leader's memory for faces and places is legendary, but his legacy could be summed up with his watchword: 'Yesterday was yesterday, today is today'

12. Likely Lad: translator of T.S. Eliot, the man who ordered Turkish troops into Cyprus in 1974 and one of the few patently honest men in Turkish politics, Bülent Ecevit was a great hope of the Turkish left. But the Black Sea coast's nationalist *karaoğlan*, or likely lad, could never unite Turkey's fractured left or change the fact that most Turks vote right of centre

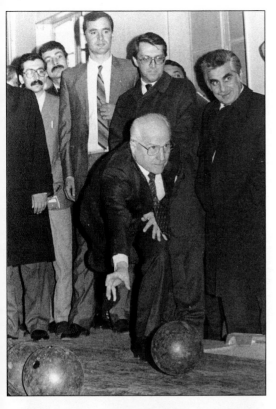

13. Implacable Pasha: the stern General Kenan Evren led the 1980 coup that temporarily crushed the squabbling politicians of the 1970s. Later president, Evren retired to the Mediterranean coast to paint, but the army's 1982 constitution still hamstrings democratic progress

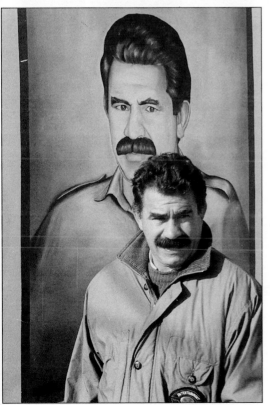

14. Brigand President: exiled Kurdistan Workers' Party (PKK) leader Abdullah Öcalan was the only Turkish Kurd nationalist ruthless enough to survive the 1980 coup and more than a decade of rebel guerrilla warfare against the Turkish army

15. Revolutionary Sultan: the late President Turgut Özal was lucky to survive a 1988 assassination attempt, but the attack at the peak of his reforming premiership came at a watershed as he began to compromise the brave principles with which he internationalized Turkey

16. Sex and Power: Turkish fig farmers near the western town of Aydin extol the virility that can be stoked up by eating their prize dried fruit and its fast-dissolving fructose

17. Commercial Spirit: Turgut Özal's 1980s reforms unleashed an unprecedented zest for business among Turks. Brokers outside the old Istanbul Stock Exchange helped lead a revolution in mentality: turnover at the new all-electronic market now ranks among the top half-dozen in Europe

18. Police State: a May Day demonstrator lies dead after being shot by a policeman (not shown) in Istanbul in 1990. Militant provocations, police arrogance and disrespect for the law on all sides mean Turkish street protests quickly become volatile and violent

19. Kurdish Agony: a Turkish Kurd woman screams in her burned-out house after a murderous raid of the kind that has depopulated south-eastern Turkey. This raid was blamed on the rebel PKK; other villages were destroyed by the Turkish security forces

20. Tough Neighbourhood: with ten often difficult neighbours, Turkey's foreign policy is a standing exercise in crisis management. Here some of the 500,000 Iraqi Kurd refugees who appeared on the Turkish border in 1991 are led out to a holding camp in northern Iraq

21. Fundamentalist Nightmare: in 1993 a Sunni Muslim mob burned down a hotel in Sivas hosting a congress of Alevis and intellectuals, killing thirty-seven and striking fear into the hearts of Turkey's secularists. Famed satirist Aziz Nesin (on fire ladder) narrowly escaped with his life

22. Shameless Ambition: Tansu Çiller became Muslim Turkey's first woman prime minister in 1993 and turned out to be a tough politician, manipulating a love-hate relationship with the public and defying charges of patchy competence and corruption

23. The Hoca Makes Good: old-world gentleman, Muslim dreamer and a charismatic, ruthless leader, Necmettin Erbakan, known as the *hoca*, or teacher, skilfully side-stepped the secularist military in 1996 to become the first Islamist prime minister of Atatürk's republic

24. Flying High: many Turks have synthesized the Muslim and European parts of their identity, and few would feel any contradiction at the sight of this girl in a bikini paragliding past a waterfront minaret on the Bodrum peninsula

25. Whose Atatürk? After decades in which republican secularists repressed all but the most controlled forms of Islamic education, religious instruction is back with a vengeance. Sometimes open-minded and progressive, sometimes fundamentalist and reactionary, Turkish society is at last feeling its way forward more freely

was used to try to sort out the budget, it later became a lever to gain political advantage. Evren was to write that he believed Özal got a sadistic kick out of raising prices. Inflation ticked inexorably upwards, but Özal was unconcerned. Growth was his panacea, as he asserted to anyone who remonstrated with his policies.

'He didn't really speak English. He spoke economics,' said John Golden, the man who shared his office in the World Bank. Throughout his period in power, Özal could never resist the temptation to lecture. His powers of free-market persuasion did not charm just the military. Cabinet meetings and press conferences turned into long seminars on his economic theories. Even when the glow had long gone off his popularity, he ruthlessly used info-documentaries broadcast on state television to drum in his message of economic progress.

The result of these policies was an astonishing success in converting the Turks into a thoroughly business-minded people. Despite the red tape, poor infrastructure and widespread corruption, modern factories began to spring up, gradually exporting clothes, leather goods and even trucks and buses all over the region. By the 1990s, international manufacturers like Renault and Opel found to their surprise that the quality of Turkish production and even management was some of the highest of their factories anywhere in the world. Shopping centres, glossy magazines, tyre factories began to win prestigious international prizes. Of the nine F-16 warplanes out of 3,000 produced around the world to be awarded a 'perfect' grade, three were assembled in Turkey. Tourism meanwhile spread sophistication and new business along the Mediterranean and Aegean coasts. In 1987, there were still only one or two five-star hotels in Istanbul worthy of the name. A decade later, more than twenty were often filled to capacity.

To illustrate Turkey's and his own success, Özal liked to tell a story from one of the interminable meetings in 1980 during which he used to do battle over the rescheduling of Turkey's foreign debt.

'I went to fight for our debts at the OECD. It was a huge room. I could feel my heart misfiring slightly. Behind me waited a doctor. All Turkey's creditor countries were arrayed around the table,' he remembered. Feeling the atmosphere a little tense, he tried to brighten up the tight-lipped bankers with a joke about the legendary Turkish figure of fun, Nasruddin Hoca. In it, the *hoca* proposes to his creditors that he plant thistles in the path of passing flocks of sheep. Then, the *hoca* suggests, he could collect wool from the prickles and sell it to pay off his debts. Silence greeted Özal's attempt at humour. The Paris Club was not amused. The joke was much too close to their perception of Turkey's future prospects of earning money. 'They didn't take it well. They just thought: "He's not going to pay." The atmosphere froze,' said Özal. 'But six years later I was the man chairing an OECD meeting, there in that same room.'

By the mid-1990s, it was possible to see that Turkey was ready for a new leap forward. Turkish designers and engineers had started to create their own products rather than simply fill orders for foreign firms. Others had established themselves as regional commercial powers in their own right, investing in factories and franchises in neighbouring states. Individual Turks were also setting out bravely on their own to make their fortunes with nothing more than a bakery oven or the secret of how to marinate a *döner kebab*. All of this followed naturally from the movement that Özal had set in train.

If food, pharmaceutical and contracting companies got off to a quick start in the Middle East, they were soon followed by another success story, the textile industry. Starting by building up the processing of Turkish-grown cotton into thread, cloth and then fashion clothing, the garment industry became one of Turkey's biggest export earners.

A similar process transformed the leather industry, which started the 1980s in tanneries that had festered outside the walls of Constantinople ever since their medieval origins as manufacturers of boots for Ottoman armies. The evil-smelling quarter has now been demolished to make way for a grassy park. The tanners have branched out from making rough hippie coats for 1970s students on the trail to Katmandu into state-of-the-art factories. They now manufacture many boutique items sold by grand houses in Paris and Milan; their own brand names are also steadily growing in repute.

Figures for trade and production have soared since 1980. Exports rose from $2.9 billion in 1980 to $21.6 billion in 1995, while imports grew likewise from $7.9 billion to $35.19 billion. The number of cars on the road and of telephone subscribers doubled between 1990 and 1995, while the number of tourists grew from 5.4 million to 7.7 million. GNP growth, despite zigzagging ups and downs, has officially averaged about 5 per cent a year. Unofficially, it may have been more.

One way or another, during the decade in which he was a political force first as prime minister and, after 1989, as president,

Özal achieved a significant number of the dozen pledges of reform that lay at the core of the January 1980 measures and which were read out to parliament after he took power in 1983.

A key change of policy by Özal's administration was to drop state investment in factories and to concentrate on the infrastructure of the country. Huge amounts of money were spent on new motorways, dams, bridges, airports, yacht marinas, telephone exchanges and electricity pylons, which reached far up into the mountains of the Kurdish south-east.

The stock-market was next off the mark, reopened and reorganized from 1985 on. For nine years the new market grew up in Karaköy, an ancient quayside at the mouth of the Golden Horn. At first, apart from the main trading floor, impromptu dealers built up a business in colourful bearer stocks from picnic tables on the pavement or over the green baize card tables of the smoky Café de la Bourse. Here a grizzled former tyre salesman earned the title 'professor' for his analyses of company accounts – at first considered a bizarre approach in the rumour-driven market. There a former shoe-maker secretively kept track of prices in old Ottoman numerals. 'Tipster' Mehmet in the corner was rumoured to be worth a million or two. By the time a new generation of cellphone-wielding stockbrokers, half of them women, had moved into a powerful marble-clad Stock Exchange building in 1995, stock turnover of up to $400 million a day had propelled the Istanbul Stock Exchange into the top half-dozen in Europe.

Dealing in foreign currency, treasury bills and gold moved likewise into a bigger league. Astonishing amounts of hard cash and bearer bills have always moved around Istanbul in suitcases and brown paper bags, and as late as 1988 there could be a 30 per cent difference in foreign rates of exchange between the Central Bank and the black market. Youths representing underground dealers and market-makers among the shops and jewellers of the Grand Bazaar still trade kilos of gold and 'whole ones', 'priests' or 'chocolate' (American dollars, German marks or Swiss francs) by open outcry in a warren of streets by the Swordmakers' Gate. But with the lifting of exchange controls in September 1989, the availability of electronic trading screens and the increasing sophistication of Turkish banks, the bulk of business has now moved into the official arena of interbank trading. Margins have become as thin as any other major market. In fact, Turkey suddenly had one of the freer foreign exchange regimes in Europe, permitting the repatriation of stock-market profits and the principal, capital gains and rent from investments in real estate. In April 1990, the

IMF accorded Turkey Article VIII status, making the Turkish lira an officially convertible currency. The idea would have seemed preposterous a decade before.

By the late 1990s, foreign travel had been freed as promised. Consumer goods became incomparably better and more freely available. Housing and apartments were built at an amazing pace all over the country, 800,000 of them with Özal-style special funds. Even the old bungalow-style *gecekondu* dwellings mushroomed upwards into *apartkondu* blocks of flats. Real power was beginning to decentralize as independent magnates emerged to make provincial cities into 'Anatolian tigers'. Özal's simple new value added tax became the government's biggest single source of income. The main Atatürk Dam of the massive South-East Anatolian Project (GAP) had started producing electricity, and irrigation tunnels were near completion.

The banking system and laws on foreign investment were revolutionized. Although the Menderes government in 1954 had introduced one of the most liberal direct investment laws in the developing world, the bureaucracy had seen to it that foreigners were rarely able to take advantage of it. In the twenty-four years between 1954 and 1980, a total of only $230 million dollars was invested. By the 1990s, the annual flow of investment was several hundred million dollars. More than a dozen international banks flocked to Istanbul in the 1980s and made large profits out of the inefficiencies of the inexperienced markets. But local banks soon built up capital and learned to copy their tricks, often hiring back Turkish managers trained by the foreigners. By the 1990s, the foreign banks' role had largely reverted to specialist functions. The pattern was repeated in other services like accounting. Big foreign-backed factories making Japanese cars, French television tubes and German clothing were built. Even so, the overall inflow of foreign investment was always disappointing, held back by the constant political uncertainty in Ankara, the weak legal framework and worries about Kurdish separatist and leftist radical violence.

The deep shock occasioned by the country's virtual bankruptcy in the late 1970s was the key to popular support for the austerity programme between 1980 and 1987. The man Özal chose to be his Central Bank governor, Yavuz Canevi, in his book about the Özal revolution, also listed as contributory factors the administration's commitment to reform, public confidence in the government's intentions, the speed with which its tougher measures were implemented, the return of skilled workers from Europe after 1983, the availability of export markets in the 1980s world boom, the fact that most of Turkey's debts were owed to understanding governments, the new-found social order imposed by the military intervention, the real wage cuts accepted by or dictated to the previously militant trade unions and the natural wealth of the country. The impression of rapid growth was helped by the fact that, in 1980, many factories were working at less than half their capacity.[4]

But Özal also had his failings: as Süleyman Demirel often taunted, he could pilot a plane at take-off but was unable to land it. His principal weakness was a failure to control inflation, even if that was almost a conscious choice. 'It's not that I don't think inflation important. But I attach more importance to Turkey's development,' he said in May 1987, as the annual rate began to tick back towards 40 per cent. As his popularity faded, so did his will to enforce the politically painful discipline of tight control on spending. The rate would soon shoot up much further.

The income tax system was also never properly reformed, leaving the black economy untaxed. The main tax burden of the system, as usual, fell on the salaried middle and working classes and on those companies that chose to try to be honest. Foreign investment did rise sharply in Özal's early years, but it was never sufficient. For their part, investors resented having to negotiate tough bureaucratic obstacles and face constant legal challenges from opposition politicians as a result of sloppy work on the fine print by Özal's team. Others were put off by the poor handling of the privatization programme.

The benefits have probably outweighed these failings. Özal was already predicting this in the early 1980s, but it took a long time before ordinary Turks, patiently waiting and working, saw any concrete results. As time went on, he came under increasing political pressure. He needed a better goal than that of shop windows full of goods taunting people without the money to buy them. He wanted a symbolic confirmation of Turkey's Westernizing vocation and his own international popularity and importance. In April 1987, against the advice of almost every ambassador in Ankara, Turgut Özal applied for membership of the European Community.

12

A Bridge Too Far

As a result of our revolutionary change of
script, our dear Turkey looks completely like
Europe. In less than one year it will have the
true key of civilization and knowledge in its
hand.

Cumhuriyet editorial, 1928

AN AWKWARD SILENCE from Brussels greeted Turgut Özal's
hastily drawn up application to join the European Community on
14 April 1987. Even if Turkey might one day become an economic
Cinderella and a dream partner for European businesses, the
European establishment reacted as if one of the ugly sisters had
asked the prince for a dance. Their strained response missed the
point of Özal's approach. It was not the intention that Turkey
should enter upon a marriage with Europe right away. The application was rather another expression of the age-old Turkish concern
that it should not be excluded from the official European invitation list.

At his desk before a wide window overlooking a panorama of the
Bosphorus waterway separating Europe and Asia, Orhan Pamuk is
an eloquent exponent of the Turkish point of view, as representative as it is unofficial. Now in his forties, often bitingly critical of
the state, Pamuk's erudite prose has made him the leading novelist
of Turkey's younger generation, often exploring the relationship
between Turkey and the West. 'Turkey is constantly moving
towards Europe, becoming more Westernized. But a union will
never be realized. Turkey's place is in continuous flux. This limbo
is what Turkey is and will stay for ever. This is our way of life here,'
he explains to his visitors.[1]

Behind him floor-to-ceiling bookshelves overflow with stacks of publications, including Persian mystic poetry, American novels and Russian philosophy. Between the view of freighters, tankers and ferries moving on the waterway and Pamuk's study are the twin stone minarets of an Ottoman mosque. The balcony of one is adorned with loudspeakers, and, five times a day, the muezzin lets everyone in the quarter know at some volume when it is time to pray. Pamuk gives one of his deep laughs as his office echoes with the racket. Flopped in an easy chair, he clearly feels little of the tension between the Christian West and Islamic East that causes such anguish among intellectuals in Europe, Turkey's old-fashioned Kemalist élite, and, indeed, among radical Islamic fundamentalists.

'People are always asking me about the supposed paradox of girls in headscarves happily walking alongside girls all made up,' Pamuk says. 'But what is important is the way things combine, elegantly, without fuss over their origins. This country, this Istanbul, is a coming together of things. People are comfortable with that.'

The momentum of this convergence between Turkey and Europe in the past two decades is often overlooked, being the sum of many small parts. Mutual trade and investment have expanded greatly. The numbers of travellers both ways between Turkey and Europe have risen fast. The children of over two million Turkish guest workers in Europe, despite prejudices on both sides, are beginning to see themselves more as a part of their new countries than mother Turkey. There is the cumulative effect resulting from years of competition in European sports, in which Turkey is beginning to move up the rankings. If it is a test of Europeanness, Turkey can now usually count on an at least respectable score in the Eurovision song contest. For forty years, its military has intermingled with NATO. Even its younger generation of police officers are likely to have been on courses in the West.

Turkey is sometimes taken for granted because, unlike Iran, it has not so far frightened the West with outright Islamist hostility, even if its weak secular politicians like to appeal for Western support to counter a purported Islamic fundamentalist threat. Turkey is even resented because of what are perceived as shrill and unceasing demands for full membership of the European club. Also, unlike other Muslim states such as Saudi Arabia or the princedoms of the Gulf, European trade with Turkey is not usually done on the back of huge arms transactions or showy government-to-government deals. The trade is a broad web of smaller partnerships. And although Turkey's official GNP in 1995 was about 167

billion dollars, according to the OECD the real figure is closer
to 250 billion dollars or more – more than the economic strength
of oil giants Iran or Saudi Arabia, and indeed well over half the
World Bank's estimate of 400 billion dollars GNP for the entire
Arab area of the Middle East and North Africa. Moreover, it is
earned by a country that produces less than a tenth of its own oil
consumption.

At a popular level in Turkey, there is a kind of love–hate
relationship with Europe. At the same time as trying to Westernize
the Turkish people, for decades the Kemalist republicans deliberately isolated Turkey from the outside world, making information
from abroad difficult of access. Few Turks had met foreigners and
fewer still could speak their languages. Now the populations of
cities and tourist resorts are busy forming more natural relationships with foreign visitors. From close up, a weatherbeaten Turkish
peasant at a provincial bull-wrestling festival is perfectly likely to
clap his hand on a friendly European's back and proclaim a
common sense of identity. But from a distance, travellers may still
meet local hostility as they pore over their maps. Uneducated
local people can be heard suspiciously speculating whether these
elaborately equipped visitors are locating long-hidden gold, plotting an invasion route or investigating the site of an Armenian or
Greek grandfather's house with a view to establishing a claim.

A sense of both belonging and not belonging to Europe is
perhaps most powerfully expressed by home crowds at key European soccer games. Hours before an important match in Istanbul,
much as in Byzantine times when public life was dominated by
the green and blue factions of the Hippodrome, a sense of expec-
tation fills the air. A burst of heavier traffic clogs the arteries of
the city as people rush home. A strange quiet then falls on the
city as families gather around television sets. National honour is
at stake, and it is as if the nation is holding its breath. From
the outside, the stadium itself looks battered, grey, and grimly
overshadowed by spiralling motorways. Inside, it turns into a boiling cauldron of roaring crowds and billowing smoke from
coloured flares. If the Turkish team wins, delirium breaks out all
over the country. Trucks loaded with entire families from poor
gecekondu districts career along the ringroads. Young bloods in the
rich districts of town set up roadblocks and demand tributes of
joy from passing cars. The hooting cavalcades of merry-makers
need no encouragement, and, until new laws, mounting child
casualties and safety-conscious footballers persuaded them to stop,
the more exuberant men would often shoot their pistols into the

air. Typical headlines after a victory against a European team show how blurred is the Turks' sense of being inside or outside Europe. 'Galatasaray roared, Europe groaned, the Earth was shocked', or 'We have become Europeanized', or 'We have entered the European Palace Accompanied by our Lion'.

Lions or no lions, however, Turkey has not been allowed to enter the European palace. Rather, the 1996 Customs Union accord between Turkey and the European Union confirmed Ankara's place in the European back garden, too big and too wild to be let through the door. It is unlikely to be allowed inside in the near future. While optimists see the Turkish economy as the equivalent of Italy twenty-five years ago and Spain fifteen years ago, realists see that Turkey will have to wait until the European Union digests a whole series of newly independent East European states before it looks at Turkish membership again. And that fact of life rankles with Turkish diplomats a great deal.

Turgut Özal was, after all, technically within his rights to make the application for full membership. The Ankara agreement of 1963, the foundation of Turkey's relationship with Europe, signed at the height of Turkey's strategic importance during the Cold War, specifically mentions Turkey's right to eventual accession to the European Economic Community. The association agreement's stated objects were the progressive establishment of a customs union within twenty-two years and the alignment of economic and social policies. These documents also date back to Germany's urgent need for cheap labour to rebuild its post-war economy, and in the Additional Protocol of 1970, they also foresaw the free movement of labour by 1986. European diplomats did not disguise their later regret over the clauses relating to full membership and circulation of labour. By the 1980s, every official visitor from Germany was raising the question of how to persuade Turkish immigrant workers to return to their own country. The Turks were not impressed.

'Our German friends used our workers very cheaply. They squeezed the orange and now want to get rid of the skin. They are being selfish,' President Evren commented in 1983. That was not the whole story, of course. The Germans were not threatening to use force, and were offering compensation and the possibility of 'bringing the factories to the people' in Turkey.[2]

The Turkish authorities ultimately understood and took into account the Europeans' concern at a possible flood of immigrant workers, biting their lips as they noted how Turkish workers were still apparently thought good enough to clean the floors in the Commission buildings in Brussels. The Turkish élite, however, was not ready to drop the idea that Turkey should one day be accepted as an equal by Europe. Western Europe, they argued, could not claim a monopoly on a Europeanness to which Turks also aspired, a Europeanness representing social advances, justice and technological progress. Even though only three per cent of Turkey's landmass lies in the Balkans, most Turks feel at least partly European.

A minority of Turks, it must be said, reject Europe – a perception shared, ironically, between the more radical Islamists and Kemalists. This minority flourishes at times of criticism from Europe, of official rejection by Brussels or when a sense develops that Europe is not living up to its avowed ideals of fairness. Angry reactions have been especially common over the handling by Europe and America – the two are sometimes not clearly distinguished – of modern conflicts involving Muslims in Bosnia, Azerbaijan or Israelis and Palestinians, all of which involve co-religionists or ethnic kinsmen of the Turks only a few hundred miles from Turkey's borders.

Suspicions have often crystallized around Turkey's Kurdish problem, the subject of an official European Union protest note in 1992 and a constant concern of the European Parliament. Things were made worse by Turkey's official culture of denial and the habit of right-wing Turkish politicians of hitting back below the belt. Government minister Ayvaz Gökdemir called three respected women leaders of the European Parliament 'whores' during a 1995 coffee-shop campaign stop. 'I don't know if they are whores or not. It's not a serious insult. What words do the Turks have for those who threaten their own country?' the minister said afterwards. This was by no means a mainstream view, however, and the Turkish press howled in protest. 'Gökdemir is a standard-issue Turkish male, a deputy served up by the lottery of democracy, a hard-line, rough guy who uses his moustache as a filter to breathe through his nose. The real problem is that those like Gökdemir view all women politicians in the same way,' said the leader writer of the popular newspaper *Sabah*.

A lingering mutual suspicion is natural enough, given Turkey's history. For centuries, the Europeans were seen as Christian infidels who were the object of either actual or suspended holy war. In practice, however, a state of peace usually prevailed, during which the Ottoman sultan might unilaterally grant boons such as trading concessions. The military and technological rise of Europe, however, forced the Ottomans to revise their opinion of their neighbours and to embrace as many of these new developments as they could.

The Ottomans had initially refused to join the Concert of Europe early in the nineteenth century, believing it demeaning to co-operate in the Christian desire to guarantee Ottoman borders in order to block their partners from obtaining any 'unfair' advantage in the Eastern Question. But having joined forces with the British and French in the Crimean War, the Ottomans were theoretically entitled to admission to the high table of European politics. European signatories to the Treaty of Paris in 1856, including Britain, France, Prussia and Russia, engaged jointly to respect and guarantee the integrity and independence of the Ottoman empire and declared that the Sublime Porte had been 'admitted to participate in the advantages of the public law and system [concert] of Europe'.[3] This concession was never much more than theoretical as far as the Europeans were concerned, however, and they soon started picking off parts of the Ottoman empire again.

The legal umbrella of the European Union today is what attracts some Turks, frustrated by the growing inefficiency and injustices of the judicial and governmental system in Ankara. From customs regimes to personal justice Brussels, they believe, could organize things better. Perversely, the republican state machine sometimes seems to believe the same, as if Turkey needed an outside control mechanism to keep it on the straight and narrow. In the run-up to the 1996 Customs Union agreement with Europe, bureaucrats and deputies were suddenly able to overcome resistance to much-needed new legislation on tax, patents, trade marks, copyright, environment, labels of origin and industrial design. And each time a Turkish court provoked outrage with a judgement in blatant disregard of human rights, usually firmly rooted in oppressive laws, official spokesmen, sometimes privately embarrassed, would repeat like a mantra that all was well because Turkey had accepted an individual's right to appeal to the European Court of Human Rights.[4] Turkey would sometimes even settle out of court – for instance, paying damages to a group of Turkish Kurd villagers, one of whom had had his face smeared with animal excrement by Turkish security forces.

The economic momentum of the convergence with Europe has been more impressive, with the overall volume of business nearly doubling every five years since 1980. In 1981, two-way trade with

the European Community was well under a third of Turkey's
imports and exports. By 1995, it had reached 28 billion dollars
and represented more than half of Turkey's trade with the rest of
the world. Two-thirds of foreign investment in Turkey was also
European.

The burning desire to become members of a club that seemed
so reluctant to accept them drove Turks to blindness in many
respects. At conferences sponsored by the European Commission
to enable both sides to become acquainted, Europeans would
point to the contradiction between proud assertions of Turkish
sovereignty and the exigencies of the new European structure. 'Of
course, we will not stand for anybody messing with how much
sugar we put in our coffee,' the minister of European affairs told
participants at one such get-together. 'But that,' pointed out the
editor of a Dutch newspaper on the other side of the table, 'is
precisely what membership of the European Union is all about.'
The Turkish minister did not get the point.

The Turks' faith in their own economic progress has also made
them reluctant to appraise their economic and social standards
from the European point of view. To Europeans, Turkey's inflation, population growth, unemployment, budget deficits, social
indicators, regional disparities and farming subsidies looked hair-
raisingly out of kilter with their own mellow, stable economies.
Turkey would qualify for unimaginable amounts of aid if it was
accepted as a member on equal terms. It also escaped nobody's
attention that Turkey was a country that already had a larger
landmass than any European state and, within a generation, would
probably also have the largest population.

Turkey's case has not been helped by the fact that Europe does
not feel the same strategic imperatives as does the United States;
indeed, Europeans have been put off by Washington's constant
lobbying on behalf of its ally. For Washington, having nuclear
missiles and military listening posts in Turkey, within easy range
of the southern underbelly of the Soviet Union, was a good coun-
ter-weight to Moscow's relationship with Cuba. Later Turkey also
served as a useful logistical base for missions in the Middle East,
from Lebanon in 1958 to the Gulf War of 1991. In fact, as far as
the Europeans were concerned, Washington had already taken
care of most of their strategic worries. Even so, when the time
came, European chanceries ensured that Turkey was given a good
seat as an observer at the Western European Union, the defence
arm of the European Union. And in the mid-1990s, European
Mediterranean strategists began to take more account of Turkey's

importance in their drive to stem the rise of Islamic fundamentalism and to encourage economic growth among their southern
neighbours in order to create new markets and reduce immigration to Europe.[5]

From the vantage-point of his reception room in the heart of
the headquarters of the Turkish General Staff, General Doğan
Güreş spelt out the Turkish military argument. 'Turkey is the
bridge between Europe and the hazards of the Middle East. The
whole region around Turkey is unstable. Without us, you can't
have any security. Fine, the Europeans can go on getting rich
together. But all around them will be poorer nations, who will get
them in the end,' he said.[6]

Haunting Europe still are age-old suspicions about the Turks,
the horde at the gates of Vienna, a people with an alien Muslim
tradition, a police force with an appalling record of brutality
towards its own population, a country that was both visibly poorer
and different. 'We went to Süleyman Demirel's house today. No
European would live in a house like that,' confided one Spanish
Eurocrat after a visit that like all others seemed to turn into a
critical tour of inspection. The Eurocrat couldn't put his finger
on what he objected to: the kitsch sculptures everywhere of the
white stallion (the symbol of Demirel's party), the Middle Eastern
baroque furniture in the drawing-room favoured by older and
wealthier Turks, the books piled up in abandon all over the work
desk. For him, the sum of the parts was non-European.

This sense of otherness found vivid expression in the debate
about human rights, particularly in relation to the Kurds, which,
as we shall see, came to a head in the final period of bargaining
prior to the Customs Union agreement of 1 January 1996. Europe's
attitude had started hardening well before then.

The 1980 military coup was a watershed in Europe's perception
of Turkey. The Council of Europe, of which Turkey was a full
member, and which at the time saw itself as the main keeper of
Europe's conscience, seriously considered throwing the country
out. Relations with the European Community also went into deep
freeze. The Association Council, the main inter-state body governing the relationship, was suspended until 1986 and was subject
to frequent other blockages. A Joint Parliamentary Committee,
suspended between 1980 and 1988, never managed to achieve a
smooth dialogue. The political relationship worsened as the core
states of the European Union started to concentrate on a deeper
political and social union.

If European foreign ministers had to select a moment at which they were at their most spiritually united, one of the contenders would have to be their discussion in 1989 of the edict issued by Iranian revolutionary leader Ruhollah Khomeini against the British writer Salman Rushdie. It would also have been a moment when a Turkish minister would have felt at his most awkward. The representative of a Muslim and socially conservative country like Turkey, where people are still dangerously ready to kill and die for intellectual, religious or political concepts, would never have been able to join unreservedly in the moral indignation felt by European Christians, who had been brought up in an established, hard-earned and well-protected tradition of free speech.

'*The Satanic Verses* is a blasphemous book. We support free speech, but it must not infringe other people's rights. Turkey is a broad society, not like France. We are the world's transit area, a mixture of east and west,' Özal said.

Thanks to the coup, the European Union's financial assistance to Turkey was suspended in 1981. More surprisingly, as a result mainly of the objections of Greece, the core financial aid programme had still not been restored by 1997. Between 1964 and 1981, a total of nearly one billion dollars had been allocated to Turkey, almost all reduced interest rate loans intended for industrial and infrastructure development like coal mines and power stations. A dribble of Special Aid Funds once again started to be distributed after 1987 to university programmes, health projects, business conferences and vocational training. In the mid-1990s, more substantial money started being lent by the European Investment Bank, the European Union's funding arm, but only as part of Europe's new Mediterranean policy. In 1996, even this was questioned by a European Parliament angry at Turkey's continued human rights abuses. Thanks to Greece, the main package of loans remained blocked. Both sides knew that occasional project-based loans were not the same as a dependable, formal relationship.

European governments had however kept open their gates to the free trade they had promised Turkey. This was despite the fact that Turkey, pleading special circumstances, had suspended its own promised tariff reductions for eleven years until 1988 and after 1984 had also started adding on tariff-like levies to fund Özal's many extra-budgetary projects. This gesture of goodwill was a vital door of opportunity that allowed Turkish industry, particularly the textile business, to establish itself in European markets, although there was continual struggle as Turkish producers were perceived as dumping goods.

Individually, in pairs and even troikas, some major European governments had worked hard to be helpful as well as to gain advantage. Most showy and sophisticated was France, whose revolution inspired the more Jacobin elements in the early Kemalist revolution and whose culture dominated the late Ottoman and early republican élites. Hoping to broaden support for Turkey in Europe, Özal deliberately awarded big contracts for satellites and infrastructure projects to France in the 1980s.

Britain's Margaret Thatcher was fond of Özal, famously declaring, just before the anticipated award of a contract to build a third Bosphorus bridge, that their shared free-market creeds meant that 'I am an Özalist'. Thatcher also saw European Union membership for Turkey as a useful trump card to play against Europe's integrationist tendencies. Britain did not win the bridge contract, nor was the bridge built, but a curious special relationship remains between the two countries thanks to the growing power of the English language. While most of the younger pro-Western generation in business have finished their education in America, many up and coming mayors and officials in the pro-Islamic Welfare Party have done courses at universities in provincial Britain.

Of all the states of the European Union, however, it is Germany that has by far the closest and broadest relationship with Turkey. It is an interaction as uneasy as it is historic. From the time that Ottoman armies first arrived before the gates of Vienna in 1529, it was the Germanic and Ottoman worlds that divided the Balkans and Eastern Europe between them. Above all, the Turks admired the success of the German armies, and called most often on German military advice. In the First World War, the rulers of Turkey allied the Ottoman empire with Germany as the best guarantee against Russian expansionism. During the Second World War, the Turkish right also put pressure on the neutral Inönü regime to accept that an alliance with Hitler's Germany would be in the country's best interest.

Although the centralized government of the Kemalist republic now most resembles that of France, Germany and Turkey also have much in common. Both states share a racial sense of nationality based on blood, not residence. Germany is Turkey's biggest trading partner by far, taking more than a fifth of Turkey's exports and supplying nearly a sixth of her imports. And the relationship is both cemented and complicated by the presence in Germany of nearly two million Turkish *gastarbeiter*, or guest workers, perhaps a quarter of whom are ethnic Kurds.

Some of these guest workers have returned to Turkey, bringing with them the skilled labour, working discipline and know-how that helped fuel Özal's economic miracle. But they have also been an integral part of Germany's success, and still supply, for instance, a quarter of the workforce in the legendary German car industry. Most Turks seem likely to stay there, despite a second-class status as *mitbürger*, or fellow citizens. Neither able to become assimilated nor wishing to abandon their Turkishness, they also seem culturally adrift from the mother nation.

From 1961 on, the Turkish government had assisted this drive, encouraging workers mainly from deprived villages in Anatolia to go to Germany. The community there developed separately from 'mainland' Turkish society, stuck in a time-warp that missed out on social advances at home. Also, homesick and challenged by the rejection they felt from the German Christian society around them, older members of the community turned in on themselves and reformulated their traditional, rural Islam into something tougher. Just as ethnic Kurds in Germany became more radical than those in Turkey and more munificent in their support for Kurdish nationalist groups, tens of thousands of Turks joined pro-Islamic organizations that proved a goldmine for the pro-Islamic Welfare Party in Turkey. By the 1990s, a charter plane from Düsseldorf landing at Istanbul airport would disgorge a people whose clothes, bearing and attitudes all seemed to belong to a different line of development.

This difference was felt most keenly by the German-educated children of the workers, which even earned them a nickname in Turkish, *Alamancı*, a playful pun on the word for German, *Alman*. Some started a new kind of Turkish German culture, winning recognition as writers, businessmen or artists. But misunderstandings were always common in this hybrid community. The hot-selling *Alamancı* rap group Cartel were surprised to find their basically defensive nationalist message immediately adopted in Turkey by the aggressive far right. Turkey had to set up special courses in schools to squeeze *Alamancı* children back into the rote-learning Turkish mould. One 15-year-old *Alamancı* found himself in gaol after being denounced for simply carving a Communist symbol on his desk.

Even the older guest workers seem inclined to stay in Germany in order to remain close to their children, rather than to carry out their original plan of retiring to Turkey in comfort. This tendency survived the notorious arson attacks by German neo-Nazis on the homes of Turks that led to the deaths of more than twenty guest workers in a year between 1992 and 1993. The Turks could after all take some comfort from the fact that many Germans rallied to the arson victims, and that subsequent anti-Turkish attacks appear to have been mainly the work of radicals among the ethnic Kurdish community, not of Germans.

The German government has offered rich incentives for the Turks to return, but there are many economic and social reasons for them to stay. More than 800 mosques have been built, tens of thousands of homes have been created, four television channels have been set up and more than 13,000 Turks attend German universities. About 40,000 Turkish-owned businesses have been registered, mostly shops or restaurants. These entrepreneurs have invested five billion German marks and do more than 25 billion marks' worth of business every year. Their companies employ more than 125,000 people, sometimes Germans as well as Turks.

Yet the Turkish republic remains wary of Germany, believing it to be publicly for, but privately against Turkey's full membership of Europe. Former Prime Minister Mesut Yılmaz told *Die Zeit* in May 1996 that 'we hear everywhere that Germany's attitude is the biggest obstacle, not that of Greece.' Others point to the line that Hitler's Germany drew at the Bulgarian border between Turkey and its planned European system. Another permanent irritant is the close tracking of Turkey's human rights record in the German media, often to the exclusion of all other aspects of the country.

For all these reasons, but above all because the current European priority was to develop a deeper and fuller union between existing member states, the European Commission in December 1989 gave a polite cold shoulder to Turkey's application for full membership. It stated its opinion that negotiations for Turkey or any other new country to accede should not be considered until at least 1993. At the time Turkey was disappointed but did not react strongly. The opinion reaffirmed Turkey's fundamental eligibility to become a full member, and encouraged it to draw closer to Europe.

The picture had changed significantly for Turkey by the time of the Lisbon declaration by European leaders in June 1992. By then, following the collapse of the Soviet Union, seven other would-be members had applied to join. Europe now developed three new basic conditions for membership, none of them in Turkey's strong suit – European identity, democratic status and respect for human rights. The reference at Lisbon to Turkey's ambitions became even cooler. Other states would clearly be allowed to overtake Turkey in the queue for membership.

Even in 1991, Turkish leaders could see which way the wind

was blowing. 'When Europe says that your democracy is not the right kind of democracy, that would be true, or that you are poor, that would be true too,' said Süleyman Demirel after winning the October 1991 general election. 'But if they say we don't want you because you are Turks in Europe, then we shall resent it. When the defence of European civilization [against Communism] was at stake they didn't say we were Turks and Muslims.'[7]

Such feelings were sharpened when Turkey finally consummated the intimate and unique Customs Union with Europe in 1996, and yet found itself formally placed behind a whole list of East European states for discussion of full membership. This rankled especially when Turks saw that, despite forty years' service guarding the southern third of NATO's flank against the Warsaw Pact, Turkey was now on the same list as Russia or the Ukraine, at least as far as Brussels was concerned.

Turkish governments since the 1980s, even that led by the pro-Islamic leader Necmettin Erbakan in 1996, may have always directly or indirectly listed pursuit of full membership as one of their major goals. But as Nihat Akyol, a senior Turkish diplomat who spent years managing the relationship with Europe, has pointed out, after Özal's initial application, there has been little real Turkish pressure to open negotiations on the point.

'It's when we see the way closed that we react,' Akyol said. 'The perspective must be open, defined. As we go in this direction, there must be something concrete in view.'

Nothing, however, seemed to be more consistently and reliably concrete than the principal obstacle to Turkey's diplomatic integration with Europe: Greece.

It is not true that Turks and Greeks are invariably enemies. But the rivalry between the two nations is now so ingrained that nobody knows how to break the habit. Greece routinely holds every other country in the European Union to ransom on the question of Europe's ties with Turkey. Diplomats from other countries roll their eyes and vent real anger at the way each fresh bilateral spat wrecks supposedly long-term multilateral processes. But given the veto rights in European voting, there is almost no way around it, and no way to expel Greece either.

Greek-Turkish relations were in fact surprisingly good during the Turkish republican period. At the peace negotiations at Lausanne after the bitter Turco-Greek war of 1919–23, advisers even had to step in to stop Ismet Inönü from having a friendly dinner with his Greek counterpart, Eleutherios Venizelos, the man who had ordered the Greek invasion of Anatolia that started the war. With the Ankara Treaty of 1930, Atatürk and Venizelos succeeded in forging a détente that lasted until the Cyprus problems of the 1950s. In the 1980s and 1990s, Greek and Turkish musicians would make joint records and groups of civilians would try to meet to overcome the ill will generated by their leaders' political disputes. Their shared traditions included aniseed-flavoured drinks like *rakı* and *ouzo*, vegetables served in succulent olive oil and a love of singing and dancing at restaurants late into the night. Academic meetings gathered pace in 1994–6. But somehow Greek-Turkish encounters always turn into tense high-wire acts as participants tiptoe around the many sensitive political subjects that could unbalance the process.

Periodically Turgut Özal would hack at the tangled knot of interrelated disputes in a fashion worthy of the country that preserves the remains of the ancient city of Gordion. The first occasion was on the eve of the press conference following his 1983 election victory. As he sat up late with his intimates trying to work out an eye-catching announcement to make, an idea formed in their minds – why not unilaterally lift visa restrictions for the Greeks? Özal, with typical panache, went ahead and did it. None were more surprised and shocked than the hardened diplomatic wrestlers of the Turkish foreign ministry, the *statukocus* (Özal's word for the defenders of the *status quo*) who had not been informed in advance. Soon the old *meyhane* tavernas of Istanbul enjoyed an upsurge of business, as did the suppliers of the white plates that are customarily broken during riotous Greek evenings. Özal also eased the law to allow Istanbul Greeks living abroad to sell their land and properties. It was Özal, too, who finally gave the Orthodox patriarchate the go-ahead to restore its buildings in 1987; he perhaps saw the advantages of having the patriarch on Turkey's side, a symbol adding to the *gravitas* of Istanbul as a regional centre.

Özal, like Greek leaders on the other side of the Aegean, could also adopt an aggressive posture when engaged in populist politics. As he told a provincial audience a year after coming to power, 'Turkey is not the old Turkey. Greece is frightened of us. We see it as a small state. They came and were taught a lesson twice. That was enough.'

But he reacted fast to defuse a crisis that blew up in March 1987, when, on returning from heart surgery in Houston, the television in his London hotel suite started broadcasting the news that Turkey and Greece were on a collision course yet again in the Aegean Sea.

Güneş Taner, then operating as Özal's chief of staff, records: 'I was eating breakfast in his drawing-room. He was asleep in his room. I was watching TV. Suddenly I saw the Turkish army issuing declarations and ultimatums, there on the TV. The Greeks had been pushed into a corner.' The whole dispute, he suspected, had been stirred up by the leader of a conservative faction within Özal's own party. 'I went into Özal's room, started shaking him. He asked, what the hell is going on? He called everyone, the General Staff, President Evren. A BBC crew had come. I brought them up, got him talking to lots of TV stations. Things started to cool down. After the last interview, he could barely stand up.'

Ten months later, Özal and Greek Prime Minister Andreas Papandreou came together at an economic meeting in Davos, Switzerland, engendering what became known as the 'Davos spirit'. The two leaders agreed on a long-term process for overcoming their differences, meeting again in March 1988 and in June, when Özal paid the first visit to Athens by a Turkish premier in forty-six years. They agreed not to threaten each other with war, to set up a hot-line telephone link, to hold annual meetings and for political and economic committees to work out new initiatives on cultural affairs, tourism, trade and investment. But the political committee failed even to draw up an agenda, and Turkey withdrew from it. Özal and Papandreou met again in May 1989, but the Davos spirit was dying. Greece and Turkey were soon at loggerheads again over the old issues of Cyprus and territorial rights in the Aegean Sea.

Successful Turkish-Greek rapprochements only seem to happen in periods of strong leadership, as under Atatürk or Özal. Strong American pressure can also do the trick, as when the two countries joined NATO in 1952 while in need of strategic support against the Soviet Union. The United States was also behind joint economic support after the Second World War in the US-funded European Recovery Programme, and its pressure was behind General Evren's decision to allow Greece back into NATO in 1981.

Increased tension between the two sides, however, was usually the result of weaker, populist politicians trying to stir up domestic support or trying to justify anti-NATO policies. Tension may also have been exacerbated during the Cold War by superpower politics. For the Soviet Union, the squabbling between Turkey and Greece was always something to be subtly encouraged in order to undermine NATO; some even believed that the United States followed a similar policy in order to sell more armaments to both sides.[8] But once such stirring-up starts, given the hostility cultivated from the earliest years at schools in both countries, it proves very hard to stop.

'We don't want to love [the Turks]. I don't imagine any Greek of my generation wants to love them. Friendly relations are impossible,' said Theodore Pangalos, the Greek foreign minister, after the United States had just managed to damp down another Turco-Greek confrontation over two uninhabited outcrops of rock in the Aegean Sea in January 1996.

One or two well-researched Turkish books did appear in the 1990s representing some of Ankara's policies towards the Greeks as counter-productive and sometimes ugly. But when Turkish journalist Özdemir Kalpakçıoğlu was looking for a title for his book of memoirs after six years of reporting from Athens, he chose *A Greek Can Never Be a Friend*. 'I just didn't find a positive side to them,' he went on to explain in his foreword. 'I could have forced myself to see the Greeks with another eye, to take on board the old Western romanticism, to write about tavernas, songs, dances, whatever, or to accept modern Greece as if it were the Greece of antiquity. But it would have been false. It's not that I don't like the Greeks. I see the Greek as an enemy, and love him as such. The strange part is that the Greek feels no love for me. He sees me purely as an enemy.'[9]

The psychology of the relationship is certainly strange, as is the pattern of their foreign relations. Despite a perception that Greece is naturally in the Western camp, two centuries of patronage by outside powers on top of a religious schism between Constantinople and Rome since 1054 has made the Greek élite arguably more anti-Western than the Turkish élite, which for nearly two centuries has taken the West as a model.[10] It is equally difficult for outsiders to untangle right and wrong on the most contentious issues. The problems are not restricted to Cyprus, the patriarchate and the treatment of each other's ethnic minorities. The dispute that brings the two countries closest to war involves the territorial waters of the Aegean Sea.

Although the new International Law of the Sea allows a theoretical 12-mile limit to territorial waters, Turkey has not accepted Greece's right to this limit in the Aegean. With more than one thousand Greek islands and outcrops in existence, Turkey calculates that under this rule the Aegean would be turned into a predominantly Greek lake, in which they would hold about 71 per cent of the waters as opposed to about 44 per cent as at present.

Turkey has threatened Greece with war if it extends the limit. So both sides, complaining loudly, formally stick to a 6-mile limit. However, Greece does claim 10 miles of territorial air space. As a result, almost every day Turkish pilots test what they consider to be 'international' air space between the accepted 6-mile and the Greek-claimed 10-mile limit. Greek pilots scramble to intercept planes they consider to be 'intruders'. There are regular incidents in the fierce mock-dogfights that follow between the supposed NATO allies.

The continental shelf is also in dispute. Every ten years or so – taking them to the brink of war in 1974 and 1987 – both countries have sent seismic research vessels out into the Aegean. Their purpose is supposedly to search for oil but in fact to test the other side's resolve on the question of what belongs to whom. As such escalations calm down, Turkey will usually offer some form of a 'dialogue without preconditions'. Greece will then generally respond that there is nothing to discuss, except in court or an international forum, apparently fearing that even to engage in debate will open the door to Turkish territorial designs. This fear can assume bizarre dimensions. Even in 1996, European diplomats on the islands were arrested for 'spying for Turkey'. For years, Greece actively discouraged tourist exchanges with Turkey using all kinds of restrictions, although that has moderated since a mid-1990s shift in European holiday-making habits away from Greece and towards Turkey. Pettiness abounds. Passengers arriving by ferry from Turkey at Lesbos are made to walk through a symbolic bath of disinfectant, or, if none is available, bathroom detergent.

The risk of conflict is real, however. The Turkish military's motive in pushing for an expensive package of 160 F-16 warplanes was to strengthen air defences in the Aegean against Greece. And Turkey is right that Greece, contravening the Lausanne Treaty, has militarized the Aegean islands lying off the Turkish mainland. Greece has also used its privileged relations with Europe and the West to great advantage. The most glaring example of the imbalances that have resulted is the 7:10 ratio officially adopted in 1983 by the US Congress on the question of arms supplies to Greece and Turkey, even though Turkey at the time guarded a third of NATO's flank, had a far larger population relative to Greece and was significantly poorer in terms of GNP per capita and foreign income.

Athens knows that Greece cannot fight Turkey on its own. Even back in the 1820s, the disorganized and feuding Greeks won their confused war of independence from the Ottoman empire mainly by means of outside help. An expansionist Russia encouraged most of the early preparations for rebellion. Philhellenes like Lord Byron did much to persuade European opinion of the justice of the Greek cause and to mobilize loans for Greece in London. British officers played key roles in uniting the Greek campaign. And all might have been lost for the Greek cause had not Western navies sunk the Ottoman fleet in 1827 at Navarino Bay. Similarly, independent Greece usually only did well against Turkey when acting in concert with the Great Powers or local allies. Its defeat in the Turco-Greek war of 1897 showed the folly of trying to take on Turkey alone. Greece today is therefore quick to expand every bilateral conflict into one involving the European Union as a whole, and, while benefiting vastly from EU agricultural subsidies and other European aid, does its best to make sure that Turkey gets none.

Özal, however, always looked on the bright side of such economic problems. He believed it was a blessing in disguise that Turkey had minimal reserves of oil and other natural resources. Hard work, he would argue, was forcing the country to develop properly. Unfortunately for him, even as he tried to win the promise of European membership and to capitalize on the Davos spirit to guide the relationship with Greece into calmer waters, he was beginning to face increasing political turbulence at home that threatened to undo all his achievements.

13

Özal Stumbles

There is no salvation for the country where
the upholders of the law are not as brave as
the brigands.

Ismet Inönü (1884–1973)

THE TRANSFORMATION OF Turgut Özal the Turkish technocrat
into Turgut Özal the Turkish politician dated from his first experience of the full force of Turkish politics, the parliamentary by-
elections of September 1986. The main pre-coup leaders were still
theoretically banned from holding office, but were increasingly
speaking out, and their proxy parties were in play. In the poll,
support for Özal's Motherland Party tumbled from 45 per cent in
1983 to 32 per cent. Its main rival on the centre-right, the True
Path Party, guided by Süleyman Demirel, came storming in at 24
per cent. Özal told his party group: 'The 1988 general elections
have started.'

This decision to try to beat Demirel at his own game was a
fateful one. Özal was to play valiantly, and the Turkish people still
wonder which one of them won their hearts. As the 1990s became
dominated by their futile conflict on the centre-right, it was the
Turkish state that lost out. Their egotistical battles proved a major
impediment to economic reforms and stable government, pushing
disillusioned voters towards both far-right and pro-Islamic
alternatives.

Instead of sticking to the rigorous high road that had put the
Turkish economy back on the rails, and counting on the public
to support him for that, Özal gave into the temptation to work
political levers in the time-honoured manner. As the conservative
former mayor of Konya, Mehmet Keçeçiler, whispered in his ear

as new elections approached: 'Don't let's fill the treasury up just so that Demirel can spend it.' Slowly but surely, the fiscal reins began to loosen. Extra money started to irrigate the traditional areas of voter support, the farmers and state workers. The net of patronage was widened.

'When my brother took over the government in 1983, it had been sanitized by the army. Politics were no longer conducted in the traditional abrasive Turkish style. But by 1986, all the old politicians were back in the market,' Özal's younger and more politically experienced brother Korkut remembered. 'When it came to political struggle, Özal was a greenhorn. In his period as statesman-reformer, he used to say "I won't sacrifice truth for the sake of politics." But then in mid-1986 came his period to turn politician. I saw the financial indicators heating up. I remonstrated with him. He told me: "You are the only one telling me that I am doing things wrong." I told him: "I'm your only friend now." '[1]

The importance of Özal's choice of friends was soon to become clear. In November, his wife Semra called up Güneş Taner, his gung-ho associate from the early days of the Motherland Party, who had decided to keep his banking job rather than run for the 1983 parliament.

'She told me, he needs you, but he is too proud to call,' Taner, who was to become Özal's right-hand man, later recalled. 'I went over. It was midnight. Özal was reading the papers. He was not talking to me. Semra said: "Come on, both of you, talk!" We said, we are talking. Semra grabbed the papers from both of us and said, "You're not talking. Talk!" I said, "I am prepared to join him, but only as his chief of staff, at his side for every minute of the day except when he's in his bedroom." I wanted to be in on every single thing. So from January to November 1987 I was in the ascendant. We started changing the way things were done.'

The change was not for the best in what Özal was to call 'the critical year in my life'. Özal had to have triple heart by-pass surgery in February, a traumatic event that left him an occasionally more difficult, more intolerant man, someone who would increasingly rely on a kitchen cabinet of Motherland Party associates like Taner and above all his family. His brother Yusuf, an electronics engineer, was made minister in charge of the economy and his cousin Hüsnü was put in charge of the ministry of defence.

Having revived the old populist economics, by mid-1987 Özal also faced a test of his democratic credentials. Would he give in to the growing pressure to lift the military-era bans on more than 700 pre-coup politicians? Özal probably could have pushed a measure through parliament to give them their freedom. But such an act of grace would have been politically dangerous. He hesitated. For a while, he was able to shelter behind vague statements about military pressure not giving him freedom to move. But President Evren resented that, and let it be known he did not want to be blamed for keeping the bans in place. So Özal ordered a referendum, although it did not free him from his dilemma.

'Özal felt as though he was going to have to fight Demirel and company at some stage. He wanted one victory over Demirel in order to knock him off balance. He had to take them on, but he could not campaign against democracy. The party lost morale. It looked as if the end was near and we would be out. The media was supporting Demirel. What Özal didn't realize was that once they won their political freedom they would campaign against him. Özal was not prepared for this,' Taner recalled.

'Then I came up with the idea from a PR person of using orange as a negative colour: I ordered 14 kilometres of the stuff for the campaign. We ended up on a boat going from beach to beach along the Mediterranean coast flying an orange ensign, hailing people with a megaphone. "Do you want to go back to the era of shortages?" They would shout NO. "Do you want to go back to killing?" NO. "Electricity cuts?" NO. We weren't anti-Demirel. But we were forced to do it in self-defence. The idea was to keep the press from talking up Demirel.'

Taner's ideas and style were bizarre, as was his own personal T-shirt, donned after much debate at the height of Özal's non-campaign campaign. The T-shirt bore the following message to the Turkish people: 'No, No, No, Yes' – supposedly, an emphatic no to Demirel and the past, and a yes to democracy. This ambivalent position blighted Özal's reputation as a democrat, whether the bans were lifted or not. Özal had called up journalists to say he was in favour of lifting the bans, but in the end he went on television, looked Turkish voters in the eye and told them he would be voting 'no'. This turned out to reflect a strong ambivalence among many Turks towards Demirel and the old politicians as well. The result of the 6 September 1987 referendum was a razor-thin victory for lifting the bans: 50.24 per cent said yes, 49.76 per cent no.

'I voted for myself to be allowed to return to politics,' Korkut Özal noted wryly. 'But I have to say that the return of the old politicians was a bad thing.'

As the results came in, Özal realized that he had to act quickly to regain the initiative. He brushed aside the belief of Taner and others that they could win the referendum with protests and a recount. He immediately announced early general elections.

Özal took no chances. Using his majority in parliament, he pushed through an election law that stacked all the cards in his favour. He also campaigned furiously, towards the end running the constant risk that the retina would detach itself from an eye blinded by pressure that he refused to treat until after the vote. He never lost his faith in others' interest in him, however. He finally flew to see doctors in the United States when the election was over, and his present to a nonplussed President Evren afterwards was a video recording of his eye operation.

The results of the November 1987 election handed Özal a remarkable majority. With just one-third of the national vote, his Motherland Party had managed to win two-thirds of the seats in parliament. Thinking that he had restored the natural order of things, Özal felt free to stamp on the fiscal brakes to restore the economic order which had made his reputation. In February 1988, he announced a raft of austerity measures. But his political spell over the Turks had been broken, and the belt-tightening was resented. Özal had pumped election-era money into the economy, causing it to expand by 6.8 per cent in 1986 and 9.8 per cent in 1987, but now the growth rate plunged to 1.5 per cent in 1988 and 1.6 per cent in 1989. This was effectively a contraction, since the population was growing proportionately faster. The real wages of most workers fell by a quarter in 1988 alone, and state sector investment went into a decline from which it has still not recovered.

Turks became more outspoken in their discontent. One man, Kartal Demirağ, went so far as to open fire on Özal with a pistol at the Motherland Party congress in June 1988. Demirağ claimed to be acting alone on a personal suicide mission of protest against a Turkey in which people were 'walking around hungry and without water'. Demirağ however confessed that he had been trained as a commando by the Grey Wolves in the 1970s, a common recruiting ground for hitmen by Turkey's many mafias. The Özal family believed it was a plot, perhaps connected to cigarette smugglers put out of business by the import reforms. Whatever the truth, Demirağ fired from a distance, and by his own admission, he was not much of a shot. Before his pistol jammed on the third round, he had only hit Özal in the thumb. Unfortunately, many more people were wounded as police opened fire in the panic: Demirağ was hit four times. Özal quickly recovered. He went back to the tribune to finish his speech to wild applause from the party faithful.

Özal was not so lucky with the Turkish public, which gave its response to the situation in the local elections of March 1989. By then its mood was punishing. The Motherland's share of the vote plummeted to 21 per cent. The relatively popular and active Motherland Party mayor of Istanbul, Bedrettin Dalan, was left with a victory banquet laid on at the city hall by a five-star hotel, and nobody to eat it. Secretaries wept loudly in the background. The surprise winner, Social Democrat outsider Nurettin Sözen, was also astonished, as were many inhabitants of the city.

The Özal family gathered to listen to the election results come in. Initially the atmosphere, according to an account by columnist Hasan Cemal, was high-spirited, full of jokes and bravado. But there was a strange lack of callers after the polls closed. Silence fell on the room. Semra Özal sat in a corner doing puzzles in a newspaper weekend supplement, sipping at her whisky. Güneş Taner puffed at a big cigar, his hands in back pockets, studying a point on the wall. Turgut was silent, drinking cognac from time to time, watching the television. The guests began to bicker: building contractor Selim Edes, later disgraced in a corruption scandal, suggested that a recent dispute over women wearing headscarves to university had cost them the election. Korkut Özal snapped back that the headscarf suited Turkish women. The secularist-minded Semra shot her brother-in-law a dirty look. It was not a happy evening.[2]

Özal soon pulled himself together. He declared at the time that he could 'never, never, never go into opposition', although years later he would sometimes muse that it might have been better to do so. His ambition was set on something much higher: the presidency of Turkey, to be vacated by Kenan Evren seven months later. Getting on the phone, Özal gave directives that local elections were to be presented as completely separate from national ones. There were to be no resignations or admissions of defeat.

Özal's determination to overcome this political setback and to prove himself a great leader had tragic consequences for one group of people. The one million ethnic Turks of Bulgaria, a relic of the settlers of early Ottoman times who by the 1980s formed some 10 per cent of the population, had since 1984 been subjected to a campaign called 'Rebirth' as the Communist authorities tried to assimilate them into Christian Slav culture, changing names from Muhammad to Christos, banning circumcision ceremonies and even forbidding the use of the Turkish language. Protests against this reached a height in 1989 as the Bulgarian Turks, like many in the old Eastern Bloc, scented freedom coming. Mounting demonstrations in May 1989 were harshly suppressed. Turkey protested. Bulgarian leader Todor Zhivkov retorted that Turkey could have all its ethnic Turks if it wanted, adding some pointed comments about Turkey's treatment of its ethnic Kurds. Turkey opened its gates, with Özal proudly announcing that he had called Zhivkov's bluff.

Nothing, unfortunately, could have been further from the truth. A kind of hysteria seized the ethnic Turks, who knew little of Turkey or the West save that previous immigrants seemed to have done well in the forbidden paradise outside. Whole villages and quarters of towns applied for passports, and nationalist activists went from door to door to persuade everyone to leave. Anyone wanting to stay was branded a traitor, and no members of extended families wanted to be left behind. Thousands came, then tens of thousands. Soon the Turkey–Bulgaria border presented a latter-day vision of all the Balkan refugee movements of the past, as small Soviet-made cars and even carts arrived with short, stocky, weather-beaten villagers surrounded with their belongings – bedsteads, mattresses, pickled vegetables, wooden buckets and even village water-pumps.

The Turkish authorities began to get cold feet: not even their prodigious powers of crisis organization could deal with the 330,000 people who arrived within several weeks. The first refugees found relatives initially welcoming and sympathetic. Industrialists, keen to employ their disciplined working skills, sent buses to the border to bring them back to temporary encampments set up near their factories. Most active was the city of Bursa, a car- and textile-making centre built by generations of Balkan refugees and, paradoxically, home to the mosque of Sultan 'Thunderbolt' Beyazıt, erected after the battle of Nicopolis that confirmed the early Ottoman grip on the Balkans in 1396. But soon everybody was overwhelmed. The high hopes of the refugees gave way to a crushing sense of disappointment.

Most obviously distressed were those who were sent to camps or townships in the east thought to be in need of more well-qualified 'Turks', for instance the ethnically Kurdish town of Van, where hotels were requisitioned for the refugees. The new arrivals were cursed openly in the street, and most left as quickly as they could for the western Turkish towns where they had originally wanted to go. A more subtle problem was the clash of cultures when well-educated young Bulgarian Turks, without money, found themselves forced to live in the rougher areas of Istanbul. Young women used to the boulevards and summer evening cafés of Bulgaria found themselves in tight-packed urban jungles where they were either frowned at by traditional Islamists or gawped and grabbed at by *magandas*, a 1980s term for the macho, gold-braceleted, unbuttoned Turkish street male.

More fundamentally, the Bulgarian Turks had made the same mistake that the Turkic Muslims of the Soviet Union were to make as they rushed into independence in 1991. Locked up behind the Iron Curtain for generations, occasionally catching rich glimpses of the West, no longer believing their own state propaganda, they thought that a new life in a non-Communist Bloc country would give them all the old certainties socialism had given them, as well as new freedom and new wealth. Instead, they found themselves grappling for the bottom rung of the capitalist ladder. Few had more than the most threadbare safety nets of support from distant relatives or the Turkish state.

Özal did not know what to do. He organized a 'mass' demonstration on Taksim Square designed to whip up martial spirit, more to show that he was doing something on behalf of the Turks than an indication of possible military action against Bulgaria. The state television channel broadcast mournful soloists serenading the antique armaments, Ottoman campaign tents and blood-stained shirts in Istanbul's military museum. But none of this did any good, and the Özal government was forced to admit silently that it was Zhivkov who had called its bluff. The Turks began to limit the flow of refugees.

Indignity was compounded by humiliation as many of the refugees started to return to Bulgaria. The packed trains that had drained the east Bulgarian countryside of its inhabitants had been dubbed by the Turks the 'trains of shame'. The real shame could now be seen in the faces of those refugees heading back to Bulgaria, hounded by the insults of the Turkish border guards who had only recently welcomed them with militaristic music blaring from the tannoys. A few even kissed the Bulgarian soil. Others went to those 'trains of shame' still headed for Turkey to try to explain to people what to expect. But there was no stopping the flood: after all these years of thinking and talking of Turkey as the promised land, everybody had to see it for themselves.

In the end, about half of the 330,000 refugees went back to the familiarity of their grid-planned towns and neat collective villages in Bulgaria. But, despite the relative open-mindedness of the post-Communist Bulgarian government, many no longer found happiness there either, and once they had made sufficient preparations, returned again to Turkey.

Turgut Özal never acknowledged the traumas he had inflicted on the Bulgarian Turks in that terrible summer of 1989. His eye was firmly fixed on Turkey's ultimate political prize, the presidency. Naim Süleymanoğlu, the diminutive Bulgarian Turkish weightlifter, was to learn the priorities of the man who had spent a million dollars from a state secret service fund in the 1980s to buy him from the Bulgarian government. As soon as Süleymanoğlu won his gold medal at Seoul in 1992, Özal ordered him to fly back to appear with him at a political rally; Süleymanoğlu could only faintly protest to reporters that he would have liked at least a day to see the rest of the Olympic Games.

Özal did not have to be subtle in his plan of campaign for the presidency. In theory, if he wanted it, and his party supported him, he could have it. A two-thirds majority vote in parliament was needed to win in the first two rounds, but the Motherland Party had the absolute majority that the constitution required in the final round of voting.

The atmosphere in parliament that day in October 1989 was tense as Özal arrived between its heavy, square columns with a swarm of followers in tow. The opposition boycotted the proceedings, their deputies sitting outside the chamber in the wings. The Motherland deputies went through the voting on their own. It all felt wrong. But by the time he had reached a celebration party in Atatürk's pink palace on Çankaya hill, the cloud on Özal's brow had cleared. Standing side by side with his wife Semra on the terrace, he turned round, surveyed the grey concrete blocks of the city spreading over the plateau and hills below, and told a visitor: 'Don't worry. Everything will be all right.'[3]

But all was not well. The half-empty parliamentary chamber symbolized a sense that the Özal presidency lacked legitimacy. Özal himself felt it, cutting the normal live television coverage of parliament so that the empty seats would not be seen. Even so, he continued to press ahead with his plans for a presidential system and deployed the theoretically wide powers of the presidency to maximum effect. Significantly, the Turkish bureaucracy began to seize up, having a rhythm all its own that slows during times of domestic uncertainty as it waits to see which way the political wind will blow.

Özal could not let go of his Motherland Party, and the party grew restive. Pulling the strings he still controlled in the party, Özal managed to install Yıldırım Akbulut as leader and prime minister. A bluff, slow-spoken lawyer from Erzincan, an eastern Turkish town regularly devastated by earthquakes, Akbulut never attempted to shake Özal's grip on power. Though a man of no obvious vices, his puppet status rendered him such a figure of public ridicule that a whole class of jokes was named after him. Anthologies of these jokes sold out edition after edition.

'Every man eats yoghurt in his own way,' Özal said of Akbulut, trying to allay disquiet. But things were clearly getting out of hand. In parliament, scornful deputies hurled yellow-bound copies of the government programme at Akbulut during the vote of confidence debate on his government. Everybody knew that Özal was still in charge. Ministers came and went at Özal's say-so. Monthly 'briefings' in his Çankaya palace dealt with the economy, although Güneş Taner claimed to be the power behind the throne. 'Everything was in my hands. I was the *éminence grise*. Akbulut was prime minister in name only. Özal could rule through me very easily. We would meet from midnight to four a.m. every single day. Now there are six ministers doing the job I did alone,' Taner said.

Not everybody in the Motherland was happy as the party's popularity slumped to about 12 per cent in two newspaper polls in early 1990. Özal's only political base of support was slipping away. Sensing opposition to his one-man style of rule, and later trying to capitalize on his strong image as a national leader following the Gulf War crisis of 1991, he and his wife Semra embarked on an ultimately damaging course.

To some Turks it looked as if he was setting up an Ottoman-like court; others simply called it nepotism. Not content with frequent ministerial assignments for his relatives, Özal encouraged his son Ahmet to set up Turkey's first private television station, broadcasting by satellite from Europe after 1989 through a loophole in the Turkish telecommunications law. Star Television turned out to be an ice-breaker for an information revolution in Turkey; but it was also a thoroughly political move. Not content with that, in 1991 Semra Özal put her name forward for the chairmanship of the key Istanbul branch of the Motherland Party.

Semra had long acted as Özal's chief confidante and her friends credited her with a lively intelligence capable of stiffening her husband's resolve when it wavered. The daughter of an Istanbul ship welder, she had quickly acquired a taste for the more expensive things in life. Her Foundation for the Empowering of

Turkish Women (Türk Kadın Güçlendirme Vakfı) may have been set up with the best intentions, but it soon became a society of flatterers dubbed the 'daisies' by the Turkish press. By 1991, it was throwing lavish parties, but only had four modest vehicles, one clinic and a slick news-sheet heavily subsidized by state bank advertising.

Like Turgut Özal, Semra was tough, ambitious and a media-flirt. As her political ambitions emerged, she cast herself in the role of the Kemalist republican standing against the party's 'Holy Alliance' of right-wing nationalists and Islamic conservatives. Pro-Islamic politicians like Korkut Özal were appalled. 'Semra was a bad influence,' he said. 'She was even toying with the idea of becoming overall party leader. They tried to change this party from a broad base to what they called liberal. The Motherland lost its identity. We were moderate, tolerant and very progressive, but had respect for Islamic values. If you don't respect these values, you can't engage in politics in Turkey.'[4]

Semra battled royally for the Istanbul post. For days before the branch presidency ballot in March 1991, ministers had been in Istanbul to twist every available delegate's arm and to distribute whatever their patronage could deliver: beepers, mobile phones or choice job transfers for relatives in the bureaucracy. While the President's wife led the campaign from the top floor of a luxury Istanbul hotel, her opponent used the modest Motherland branch office in the conservative district of Fatih around Mehmet the Conqueror's mosque. But despite his disadvantages, he ran a very close race on the night.

What a night it was. The Hilton Convention Centre was filled with smoke, men in suits and the scent of sweat. Delegates queued to kiss Mrs Özal's hand. A bank of television sets played lurid videotapes of Özal-era economic achievements. Poems blared out with lines like 'Semra Mother, God gave you light, in your hands roses open'. When opponents started to shout demands for her resignation, the sound system was simply turned up to full volume belting out the song 'My paradise country, how lovely is Turkey'. A batch of thirty extra votes, enough to change the result, found their way into the ballot box. Riot police, directed by the operatically tiny Istanbul police chief of the day, had to calm passions that broke out into fist-fights. In another corner, victorious pro-Semra delegates held hands, hopped and danced in traditional Turkish lines. And, monitoring the scene on a close-circuit television in a nearby hotel suite was President Turgut Özal himself.

'You'll get used to me,' was the phrase that Özal famously used

to try to calm voices in the Turkish republican establishment raised
in outrage at such scenes. But Özal could not get used to the way
the opposition grew bolder in its calls for impeachment. 'It doesn't
trouble me much,' Özal insisted.[5] A high-flying young army lieutenant discovered differently when he tried to send a telegram to
Özal complaining about the Motherland's concessions to Islamic
education, corruption, and the collapse of the state health system.
Finally he stated his belief that Özal was not a worthy heir of
Atatürk: 'You said I'd get used to it, but, Mr Turgut Özal, I have not
got used to you being president.' The telegram was sent straight to
the state prosecutor. The lieutenant was frog-marched out of his
unit and committed to hospital for psychiatric treatment.

Seeking to buy back popularity in 1990, Özal's men forced Akbulut
to push through an extravagant series of public sector wage rises.
The young and shallow stock-market, urged on by an advertising
campaign featuring Larry Hagman re-creating his role as JR, a
ruthless oilman in the American television series *Dallas*, was
encouraged to continue a storming rise that had started in 1989.
But while the main goals of the Özal revolution of the early 1980s
had been achieved by 1989, including key legislation on con-
vertibility, one item remained stubbornly difficult to solve: privatization of the state sector industries.

Turgut Özal had been one of the first leaders of developing
countries to espouse publicly the idea of selling off government-
owned industries to relieve the strain on the state budget. It was
a major topic in his first administration from 1984 on. Even so,
the first privatization came only in 1988, when 22 per cent of a
telecommunications company was sold off. 'The bureaucracy was
not ready for it. The market did not have the money or resources
to take it on. The only option was investment from outside the
country. But they also thought Turkey was not ready,' said Güneş
Taner.

Institutional and political suspicion within Turkey of such
foreign investment dates back to memories of economic subservi-
ence to the system of capitulations in the Ottoman era. Süleyman
Demirel spotted a chance to humble his former protégé. In 1989,
he and his True Path Party deliberately derailed the programme
by opening a court case to block the sale of five state-owned cement
factories. He admitted candidly to foreign diplomats that he was
only doing it to cut Özal down to size. Unfortunately it set a
precedent that was to be followed again and again. As a result,

while investment banks got rich advising the Turkish government
what to do, a foreign investor needed nerves of steel to venture
into the legal and political minefield. Turkey missed a golden
chance to cash in. In the early 1990s, Eastern Europe arrived
in the market-place with its own forceful privatization programmes.
And although Özal invented a model called Build-Operate-Transfer
(BOT), essentially a revival of the nineteenth-century idea of the
commercial concession, it saw more service when copied outside
Turkey than in it.

Meanwhile most Turkish state companies became less attractive,
starved of investment and demoralized as they waited to be privat-
ized. A few benefited from management reforms: some went back
into profit and the manager of the small Etibank proudly
announced that, after two years' work, he could now actually read
the accounts. The state's consolidated budget saw little benefit.
Most of the privatization income went towards preparing other
companies for sale, and only amounted to 2.8 billion dollars after
eleven years of talk.

The legal wrangle resulted partly from Özal's notoriously sloppy
legislative style. Bureaucrats remembered him taking momentous
decisions while being served breakfast by Semra in her house-coat
as his youngest son played with a train set on the floor. Özal
even felt free to comment: 'What does it matter if we breach the
constitution just once?' But it did matter. In his first four and a
half years in power, out of 364 laws thirty-seven were ruled invalid
by the Constitutional Court.[6]

Instead of starting divestment with the small, easily sold parts
of the more than 400 state-owned enterprises, politicians like Özal,
and later Tansu Çiller, were often tempted to sell off huge, eye-
catching items like the state telecommunications monopoly that
immediately aroused Turkish fears of corruption and possible
foreign domination. Even more important was institutional resistance among both politicians and the bureaucracy to the dismant-
ling of the state structure that fed them and their networks of
patronage. The net result was that, for most of the 1980s and early
1990s, it would have cost the state less to close down the perilous
Zonguldak coalmines on the Black Sea coast and pay the 30,000
miners to stay at home than to keep them running (a freeze on
hiring and restructuring later improved the picture). In the south,
a private steel mill could operate beside a state steelmaker and
produce more steel with a fraction of the personnel, at the same
time as profiting hugely from artificially high prices maintained
by the state to keep its own steel mill profitable.

As a result, the state's share in economic output did not immediately decline: it was rather that many state factories withered on the branch while the private sector flourished, hiring their best personnel, attracting new investment. There are no official statistics to determine how much of Turkey's overall economy is in state or private hands. The best indicator available shows that while the state controlled one-third of the output of manufacturing industry in 1986, that figure had fallen to one-quarter by 1992.[7]

But the state still had a massive, dragging presence. By mid-1996, a special report in the newspaper *Sabah* showed that 1,830,366 workers were on the state's permanent payroll, 261,000 working as teaboys, cleaners and messengers. State factories produced pickles and ice-cream, state companies ran restaurants and hotels. The state owned 71,000 buildings, 298,000 official lodgings and 152,000 vehicles. Ankara has new boulevards lined with huge Orwellian ministries full of people paid a pittance for doing virtually nothing. Similarly, monstrous concrete government houses rose from the heart of provincial towns. 'The Turkish state is like an Ottoman princeling frittering away his huge inheritance while living in poverty himself, someone who has got so fat they puff when they walk, who has arteries constantly liable to get blocked, who has high blood pressure and a cholesterol level that is at danger point,' the *Sabah* report concluded.

The problem is not that the state is poor: various reports estimate that between one-half and two-thirds of all land in Turkey is owned by the state. Not counting forests and mountains, the *Sabah* report counted 206,000 plots of land, 877,450 farms and fields and 59,000 orchards. One newspaper estimated that 16 per cent of the capital, Ankara, is owned by the military alone. The problem is simply that as in Ottoman times, to reduce the size of the state would involve putting thousands of people out of work, and eliminate the possibility of paying off one's supporters with jobs. A well-worn Turkish saying has it that 'the state's wealth is a sea; he who does not eat of it is a pig.' So instead of selling off assets, running down debts and laying off workers, the state machine carries on taxing and borrowing money to keep itself going.

This inertia is closely linked to the politicians' conception of democracy. Not content with allowing themselves spending binges before elections and fiscal crash diets afterwards, they openly used the state sector as a kind of employment agency for their constituencies. Stories abound of busloads of party workers turning up at factory gates to be put on payrolls at the orders of a minister or even a parliamentary deputy. If the factory manager resists, the politician simply has him or her transferred. The huge state banks were an even more tempting source of abuse, since the right kind of pressure could produce a loan that, in some circumstances, nobody ever expected to be paid back. 'Even those politicians who seem most strongly in favour of privatization are reluctant to go ahead, just in case they need the state economic enterprises in the future,' said Uğur Bayar, head of the Privatization Administration Office.[8]

The period after 1989 would have been difficult at the best of times. A drought hit Turkey, obliging Istanbul residents to queue through the night to stock up with water at old Ottoman fountains, forcing hospitals to send patients home and adding a billion dollars to the country's wheat import bill. This was followed in 1990 by the devastating effects on Turkish patterns of trade of the Gulf War. On top of that, serious labour unrest hit the country. In January 1991, about one and a half million unionized workers refused to go to work – resulting, effectively, in the country's first, if brief, general strike. Turks were also broadly sympathetic to an epic march on Ankara undertaken in January 1991 by tens of thousands of miners from Zonguldak wanting the government to raise their pay of between five and ten dollars a day.

By 1991, the ratio of Turkey's budget deficit to GNP had soared to 12.6 per cent. The governor of the Central Bank was openly warning the state not to carry on printing money to cover the deficit. The state's dire need for cash also forced up interest rates. This in turn made it more profitable for many companies simply to buy treasury bills rather than to invest. Foreign investors started betting on the lira, taking advantage of huge real rates of return as the Turkish government was forced to keep the lira unnaturally strong against the dollar. A massive correction, financial crisis and recession was to result in January 1994 – a financial crisis in which the lira's value halved in a matter of months.

Luckily for Turkey, by 1994 the early reforms brought in by Turgut Özal the technocrat and his team had themselves become institutionalized. The foreign exchange and banking freedoms survived, even though, perhaps not too mysteriously, the government of the day allowed banks in which the Özal family had interests to go to the wall. Foreign currency reserves plunged from 12.5 billion dollars to 2.5 billion dollars. Planeloads of foreign currency had to be flown in to supply anxious depositors who withdrew their money and put it under their beds (Turkish mattresses are still made with a special zip for valuables). But those who panicked were the ones who lost out. Most people who kept their nerve and had chosen reputable banks over those who gave unnaturally high rates of interest did well. Soon currency reserves were back to normal again.

By the later 1990s, the Turkish jury was still out on Özal and his methods. In previous eras under the republic when the bureaucracy was in full control, little may have got done, but there were rules that prevented serious abuse of the system for personal advantage. An obvious change in personal circumstances would also have been quickly noticed. Özal, however, had slashed away at the bureaucratic red tape which he believed was holding the Turkish economy prisoner. His era came to symbolize a get-rich-quick mentality called 'turning the corner' in Turkish.

Özal himself, like Süleyman Demirel, seemed more interested in power than personal riches, but many around him, whether in his family or close by, seemed to have become rich very fast. After Özal's death and the family's fall from grace, many of them became entangled in a network of court cases, scandals and underhand dealings.

Turgut Özal boasted of using the economic power of state advertising for personal political advantage, forcing an editorial writer off one struggling pro-Demirel newspaper and telling a Motherland congress, 'I know when to put up the price of newsprint.' His wife Semra was once found to have arranged for a military helicopter to bring her tailor to her summer residence. His eldest son Ahmet was outwitted in his television partnership, fell deeply into debt, was charged with corruption and for a year felt obliged to live in exile. His daughter married briefly a rock drummer and made the mistake of accepting the gift of a Jaguar car. His youngest son Efe became a stockbroker in a market where the state could have a massive impact, and he was soon living in a luxury flat by the Bosphorus. On their own, perhaps none of these events would have raised many eyebrows. But the cumulative effect could not be brushed aside by Özal's riposte: 'I am a father. What father can make his children do exactly as he says?' None of the scandals, however, had a more devastating impact on the Özals' reputation in Turkey than the affair known as Civangate.

The Civangate affair revolved round loans given by a big state housing bank, Emlakbank, to a close associate of Özal's, Selim Edes, and the kickbacks paid in gratitude for those loans. The scandal takes its name from the bank's manager, Engin Civan, who took over in 1989 from Bülent Şemiler, one of the young US-educated 'princes' brought back to Turkey by Turgut Özal. Özal was forced to move Şemiler on from the bank after he had fallen foul of the Motherland Party élite. Özal did not move him very far; he was often to be found in the president's entourage and was later the co-defendant in a big bribery case with Özal's son Ahmet. In 1989, before handing over to Civan, Şemiler had been outspoken about the way business was being done.

> Here in Turkey we have eleven government banks. Even the Soviet Union only has two. And it takes six months simply to work out the interest on some of the bad loans. Basically, only people who can't borrow from the private sector come to us. Members of parliament are forever trying to get people jobs, or exert pressure for new investments. Refusals bring complaints. Eventually a negative picture builds up of any manager who does not play along.

For several months during one particularly tense period, after he tried to start forcing people to pay their debts by seizing houses, yachts, antiques and buildings, Şemiler had to resort to carrying a pistol.[9]

Şemiler's successor at Emlakbank, Engin Civan, was also to learn the benefits of carrying a pistol, just as he was to come to regret his association with the Özal family and their circle, particularly the contractor Selim Edes. Property business between Emlakbank and Edes went sour. By the end of the tragi-comic drama – at one point television cameras filmed the arrest of a mafia gunman planning a courtroom assassination wearing a wig, false glasses and a lawyer's gown while carrying a gun smuggled into court in his female accomplice's underwear – both Civan and Edes had to serve brief stints in gaol. Civan had also been shot and wounded by a hitman, whose mafia godfather hinted that his services had been requested by the Özals. The mafia godfather's daughter then publicly alleged that it was in fact Semra Özal who made the request, but, only days before she was due to testify in court, she was shot dead at Turkey's main ski resort, Uludağ, near Bursa.

Semra Özal still appears in Istanbul society, resplendently trim after visits to clinics in the United States. The former businessmen-courtiers and their 'daisy' wives who once queued to be photographed kneeling in front of her treat her with some wariness, however. They are probably right to take care. Semra likes pistols too. As she told one interviewer, 'I am a good shot. I sometimes go shooting with Turgut, sometimes alone. I like Magnums a lot, and I always carry a little gun around with me in my bag. God forbid, but anything can happen in this world.'[10]

Turgut Özal had one final line of defence against those critics who taunted him with corruption during his period of office. Corruption, his argument ran, happened everywhere all the time, and at least he, Özal, had done a lot for his country. Coming from the liberal right of Turkish politics, Özal would always take aim, in turn, at the Inönü family, particularly Ismet Inönü's brother and what he called the 'skyscrapers' built by the family in the gardens of the grace-and-favour 'Pink Kiosk' given to Ismet Pasha.[11] There is indeed no lack of examples of the seamy side of Turkish politics, although the word 'mafia' has become diluted to mean almost any business in which a handshake carries more weight than a tax-registered contract. One businessman-godfather plausibly claimed an intimate acquaintance with the fortunes of Süleyman Demirel, and Süleyman's brother Hacı Ali became a rich man with a wide network of contacts. When a famous car-dealer and loan shark was killed in a hail of bullets in Ankara in 1996, Hacı Ali was on the scene within an hour.

Perhaps encouraged by such examples at the top, corruption has become a chronic and integral part of Turks' perception of government. *Rüşvet*, ranging from a small present to a cash bribe, can smooth and quicken many transactions relying on the power of officials – from postmen and policemen to judges and ministers. A whole class of *komisyoncus* exists to oil the wheels in places such as customs offices. On country roads, particularly in the east, policemen can be seen holding up traffic almost like highwaymen, pocketing bribes or demanding goods-in-lieu from ice-creams to tea-sets. The policeman, like other officials, does this because his colleagues do too and it helps him make ends meet. Once the bribe has been asked for, the driver, while cursing under his breath, is ultimately relieved to pay it because it is cheaper than a fine. He knows his car or its documents would probably not stand up to inspection, since it is almost impossible to have all one's papers completely in order in Turkey.

This vicious circle is deeply engrained. Nothing happens to break it because so many people are involved and are tarred with the same brush, from the lowest to the highest in the land. Neighbours will rarely protest at an illegal building extension because they may fear retribution against their illegally glassed-in balcony; if the good citizens persist in their protest, a fiercely brandished pistol can see off the municipality's *zabıta* guards and even gendarmerie reinforcements with semi-automatic rifles. Even in parliament, self-righteous Islamist leader and millionaire Necmettin Erbakan cut a deal in 1996 with his richer rival, the conservative Tansu Çiller, not to investigate how they both came by their fortunes. Unfortunately, because laws have become so antiquated, because few expect justice from the courts, and because nobody cares to involve the much-feared police unless they positively have to, this state of affairs is not likely to change unless a truly honest, strong leader takes power.

'If there is corruption, there cannot be justice. If there is no justice, there can be no competition. And if there is no competition, there can be no quality in any area of life. In societies where corruption is a semi-official tax, why is there terrorism and torture? It's all part of the same vicious circle,' trumpeted the daily newspaper *Milliyet* as it launched a clean-hands campaign, one of Turkish society's periodic attempts, like a smoker trying to give up cigarettes, to purge itself of the habit.

Meanwhile, life in Turkey goes on. An importer of Japanese electronic goods even factored into his budgets a calculation for *rüşvet* bribes which ran to about two per cent of his business costs. Perhaps to compensate for these unpleasant necessities in public life, most Turks take great pride in personal honesty. Taxi-drivers, for instance, will often go to great lengths to return lost valuables and dropped wallets, and there are legendary stories about the code of honour of individual members of the Turkish mafia.

By early 1990, tolerance was wearing thin both among the people and the élite for Turgut Özal and what the media called Semra's *hasbahçe*, or palace garden. High officials avoided attending ceremonies with him; at one, a lowly mayor refused to stand in his presence, and was duly relieved of his post. At a speech in an Ankara hotel, Özal had to rebuke his chattering audience with the words, 'Even in the country they listen better than you.' In the bureaucracy, his first Central Bank governor talked of 'reform fatigue'. One of Özal's ministers, Kamran Inan, admitted that power had simply corrupted the government. 'We are a young people. Things go out of fashion easily,' he said. 'You can't hold the stage for ever when people are looking for change.' Özal had been preaching too long a new-fangled form of economics that ordinary people did not understand, and, by 1991, these innovations had not yet appeared to have done them much good. In reaction, when they got the chance to have their say in the elections of October 1991, the electorate were to turn back to old names.

Özal tried to tinker with the Motherland Party, ousting Yıldırım Akbulut and tilting the balance towards the 43-year-old Mesut Yılmaz at a 1991 party congress. The smell of defeat was almost tangible among the provincial delegates squatting to eat their *döner kebab* sandwiches. From the platform, pious undertakings to open up Ayasofya to Muslim prayer competed with a stand-up fight between a burly minister of state and the minister of culture. The dour Yılmaz was a disappointment too. Calling early elections could not postpone the fate long evident for all to see.

'Who will you vote for, donkey?' asked Ismail Gülgeç of the ass that represented the populace in one of his regular cartoons for the daily newspaper *Cumhuriyet*. 'Well, as you know, lots has been done in the past ten years. We've jumped an age, we're twice as well off, the villages now have telephones and the workers now have megaphones,' the donkey replied. 'Still, I think I'll do something asinine again and give my vote to the opposition.'

And so the people did. At the poll of 20 October 1991, the vote splintered between the parties. The Motherland vote fell to 24 per cent, down from 32 per cent in 1987. Süleyman Demirel's True Path Party came first with 27.4 per cent, after beguiling the electorate with promises of a new start on human rights and the keys to a car and a house for every family. Demirel was able to put together a coalition with the Social Democrats of the gentlemanly Erdal Inönü, the son of Ismet Pasha, a university administrator and nuclear physicist.

The Demirel–Inönü government soft-pedalled on its early promise to oust President Özal, but steadily chipped away at his authority. At the time of his unexpected death in April 1993, Özal seemed likely to lose several of his important powers of official appointment. Angry with Yılmaz, who had turned against him, he was talking half-heartedly to his intimates of resigning to form a new party and starting again.

In reality, the Özal era in domestic politics had been in a state of suspended animation ever since his disputed election to the presidency. The obstinacy, egotism and short-sightedness he showed as he clung to office is something of a national political sickness. The fact that he had been able to hold on to power for so long was largely due to unforeseen factors that both made him famous in the outside world and also gave him greater legitimacy at home. He was saved by his seizure of the initiative when, on 2 August 1990, Saddam Hussein's armies rolled into Kuwait and set in train the Gulf War crisis, a regional realignment that was also to work a major change in Turkey's perception of its place in the Middle East.

14

A Place at the Feast

It's not a wedding and it's not a feast day. So
why is my uncle kissing me?

Turkish saying

SADDAM HUSSEIN'S INVASION of Kuwait in August 1990 was
a godsend for Turgut Özal, and the Turkish president rose to
the occasion. Exploiting a sense of national emergency, he
transcended his domestic failings and growing unpopularity. He
dispensed with the normal cabinet process as he despatched
the nominal head of the executive, the stoical Prime Minister
Akbulut, to open sugar factories in the east. Özal commandeered
the crisis to inject the same dynamism and hungry ambition
into Turkey's foreign policy that he had brought to the Turkish
economy. Frustrated in his application for full membership of
the European Community, he now wanted Turkey to take a
position in the Middle East, to throw its new-found economic
weight around a little. This activism was a radical departure from
the strait-jacketed neutrality of the foreign ministry bureaucrats
in charge of Middle Eastern affairs. As ever, Özal felt obliged to
dress his personal policy-making up with the sacred legitimacy of
Atatürk.

There are two political lines [Özal would say]. One is Atatürk's, the
other Ismet Inönü's. They are very different. Atatürk's line is reformist,
attacking, risk-taking. It brought results like the taking of Hatay [from
Syria]. Ismet Inönü's is the line of the *status quo*: don't interfere with
them, they won't interfere with you. We have chosen Atatürk's line.
If Ismet Pasha had entered the Second World War, Turkey could have
had the Dodecanese Islands. The West offered them to us. What we

are saying is this: let's not be with the losers all the time. Let's be with the winners.[1]

Özal's motives were mixed. There was an element of the gambler in him: he talked of betting one and getting five times, even twenty times the return on his political investment. He wanted to send Turkish troops to join the coalition forces in the Gulf and to open up a second front against Iraq. He was only stopped by deep resistance in the military, the bureaucracy, the media and the population as a whole. He may well also have wanted to annex the oil-rich provinces of northern Iraq. He needed to win the domestic accolades that would flow from military success. He longed for Turkey and himself to be seen as regional and even world players. Posing in a tank as the war approached, he told reporters, 'No, I'm not going on pilgrimage to Mecca. I'm taking the short cut to the European Community.'

Özal spared no effort to find what one of his cabinet ministers called 'a place at the victory feast, not on the menu'. He stumped up and down the country trying to stir up the warlike spirit of the Turks. 'The ground shakes when we move,' Özal said as Turkish troops massed on the Iraqi border a month before the outbreak of war in January 1991. He stepped up his rhetoric as hostilities began. 'We have got used to luxury and we don't want to lose it. But war is nothing to be afraid of. Don't forget we are a martial nation,' he said in one speech. 'Saddam executed the Kirkuk Turks, he crushed the Kurds, he used poison gas. Won't he do the same to us next? We must remove such dangerous regimes. Let's finish it quickly and break the man's back,' he told a group of provincial businessmen.

It was not only Turkey's diplomats who were horrified by such aggressive talk, especially in relation to the Middle East. Anti-war meetings attracted considerable support. Famed Turkish Kurd novelist Yaşar Kemal made an impassioned speech, recalling the Ottoman's First World War retreat from Yemen and reminding his listeners: 'The Arabian deserts are already full of our bones.' Retired Turkish generals protested that Atatürk's foreign policy was based on Turkey keeping itself to itself, that the army was trained for defence not attack, and that if Turkey went out on a limb it would find itself alone. The United States, they warned with some prescience, had no long-term plan other than its tactical objective in Kuwait. Opinion polls showed that between 68 and 90 per cent of the population opposed entry into the war. On one January day, nine out of ten columnists in the Kemalist daily

Cumhuriyet attacked the approaching conflict, with front-page editorialist Uğur Mumcu equating the Americans to the Germans who tricked the Ottomans into the First World War.

First the foreign minister, then the defence minister, then Chief of General Staff Necip Torumtay resigned over both the content and form of Özal's management of the crisis. His autocratic style was clear from the moment he took the first action of the conflict, closing down a double oil pipeline that carried half of Iraq's oil exports. 'I learned of this decision through an announcement on television. So did the foreign minister. Thus we entered a highly critical period with an idiosyncratic, centrist attitude that brushed the established order aside,' General Torumtay later wrote in his memoirs. 'Prime Minister Akbulut maintained a stony silence at crisis meetings. He did not issue any orders for the chief of staff to comply with. Özal worked from watching TV and chatting with heads of state, with no knowledge of military matters. He insisted that the army push into northern Iraq. He believed that the Iraqi regime would fall and Turkey would benefit.'

Özal was unrepentant, declaring, 'We need generals who will fight.' Even in the cabinet, on the few occasions when it was allowed a say, some people tried to remind him of Enver Pasha's reckless expedition to the Caucasus in 1914. 'There was a lot of shouting,' Güneş Taner remembered. 'Özal wanted a second front, to be at the "table of the wolves" when they were dividing the spoils after the battle. The Americans were all for it. I was strongly opposed, and spoke against it in the cabinet. The hard part, I said, was not fighting a war, but afterwards. We were gambling that we were going to get the oil in Kirkuk. But there was not enough oil left to make it worthwhile. The United Nations, too, would insist we get out, and because of internal politics, we wouldn't be able to. And where was the money to do it with? It was suicide. On top of that, the General Staff plan forecast that 40,000–50,000 Turkish lives would be lost in an offensive.'

This institutional opposition prevented Özal from opening a land front, although when the air bombardment of Baghdad started Allied warplanes were promptly given permission to bomb targets from the big NATO airbase at Incirlik near Adana. But it was significant that, for the first time, it was the Turkish chief of staff who resigned over a disagreement with the politicians, not the army that forced the civilian ruler out of office. Indeed, Özal's posturing never completely lost him support. Despite public opposition to Turkish involvement, polls showed that nearly two-thirds of the people supported the Allied intervention and believed that

Saddam Hussein and his long-range missiles were a threat to the country. Even though it had the biggest standing army in NATO after the United States, Turkey in the mid-1990s could only field under-equipped aircraft capable of delivering a warhead no further than 50 kilometres.

Özal was also not alone in defending one aspect of Turkey's growing regional impact – an aspect that could not avoid its being drawn into active political engagement with the Middle East: the growing Turkish determination to control and exploit its water resources. This was an issue that had proven potential to unite Turkey's Arab rivals, especially Syria and Iraq. On the day after the Iraqi invasion of Kuwait, Turkey's state television echoed general relief when it gloated, 'The Arab bloc opposed to us on the water question has effectively split up.' Almost everybody in the Turkish establishment, in the military, politics and bureaucracy, is proud of their role in building the $32-billion-dollar, 22-dam South-East Anatolian Project (GAP) to harness the headwaters of the Tigris–Euphrates river system. Even General Evren pushed ahead with the project during his austere period of military rule between 1980 and 1983, believing that the war between Iraq and Iran provided a unique opportunity for Turkey to act while other Middle Eastern states were busy elsewhere.

About 70 per cent of the flow of the two rivers comes from Turkish territory, although since antiquity, populations living in Syria and Iraq have consumed most of the water – a volume equivalent to about two-thirds the flow of the Nile.[2] Turkey does not plan to do much more than generate electricity from dams on the Tigris river, but has built irrigation tunnels near Urfa that can siphon off one-third of the flow of the Euphrates. By the late 1990s, concrete irrigation canals to divert the water were only about one-third complete and unlikely to be finished until well into the twenty-first century. When they are finished there will be almost 1.7 million hectares able to receive irrigation, allowing double or triple cropping on the rich soil of the old Fertile Crescent, a vast area north of Syria that is equivalent to the surface area of Wales or New Jersey.

In a 1987 protocol Turkey gave an undertaking to Syria that at least 500 cubic metres of water per second would cross the Turkish border, about half the historic flow of the Euphrates. Turkish diplomats will not write this guarantee into a treaty, fearing that droughts or climatic changes could one day lower the overall flow of the river, as has happened in the case of the Nile since the turn of the century. The Turks are also pushing for deals on better irrigation practices by all who use the rivers, which currently lose 10 per cent and could soon lose 20 per cent of their flow to evaporation from canals and dams, especially in the floodplains of Iraq.

To show a spirit of compromise, Özal often dusted off plans for what he called a Peace Pipeline to bring water to the Middle East from the southern Ceyhan and Seyhan rivers, through Syria and Jordan and then splitting in two to the Gulf states. The total distance covered by the two routes would be more than 5,000 kilometres and cost some $15 billion to build. Not surprisingly, Gulf states rarely showed much interest in the project, fearing dependence on unreliable neighbours. Other ideas developed in the Özal era included shipping water from the Manavgat river to Israel and elsewhere in vast floating nylon mesh balloons, each of which could contain two million tons of water. In 1991, many Allied troops marched into battle in the Gulf with Turkish bottled water in their backpacks, and there is no doubt that Turkey is determined to exploit this increasingly valuable resource. 'The day of the impotent Turk has gone,' Özal declaimed as he pressed a button in January 1990 to lower an 87-ton concrete plug into the bottom of the centre-piece of the GAP project, the Atatürk Dam. His minister Kamran Inan went further. 'We didn't get our share of oil, but we have our share of water. We must know how to make best use of this.'

Repeatedly Özal and his ministers represented Turkish control of the sluice gates of Middle East water as the equivalent of the Arabs' and Iranians' control of oil. The economic impact on the GAP area around Urfa is already great. Urfa itself is booming and growing by some 10 per cent a year. In the end the GAP project's hydroelectric plants will have added more than 70 per cent to the country's electricity output. The nation's cotton, pistachio and wheat crops could double.

Few Turkish commentators recalled to mind the old Anatolian peasant rule about not cutting off your neighbour's stream. If Arab nationalists, particularly in Syria, have never forgotten the clashes that marred the last decades of four centuries of Ottoman Turkish rule, neither have the Turks forgiven the Arabs for their betrayal of the Ottoman caliph and empire during the First World War. The progressive newspaper *Sabah* still carries a daily cartoon strip featuring the adventures of the 'Last Ottoman' against the likes of Lawrence of Arabia. Another of the problems underlying relations between Turk and Arab is that the division of borders with the Arab world following the First World War was not as clean as on other frontiers. The decision which incorporated the oil-rich provinces of Mosul and Kirkuk into British-mandated Iraq, rather than Turkey, was not settled until 1926. And Syria has never accepted Turkey's 1939 take-over of Alexandretta, a half-Turkish, half-Arab populated province known in Turkish as Hatay, a transfer sanctioned by the French authorities as they tried to tempt neutral Turkey on to the Allied side on the eve of the Second World War.

The Turkish republic and the Arab world have also not seen eye to eye about Israel. After an initial reluctance, Turkey in 1950 bowed to its need for American support against the Soviet Union and recognized the Jewish state. Turkey's image as an agent of American imperialism and aircraft-carrier of American weaponry appeared confirmed to Arab nationalists when in 1955 it organized the Baghdad Pact, a short-lived, US-backed attempt to bring every nation in the region into an alliance against the Soviet Union. By 1958, Turkey had signed a secret accord with Israel and Iran, joining forces against the Arabs. Then Turkey took France's side in opposing Algerian independence. The Arab attitude was summarized by President Nasser when he publicly declared Turkey *persona non grata* in the Arab world – apparently justifying a similar Turkish prejudice summed up in the folk proverb: 'Never get mixed up in the affairs of Arabs.'

This pro-active period of Turkey's Middle East policy in the 1950s reflected both Prime Minister Adnan Menderes' uninhibited style and his belief in the need to remain loyal to the United States. Turkey began to widen its options in 1964, stung by the harshness of the letter from President Johnson warning the Turks not to use American arms to fight in Cyprus. This was at a time when the Turks had virtually no other useful weapons. From then on, Turkey pursued a policy of more even-handed neutrality between the Arabs and Israel in the late 1960s and early 1970s, inclining further towards the Palestinians in the 1980s as its Arab commercial interests grew. During the years of the Iran–Iraq war and up to the Gulf War, Iraq had become Turkey's second biggest trading partner, although Turkey was always careful to balance its interests with those of Iran, to which it sold almost as much.

Turkey's policies towards Iran have always been in a class of their own, separate from the rest of the Middle East. Reza Shah and Atatürk shared a taste for autocratic methods of modernization, earning them the title in the 1930s of the 'two dictators of the east'. But the ways of these perennial rivals for domination of the Middle East parted. Oil wealth transformed Iran, while Turkey wrapped itself in its Kemalist isolationism and then plunged into political and economic confusion in the 1970s. This distance turned to wariness after 1979 when the Islamic Revolution overtly threatened Turkey's secular order, whilst a new Great Game emerged after 1991 as rivalry developed between them for trade and influence in the Caucasus and Central Asia. Iran has frequently accused Turkey of spying and harbouring opposition groups such as the Mujahedin-e Khalq, who were active among the tens of thousands of Iranian refugees in Istanbul during the Iran–Iraq war. Turkey for its part has strong evidence of Iranian tolerance of Turkish Kurd rebels and Iranian links to a series of assassinations of secular Turkish intellectuals between 1990 and 1993. Such problems reinforce age-old prejudices in which Turks tend to view the Iranians as fickle, arrogant and unpredictable, while Iranians tend to scorn the slow-witted, over-loyal 'Turkish donkey'.

There is nevertheless a long and stabilizing history to the relationship. The two states are separated by borders that have been established for more than four centuries. After more than a millennium of sparring between Persian Iran and Turkish Turan, their cultures share many links, especially in poetry. Although the two nations appear neatly split by Turkey's Sunni Muslim and Iran's Shia Muslim identities, there are cross-overs. The 10–20 per cent of the Turkish population who are heterodox Shia Alevis are matched by Iran's similar number of ethnic Azeris, who share Iran's mainstream Shia faith but speak Azeri, a close cousin of Turkish. The spiritual leader of Iran since 1989, Ali Khamenei, is a Shia Turk from eastern Iran and other senior Islamic republican officials have come from Turkish stock. And as a vestige of the days of the Turks' martial role in the medieval Islamic world, the post of head of the Iranian army is still usually reserved for an ethnic Turk.

Balancing Iranians, Arabs and its interests in the fifty states of the Organization of the Islamic Conference, the Turkish bureaucracy generally pursued a set policy from the time of the fall of Menderes until Özal's seizure of the initiative in the Gulf War. They avoided regional Arab institutions and emphasized bilateral links with all parties, to the point of defying the United States and currying favour with oil-rich Libya. They tried to live down their slavishly pro-American reputation of the 1950s, and also to stay out of inter-Arab disputes, partly in order to avoid raising fears of Ottoman-style ambitions of regional hegemony, and partly because they lacked the expertise to exploit these disputes.[3]

'One thing that particularly strikes me during my talks with

Arab leaders: almost all of them have fallen out with one another,' noted a bemused General Evren, who had the politeness to keep his thoughts to himself until he wrote his memoirs. Not so Özal. He could be tactless. Once in the 1980s, when Saudi Prince Abdullah protested to Özal that he had seen an Israeli El Al plane at Istanbul airport, Özal was ready with a reply that was sure to make his interlocutor bristle. 'Oh, yes,' he said. 'But we have one very strong principle. We never interfere in affairs between former provinces of the empire.'[4]

This neo-Ottoman spirit is strongest in the circles where Özal made his political début, Necmettin Erbakan's pro-Islamist National Salvation Party, now called the Welfare Party (Refah Partisi). The Welfare Party has promised a genuine revolution in Middle East policy, reducing ties with Israel to a minimum, embracing fellow Middle Eastern states in a new Muslim commonwealth and dropping the policy of integration with Europe. 'We don't want to be the last of the foxes. We want to be the head of the sheep,' said Abdüllah Gül, a leading member of the party's younger generation.[5] 'We led the Islamic world for a thousand years. Turkey should resume the leadership of this world,' intoned Şevket Kazan, a stalwart of the Welfare old guard.[6]

The Welfare Party learned the traditional difficulties on the path to Muslim unity, in the case of Turkey's Arab and Iranian neighbours at least, in a series of snubs delivered after it came to power in July 1996. Such a goal flies in the face of all the republic's accumulated experience of Arab suspicion and hostility, especially as regards Syria, with whom Turkey has always preserved a balance of threats rather than of interests. It also disregards the way Turks have voted with their feet. The number of Turkish workers in the Arab world peaked at 180,000 in the 1980s – most of them construction workers who rarely took their families to remote, hot building sites. Meanwhile more than two million Turkish workers have settled in Europe and show every sign of making their homes there. Even a new wave of Turks who headed off to the Caucasus and Central Asia in the 1990s did so with more enthusiasm and ideas of permanence than those who sought work in Arab countries. Turkish trade with the Middle East has followed a similarly opportunistic pattern. Oil purchases dominate the picture and brought a substantial rise in Turkish exports in the 1980s, but the Middle East share of Turkey's overseas business fell back to 10–15 per cent of the total in the early 1990s.

The Welfare Party's unguarded statements of an Ottoman-like ambition to lead the Muslim world seem as certain to arouse the

suspicions of Arab states as the martial spirit Özal tried to drum up
in the country during the Gulf crisis. Other factors causing friction
in Turkish-Arab relations were also unlikely to change: Syrian support for Turkey's Kurdish rebels, Turkey's determination to take a
larger share of rivers flowing into the Middle East, and a genuine
sense of common cause between the Israeli and the mainstream
Turkish establishments. And, both in the prelude to the Gulf War
and after it, Arab states could find much to wonder about in Turkey's
ambiguous attitude towards northern Iraq.

Özal had been quick to explore the idea of an expanded Turkish
role in the area. Visiting Washington's National Press Club for
dinner before the Gulf War, he spent most of the evening briefing
correspondents at his table about Turkey's rights to northern Iraq.
In September 1990, he openly told the newspaper *Sabah* that 'after
the crisis, the map of the Middle East will change completely . . .
if there is a better place for us in the world, we must take it.'
Defending existing borders was a principle that 'should be reas-
sessed according to the conditions of the day', he said.

On paper, Turkey had accepted the League of Nations' decision
in 1926 that had lost it Mosul and Kirkuk to the encroaching
British protectorate over its oil-supplier, Iraq. But a moral claim
to the old Ottoman territory persists in the minds of many Turks.
Income from the oil would have made a great difference to the
country, however much Özal argued that 'oil has made some countries lazy. Turkey is a dynamic country. We need technology, not
oil.' But as Turkish foreign ministry textbooks point out, Mosul's
loss was accepted only because the young republic was too weak
to fight for it. Atatürk himself declared the region to be within
the near-sacred 'National Pact' boundaries of the republic.[7]

Turkish officials began to adopt the contorted doctrine of 'protecting the brothers of our brothers' – that is, the Iraqi Kurds, as
brothers of the Turkish Kurds – as well as reviving a strategic
interest in the ethnic Türkmen of Iraq, descendants of Central
Asian Turcoman nomads and Ottoman immigrants who once
formed a substantial part of northern Iraqi urban populations.
Their numbers dropped during the Arabizing campaigns of
Saddam Hussein, who publicly referred to them as 'guests', not
Iraqis. But to this day, older merchants in the downtown bazaars
of northern Iraq often still speak Turkish.

Young soldiers on the Turkish Airlines planes filled with
reinforcements going to the front in late 1990, questioned about
what they were going to fight for, were as likely as not to reply,
'Well, Mosul and Kirkuk, I suppose.' While the Kemalist daily

newspaper *Cumhuriyet* was running advertisements signed by dozens of intellectuals with slogans like: 'No to the Second Front! USA out of the Middle East! No more war!', the marginal right-wing newspaper *Yeni Nesil*'s headline proclaimed: 'Mosul and Kirkuk Await Us'. A drunken Turkish businessman in an airport bus could deliver the opinion that 'this business has to be finished with the bayonet. The Americans haven't got the guts for face-to-face fighting. The Turks know about bayonets, they should go in to finish this. But they will never withdraw from territory for which they have spilled blood.'

The age of trench warfare certainly came to mind during the first press view of exercises on the Turkish army front lines before the Gulf War. With bayonets fixed and bloodcurdling yells of '*Allah, Allah, Allah*', Turkish paratroopers charged at each others' lines. The soldiers were disciplined and tough, but, although they loosed off a few anti-armour rockets, their machinery of war seemed dated. As Turkish armoured columns moved up the border, their labouring trucks not infrequently broke down. And it was hard to know what to make of a tour of a Turkish logistical base camp. With little stencilled signs to explain their functions, soldiers kneaded dough, baked bread or mimed the cooking of meals. Some wore gas masks, sensibly enough in view of Iraq's chemical warfare capability. But gas masks looked out of place on waxwork-like privates polishing boots, minding trays of military soap or sitting stiffly draped in towels while others scrubbed themselves by numbers in a steamy canvas-walled bathhouse designed along the lines of a Turkish hammam.

Whatever reservations the military commanders may have had about President Özal, some 100,000 Turkish troops were arrayed along the border with Iraq by the eve of the war. Their mere presence performed a vital task for the Allies, pinning down eight Iraqi divisions in northern Iraq. Turkish tank and artillery units dug in amid the mud and volcanic boulders on the bare, misty hills that dominated the only obvious theatre of battle, the strip of land alongside the Tigris river at the westernmost point of the border. No major military movements were thought possible farther to the east, where the imposing snow-capped peaks of Kurdistan rose from the north Syrian plain. Little did Turkey realize just how possible the mass movement of Iraqi Kurdish refugees through the narrow and heavily mined mountain passes would prove to be.

Meanwhile the inhabitants of Turkey's south-east took their pre-
cautions. The population of some towns halved. The panicky few
who remained bought rolls of plastic sheeting with which to seal
their windows from the feared chemical weapons of Iraq. Others
perched caged cocks on their window-sills as a warning system.
Behind the tall sandstone walls of the Syriac Christian monastery
of Mar Gabriel, not far from the border, monks calculated that
thirty-eight wars had already ravaged this land in the 1,600 years
of the monastery's history. An ancient crypt among the graves of
12,000 holy men was neatly converted into a bomb shelter, complete with emergency supplies. If the nuns for whom camp beds
were laid out in the dank inner sanctum needed comfort, they
had only to reach into the tomb of John the Arab and extract his
femur, already burnished by the kisses of centuries of devotees.

In the event, these preparations were unnecessary. No Iraqi
response came as American fighter-bombers bristling with
weaponry roared into the air like great wasps from the Incirlik
base and sped off towards Baghdad and other targets. The only
Turkish 'war' casualties were from three Patriot missiles fired off
by mistake. But after Iraqi troops had been expelled from Kuwait,
President Özal found out that he had only been half-right in his
decision to back President George Bush. 'Bush was hesitating
about going on to Baghdad,' Güneş Taner recalled. 'Özal called
him and urged him to press on. Bush said he would stop and let
the people do the rest to topple Saddam. Özal told him: "The
Iraqi people? What have the people got to do with it? Did the
people elect him, that they can bring him down now?" '

The American president ignored Özal's warning, stopped the
Allied advance and issued his famous call for the Kurds and Shia
Muslims of Iraq to take events into their own hands. For a while
the uprisings had some success. But when it turned out that the
Allies' no-fly zone did not include any ban on Iraqi helicopter
gunships, and that Iraqi tanks were free to move, the rebellions
were doomed to failure. The Shia were brutally crushed. The Iraqi
Kurds knew what to expect. In the preceding decades, Saddam
Hussein's regime had murdered 180,000 of their people, razed
more than 4,000 of their 5,000 villages, methodically tortured
them and used chemical weapons against them. They abandoned
their brief spring of freedom. By the end of March 1991, whole
cities were streaming along the roads into the mountains. About
one and a half million people headed east to Iran. Another
500,000 Iraqi Kurds, Christians, Türkmens and Arab deserters
arrived at remote outposts in the Turkish mountains, where they

were met by a determined refusal on the part of the Turkish soldiers to let them across.

Turkey had been here before. In 1988, about 55,000 Iraqi Kurdish refugees fled over the Turkish border as Iraq re-established its control of the north at the end of the Iran–Iraq war. Three years later, nearly half of these Iraqi Kurds were still in Turkey, squatting in south-eastern housing projects, camps and bungalows set up for earthquake victims. The West had initially promised much help, but lost interest after accepting the educated cream of the refugees. On top of that was the well-justified Turkish fear that the nationalism of the Iraqi Kurds was spreading to their own Kurdish community. The idea of looking after 500,000 more Iraqi Kurds raised the real possibility that Turkey would face a highly destabilizing and expensive Afghan- or Palestinian-style refugee problem. Turkey resolutely refused to allow this to happen. 'Western television stations find it easy to make speeches in front of maps of Kurdistan. But they too find it hard to open their arms to these displaced, homeless people,' wrote the late Uğur Mumcu, front-page columnist of the *Cumhuriyet* daily.

Events proved in the end that, knowingly or not, the Turks acted in the Iraqi Kurds' best interests, at least in the short term. But it was a harsh trial for everybody involved. The human and public relations cost of keeping the Iraqi Kurds in the cold, sometimes snowy mountains was immense. Exposed at heights of 2,000 metres, the refugees were desperate to reach better shelter and to find food. Mothers carrying sickly babies charged the Turkish lines. Men dragging dying grandfathers begged to be allowed through for medical assistance. Children lost limbs as they crossed minefields to collect firewood. But the Turkish soldiers had firm orders not to allow down from the mountain passes refugees not obviously suffering from life-threatening wounds. They beat them back with rifle butts. When that failed, shots would ring out and refugees were killed. The conscripts knew no other way to stop them, and even that barely worked.

Unlike Iran, Turkey left the world's media free to cover what it wanted as the crisis developed. The heart-rending scenes had a huge impact on television viewers who were shown the funerals of the many children who died of diarrhoea, the wheels of aid trucks turning impotently in the muddy mountain tracks and the frustration of foreign aid workers who could not understand why Turkey refused to let the Iraqi Kurds through. A major international relief effort went swiftly into action, partly fuelled by a sense of Western guilt at allowing the disaster to happen. World-

wide publicity was given to air drops of ex-Gulf War troop rations
on to the crowded, fetid camps. Few of the Iraqi Kurds knew what
to do with the packets of supplies, some were crushed by them
as they landed and some Muslims rightly worried that the fussy
individual packs of American 'Meals, Ready-to-Eat' contained
pork.

In fact, some of the fastest, most effective and unsung aid was
given from the Turkish side, often by Turkish Kurds. Spontaneous
door-to-door collections and donations in nearby towns brought
truckloads of food and clothing that was more readily of use. Local
men laboured up the steep mountainsides under sacks of sugar
and flour. Sick refugees could be found smuggled through to the
houses of mayors. In the more easterly border areas, many Turkish
Kurds came from tribes that were related to the Iraqis. 'We hold
them as close to our hearts as pistachio nuts,' said a minibus driver
who had volunteered to ferry helpers from the Turkish Kurd town
of Hakkari to the border. 'Today it's their turn to suffer. But
tomorrow it could be ours, you never know.'

Özal realized that something had to be done quickly. All the
Western goodwill earned by Turkish support for the Gulf War was
being eroded by a growing perception in the media that Turkey,
not Saddam Hussein, was somehow responsible for the Iraqi
Kurdish refugee problem. Özal called up President Bush with a
new idea. He was proposing to push into northern Iraq to resettle
the Iraqi Kurdish refugees on their side of the border. 'When he
realized that I was serious about entering Iraq, he stepped in and
solved the problem. Sometimes you have to scare people a little,'
he remembered later.[8]

Britain's John Major quickly supported the idea. Soon a force
was on its way that would number more than 16,000 troops from
the United States and several European countries.[9] Gradually the
refugees were tempted back to their homes by reassuring Allied
outposts known as 'way-stations' and military trucks to help them
along the roads. They tramped out of camps littered with plastic
trash and discarded gifts of European second-hand clothes, back
across the mountain passes and past the wreckage of all that they
had abandoned in their haste on the way up: the cars, the municipal buses, the tractors, the fire engines and the impromptu graves
of relatives.

The security zone was initially envisaged as a relatively small
affair, a space for large camps for the Iraqi Kurdish refugees. More
important, however, was the accompanying Allied threat to shoot
down any Iraqi aircraft, including helicopters, that breached a

no-fly zone north of the 36th parallel: that is, most of Iraqi Kurdistan. This was a crucial move, and one that could have prevented the whole catastrophe had the United States articulated it a few weeks earlier. Even after the security zone was set up, there was still much uncertainty. Iraqi government police remained in place, but were required to do the Allies' bidding. US soldiers forced the Iraqi district prefect's office to issue visas for reporters and aid workers in the border town of Zakho virtually at gunpoint.

The energetic and confident American officer who ran the Allied liaison office for the first year, Colonel Richard Nabb, then went further. He decided to push slowly down the road from Zakho towards the western Kurdish provincial capital of Duhok. Not surprisingly, perhaps, there was no resistance. The Iraqi army pulled back behind the last ridge before the Mesopotamian plain. In the east, the situation also improved. When Allied intervention had halted the fighting at the end of March, the Iraqi Kurdish guerrillas still controlled much of the north-eastern corner of Iraq. Cautiously they started moving back south, taking control once again of the eastern provincial capital of Suleymaniyeh, as well as Arbil, the capital of Iraqi Kurdistan as defined in the Kurds' benchmark 1970 agreement on autonomy with Baghdad's Baathist, or Arab nationalist, regime.

Saddam Hussein then made a crucial move. In October 1991, he ordered his governors and other high officials to leave Iraqi Kurdistan. He also stopped paying state and municipal salaries and pensions, stopped supplying schoolbooks, stopped fuel shipments and stopped the rations on which Iraqis had become dependent during a decade of fighting his wars. Hundreds of thousands of the 3.5 million people of Iraqi Kurdistan were suddenly without income. 'Saddam thought everyone would leave. But only the top five per cent of Baathists and Kurds went. The Kurdish front had to move into the government's shoes. Now there is no Iraqi government authority in northern Iraq. Saddam lost,' Nabb noted with satisfaction.[10]

Saddam went one step further in May 1993. He withdrew the 25 Iraqi dinar note from circulation, taking one and burning it on Iraqi television to underline his malignant intent. This was the note of highest value in Iraq, and its cancellation wiped out the main vehicle of savings and trade in northern Iraq (and also ruined merchants in Jordan and elsewhere). It was another devastating blow, but somehow the Iraqi Kurds bounced back. Cars and houses began to be traded for American dollars and German marks, while the majority of transactions were carried out in the currency of the better pre-Gulf War days, printed on stout paper in Britain. The Iraqi Kurds avoided the new post-Gulf War notes issued in Baghdad, quickly nicknamed 'photocopy' money. As time went by, the old notes became a virtual Iraqi Kurdish currency, with a floating, free and far stronger rate of exchange against the dollar than Saddam Hussein's own.

Other signals of a deepening line dividing Iraqi Kurdistan from the rest of the country were the so-called Law Number One issued by the Kurdistan Front setting up an assembly for Iraqi Kurdistan, and the Front's later assertion of the region's status as a federal state. Turkey's old fears of an independent Kurdish state revived, even though it was Saddam Hussein who, by a process of exclusion, was forcing the Iraqi Kurds to take action, and Iraq that had agreed to the autonomous Kurdish arrangement in 1970, even constructing a parliament building in the Iraqi Kurdistan capital of Arbil.

Despite stern warnings from Turkey's foreign ministry, the Iraqi Kurds went ahead and held the country's first free elections in May 1992, in which 100 seats in parliament were contested by Kurdish parties and five seats contested by the chief minorities, the Assyrian Christians and Türkmens. (Few Arabs remained, since most of the Saddam Hussein-era settlers had been evicted soon after the Kurdish guerrilla take-over.)

The election result was so close that the two main Kurdish leaders split their 100 parliamentary seats equally between them. This arrangement did not last long. Within two years they were fighting each other and parliament dissolved itself in a mêlée of street fighting. Soon the area was effectively divided into cantons, the easternmost, Surani-dialect area run by Jalal Talabani, and the western, Kermanji-dialect area run by Masoud Barzani. This development did not displease Turkey, which schemed and encouraged these divisions as part of its sporadic efforts to persuade the weakened Kurds to resume public negotiations with Saddam Hussein.

Turkey could not help being worried, however, when a sign just over the border welcomed visitors to 'Kurdistan'. But there was little Ankara could do. Iraqi Kurdish society was managing to put itself back together, despite the Iraqi Kurds' uncertain international status, internal feuding and the suffering of the formerly privileged and salaried urban middle classes. In five years of Allied military protection and aid from the United Nations and many countries, including Turkey, enormous progress was achieved. Journeys from east to west that once took whole days on bumpy dirt roads were reduced to hours by repaved tarmac highways. New bridges paid for by British charities ended perilous crossings of flooded rivers on rafts lashed together from oil drums. Gradually the shelters made of Allied parachutes and tents disappeared from the sweeping highland valleys. Hundreds of villages rose from the dynamited ruins left by Saddam Hussein. Flocks of sheep and herds of cows grew in number from year to year. Towns could boast up to fifteen television stations and some restaurants showed signs of visible prosperity, filled with customers at tables groaning with food. Kurdish archaeologists even started exploring once-forbidden aspects of their non-Arab, non-Turkish past.

Emerging symbols of Iraqi Kurdish statehood were intensely worrying to Turkey's strategists, who saw them as proof that an independent Kurdistan was on the way. This, they rationalized, would make it impossible to keep control of the Kurds in Turkey's south-east. Schooled in the lessons of Turkey's struggle for ethnic self-determination, they could not believe that the Kurds did not want an independent nation-state. Most ordinary Kurds in Iraq, and in Turkey for that matter, had serious and sustained objections to the economic and internal political desirability of such a project. The years of blockades after 1991 reduced some Iraqi Kurdish townspeople to trading old planks and second-hand towels, and many longed for a return to the economic comforts of a federally organized, oil-rich Iraq. The Turks were not reassured by the apparent caution of the Iraqi Kurdish leaders, who confined their publicly voiced ambitions to the hope for no more than regional autonomy or federal status.

'Every Kurd has a dream of living like other nations. But it is a dream. We must live with reality not dreams. I doubt if we can change that reality by force. We are surrounded, landlocked, and cannot gain freedom through violence. The Kurds, I believe, must gain their freedom within their existing states, defending their own rights. Our view is that the problem must be resolved within an Iraqi state,' guerrilla leader Masoud Barzani said in a classic statement of the Iraqi Kurdish case.[11]

The Turks were not convinced. It was true that in the year before the Iraqi invasion of Kuwait, a sense of momentum had built up behind attempts to bring together the various Kurdish guerrilla groups of Iraq, Iran, Turkey and Syria: Barzani's spokesman Hoshyar Zibari had said, 'We want to broaden the Kurdish issue. We are trying to have a united front, something along the lines of the Palestine Liberation Organization.'[12] The Turks could also point to the more nationalistic statements of Barzani's rival

Jalal Talabani. Even the normally diplomatic Kurdish negotiator Sami Abdul-Rahman could state in the heady days of Western protection in September 1991 that

> All we lack is international recognition. For the first time since the First World War, international borders are changing. If the Soviet and Yugoslav borders are changing, why should borders here be sacred? The Turks are so short-sighted and nationalistic, they don't see what is going on in the world. Of course it makes you think of alternatives, even if it is a pipe-dream.[13]

The likelihood, or otherwise, of Iraqi Kurdistan achieving independence was, however, only one part of a complicated set of dilemmas which northern Iraq posed for the Turkish political establishment, dilemmas that brought them into direct conflict with their principal allies in the West.

Turkey's problems over northern Iraq were made worse than they should have been by friction with its Western allies, a growing suspicion fed by misunderstandings, shallow media coverage on both sides and the unprincipled exploitation of the Kurdish question by Turkish nationalist politicians.

Clouding Turkish judgement has been an inability to rise above suspicion of the real intentions of their supposed allies in the West. The Turks have never forgotten the West's scheme to create a protectorate for Kurdistan in their proposed carve-up of Anatolia following the First World War. Such a goal has been consistently denied by modern Western governments. No Western strategist of note thinks that an independent Kurdistan, implying as it would the dismemberment of Iraq, would make for a stabler Middle East. But that is only part of the picture seen by the Turks, unable to view the Kurdish question clearly after years of propaganda and brutal republican repression of even modest Kurdish demands.

Turks find it hard to differentiate between overwhelming support for Kurdish rights among European intellectuals and support for an independent Kurdistan, especially as some seem to be advocating that goal, with the description of the Kurds as 'the world's largest nation without a state'. This clash between Turkish and European perceptions first became a real and practical problem during the April 1991 Kurdish refugee crisis, partly because of the Turks' shocked reaction to Western media coverage of the international aid effort.

Most of the reporters who flew in had never before been to Turkey, let alone south-eastern Turkey. They had little sympathy for the complexities of Turkey's position. Some were so carried away by a perception of the romantic nobility of the Kurdish cause that they arrived wearing the Kurds' traditional baggy trousers. They naturally tended to give credence to the press briefings of the highly organized Allied military operations. The Turks, for their part, failed to comprehend the gravity of the situation. They sent just one senior civilian official to deal with several hundred representatives of the world's media. The first holder of the post had never been to south-eastern Turkey before. He gazed wide-eyed out of the aircraft window on the landing approach to Diyarbakır airport as if it was his first trip to a foreign land, which, in many ways, it was.

Not surprisingly, Turkey found it impossible to get across its reasons for preventing Iraqi Kurds from settling on its side of the border. As a result the Turks fell naturally and somewhat unfairly into the role of the barbarians of the piece – especially those cold and hungry conscripts manning the Iraqi border for weeks on end and obliged to keep the refugees at bay in conditions that in some cases differed little from those of the Iraqi Kurdish refugees themselves.

Turkey's moral position in foreign media eyes was also fatally weakened by its oppression of its own Kurdish community. Tragicomic situations had already arisen in course of the short-lived military briefings given during the Gulf War itself. When an American correspondent asked about the situation of the Turkish Kurds, the Turkish colonel stormed out of the news conference declaring that he would 'eat his uniform' before answering the question. On another occasion, a Turkish colonel accepted a barrage of questions before silently writing in the reporter's notebook, 'My briefing is at 10 a.m. tomorrow.' The briefing was then cancelled.

Misunderstandings multiplied as the Kurdish refugee crisis took hold. Despite decades together in the NATO alliance, the Turkish and Allied military were not getting on well together either. British officers had at least warned their men that for the Turks, allowing the Allies to feed the Kurds was the equivalent of the British allowing logistical supplies to the Irish Republican Army. But even among the British such sensitivity was in short supply. Young helicopter pilots beamed with excitement while swooping in and out of Turkish mountain valleys whose snows were marked with greasy grey stains borne on the wind from the oilfield fires in Kuwait, 700 miles to the south. The military missions of the major powers were used to taking charge and British liaison units blithely organized media trips and events with tent-front advertisements like 'See the Iraqis by Night!'

The Turkish military, insecure and resentful, loathed it when their visitors ran up their flags higher than theirs in a region that only a generation before had been completely closed to foreigners. The Turkish air force vented its anger by starting dive-bombing practice with concrete bombs on the target range just alongside the strip of land used as the main Allied camp at Diyarbakır airport. The British riposted by calling one of its bases in northern Iraq 'Camp Allenby', named after the First World War British general who drove the Ottoman Turkish armies out of the Arab world.

These strains communicated themselves quickly to visiting reporters, whose stories fuelled a vicious circle of conflict. Finally, a burning story appeared in bold print on the front page of a British newspaper alleging that Turkish soldiers had gone on a 'rampage of looting among thousands of Kurdish refugees'. Allied troops were flying supplies away to save them from the Turks. Turks were feeding refugees only once every three days in a 'prison camp'. Turks were starving frightened refugees to make them easier to control. Turks were denying foreign medical teams access to the camps. Christian refugees were 'almost as frightened of the Turks as of the Iraqis'. British and American troops had cocked their weapons in a confrontation with Turkish soldiers while Turks had stolen blankets, sheets, food and water. 'Every British and American soldier I spoke to reported Turkish army looting of refugee supplies over a period of two weeks. "The Turkish soldiers here are shit," a British soldier said with venom.'[14]

British officials later gave a much less dramatic version of the incident in question, but the damage had been done.[15] Seeing themselves portrayed as uniquely and unmitigatedly evil, the Turks lashed out. The British newspaper reporter was bundled out of the country. Turkey tightened its controls on the chaotic inrush of non-governmental organizations trying to aid the Kurds. A counter-campaign in the Turkish media got under way accusing the Allies of colonial arrogance, imperialist ambition and designs to cut up Turkey. Growing Turkish ill-will added to the delays in getting aid supplies through. 'It is the considered opinion of all diplomats that the media coverage of the situation, on both sides, is about the worst we've ever seen,' said the European Union's ambassador to Turkey, Michael Lake.

Nevertheless, the situation of the refugees themselves quickly stabilized. The early days were a disaster of tragic proportions: the late American disaster expert Fred Cuny reckoned that at this period death rates in the border camps briefly reached a rate of 7.2 per 10,000 people, or about 360 refugees dying each day. Within a few weeks, the refugees were relatively safe and well fed. The improvement was due partly to the great momentum of the relief effort – foreign states alone spent more than one billion dollars in the first year – and partly to the order banning Iraqi air movements and the Allied defence of the security zone.

It was at this stage that the war of words between Turkey and its Western allies began to do long-term harm. Worst of all were Turkish politicians, who deliberately fanned ill-informed popular Turkish suspicions of Allied intentions towards northern Iraq in order to embarrass the government of the day. As they came in and out of power, such supposedly nationalist leaders – Süleyman Demirel, Mesut Yılmaz, Deniz Baykal and others – would simply perform a quick U-turn. Whether it be a question of privatization, European integration or attitudes to the Kurds, such politicians have thought nothing of sacrificing serious policy questions for ephemeral domestic political gains. This short-sightedness has been a constant source of friction with Turkey's Western allies.

Turkey for its part was angered by Western insensitivity. The chief issue for Ankara arose in July 1991 when the main Allied force dealing with Iraqi Kurdish refugee relief withdrew from northern Iraq. It was replaced by another deterrent force based in Turkey and eventually called 'Operation Provide Comfort II', although the Turks never let go of its catchier original name, 'Operation Poised Hammer'. It consisted of some eighty American, British and French warplanes and support aircraft that patrolled the no-fly zone above the 36th parallel in northern Iraq. A small group of officers based in Zakho patrolled the security zone until Iraqi Kurdish in-fighting persuaded them to withdraw in September 1996. As time went by, and in response to Turkish demands, Turkish officers became more and more dominant in setting the force's operational parameters, flying with its missions and sitting in on meetings with Iraqi Kurdish leaders.

The Turkish military and foreign ministry had no doubt that Operation Provide Comfort II had many advantages. It ensured that an international deterrent was in place to prevent Saddam Hussein from trying to repeat his 1991 stampeding of Kurdish refugees towards the Turkish border. The fact that it was based primarily in Turkey meant that Turkey had a strong measure of control, which it would not have had if the force had moved to, say, Cyprus, Jordan or an aircraft-carrier in the Gulf. And yet at the same time Turks felt that the longer the force was there and the longer the Iraqi Kurds were allowed to develop outside Baghdad's control, the more possible it was that an independent Kurdistan would result.

'Today they call it a security zone. Tomorrow they will be calling it a Kurdish state,' warned former President Kenan Evren. As time wore on, Süleyman Demirel voiced the opinion that the West wanted to add the Kurds to a list of 'front-line forts' that included the 'Armenians, the Greeks and the Jews' – conveniently forgetting, of course, the Turks' own role in that regard.[16]

A parallel and inextricable issue was the question of Turkey's Kurdish rebels, the Kurdistan Workers' Party (PKK), who picked up a windfall of weaponry in the chaos of northern Iraq after the Gulf War and quickly took advantage of the power vacuum there. Estimates of their presence in northern Iraq in 1991–2 went up to half of their then total strength of 10,000 guerrillas. From August 1991 they started mounting substantial cross-border raids, culminating in a massive and suicidal attack on a Turkish border post by 500 guerrillas in October that year.

The Turkish military had various options for guarding the difficult mountains of the 331-kilometre-long border with Iraq: to order Iraqi Kurdish groups to strengthen their control of the border, to try to control the area beyond the border themselves, to work with Iraqi Kurdish guerrilla groups, to co-operate trilaterally with Iran and Syria, or to set up an Israeli-style electronic border monitoring system. Ankara experimented fitfully with all of these options, but none of the combinations quite worked. The Turkish military command was reluctant to do anything to reinforce Iraqi Kurdish strength and unity, undermining the effectiveness of any alliance with them. And doing the work on their own, as shown during a 35,000-man offensive into northern Iraq in March 1995, proved both inconclusive and unacceptable to the world.[17] Civilian casualties that went unnoticed in internal Turkish-Kurdish or Iraqi inter-Kurdish wars suddenly became an international issue. Paradoxically, the Americans were at the time trying to persuade the Turkish high command to apply the same scrupulous rules of engagement it was using inside Iraq to its far dirtier war in south-eastern Turkey.

Turkey also flirted with softer policies that reflected the country's ambiguous view of their links to and rights in northern Iraq. This approach was summed up by Özal in the summer of 1992: 'Let's go and help them in northern Iraq. Let's take our television stations and our electricity there. What will we lose by spending $30–40 million dollars? We can fight the PKK better this way. As long as Turkey opposes it, no Kurdish state can be formed. But many kinsmen of our own [Kurdish] citizens live there. We should protect them as much as we protect the Bulgarian Turks.'

The Turkish media floated the idea that the Turkish lira could replace the cancelled Iraqi currency. The Turkish Red Crescent was given significant funds for aid, even though this was mainly directed towards the Türkmen minority. Public and covert links to Iraqi Kurdish groups multiplied, sometimes thanks to shared interests. Iraqi Kurd guerrilla leader Masoud Barzani had to fight his own war with the PKK as its uncompromising pan-Kurdish militants struggled to win hearts, minds and territory in northern Iraq. Even Jalal Talabani was ready at times to play with the idea of an informal Turkish protectorate.

'Don't compare Turkey with Britain. Compare it with Iraq. Which is better? In Turkey, you can have newspapers, you can have a party, you can have deputies in parliament, you have freedom to speak and shout. In this country [Iraq] they will kill you. Look, don't misunderstand me. I'm not saying Turkey is the model. We are living in the Middle East. Is it good? Yes. Is it enough? No. But it is certainly a step forward,' Talabani said in December 1992.[18]

At that time, Özal was still alive and Turkey's Kurdish nationalist deputies had not yet been dragged out of parliament and into gaol. Barzani and Talabani could travel on Turkish diplomatic passports. They opened parallel missions in two mirror-image apartments on the same floor of a building in Ankara's diplomatic district of Çankaya. They visited Turkey's top politicians, leaders and even generals as they passed through Ankara. In the most bizarre illustration of Turkey's inability to come to terms with its dilemmas over Iraqi Kurdistan, two of the most outspoken champions of Iraqi territorial unity, Bülent Ecevit and Süleyman Demirel, have also at various times publicly backed the idea that the Iraqi border should be moved up to 40 kilometres southwards to make it 'easier to defend'.

But none of these options could be seriously pursued as long as the Iraqi situation was conditioned by circumstances beyond Ankara's control: US feuding with Saddam Hussein, UN sanctions against Iraq and Turkey's need to respond to regional rivals Iran and Syria. The running political sore of northern Iraq was far from the recompense that Özal and Turkey had counted on for taking the West's side in the Gulf War.

*

The Gulf War crisis suddenly cast Turkey in a new light, just as its old strategic importance seemed about to recede with the end of the Cold War. It seemed as though Özal could do no wrong. 'Turkey's New Image is Suddenly Making it a Mideast Role Model,' the *Wall Street Journal* gushed. 'A Friend on the Front Line,' said the *Financial Times.* 'In its meandering way, the European Community has begun to accept that Turkey matters to Europe,' opined *The Economist.* Özal and Bush communicated often by telephone, with the American president once absenting himself to speak to his Turkish counterpart in the middle of a press conference being transmitted live to the world. Özal frequently made important announcements first on international live satellite television. 'We have no ally who has acted more boldly and determinedly against Iraq's aggressive attitude than this man sitting on my right,' Bush told reporters when a glowing Özal came to Washington to visit him.

Bush remained personally loyal to Özal for what he had done during the Gulf War, inviting him to spend the night at Camp David after it was all over. 'Bush liked me a lot,' said Özal with his characteristic immodesty. But Bush was voted out of office in 1992 and the economic, political and military benefits to Turkey as a whole fell short of what Özal was gambling for, however much his supporters greeted him with placards reading 'Conqueror of the Gulf' and 'Guardian of the Middle East'. Social Democrat leader Erdal İnönü turned out to be correct in his early judgement of this outpouring of unwonted foreign attention. 'Of course if you defend Western interests, there will be nice editorials. It's like this in every crisis. Afterwards they all disappear,' he said.

The United States promised to double Turkey's $300 million textile import quota, which it did; to protect Turkey's military aid budget, which it only did for a year; and to lobby for Turkish membership of the European Union, which arguably made little difference. Only part of Özal's boast of an 8-billion-dollar windfall of new and hand-me-down Western weaponry materialized.[19] Gulf states promised compensation, and a few billion dollars of cash and oil-in-lieu was forthcoming. But as the years went by, this did little to compensate for Turkey's very real losses.

To take just one example, about one-third of Turkey's 300,000-strong trucking fleet used to work on the Baghdad route to Iraq and the Gulf, with about 5,000 trucks a day passing through the border to Iraq. This stopped as the world clamped sanctions on Saddam Hussein. The disappearance of this source of wealth on the 'old Silk Road' through south-eastern Turkey was one reason why disgruntled Kurdish youth began to join the well-funded and well-organized PKK rebels after the Gulf War. The hard-bitten truck-stop towns of Silopi, Nusaybın and especially Cizre soon became the scene of the hottest opposition to the Turkish security forces, an opposition that only began to be defused when trucks started to use the route again in 1995.

Officials in Ankara exaggerated the overall figure of Turkey's losses when they talked of an annual loss of seven billion dollars. But, not counting large quantities of Turkish dam-making equipment sold off to Iran by Kurdish feudal lords at one project site in northern Iraq, the most conservative figures amounted to between two and two and a half billion dollars a year. This added up to a real loss of trade, transit dues and other gains of between 12 and 15 billion dollars by December 1996, when the locomotive of Turkish-Iraqi trade, the oil pipeline, was conditionally and partially reopened.[20]

Strangely, too, the realignments after the Gulf War that gave rise to a new Middle East peace process did not, as Özal expected, throw up Turkey as regional leader of the Arab states. Instead, peace-making between the Palestine Liberation Organization and Israel made it possible for Turkey publicly to improve its relationship with Israel. This blossomed so quickly from late 1993 onwards that at first Israeli diplomats had to beg the Turks to go slower, partly for fear of upsetting Syria.

Indeed, outflanking Syria was the Turks' main objective. Ankara had been unable to crack the Kurdish rebellion by force, unwilling to solve the Kurdish problem by political reforms and unsuccessful in its efforts to persuade Damascus to clamp down on the PKK in return for guarantees of a minimum water flow in the Euphrates river. Believing its own propaganda that 'foreign forces' were the mainspring of the rebellion, Ankara had then tried to involve the United States in putting pressure on Damascus, but this too met with only mixed success. Amid persistent reports of intelligence co-operation with Tel Aviv against Syria, Iraq and the PKK, the Turkish military then took the major step of signing a military training co-operation accord with Israel in February 1996. Soon Turkish and Israeli pilots were flying in each other's countries and Turkey came close to signing a vital electronic warfare deal with an Israeli company to upgrade its F-4 Phantom fighter-bombers.

That Turkey should be the first Muslim state to sign such a deal with Israel was perhaps not surprising. Turkish and Jewish communities have lived side by side since the conquest of Constantinople, when Mehmet the Conqueror signed a decree offering

them safety. Their contribution to imperial prosperity was such
that his successor invited them to his domains to escape the oppression of the Spanish Inquisition in 1492. They survived the transition to the republic, since, unlike the Greeks and Armenians,
the Jews made no territorial claims on the disintegrating Ottoman
empire. The republic maintained Ottoman traditions, protecting
some Jews from Nazi Germany by giving them Turkish passports
and welcoming 150 Jews among more than 200 German professors
who took refuge in Turkey during the Second World War. A
'wealth tax' during the war fell heavily on the Jewish business
community, however, and the general depression of the times
encouraged many Jews to emigrate to Israel after the war. There
they maintained strong links with their mother country, sometimes
receiving visiting Turkish politicians with more enthusiasm than
the politicians could count on in Turkey.

The Jewish population of Turkey had stabilized at about
22,000 in the 1990s, although their sixteenth-century Judaeo-
Spanish dialect, known as Ladino, was dying out. Their culture
was converging with that of the mainstream Turkish middle classes
and élite, with perhaps one-quarter of Jews marrying Turkish
Muslims. This closeness was symbolized by the election in 1995 of
Jewish businessman Jefi Kamhi to parliament, the first non-Muslim
deputy since the 1950s. The connections have been strong on the
Israeli side, too. When Israel's President Ezer Weizman visited
Turkey in 1996, he was able to tell his interviewers that his grandparents had spoken Turkish and that his father had been a doctor
in the Ottoman army.

Islamic fundamentalists and the sometimes scandalously anti-
Semitic leader of the Welfare Party, Necmettin Erbakan, have
vowed to uproot this budding relationship and put an end to
military co-operation. The thought of Israeli planes flying over the
Anatolian plateau was apparently the trigger for a deranged lone
Islamist to open fire on President Süleyman Demirel in May 1996,
wounding two bystanders. But when Erbakan became prime minister in July 1996 he did not oppose the military's continued
co-operation with Israel. A general confrontation with the Jews
and Israel seems unlikely, given the historic links between the two
peoples, the existing institutional interaction, and the growing
economic ties between Israel and Turkey. Such ties range from
the 300,000 Israeli tourists who visit Turkey each year to the help
given to Turkey's ineffectual representatives in Washington by the
powerful pro-Israeli lobby. If outrages committed by Israel against
the Palestinians have harmed the general image of the Jews in

Muslim countries like Turkey, especially in Islamic circles, many other Turks are also impressed by Israeli military prowess and share the Israelis' suspicions of the Arabs.

Israel, however, is also a rival of Turkey for the attention of the United States in the region, attention that Özal believed was sure to rise now that he had proved Turkey to be a key strategic player again. Once the Gulf War was over, Özal tried to overcome his disappointment at failing to gain entry to Europe by seeking a free trade zone with the United States and by offering Washington regional 'strategic co-operation'.

American officials back-pedalled fast. Their view of the Middle East was centred on Israel and Arab states such as Egypt and Saudi Arabia. Ankara had no prospect of supplanting Israel in Washington's affections, and Cairo had no intention of sharing its regional pre-eminence with a large, non-Arab state like Turkey. Nor would either contemplate losing their massive US infusions of aid, which together amounted to ten times that given to Turkey. The Americans gently steered Özal back towards the European Union.

'Unless you have it written down, you can't trust the United States,' was the advice offered by former President Kenan Evren. A decade before, Evren had admitted to a visiting German official: 'We only take US aid because we have to. The US uses aid as an instrument of pressure. If we go against their wishes, they start saying they will cut it off. I sometimes ask them, "Does the US give aid to have a strong country on the southern flank of NATO, or as a tool to make Turkey do as it wants?" '

In the absence of the Cold War that had brought the two countries together in the first place, the United States was losing its fundamental interest in Turkey. Furthermore, aid to Turkey was often politically difficult. Armenian, Greek, Cypriot and even Kurdish lobbyists constantly embarrassed and sabotaged the Administration's plans for Turkey, especially in election years, despite loud cries of foul from the State Department. Even an upsurge of US official support for Turkey as a secular role model for Turkic states after the collapse of the Soviet Union was short-lived.

'Özal envisaged strategic co-operation with the US after the Gulf War. But the United States has shown little interest in a specific military arrangement with Turkey in the Middle East,' said Morton Abramowitz, the US ambassador to Turkey during the Gulf crisis. 'The imperatives that once drove US-Turkish relations – NATO, bases, and military assistance – are rapidly disappearing.'

The American military presence, totalling some 10,000 service-

men in 1990, had been halved by 1992. In the same year, the
American government replaced military grants with loans at com-
mercial rates, thereby adding hundreds of millions of dollars to
Turkey's debt each year. Other funds that used to be critical to
Turkey's balance of payments were also becoming almost irrel-
evant. The story of the 1997 foreign aid budget is instructive. First,
American lawmakers reduced it from $49 million to $25 million
to signal their protest at the Turkish army's campaign against the
Kurds. Then Armenian lobbyists managed to get another three
million lopped off unless Turkey opened its border gates to
Armenia (Turkey was keeping them closed to put pressure on the
Armenians to give back at least some of the 20 per cent of Azerbaijan that the Nagorny-Karabagh Armenians had occupied). Turkey
then refused to accept any of the aid at all. And so the debate
went on.

Perhaps this last gesture recognized a subtle but important
change: Turkey was growing up and no longer needed the aid
very much. The days when most of the buses in Ankara seemed
to belong to the US base and when US military transfers dominated the balance of payments were over. Turkey was not exactly
free: in fact it was more integrated than ever into the Western
economic system, its trading pacts, its rating agencies and its laws.

But Turkey now had a greater margin for manoeuvre. Thanks
to new and intimate concerns in Iraqi Kurdistan and Syria, and a
growing interaction with Israel, it also seemed unlikely to return
to its old Kemalist position of rigid aloofness from Arab and Middle
Eastern affairs. And no issue dragged Turkey further into the
Middle East in the aftermath of the Gulf War than its inability to
find a solution to the related and snowballing difficulty of dealing
with its own Kurdish problem.

15

The Kurdish Reality

Say I just want death.
What unjust place am I in?
If I say I am a Kurd
Or a mountain-made Turk
  I'm a broken note.

Yılmaz Odabaşı, Turkish Kurd poet, 1990

'*HAVALO!*'

The shout of the man in a chequered turban and Kurdish *pesh-merga* guerrilla uniform carried faintly over from the Iraqi bank of the swift-flowing Habur river. He waved a white handkerchief to a group of curious Turkish Kurd villagers, gathered on the Turkish bank not far from where the Habur feeds into the Tigris. On the road behind the *peshmerga*, along the foot of what are known in Turkish as the Good-for-nothing Mountains, moved a commandeered Iraqi army jeep flying the yellow banner of an advancing Iraqi Kurdish guerrilla faction. It was a bright morning of March 1991. The Gulf War was over, the Kurds of Iraq had rebelled and the victories of that Kurdish spring tasted exquisitely sweet to long-repressed Kurds everywhere.

'That means "friends", I think,' explained one of the men on the Turkish side. But he made no response to his ethnic kinsman on the opposite bank. The sound of engines from a Turkish army patrol was approaching. The Turkish Kurds quickly dispersed to the privacy of the flat-roofed mud houses of their village to talk in hushed and incredulous voices about the extraordinary events over the border.

The excitement of those days was infectious, coinciding as it did with Nowruz, the spring equinox celebrated on 21 March as a national New Year holiday by the Kurds and other peoples in

the Iranian and even Turkish worlds, where it is called Nevruz.
There was no holding back the Turkish Kurd town of Cizre, where
news of Iraqi Kurdish success was spreading fast. In one shop on
the muddy main street, a group of men clustered around the
owner's desk. Şeyhmus – not his real name – had a short-wave
radio that could pick up the newscasts of Iraqi Kurdish guerrilla
groups, and his phone never stopped ringing with requests for
updates from near and far. Never mind that half of the scratchy
transmissions were unintelligible and that Şeyhmus did not always
understand their Kurdish dialect. Excitement thrilled in the voices
of the presenters as they broke into programmes to announce the
liberation of another town in Iraqi Kurdistan.

Turkish troops in Cizre were right to be nervous of local Kurds
catching the spirit of rebellion. They pulled back to their barracks
as night fell, leaving townspeople feeling as though they, too, had
somehow been liberated. Not that Cizre was a tame town in the
first place. Wolfskins could be bought behind the grimy strip of
primitive repair shops that served the trucks that until the Gulf
War had rumbled through this ancient junction of the many Silk
Roads across south-west Asia. Crossing the Tigris, the routes led
south into Mesopotamia, north to the Caucasus, west to the plains
of the Fertile Crescent or east to climb into the steep mountains
of Kurdistan. The 50,000 Kurdish inhabitants reflected this mixed
heritage. The men wore the baggy trousers of the Turkish Kurds,
the headcloth of the Arabs, and, on top, the flat cloth cap that
Atatürk imposed on all Turks. Perched on the crumbling stone
walls of the town, the keep of a former Kurdish prince's stone
castle overlooking the Tigris had been levelled to make way for a
concrete set of Turkish army barracks.

One by one, passage through Cizre's streets were cut as traditional Nowruz fires started to blaze, symbolically burning away
the impurities and memories of the past. They could be seen on
the flanks of the mountains nearby, presumably lit by Turkey's
rebel Kurdish guerrillas. Nationalist youths and young women
took to the streets in impromptu processions shouting 'Long Live
Kurdistan' or 'Long Live Apo' (guerrilla leader Abdüllah Öcalan).
Their parents felt the same. After showing his guests a pirate video
of the aftermath of the 1988 Iraqi gassing of Kurds at Halabja,
Şeyhmus watched the Turkish evening news. Turkish politicians,
unsettled by the rising strength of Kurdish feelings, were rehears-
ing the official line that 'all citizens of Turkey are first class citizens'. The audience in Cizre was not impressed. 'They're all dogs,'
spat Şeyhmus, switching off the television and heading up the

stairs to his flat roof. The whole population seemed to have done the same. Smoke from hundreds of burning tyres had completely blocked out the stars. Deafening volleys of celebratory shots rang out in the putrid blackness; it was as if everybody wanted to show they had a gun.

'The arrow has left the bow,' mused Haşem Haşemi, Cizre's mayor from the pro-Islamic Welfare Party, which wore its local Kurdishness more lightly than the pro-rebel nationalists. Despite harassment from far-away Ankara, and bans on the Kurdish language, Haşemi's municipality, like many others in Turkey's Kurdish south-east, had quietly gone about its work in its native tongue. But he was still trying to digest the news that the President of the Republic had admitted that there were 12 million Kurds in Turkey. In one sentence, Turgut Özal had broken the spell of decades during which the Kemalist state had entirely denied the Kurds' existence. Haşemi was both perceptive and pessimistic. 'It's a big event. But who knows how far it will go. All I know is that it will not lead to independence.'

If there is a constant in nearly three millennia of Kurdish history, independent statehood is certainly not it. Instead, the world's largest nation without a state – about 25 million people now split between Turkey, Iraq, Iran, Syria and the former Soviet Union – has endured an apparently never-ending cycle of uprisings and suppression. The power of Kurdish princes and rebels has usually only grown when the established states around them – Persian, Arab or Turkish – have weakened. A Kurdish chief could win control of a region, perhaps conquer one or two rivals, perhaps dominate the surrounding plains. But it never lasted long. Sometimes a neighbouring state would regain sufficient power to crush the upstart. At other times a quarrel would emerge in the Kurds' own ranks, encouraged either by gifts and promises of preferment from scheming outsiders or by the feuding tribal traditions that prevailed in their remote and beautiful mountain valleys.

So it was to be in the 1990s. The slim opportunity for an independent Kurdish state in northern Iraq in 1991–2, if it was ever really wanted by the Iraqi Kurds, was soon frittered away by quarrelling between the two main Iraqi Kurd leaders. The Turkish Kurd rebellion, which had a particularly murderous edge to it, looked headed for a more traditional fate: legal harassment, a dirty war of assassinations and suppression by sheer military force. The Turkish treasury became depleted, the south-eastern countryside devastated and, thanks to the security forces' blatant disregard for human rights, Turkey's international reputation was left in tatters.

Worst of all, the struggle never looked likely to have a clean ending. In the first decade of fighting, millions of Turkey's Kurds have been displaced into the poorest quarters of big cities, where resentment can only fuel the anger of a future generation of rebels.

The Kurds are some of the most ancient inhabitants of the Middle East, and have lived there for much longer than the Turks. Their origins go back to the Medes and the earliest Indo-European Bronze Age migrations. But the first famous Kurd is perhaps Saladdin, the brilliant leader of the armies of Islam who captured Jerusalem in 1187. One of his descendants, Mir Mohammed, led a great revolt in what is now northern Iraq against the Ottoman empire in 1836–8. Mention of Saladdin's origins is conspicuously absent from Turkish textbooks: instead an odd stress is laid on the Turkish character of his state machine. Only in 1995 did a growing understanding of reality allow a Turkish newspaper to print a correction to a story that asserted that Saladdin was a Turk, and to recognize, with an apology, that he was indeed a Kurd.[1]

The mistake was probably made in good faith. Turks have long suffered from enforced ignorance about the history of the Kurds, to the point where a frustrated former governor of Turkey's Central Bank was ready to corner a foreign reporter at a reception and beg him to explain exactly what the truth of the matter was. Block-headed quarrels could even break out on the floor of parliament between Turkish and Kurdish deputies, cuffing each other in arguments about 'who got here first'.

It was Turkey's foremost Ottoman historian, Halil Inalcık, who finally had the courage to point out in public that the Kurds were in Anatolia first. Xenophon is recorded as having been harassed by the *Kurduchoi* not far from Cizre as he retreated up the Tigris towards the Black Sea in 401 BC, while the first truly Turkish raiders only started to penetrate into Anatolia thirteen centuries later. Denial and a refusal to conduct academic research was counter-productive, he believed. 'In the past half-century we have only touched the regional problems with the tip of our finger. Because we've hidden our heads in the sand, we have reached a point where we understand nothing,' Inalcık wrote.

The Ottomans were careful to guard against the emergence of a single Kurdish entity, and shared with the Kurds the important bond of Sunni Islam. Until the nineteenth century the sultans recognized the rule of dozens of virtually independent princes in inaccessible mountain valleys. The rulers of this feudal society often ran glamorous courts, and a distinct Kurdish culture developed, although dialects could vary markedly from place to place. Their only obligation was not to change sides and to fight when required for the sultan. For long centuries the system worked. Their romantic redoubts still dot the Kurdish landscape, and indeed one of the main Kurdish nationalist leaders of the 1990s was himself a feudal lord who lived in a castle.

The Turkish republic did not always deny the existence of Kurds. The first assemblies of 1920 and 1923 referred to deputies from Kurdistan (as well as from Lazistan, the north-eastern corner of Turkey inhabited by a Black Sea people related to Mingrelian Georgians). At Lausanne at the same time, Ismet Inönü presented himself as a negotiator on behalf of both Turks and Kurds, 'whose motherland is Turkey'. In January 1923, Mustafa Kemal told journalists that 'instead of thinking of Kurdishness as a thing in itself, our constitution will provide for a kind of local autonomy. Thus, wherever the people of a particular province are Kurds, they will administer their affairs in an autonomous manner.'[2]

But Turkish suspicions lingered. Turkish leaders could not believe that the Allies had given up the hope expressed in the unratified Treaty of Sèvres of founding an independent Kurdistan. They blamed small-scale Kurdish uprisings on British scheming to do them out of oil-rich Mosul. Mustafa Kemal's government began to act against the Kurdish nationalists in Anatolia. Kurdish intellectuals were split between those who wanted independence and those merely wanting autonomy, but in Mustafa Kemal's time as much as in the 1990s, their fate was to be the same. On 3 March 1924 – the same day that he forced the abolition of the Muslim caliphate through a protesting assembly – Kemal banned all Kurdish schools, publications and associations.[3] The symbolism was apt: the four-month-old Turkish republic's first major act was an attempt to crush the two forces with which it would do battle, increasingly defensively, throughout the next eight decades.

Sensing which way the wind was blowing, and provoked into premature action by Turkish expeditionary forces, the Kurds rebelled in force on 13 February 1925. Many other Kurdish leaders having been arrested, the revolt was led by an impromptu figure, Sheikh Said, both a Kurdish nationalist and an Islamic leader. A Kurdish rebel force of 3,000–5,000 men quickly captured Elaziğ and Lice, occupying a third of the Kurdish provinces and even threatening Diyarbakır. The fledgeling government in Ankara correctly judged this to be a severe threat. Within two months Turkish troops had brutally suppressed the uprising. 'Independence

courts' hanged Sheikh Said and dozens of his folllowers in Diyarbakır and other south-eastern towns in September 1925. After that,
the Turks never forgave or trusted the Kurds. A key question in
a secret government report on Turkey's 700-odd Kurdish tribes
and clans leaked to a dissident magazine in the 1980s was still
addressing the question 'Did they join the rebellion?'[4]

The Kurdish language was officially outlawed by the 1923 Treaty
of Lausanne. The right to speak any language other than Turkish
was reserved for the non-Muslim Armenian, Greek and Jewish
minorities only. In March 1925, a law was promulgated 'For the
Re-establishment of Order' that gave Mustafa Kemal the right to
ban organizations and publications at will. His regime embarked
on a reign of terror. Hundreds of villages were destroyed and
hundreds of thousands of Kurds deported. The total number of
victims of the 'independence courts' is still not known, but probably includes several hundred people hanged, most of them Kurds;
only in the 1990s did families dare to speak openly about their
suffering.

By 1930, most of the Kurdish revolts had been crushed. With
one stroke of the pen, a law remitted all the murders carried
out by the Turkish security forces. Two years later, another law
envisaged the emptying of inaccessible areas, and the demarcation
of areas where culturally Turkish people should be brought in
and those 'in which it is deemed desirable to establish populations
which must be assimilated into Turkish culture'.[5] Even so, one
mountain outpost in the central eastern highlands held out:
Dersim. It took two years, from 1936 to 1938, for the Turkish army
to pummel the Kurdish population there into submission. When
the soldiers had finished, the blighted province was renamed
'Tunceli', or 'fist of bronze'.

An example was made of Sheikh Said's family. They figured
among the fifty of his closest companions who were hanged in
front of him before he died with a defiant plea in Kurdish for
future generations to be proud of their struggle. Many of his other
relatives met the same fate. One brother and his men fought their
way through to Iran, but were treacherously machine-gunned in a
barracks by the troops of Mustafa Kemal's ally Reza Shah. Another
brother led a mountain guerrilla band for years, but was betrayed
by a renegade Turkish officer in his ranks on his way back from
refuge in Syria to join the Dersim rebellion. Two of Sheikh Said's
nephews were bayoneted. Sheikh Said's eldest brother was beaten
to death by republican troops while reading the Koran one morning. Surviving members of the family conserved his bloody shirt

throughout their 23-year internal exile near the Bulgarian border.
It was used as a charm against disease and a powerful reminder
of the hundred or more relatives and in-laws of Sheikh Said who
died in the struggle.[6]

'Nothing changes for the Kurds. The horizon is pitch black.
But the oppressors will drown in the blood of the oppressed,'
intoned Abdülmelik Fırat, one of Sheikh Said's grandsons. After
years as a member of parliament for the conservative party of
Süleyman Demirel, he emerged in the 1990s as one of the few
rallying points for Kurdish nationalists within the establishment.
In the uncompromising style of all the country's radicals, he
explained how a traditional pro-Islamic figure like himself could
sympathize with the Marxist rebels of the Kurdistan Workers' Party
(PKK) who emerged in the 1980s and 1990s.

'Basically, it was the Turkish Republic that invented the PKK.
Ninety-nine per cent of Turks see Kurds as the same as the
Armenians. We are offered the same choice, either assimilation
or genocide. It is a lie that the Kurds are "first-class citizens": only
if they deny their origin can they do what they want. It is the
mistaken policies of the government that have made the PKK
into the sole representative of the Kurds,' he declared, when inter-
viewed in his neat modern office in the grounds of the Turkish
parliament. 'Only two per cent of the [Kurdish] population naturally support the PKK. But because the Turks didn't approach this
democratically, the PKK got a lot of sympathy. We tried to say,
okay then, don't talk to the PKK. There are seventy members of
parliament who are Kurds, talk to us. But talking to the Turks is
like talking to a wall.'[7]

The decades in between, from the 1930s to the 1980s, are
covered by a blanket of silence. Until 1965, foreigners were banned
from even travelling to the south-east. Troop barracks, government
headquarters, police stations and prisons studded the south-
eastern landscape. Local Kurdish names of villages were changed
to anodyne Turkish equivalents. Fines were introduced for speaking Kurdish in public. Written out on victory arches in the regional
capital of Diyarbakır, picked out in whitewashed stones on hill-
sides above army barracks and posted up in school corridors was
Atatürk's message 'How happy is he who says he is a Turk'.

The Kurds were relegated to the status of 'mountain Turks'.
The denial of identity went to absurd lengths. In case a Turkish
soldier should hear the word Kurd mentioned while on duty in
the south-east, his service handbook informed him that this was
a nickname born of the '*kürt, kürt*' sound made when crunching

through the 'mountain Turkish' snow. Republican leaders issued grim warnings of bloodbaths should their mountain Turks try to imitate the Kurdish nationalist exploits of the short-lived 1946 Mahabad Kurdish republic in Iran or the uprising led from the 1960s onward by the Barzani tribe in northern Iraq.

Wary of the fate of their fathers, an emerging class of Kurdish radicals in the 1960s channelled their energies into the exciting ferment of the Turkish left. For their part, fearing that they might lose control, the republican authorities retained the Ottoman system of ruling the region. Though no longer recognizing them as princes, they continued to deal with *ağas*, or tribal chiefs, who commanded the loyalty, votes and even lives of tens of thousands of Kurds. Republican reforms in education and society thus barely scratched the surface of social organization in the south-east.

Even today, most Kurds are only a generation or two away from their ancient, semi-nomadic tribal culture of the hills and mountains. A survey of the Turkish Kurds of Istanbul showed that only 28 per cent had been born in the city, and almost all of their fathers were inward migrants.[8] Their language is mainly Kermanji, a western dialect of Kurdish, a distinct cousin of Persian in the Indo-European group of languages believed to have descended from the Medes. A splinter group in Turkey, who also see themselves as Kurds, speak another dialect known as Zaza. Some common Kurdish words are strikingly similar to English and other Indo-European languages: the words for 'father', 'new' or 'bad', for instance, are virtually the same: *peder, nev, bad*. The old-fashioned Kurdish style of dress is also a source of great pride, the men in baggy trousers gathered with elaborately knotted cummerbunds, waisted tunics and neatly tied chequered turbans, the women in gay-coloured clothes glittering with sequins, and a long white headscarf and silk headband that makes them look as though they have stepped out of a medieval illuminated manuscript.

But in Turkey this past is increasingly folkloric. Only a fraction of Turkish Kurds now wear such clothing: almost all have adopted the more Western styles of mainstream society. It is also easy for Westerners to romanticize the harsh life of remote Kurdish villages. Thousands of hamlets are buried under snow and cut off from the world for months at a time in winter. Blood feuds divide families and tribes for generations. Lack of health facilities, difficult terrain and poor soil mean that only the fittest survive. In these regions, the incidence of infant mortality, officially 80 per thousand in 1989, and probably higher due to under-reporting, far exceeds the 50 per thousand in the westernmost provinces.[9] South-eastern areas still have by far the highest birth rate – the Kurds' 'nuclear bomb', according to nationalists – and also the highest incidence of Islamic polygamy. The current record-holding Kurd, with a full complement of four wives, lives near Muş and now has more than forty children. This fecundity goes hand in hand with poverty. The worst-off province with a majority population of Turkish Kurds, south-eastern Hakkari, has just one-tenth the average income of the richest province, Kocaeli, near Istanbul.

Many Turkish Kurds live in Kocaeli too, however, and in other western provinces – accounting perhaps for one-half of Turkey's Kurdish population. Copious books of statistics give proof not only of Turkey's rapid urbanization but also of a huge shift in population from east to west, from Turkish and Kurdish provinces alike. The latest rebellion and the new wave of village expulsions since 1984 have merely accelerated the trend. Those that remain for the most part earn their living in traditional ways, often by semi-migratory sheep and cattle farming. This has always been accompanied by some smuggling – a practice that now takes the form, along the Iranian border, of the lucrative business of refining heroin.

Those who move to the big cities start on the bottom rung of the social ladder as they commute from their relatives' cheaply built homes in the concrete jungles of the city suburbs. The chatter of Kurdish or the guttural tones of Kurdish-accented Turkish is common among day labourers on building sites or roadworks. Skilled workers, Turkish or Kurd, gradually develop small businesses with their relatives: Turkish Kurds increasingly form part of the urban middle class of engineers and businessmen.

Systematic discrimination against Turkish Kurds is hard to pin down. In the military, Turkish Kurd 'Mehmets' often find themselves landed with the worst jobs, partly because they are the poorest and least educated. 'Suicides' of bullied Turkish Kurd conscripts are a distressing and recurring feature of the pro-Kurdish press. And yet western Turkish Kurds, openly boasting of their ethnic origin and their mother tongue, could often be met among Turkish army patrols in the south-east willingly hunting down the PKK.

There is little social resistance to intermarriage with Turks, since they share the same Sunni Muslim religion. Once settled and successful, the western Kurdish population generally has no intention of returning to the east. Kurdish businessmen, like their

Turkish counterparts, make most of their investments in the more prosperous and thickly populated west. Few have any wish to find themselves forced back to an independent Kurdistan in the poor and struggling east.

An element of ethnic Kurdishness has never in itself been a bar to success. The main ideologist of the Kemalist revolution, Ziya Gökalp, may have been partly ethnic Kurd. A good number of presidents of the republic, including Ismet Inönü and Turgut Özal, had Kurdish blood. Several cabinet ministers in the 1980s and 1990s have been Kurdish, some of them openly speaking Kurdish in their offices, others refusing even to mention the subject. Turkey's most famous film-maker, Yılmaz Güney, was a Turkish Kurd. The country's best-known novelist, Yaşar Kemal, is half-Kurdish. But he writes in Turkish and his intense story-telling style partly draws on the tales of the Türkmen tribes in villages near where he grew up. Such fine distinctions escaped the crasser elements in the Kemalist bureaucracy, however, and many of the Türkmen and other folk-tales that he wrote down from his early years as a travelling story-teller were burned by the gendarmerie.

If it had not been for the psychological strain of the PKK rebellion, it is conceivable that these Turkish Kurds could have been assimilated painlessly into a more pluralistic Turkish republican culture. But as the 1980s moved into the 1990s, ethnic tensions began to emerge in the western towns and cities, particularly those like Izmir that had well-defined Turkish Kurd quarters. A major cause of resentment was the insensitive and arrogant police pressure on Turkish Kurds as they tried to root out PKK sympathizers. The more established Turkish populations also resented the influx of the wilder, less educated men from the east. But as long as the Turkish economy kept growing, and everybody had hopes of personal improvement along with it, these clashes rarely got out of hand.

Much was revealed about the Kurdish community and its attitudes in a 1992 poll by the research company Konda for the newspaper *Milliyet,* one of the few serious studies ever published in Turkey. Fearing the consequences of publication, the newspaper kept most of the results secret for nearly three years. But the findings had great validity for the country of which Istanbul is the melting pot, and indeed may qualify it to be called the world's largest Kurdish city.

Of the 15,863 people living in Istanbul who were questioned, 7.67 per cent said they were ethnically Kurdish on both sides of the family, and another 13.3 per cent part Kurdish. Of those who said they were Kurdish, 30 per cent said they spoke Turkish as their mother tongue. Only 26 per cent said they definitely wanted to return to their home village; 43 per cent definitely would not. Their education was shown to be poor compared to that of the population as a whole. Fourteen per cent of Kurds were illiterate, against a 5 per cent average of those polled, and only 2 per cent had university degrees, against 8 per cent for all respondents. Even more interesting was the strictly unprompted response to the question: 'We are all Turkish citizens, but we may be of different origin. What do you feel your origin to be?' Only 3.9 per cent said they felt solely and specifically Kurdish, and 69.28 per cent of all respondents said they felt themselves to be Turkish. Only 22 per cent of Kurds said that the solution to the Kurdish problem was a separate state, while 50 per cent definitely opposed it.

Clearly some respondents may have been afraid to give an open answer to these highly political questions, but the results of the December 1995 general elections, held for the most part in a remarkable atmosphere of freedom, bear out the idea that less than half of Turkish Kurds, and possibly far fewer, supported the overtly Kurdish nationalist People's Democracy Party, the Halkın Demokrasi Partisi or HADEP. While more than half of some highly nationalist Kurdish towns like Diyarbakır voted for the party, their overall share of the vote was only 4.17 per cent.

Other polls showed great gaps in perceptions. The Turks generally saw a foreign hand behind the PKK guerrillas, supported a need for economic and military solutions and predicated on the Turkish Kurds a desire for an independent state. Most Turkish Kurds, however, did not want an independent state and thought the solution lay in more tolerant policies. But it was hard for ordinary people to find impartial information on which to base such judgements. Opinion was swayed by the way national leaders were seen to react, by the views of family elders, religious sheikhs or radical youths, or by news of bloody events. Sentiment could be very elemental. A chubby Turkish sergeant from Istanbul leant into a taxi window at a south-eastern roadblock to put some foreign travellers right on the human rights situation, pointing out with horror that 'the terrorists cut off the penises of our dead soldiers'. The Turkish Kurd taxi-driver in front remained stonily silent. As soon as he had driven well out of earshot he simply retorted: 'They cut off our penises first, you know.'

Perhaps no poll could accurately assess the confused state of mind of a people who have been subjected to so many decades of oppression from so many sources. Turkish Kurds have been oppressed by their own tribal society, by their tribal lords, by their poverty. The Turkish republic did make fitful and usually half-baked attempts at economic investment in the south-east. The countryside is littered with the bare walls and foundations of factories abandoned as soon as the businessman or contractor had done enough to qualify for a rich state incentive payment. But the Kemalist ideologues also pursued an insidious form of oppression as they proceeded to strip the mountain Turks of all cultural identity.

Kurdish first names have been banned since the first decades of the republic, with just one receiving official blessing in the 1990s. (Turkish Kurds have often rebelled by choosing Muslim Arabic names instead.) Some of the surnames imposed on Turkish Kurds during the 1930s looked quite odd on their 1990s descendants – as, for instance, that of the nationalist deputy Ahmet Türk. By many such actions, great and small, officials of the republic struck at one of the Kurds' chief sources of pride: their near sacred personal *namus* and that of their tribal or family group.

Some Turks who knew perfectly well that Turkish Kurds were ethnically different also felt they were on a mission to civilize a people who, if not watched, had a natural tendency to turn to brigandage, treachery and oppression of women. President Evren was typical of this school, even invoking the Koran when instructing Kurdish audiences to remember that the women they wrapped in swathes of black veil were humans too. Turkish Kurd historians also argue that there was a colonial aspect to western Turkish economic exploitation of eastern rivers or chromium and iron ore mines. Such sentiments could easily be evoked by the sight of pale-skinned, round-faced Turkish police and administrators in Kurdish towns, where people have longer, darker faces. Turkey rejects this analysis, and not just for historical reasons. The legal key in Turkey's international court cases against activists for Kurdish self-determination was precisely that Kurdistan was not a Turkish colony. So the Kurds are doomed to be culturally assimilated as first-class Turkish citizens.

'They think the Kurd is sick. The cure is either to give him medicine, to beat him or to give him electric shocks. The Turks are always beating us in order to make us better. But we understand what we are. You can't make people love you by force. You can't forge unity and amity from fear and prohibition,' said Musa Anter, the grandfather of Turkish Kurd letters and author of a ground-breaking Turkish-Kurdish dictionary. He was to be arrested over fifty times, to spend nine and a half years in gaol and then to be shot dead in September 1992 at the age of 76, probably by a state-tolerated death squad.

As the violence mounted, the security forces reacted with increasing anger against any symbol of Kurdish nationalism, like the red, yellow and green colours of the Kurdish flag. While going through the dusty Syrian border town of Nusaybın after the PKK's first attempt at a mass uprising for the Nowruz of March 1990, security forces not only took away red, yellow and green bead trinkets made by Iraqi Kurdish refugees but even confiscated foreign medicines featuring the offending colours from pharmacists. 'They are such donkeys about things like this. They'd remove the traffic-lights, if we had any,' joked the mayor.

Turkey eventually solved this with a tasteless but clever piece of reverse assimilation: in 1996, red, yellow and green were declared acceptable to the nation because they had suddenly been discovered to have been Seljuk Turkish colours. In the same year, Nowruz was formally declared to be Nevruz, a pan-Turkish festival that had previously been overlooked. The president himself fired the starter's pistol for a Nevruz half-marathon in Ankara, and leaders of Turkic states (but no Turkish Kurd leaders) were invited to join a Nevruz celebration. An absurd situation arose in which Turkish soldiers and officials in the south-east were now obliged to jump over fires, while Turkish Kurd nationalists told their faithful to stay at home in protest.

Cultural associations that might have preserved or developed a specifically Turkish Kurd culture never recovered from being closed down in 1924. Only one or two were strong enough to brave intense official harassment in the 1990s. Even in Ottoman times, the most successful of the few Kurdish nationalist newspapers were written in Turkish. In the late 1980s and 1990s, magazines in Kurdish only achieved marginal sales. Kurdish nationalists rallied to a series of newspapers printed in Turkish in Istanbul from 1992 onwards that carried long interviews with PKK commanders, pro-Kurdish alternative news from Kurdistan, articles on Kurdish culture and paeans to martyred guerrillas. Four were viciously harassed until they closed, but each time editors and journalists reorganized. The first, *Özgür Gündem* (Free Agenda), was closed by court order after printing an interview with PKK leader Abdüllah Öcalan. The offices of the next paper, *Özgür Ülke* (Free Country), were blown up by a high-powered car explosion blamed on a 'gas leak'. A newspaper called *Demokrasi* continued the line, although less uncompromisingly radical in tone. Its editors stated that their mission was simply to stay open. But in the first four years of their operations, 24 reporters and distributors had been murdered, 55 other co-workers had been gaoled, and more than 350 court cases started against these papers.

The lifting in April 1991 of the official ban on Kurdish resulted in a brief spurt in sales of Kurdish music cassettes: but their popularity soon waned, whether of old singers wailing of blood feuds or modern groups mixing traditional themes with songs of independence whose stanzas included recordings of the gunfire that often echoes through the south-eastern Turkish nights. The success of this experiment added to intellectual arguments that the state should legalize Kurdish broadcasting also, since that would undermine the popularity of a Kurdish nationalist satellite television station that had begun operating from Europe in 1995. But even though Turkish officials from President Turgut Özal downwards could happily ask Turkish Kurd singers like Ibrahim Tatlıses to sing in Kurdish, there remained an ambivalence. In August 1991, one of his tapes was banned, and Tatlıses rang up the relevant government minister to find out why. 'You could lose the elections by doing this,' he remonstrated. 'Yes, we might lose the elections,' the minister replied. 'But we would have saved Turkey. Send your cassettes to Iraq.'

Kurdish tribal culture everywhere has a time-honoured response to conflicts and oppression: 'to go up to the mountains'. The cultural effect of the more jack-booted policies of the Turkish republic towards the Kurds was that, in the words of Turkish Kurd historian Kendal Nezan in 1979, 'Repression has turned the Kurdish peasants into a race of outlaws.' He was soon proved to be right.

The first armed action of the Turkish republic's most sustained and damaging Kurdish revolt occurred on the night of 14–15 August 1984 – a somewhat amateurish attack in two remote towns by two groups of between twenty and thirty Turkish Kurd militants. Guerrillas strafed the garden of the army barracks in Şemdinli near the border with Iran and Iraq, killing one soldier and wounding two others. The guerrillas were more ambitious in Eruh, southwest of Lake Van. They had wanted to raid the bank, but the manager was not home and they failed to open the safe. They took over the town centre instead, killing one soldier and wounding six others before using the loudspeakers on the minaret of the local mosque to give their first propaganda speech in the name of the Kurdistan Workers' Party or PKK.

The establishment, particularly the military, was shocked. The military intervention of 1980–3 was supposed to have stamped out such terrorism; more than a thousand Turkish Kurds were still in gaol facing trial. In fact, as it was to turn out, the brutality of coup-era gaols had turned them into universities which united Kurdish nationalists behind the PKK, the only organization brutal and ruthless enough to resist the full force of the Turkish state.

The PKK leadership had managed to slip over the border to Syria just before the coup. Founded in 1978 from a group of Kurdish radical leftists who had been together since 1974, they were best known then as Apocus, the followers of Apo, the nickname of their leader Abdüllah Öcalan. They were among the most virulent of the armed groups who prospered in the late 1970s as part of the panoply of competing formations on Turkey's radical Marxist fringe. They already had a fearsome reputation stemming from the often murderous determination of their leader. The first twelve years of fighting between the PKK and the security forces were to kill 20,000 people, to injure tens of thousands more, to lead to the destruction of more than 2,000 Kurdish villages and to the uprooting of at least 300,000 people and probably many times that number.

Abdüllah Öcalan was born about 1950 in a small village near the ethnically mixed town of Urfa. One of his grandmothers was a Turk, and there may also have been traces of Arab in the family. But he felt Kurdish, even though he had to take language lessons in exile to become fluent and preferred to discuss politics in Turkish. He described his father as a colourless, weak personality, so poor that the family hardly got fed. His mother, by contrast, was strong. The defining experience of his life was when his brother was beaten up by the big boys in their village and she insisted that young Abdüllah deal with the situation. 'My mother said: "Go and take revenge, or I won't let you back into this house." She enforced this principle a lot. She was very argumentative. I went on to break a lot of children's heads,' Öcalan said.[10]

Öcalan's first schooling was to learn thirty-three chapters of the Koran by heart in a religious school set up in an abandoned Armenian village. Many Kurds used to begin their education in such small *mektebs*, where they would sometimes also secretly learn the fables and poetry of their own culture, spiced perhaps with some unorthodox Islamic mysticism and local superstitions. Eventually the Kemalists clamped down and replaced the teachers with centrally trained imams. Öcalan was clearly a bright student

when he joined the official school system, gaining a scholarship
to the Political Science Faculty of Ankara's prestigious Middle East
Technical University. The faculty traditionally trains Turkey's chief
bureaucrats. At first quiet, and known for his piety, Öcalan soon
became caught up in the anarchic and radical atmosphere of the
times.

'They were real brigands. His number two at the time lived in
a *gecekondu* area where I was working. All he could talk about was
how they had stolen wood to heat their meeting room and how
nice it was to clean a certain kind of new gun. More of my friends
were killed by his group than by Türkeş's Grey Wolves,' said a
fellow left-winger who knew him then.

As a boy, Öcalan wanted above all to become a Turkish army
officer. Even as a sworn enemy of the Turkish republic, he always
referred to Atatürk respectfully as 'Kemal'. Much of what he
appeared to be trying to achieve seemed initially to approximate
to a Kurdish copy of the Turkish war of independence and the
Kemalist state. The similarity weakened, however, the longer he
stayed abroad, chiefly in Syria, but also in former East Germany
and Lebanon. The Marxist ideology and foreign support for the
PKK made it quite different in character. 'The PKK is the representative of scientific socialism in ideology and practice, a monument to the undoing of claims that socialism is dead ... an
important force for the protection and development of socialism
not just in Kurdistan and the Middle East, but in the world as
well,' ran one bold policy statement in 1991.[11]

While the PKK kept its position on an independent Kurdistan
deliberately vague – militants in the field were all for it, while the
ordinary Kurds from whom the PKK needed support were far
from sure – the young recruits who passed through PKK camps
in Syria, Lebanon, northern Iraq and inside Turkey were indoctri-
nated in Communist principles. 'My brother Apo goes like a bull-
dozer into the brains of the people of Kurdistan and makes a
garden where a thousand roses bloom,' was an admirer's comment
that Öcalan liked to quote. The recruits were often very young
and included many girls, kept strictly separate from the boys in
the almost monastic atmosphere fostered by the PKK, which discouraged sex, alcohol and individual activity. One code-name for
girl recruits was *Melsa* – an acronym for Marx Engels Lenin Stalin
Apo. A self-appointed latterday prophet who liked to quote Zara-
thustra and Freud, Öcalan even likened himself to Jesus Christ.[12]
His charisma inspired an extraordinary devotion that shone deep
in the eyes of PKK militants as they vowed that the only guerrilla

who surrendered was one who, in Turkish official parlance, was 'captured dead'.

'I had managed to find a by now nearly forgotten relic of twentieth-century nationalism: the guerrilla army waging a war of so-called national liberation, complete with Marxist texts, wooden vocabulary, the red flags, the fervent communitarianism of collective dance, and, above all, the abdication of the self before the all-powerful leader,' wrote one visitor to a PKK camp.[13]

Anti-feudal, anti-tribal, pro-feminist and Marxist as the PKK was, it stood in stark contrast to the norms of Turkish Kurd society. As much as socialism, the driving force of the PKK was the ego of the all-powerful Öcalan. Iraqi leader Masoud Barzani compared him to the brutal Ugandan dictator Idi Amin. Barzani's nephew Nechirvan said he was 'totally crazy' and understood nothing but force. Jalal Talabani, another Iraqi Kurdish leader, commented: 'Öcalan is possessed by *folie de grandeur*. He wants to be our demigod. He is a madman, like a dog looking for a piece of meat. I counted twenty-eight pictures of him in just one edition of his paper, the *Voice of Kurdistan*.'[14] The Turks, of course, simply portrayed him as a bloodthirsty monster.

As Öcalan's influence rose in south-eastern Turkey from 1989 to 1993, however, he began to be worshipped as a hero by many Turkish Kurds. When the first major interview with him in a Turkish newspaper appeared in April 1990, the chief news-stand in the town of Nusaybın sold 500 copies in two hours instead of the usual 200 copies on a lucky day. Local people said it was mostly in order to cut out a picture of Apo. There was respect for a national leader, admiration for an outlaw who had successfully challenged the Turkish oppressors and awe for a man who did not hesitate to eliminate subordinates or to order the killing of Turkish Kurd opponents and their wives and children.

Kurdish national sentiment was gradually becoming more evident. The first wave of 55,000 Iraqi Kurdish refugees in September 1988 had raised Kurdish consciousness. Added to this was the emergence in Europe of a pro-Kurdish campaign joined by the wife of the French president, Danielle Mitterrand. Then came the crisis over the ethnic Turks of Bulgaria, when Turkish propaganda tripped over the hypocrisies of its publicly stated concept of a citizenship that was supposed to be ethnically neutral. This rising wave of nationalism could already be felt in the summer of 1989 in Balveren, a typical Turkish Kurd village of a thousand souls just north of the Iraqi border.

Balveren was perhaps the first place where Kurdish civilians rose up collectively against the Turkish state's repressive practices. They marched out of their village in protest to set up camp a few kilometres down the road 'until the torture ends'. Having made their point, the villagers went home after a few days, but were still angry. For two years, security forces had prevented villagers from herding flocks of sheep to upland pastures, believing herdsmen would feed the guerrillas. They had closed legal coalmines across the valley because they were too temptingly close to smuggling routes to Iraq, although rough piles of coal by the roadside showed that villagers had found ways around the ban, starting amateur workings of their own, 300–400 metres deep. The single school overflowed with four classes for 300 children. The stone-built, single-storey houses had no more than two rooms, one for the women to sleep and cook, the other for the men to sit, eat, talk and sleep. The atmosphere was thick with hand-rolled cigarette smoke, resentment and tangled tales of years of pressure from gendarmerie soldiers who cadged rides into town, who demanded free chopped firewood for their barracks, who conducted weapon searches in houses on tips from dubious informers ('without even taking off their boots'), who ordered the men to join the progovernment 'Village Guards' militia and who rounded up villagers for humiliating mass punishment in summer sun or winter snow. The stories of torture became more ripely embellished as the evening wore on.

'One man, they put him in a barrel in the sun and lit a fire on it. You could have lit a cigarette it was so hot,' said one man, peeling off his thickly knitted socks to show what had happened to him: a pair of feet mutilated by what he said was an excess of *falaka* beating on his bare soles.

Ironically, the resentment in Balveren was partly fed by Prime Minister Özal's 1980s programme to bring electricity to the villages of the south-east. It had arrived in Balveren three years before, and twenty proud homes and tea-houses boasted television sets. The village had then watched hours and hours of programmes in 1989 as the single state broadcaster tried to stir up Turkish nationalist indignation about the denial of ethnic rights to the Turks of Bulgaria.

'Why don't they talk about us? We also can't give our children the names that we want, we have no rights either,' said Mehmet, especially upset because he could see the Bulgarian Turk refugees fleeing in cars, then a symbol of almost unimaginable riches in a Kurdish village. 'There is some freedom these days but we want more. There are ninety-nine Kurdish members of parliament. We should shake up this parliament a bit. We don't want a separate state; we just want to live properly. But the Turks see us as enemies. They say you are Kurds, you are terrorists.'

For nationalist-minded members of the Turkish Kurd élite the defining moment seems to have been when Danielle Mitterrand landed at Diyarbakır airport in May 1989. Her official purpose was to see what she could do for the Iraqi Kurdish refugees, a vague offer that fell hopelessly short of the many hopes of aid and resettlement raised by her visit. But the Turkish Kurd radicals were not to be disappointed. Mme Mitterrand was to prove a staunch ally and to play a key role in the formation in Europe of an uncompromisingly pro-nationalist view of Turkey's Kurdish problem.

Hundreds of Turkish Kurds greeted her with rose petals as she stepped off the plane before moving on to the Touristic Hotel. Diyarbakır's nationalist society had never seen anything like it. It was as though her hotel had become a Kurdish liberated zone. Suddenly everyone started talking Kurdish, not Turkish, as one by one Turkish Kurds from various walks of life went to the upstairs restaurant where tables had been cleared for Mme Mitterrand's court. Mme Mitterrand's ideas were probably already fixed, articulated in a *France Libertés* leaflet handed out to all and sundry that declared Kurdistan a 'country of 20 million people deprived of independence for 2,600 years, reduced to slavery and death and split between five countries'. If she wanted a fresh view, she chose not to look for it.

That evening Mme Mitterrand met only those with whose opinions she was likely to agree: lawyers for PKK rebel suspects, torture victims and radical politicians. Their stories were in many ways horrifying enough, justifying in their listener a black-and-white image of brutal Turkish oppression of innocent Kurds. A typical visitor was Rahime Şahin, a 63-year-old mother who had recently tried to set fire to herself to draw attention to the fate of her son, in gaol for the past nine years, during which time he had had all his teeth knocked out and cigarettes burned into his flesh all over his body.

A hearing for the Turkish arguments about PKK terrorism was limited to icy conversation over dinner in Ankara with Prime Minister Özal's wife Semra. No Turkish Kurd businessmen or pro-Islamic Kurds were invited to meet her, even though they were arguably just as representative as the nationalists. Her first translator, a French expert on the Middle East widely known for his equal love of Turks, Kurds and Arabs, was so angered by her adoption of an exclusively nationalist perspective that an argument ensued in which he was asked to leave.[15] Even so, the Turkish Kurds thrilled with excitement. Persecuted author Musa Anter sat on a terrace in the warm evening air, sipped at his drink and gloated at the thought of the anger that must have been brewing in the Turkish officers' club two doors down and the residence of the Turkish regional governor across the road.

'Mme Mitterrand has lit a light for us,' he said.

Danielle Mitterrand formally put the nationalist flame to the Kurdish tinder-box when she arranged the first international conference on the Kurdish question in Paris in October 1989. Seven Turkish Kurd Social Democrat members of parliament joined the meeting, defying an explicit party ban on their attendance. On their return they were expelled from their party, and were forced to start working on their own pro-Kurdish political formation. Their efforts were to bear fruit in July 1990, when a big dinner party in the stone courtyard of Diyarbakır's Kervansaray Hotel celebrated the formation of the Halkın Emek Partisi, the People's Labour Party, known in Turkish as HEP. No Turks missed the similarity of its name to that of the Kurdistan Workers' Party up in the mountains; and none of its successor parties could ever avoid giving the impression that, like Sinn Fein and the IRA in northern Ireland, there was a strong but unofficial link between their actions and the aims of the PKK.

The Turks never had any doubt that the link was real, and over the years their reaction was fierce. This first attempt to set up a legal representation for Kurdish nationalist sentiment in Turkey was to meet with two party closures and three changes of name. More than 100 party activists were to be murdered, their most famous leaders would be gaoled and most of the rest were to choose voluntary exile.

Ironically, the fact that HEP was allowed to be founded at all was part of a growing sense in 1990 that the Turkish establishment was moving towards a more open policy towards its Kurds. Even though Erdal İnönü had expelled the seven deputies for breaching party discipline in attending the Paris conference, the most genuinely liberal platform was developed by this thoughtful son of Ismet Pasha, the man who had seen through Atatürk's merciless repressions of Kurdish uprisings in the 1920s and 1930s. Erdal İnönü had reached the conclusion that neither Kurdish nationalism nor Islamic fundamentalism threatened the republican order.

On the Kurdish question, this view took official form in a Kurdish report endorsed by the Social Democrat Populist Party council on the night of 15–16 July 1990.

For the first time, a mainstream Turkish party with a chance of taking power had committed itself to policies that recognized the Kurds. 'People should be allowed to accept their Kurdish identity and say I am of Kurdish origin and be able to express this identity freely,' said the report. Whatever a person's mother tongue, he should be able to teach, speak and write in it, and the state should help found an institute to study that culture, it added. The Social Democrats paved the way for a succession of similar 'Kurdish reports' that followed over the years. Most famous were those of the late Adnan Kahveci, an aide to Turgut Özal, who warned in 1992 of civil war if a democratic solution was not applied, and Doğu Ergil, an Ankara university professor, whose 1995 report showed that although not all Kurds supported the PKK, they did want respect for a separate Kurdish cultural identity.

Nothing could satisfy the chauvinism of some on the Turkish right. The dull-witted prime minister, Yıldırım Akbulut, stirred himself to deliver the opinion that 'some people have got together to write a report. But the Turks living on this soil watered by the blood of our martyrs will remain Turks. There are no Kurds, there are [only] Turks.'[16] President Özal, then still the effective head of government, scoffed at the Social Democrat report, alleging that İnönü's party was only trying to win back votes in the Kurdish south-east that it had lost by expelling the seven deputies.

But each report added to a broader Turkish understanding of the Kurdish question. Even Özal felt obliged to counter-attack, announcing himself in favour of dropping the military coup-era Law 2932 that had banned the speaking and writing of Kurdish. He then set off on a speech-making tour of the south-east, talking of his Kurdish grandmother and planned new investments. The most famous Turkish author to fall foul of the Kurdish taboo, anthropologist Ismail Beşikçi, was quietly released for a while from prison. Written rules at the Turkish foreign ministry ordering diplomats to deny the existence of Kurds were dropped and embassies started sending out information sheets referring to Turkey as a 'democratic mosaic of peoples'. In the south-east, officials were given new orders to smile when talking to local people, to take presents to their leaders and not to treat them automatically as the enemy. The word *Kurd* had first appeared in a headline on the front page of *Cumhuriyet* two years before; it now became commonplace.

At about the same time, the PKK also started to show a new flexibility. In a watershed interview with the Turkish newspaper *Hürriyet* published on 1 April 1990, Öcalan said he now believed that 'there is no question of separating from Turkey. My people need Turkey, we can't split for at least another forty years.' He vowed to stop the violence if Turkey would do likewise, prompting Mehmet Ali Birand, one of Turkey's most respected journalists, to say that the PKK wanted to legalize itself.[17] However, President Özal dismissed even the idea of talking to the rebels.[18]

This tentative convergence towards Kurdish peace in Turkey was given an unexpected boost by the Iraqi invasion of Kuwait on 2 August 1990. The regional realignment awakened Özal's ambitions to regain a say over the former Ottoman provinces of Mosul and Kirkuk in northern Iraq, an ambition that demanded more loyalty from Turkey's Kurds and a perception in the world that Turkey was a worthy protector of the Iraqi Kurds. This required certain liberalizing measures, and between January and April 1991 Özal pressed important reforms through the cabinet. The cabinet lifted notorious articles of the Turkish penal code, thus automatically freeing or reducing the sentences of thousands of political prisoners. It also freed the Kurdish language for private use. Özal nevertheless hedged his bets. The government quickly brought in the equally notorious Article 8 of an anti-terrorism law which made it an imprisonable offence to threaten the territorial integrity of Turkey 'by any means whatever'.

Hundreds of Turkish Kurds and others were thrown into gaol for minor infringements of Article 8, and this law became a major source of contention with the West until its partial reform in 1995 on the eve of Customs Union with Europe. But this was only the public face of repression. The Turkish nationalist opposition, deeply embedded in the bureaucracy, the security forces and among some politicians, was in 1991 to begin another, more secret programme of resistance to Kurdish reforms – a programme initiated out of fear that the combination of an independent Kurdistan in northern Iraq and the growing strength of the PKK could break up and bring down the Turkish republic.

At about the same time as Özal was easing the ban on the use of Kurdish in early 1991, an anonymous tract began to be distributed on the streets of the south-eastern town of Batman. It was a call in the name of Islam for resistance against the PKK. The local newspaperman who received an early copy was in no doubt that it was the work of the police. It was only natural, after all: it might seem like a complete betrayal of the Kemalist secular ideal, but

Ottoman governments, when faced with Kurdish rebellions, had always played successfully on the shared Sunni Muslim religious sensibilities of the population.

From such humble beginnings a group known as Hezbollah emerged, apparently tolerated by the local security forces. The group's name, meaning Party of God, linked it psychologically to the Islamic Revolutionary movement in Iran and Lebanon. Rooms in the village of Yolaç, a centre of Hezbollah activity, were decorated with militant pictures of Ayatollah Khomeini. The village was run by Kurdish men in fulsome Islamic beards who looked like Iranian revolutionary guards. These toughs did not hesitate to search, interrogate and lock up visitors while they checked their credentials. Such people were accused of assassinating Kurdish activists and a full-scale war developed between the PKK and Hezbollah. Concentrated in towns like Batman, Silvan, as well as Diyarbakır, this fratricidal conflict claimed hundreds of lives.

Hezbollah were not the only anti-PKK force put into action. Nobody knows quite who killed all those who died in more than 1,500 'murders by persons unknown' that first began to shock the country in July 1991 with the killing of the Diyarbakır provincial chairman of HEP, Vedat Aydın. But it was certainly convenient for the state to have Hezbollah to blame for most of them. Human rights groups had little doubt that there were also death squads operating at the very least under the protection of the security forces. Only years later when Hezbollah looked like moving its operations to the big cities of western Turkey did the state realize that the heavily armed group was turning into an uncontrollable monster. It started to crack down. The number of unexplained killings decreased. But an initial aim had been achieved: nobody who stayed in the south-east dared to be identified as a Kurdish nationalist.

'You poor people who fancy yourselves [PKK] fighters, I'll get you and kill you if you don't surrender. The wolves and birds will devour your carcasses. You brats and dogs, don't you know your friends are surrendering? If you are an armed bandit, come out and fight like a man, don't stab in the back. And never forget you cannot be saved,' said one anonymous leaflet dropped by plane over an eastern Kurdish city in September. By December, extreme right-wing leader Alparslan Türkeş had pronounced, 'We are up against a war in the east and south-east. We must declare war.'

The PKK gave as good as it got. On 25 December 1991, it staged its first action in a western city. Reporters were called to watch youths shout 'Long live Kurdistan' and then fire-bomb a department store. Eleven shoppers died in the smoke and flames. Öcalan gave a statement in support of the youths. The PKK also revived one of its more repellent methods of ensuring support: killing Turkish teachers – 139 had been murdered in the first decade of conflict[19] – and attacking the homes of those who joined the state-sponsored Village Guards militia and killing their wives and children.

Typical of such attacks was a raid and massacre on Cevizlidağ.[20] The stone-built, flat-roofed houses of this idyllic village were set in a grassy bowl in the mountains south-west of Lake Van, two hours' drive from the main road up a track that eventually turned into a path over bare rock. A few days before, 174 PKK guerrillas had been killed in a mass attack over the Iraqi border on a Turkish outpost. This appeared to be the PKK's act of revenge. About 100 guerrillas surrounded the village, defended by fifteen Village Guards dug into outposts around their settlement.

'They shouted at us to surrender, so we did,' said one of the few survivors of the massacre, sitting in a daze with his head in his hands by the village stream the next day. 'They gathered us outside the village. But then army reinforcements began to come. So they shot us, blew up our houses with rocket grenades and ran away.'

Almost all of the village's fifteen houses were still burning or smoking. A line of pale bodies of young men was being methodically washed by a nearby village imam. Just upstream, women were washing the bodies of the eleven dead women and two dead children. Then most of the corpses were wrapped in fresh white sheets, and laid side by side in a mass grave. Turkish commandos kept watch, lounged under the walnut trees or used chain saws to carve planks for coffins for those to be buried elsewhere. Two oxen also lay dead, machine-gunned while harnessed to the yoke of a wooden sledge stacked with hay. At least twenty-one, and possibly as many as forty people had died. The machinery of the Turkish state had arrived to survey the damage, with a prosecutor directing court secretaries who incongruously hammered away on typewriters set up in a small field.

The period between 1991 and March 1993 saw many such savage clashes between the PKK and an increasingly determined, well-organized and well-equipped Turkish military. The Turkish army did not hesitate to stage deep raids against PKK bases in caves among the remote mountaintops of northern Iraq. Inside Turkey, the number of troops committed soon totalled more than 200,000 men – more than a third of Turkey's army. Auxiliary forces were mobilized such as the fearsome Special Teams and the local Turkish Kurd Village Guards, a militia that by 1996 was to number 60,000 men.

In the beginning, officials saw the Village Guards as a means of both enforcing loyalty and channelling money into pro-Turkish hands in the region. Sitting on a cheap wooden bench in his fortified complex of houses overlooking the down-at-heel town of Sirnak in 1989, Ali Khan Tatar was a typical Turkish Kurd Village Guard leader who was under no illusions about what he and the state were up against. His tribe had been allied with the state since time immemorial and had helped Atatürk put down the Sheikh Said rebellion. It had profited hugely, and its lands stretched far into the distance. Nevertheless, he kept a loaded pistol beside him. His houses were all pitted with bullet holes.

'It seems as if we are the only ones supporting the government. We respect the state and obey it. If the *kaimakam* [district prefect] hit me I would just stand here. If he hit my child, I would say please go on. But ninety-five per cent of this town is pro-PKK. I don't know why. The villagers do everything they say. If there was torture, if the government cracked down on them, then this problem would end,' he said.

The critical trial of strength between the state and the PKK came at the Nowruz celebration of March 1992. Once again, the most dramatic field of battle was the town of Cizre, but unrest was widespread and an 18-year-old Turkish Kurd girl in Izmir even burned herself to death as 'a sacrifice to Nowruz'. The PKK had called for *serilhildan*, a Kurdish word akin in meaning to the *intifada* of the Palestinians. In the days running up to Nowruz, three alleged 'collaborators' with the state were found hanging from lamp-posts in the town, their mouths stuffed with banknotes. The Turkish state mobilized tanks and troops in response and the scene was set for disaster. Shots rang out when hundreds of demonstrators, with women and children pushed to the front, started to march towards the graves of PKK 'martyrs' who were buried in a specially revered section of the cemetery. How the gunfire started remains unclear, but several people died in the frightened stampede that followed. Bullets fired by troops whistled past the retreating marchers and reporters. The PKK and security forces clashed in other parts of town. More than ninety people were killed throughout the south-east during that blood-stained Nowruz.

The security forces were full of fear and bloody-minded anger, and, unable to accept any fault in their own system, tried to blame the Kurdish problem on outsiders. In Cizre, the dead included Turkish reporter Izzet Kezer, almost certainly killed by the security forces. Bystanders watched in horror as he was cut down by shots after a tank turned its turret towards his party of journalists who were slowly trying to move back to the safety of their hotel, frantically waving a white flag. Later an armed policeman stopped a convoy of human rights activists and foreign reporters on their way back from Cizre to Diyarbakır. He lined everybody up on the side of the road. Then, working himself up into a frenzy, he moved down the line, viciously kicking and punching each person in turn. Süleyman Demirel, the prime minister of the day, publicly apologized for the incident. But the policeman appeared not to have been punished. No officials seemed particularly sorry about the local people who had died.

'The PKK has declared war. There are now two courses open for us. Either one withdraws or one stays. If you are going to stay, you have to impose the authority of the state. This is what we shall do,' said Demirel. The left-wing *Cumhuriyet* agreed. 'The PKK has chosen Nevruz to drag our country into a bloody game. Their strategy is obvious ... the more blood that is spilled, the greater the possibility of international intervention. Thus the problems of northern Iraq and south-eastern Turkey will become one and the same,' the newspaper said in an editorial. Even Özal joined the chorus: 'Terrorism must be stamped out ... from now on it will be stamped out bloodily.'

Yet President Özal did not close all the doors to a negotiated solution. Perhaps he still remembered his earlier promise in October 1991 to solve the Kurdish problem as a 'last service to the nation', when he had argued that a flat refusal to discuss concepts such as a Kurdish federal solution meant abandoning the field of debate to the PKK without a fight.

Circumstances changed for the PKK too. The Turkish army's abandonment of parade-ground tactics and their offensives into Iraq forced the militants on to the defensive. With the collapse of the Soviet Union in 1991, the main sponsors of its Soviet-backed ideology disappeared. Western states were becoming less tolerant of PKK activities. Öcalan was losing support from his main protector, Syrian President Hafez al-Assad, partly because President Özal was reaching out to Damascus, and partly because Damascus needed to please Washington as the Middle East peace process got under way. From the beginning Syria had used the PKK as a cat's paw in its policy of forcing Turkey to release more water down the Euphrates: in 1987, a verbal undertaking by Turkey to ensure an average minimum flow induced the Syrians to move the PKK camps away from the border. In September 1992, after more talks with Turkey, the Syrians closed the main PKK training camp in Lebanon's Syrian-controlled Bekaa Valley.

Go-betweens began to have success persuading the two sides that the other was ready to talk peace. Foreign correspondents, Turkish journalists and Iraqi Kurdish leader Jalal Talabani took messages from one side to the other. The result was remarkable. On 16 March 1993, in the Bekaa Valley town of Bar Elias, Abdüllah Öcalan appeared in a shiny new suit and offered a cease-fire.

'We want to become a legitimate political party,' he had explained to an Arabic-language newspaper just beforehand. 'Permit me to return unarmed to Kurdistan in peace and start a dialogue. We hope that the Turkish government now realizes that the Kurdish problem cannot be resolved by military force and also realizes that it cannot ignore the existence of the Kurdish people, its rights, language and identity.'

Some Turks became hopeful at the initiative. Even though the cease-fire was not officially acknowledged, and despite much debate within the army, a big offensive into northern Iraq planned for the spring was put on hold. Prime Minister Demirel spoke positively of people's hopes. He had sat 'like a student' through briefings from the journalist go-betweens. Perhaps he also remembered an echo of his famous but soon-forgotten statement one month after coming to power with Erdal Inönü in October 1991 that he had 'recognized the Kurdish reality'. When the cease-fire came into force, Demirel declared: 'This is not something that Turkey will brush aside', although, typically taking back with one hand what he gave away with the other, he underlined that he would not negotiate with terrorists.

Even the Turkish chief of staff, General Doğan Güreş, said later that 'I felt inside me a secret joy. But of course I didn't show it. A ray of hope seemed to appear, and I wondered if this was all about to finish. They were going to leave the mountains. We were going to withdraw our armed forces. Nobody was going to die any more. Whatever happened after that would have been the business of the government and politicians. Economic and social reforms would have come.'

The Kurds made no secret of their joy. On the muddy streets of the flashpoint town of Cizre, the Nowruz celebrations of 1993 showed a new spirit. Young militants in chequered headscarves chased away any children who tried to greet reporters with the usual V-for-Victory signs and shouts of 'Down with Turkey' and

'Long live the PKK'. Flags, slogans and posters were kept to a minimum. The red, yellow and green colours could only be glimpsed woven into bands in the hair of young girls, or on jerseys or bandannas waved by the leading dancers of long lines of Kurds jigging happily to the traditional wailing reed-pipe and thumping drum.

The sincerity of the various Turkish and Kurdish leaders may well have been in doubt. But there was no doubting the palpable sense of hope and relief in the country during the two months that the cease-fire lasted. It remains a ray of hope for the future. But in 1993, all these hopes were to be cruelly dashed.

The reason for the breakdown of the Turkish-PKK cease-fire may have been President Turgut Özal's sudden death in April 1993. Or it may have been due to Turkish security forces never having ceased their local harassment of the PKK, killing scores of suspected militants. Or, again, it might have been the result of a PKK field commander rebelling against Öcalan, or a sign of anger from the PKK's godfathers in Syria over another refusal by Turkey five days before to give a written guarantee on the Euphrates water flow.

Whatever the reason, on the evening of 25 May 1993, a band of PKK guerrillas in the mountains near Bingöl set up a roadblock across a remote section of a main road. In one of the buses they stopped, they found dozens of unarmed off-duty soldiers returning from a driving course. The soldiers were marched off, lined up and mowed down with rifle fire. Thirty soldiers and two civilians were killed. Everybody involved in the peace process went into deep shock. It was some time before the PKK claimed the action as their own: finally, Öcalan admitted it. A pro-PKK news agency announced that it was 'the result of the state's violation of the cease-fire'.

The collapse of the peace initiative ushered in a second round of the war, a period of two years which would far outdo the 1991–3 period in its savagery. Within two weeks, 300 people had been killed. With Özal dead, the Turkish state machine reverted to its dream of total victory against the PKK, with no concession to the underlying causes of support for the rebels.

'If their cease-fire was sincere they should have given up their weapons and surrendered. But their attacks are like the scratches you get when you step on a cat's tail. They will end up either in gaol, in exile or in the cemetery,' said Ünal Erkan, then the governor-general of the ten south-eastern provinces under emergency rule.

For a while in the summer of 1993, the prime minister-in-waiting, Tansu Çiller, under pressure from her Social Democrat coalition partners, looked as though she might be casting about for a solution that would recognize the broad aspirations of many Turkish Kurds for an acknowledgement of their separate cultural identity. But from his new post in the presidency, Süleyman Demirel sent a shot across her bows. He warned that there could be no discussion of cultural matters until terrorism had been uprooted, otherwise there would be 'compromise after compromise with no end'. Soon her political weakness and inexperience forced her into the arms of the military and a rhetoric of nationalist bravado. Çiller capitulated in a tough speech against the PKK and Syria in an Istanbul hotel in November 1993. 'From now on, we will act differently,' she said, promising reinforcement of the much-feared Special Team units.

Challenges to state authority were now being met with massive reprisals: the murder of a Turkish general in Lice led to 400 buildings in the town being wrecked. In the town of Silopi, the district prefect summed up the essence of the new state policy of total confrontation, strongly hinting that the bearded toughs in civilian clothes all over the town had absolute freedom to torture and intimidate. 'People outside didn't understand the problem before,' he said. 'Even local people used to say "the PKK will kill me if I give in and confess without resisting." We have to take hard measures to show the full strength of the state. Personally, I regret it. But you have to fight fire with fire.'

Two policies in particular were speeded up: the crushing of all civilian manifestations of Kurdish nationalism, be they cultural associations, newspapers or political parties, and the evacuation of villages in the south-east.

The policy of relocating troublesome populations had been practised both by the Ottomans and by Atatürk's young republic. In the late 1980s, the authorities had started again to empty, burn down or blow up isolated Kurdish villages. Each individual evacuation had had a different cause: punishment for sending food to the PKK, for not joining the Village Guard militia, for having children in the PKK or simply because the villagers had left, fed up with being caught in the cross-fire.

The state policy gradually became harsher still. In 1990, officials began to talk about moving 10,000 people to clear a 600-metre security zone along the Iraqi border. Then army officers started openly to compare the PKK to 'sharks who live in water. The water feeds them. It'll take a little time but we will cut off the water.'[21] Özal had also been frank. 'Many problems would be solved much more easily', he had told one meeting of Turkish Kurds, 'if 500,000 people left here and settled in the west. We are ready to embrace you all.' Özal believed in urbanization as a natural solution, enabling Kurds to be more cheaply and easily looked after by the state. Better schools, more jobs and improved living conditions would, Özal thought, induce the Kurds to throw in their lot with the Turkish republic rather than seek an uncertain independence.

However much truth there may have been in this, those Kurds left scrabbling in the rubbish dumps of Hakkari for crusts of bread felt very differently as the new inrush of people displaced by the conflict rapidly overwhelmed the traditional safety-net of the tribe and extended family. The countryside of the south-east was devastated; even the interior minister admitted that things 'went a bit far'. Viewed from a helicopter flying over the mountains, almost every village down below seemed to consist of clusters of bare and blackened walls; one was still burning when Prime Minister Çiller flew over on her inaugural visit to the region in 1993. By the mid-1990s, official statistics spoke of 918 villages and 1,767 hamlets in twelve south-eastern provinces fully or partly evacuated, involving – with the misleading exactitude of Turkish statistics – a total of 329,916 displaced people. Nobody can know with certainty how many left, or why, but the true total is probably several times greater than the official figure.

The upsurge of violence in 1991–3 had already derailed attempts by Kurdish nationalists to form a legal party. Seventeen Kurdish deputies left Erdal Inönü's Social Democrat Party after the Nowruz clashes of March 1992, accusing it of acquiescing in a policy of suffering and tears and doing nothing for the Kurds. Most rejoined their old party HEP, which staged a manifestly nationalist conference in 1992, complete with Kurdish national colours, anti-Turkish slogans and speakers calling for the legalization of the PKK. By no means all Kurds, even in HEP, wanted such radical measures, but other initiatives never got off the ground. As far back as 1991, the PKK had ordered that no other Kurdish party should be formed. In July 1993, Turkish prosecutors caught up with HEP and closed it down for allegedly basing itself on racial differences, undermining the integrity of the state and developing cultures other than the official Turkish one.

A few days before HEP was closed down, dissident Kurdish members of parliament slipped over to a newly formed party, the Democracy Party (Demokrasi Partisi or DEP). The experiment lasted no more than a few months. DEP went further towards the PKK and suffered even harsher repression than HEP. A December congress elected the bitter radical Hatip Dicle as leader. The Kurdish problem, Dicle said, could not be solved without the PKK: 'nobody could separate the PKK from us and other friendly forces'. The last straw for the Turkish establishment came when Dicle announced that a PKK bomb which killed five off-duty military cadets in a suburb of Istanbul was a permissible act of war.

Dicle was already being pressed to resign by the Turkish Kurds of the western cities. But they were given no time to act; the military was so furious that Çiller could not resist. 'The time has now come to remove the PKK's existence from under the roof of parliament,' she declared. On 2 March 1994 television cameras captured images that are perhaps the biggest stain on Turkish democracy since the 1980 coup: the sight of secret policemen bundling two slight DEP deputies into an unmarked police car at the gates of parliament.

In fact it was only the last blow in weeks of amazing state harassment of DEP. Over the preceding forty-five days seven of their members had been murdered, several wounded by gunshots and six buildings had been bombed or damaged, one of these DEP's headquarters in Ankara, which had been wrecked by a large explosion. About 320 of their activists were taken into custody. The party was finally closed down in June 1994. The torch was picked up by the newly formed HADEP, but this party also proved unable to avoid being sucked into the vicious circle of violence. At their second party congress in June 1996, an apparently pro-PKK militant untied and dropped the Turkish flag into the crowd and hung up the banner of the PKK. The newly elected 32-member HADEP leadership council – most of them names close to the PKK – were arrested as they left the congress. Three delegates were also shot dead on their way home. Thanks to the failure of both sides to rise above their powerful radical factions, the attempts to form a legal nationalist party left Turks and Turkish Kurds badly bruised and as tragically far from a political solution as ever.

As their party faced closure in June 1994, the thirteen remaining DEP members of parliament knew they were about to lose their immunity and be prosecuted like eight fellow Kurdish nationalists who had already been arrested. They faced a crucial question: to stay and become public martyrs to the Turkish Kurd cause, or to flee the country. They decided to pursue their cause from exile. It was to prove a fateful choice.

*

The new exiles in Europe were in a position familiar from Ottoman times but difficult none the less. The longer they were away, the more their 'parliament-in-exile' risked falling into the hands of highly organized, well-funded pro-PKK networks in Europe. Also, in the years after the resumption of full-scale conflict in 1993, Turkish security forces seemed to have restored their vision of order to most south-eastern towns and to have beaten the PKK back to the mountaintops. Repeated PKK offers of a cease-fire from 15 December 1995 were ignored by the Ankara government. The PKK lost a critical edge of awe and fear that it had inspired in the population, and war-weariness did much to persuade ordinary Turkish Kurds in the south-east to look to other alternatives, such as the pro-Islamic Welfare Party, to carry their hopes. The 'parliament-in-exile' likewise never fulfilled its ambition to represent all the Kurds of the Middle East, one of the stated goals of the PKK. In fact, it remained tightly associated with the kernel of DEP deputies exiled from Turkey. 'The Kurdish parliament-in-exile is not a body overshadowed by the PKK. We are, through our efforts, the PKK itself,' said Yaşar Kaya, one of the group who was not a deputy but for a while was the publisher of the much-persecuted main pro-Kurdish newspaper.[22]

The group nevertheless succeeded in one of its aims: that of creating conflict between Turkey and Europe, carefully calculating the impact of holding each meeting in a different European city. Local European authorities could see no wrong in meetings of this apparently peaceful and oppressed Brussels-based group; Turkey, trapped by its unacceptable human rights record, had no moral ground from which to persuade anyone that these gatherings were assisting the PKK's 'terrorist' agenda. Turkey also pursued the Europe-based Kurdish nationalist television MED-TV as it hopped from satellite to satellite. The acrimonious disputes which resulted, much to the satisfaction of the Kurdish nationalists, could and did badly damage Turkey's relations with one country after another in Europe. European archaeologists were threatened with the suspension of their licences to excavate, and European companies with the loss of state contracts.

Turkey, which had previously only had to worry about Syrian support for the PKK, and to some extent the involvement of forces in Iran and Iraq, now had a whole host of new countries to reckon with. Some pro-PKK groups settled briefly in Armenia. Greek Cyprus was highly sympathetic to the PKK, as were some on the Greek mainland. Senior Greek delegations met with Öcalan; Kurdish refugee camps in Greece became thinly disguised rest and recreation areas for PKK guerrillas, and the political wing of the PKK, ERNK, was able to set up offices in Athens. Russia also opened its arms to the PKK, with Russian officials attending meetings held in government buildings that would open with readings of letters from Öcalan: as one Russian newspaper commented, it was not unnatural for Russia to support the Kurds in order to counterbalance Turkey's apparent support for the Chechens. In 1992, Europe was especially shocked by the fighting in Turkey. Germany briefly held back arms shipments and the European parliament regularly delivered sharp rebukes to the Turkish government.

Mainstream European governments, however, if not the more liberal media, were becoming more wary of the PKK. Suspicions of Kurdish organizations strengthened as local communities began to complain of extorted 'taxes'. These were reinforced in the late 1980s by the heavy Turkish Kurd hand in the European drug trade, from heroin processing in eastern Turkey to marketing in Europe. Even in the United States, 70 per cent of major heroin hauls involved citizens of Turkey. At times up to half of Europe's heroin was thought to come from Iran via Turkish Kurdistan and then on hard-to-search international trucks plying the 'Balkan route'[23] – a figure which rose to 80 per cent in Britain. Although Öcalan has claimed that the PKK has an annual budget of $100 million, the organization denies trafficking in drugs. Scandals revealed by the Turkish press have shown that many pro-government Kurdish tribes are also closely involved in the trade, often with the help of members of the Turkish security forces.

European irritation with the PKK turned to real concern at the security threat posed by Öcalan's declaration of all-out war after the end of the cease-fire in May 1993. In June 1993, Turkish Kurd militants attacked Turkish targets in six countries across more than twenty European cities, from Marseilles to Stockholm; 600 demonstrators attacked eighty Turkish premises in Germany alone. PKK threats, the kidnapping of Western tourists, and bombing of Turkish resorts damaged the noble image of the Kurdish cause, to the fury of the Iraqi Kurdish leaders who had striven to cultivate it.[24] The PKK verbally attacked German leaders.[25] When Turkish Kurd militants in Europe struck again in five countries in November 1993, and violent demonstrations became commonplace after that, European governments had had enough.

Britain and the United States had always agreed in condemning the PKK as a terrorist organization. They were now joined by France, and, critically, Germany, home to more than 400,000 *gast-*

arbeiter of Turkish Kurd origin. The Federal Government clamped down on pro-PKK news agencies and associations, accusing the PKK of being behind many of the second generation of fire-bomb attacks on Turkish homes and businesses in Germany. 'It [the PKK] is like a state within a state. It creates an atmosphere of intimidation, it levies a type of tax on all Kurds living in Germany,' said a federal prosecutor. 'It plans and directs attacks on Turkish targets and carries out reprisals against those who refuse to toe the party line.'[26]

In Ankara, Western ambassadors kept their heads down and their eye on the main chance. Contrary to alarmist Turkish beliefs of old-fashioned imperialist designs, none of them had any wish to see Turkey split up. It was true that their efforts to cultivate the Turkish government while not betraying liberal Western ideals could take strange forms, as when a junior diplomat at a British foreign minister's press conference begged reporters to ask appropriate questions to ensure that the minister's criticism of Turkey's human rights record could be publicly aired. The Americans had few such qualms. One ambassador proudly kept models of armoured personnel carriers and F-16 warplanes on the coffee table in his office in the US embassy, with its battleship-style piping in the corridors and metal-armoured shutters that often kept the mission's windows sealed off from the city outside. Advocacy of political solutions to the Kurdish problem was the official line, but the PKK was considered to be a tool of Syrian foreign policy and a strong and well-armed Turkish government was still the first priority.

Under Ambassador Eric Rouleau, when Danielle Mitterrand was in the ascendant in the early 1990s, France briefly broke faith with Turkey's Kemalist élite. At Rouleau's farewell party in the austere salons of France's 1930s embassy there were notably more Turkish Kurd figures present than prominent Turks. This pro-Kurdish nuance was rapidly corrected under the new administration. But France still kept up the Kurdish Institute in Paris, the first such international centre for Kurds, housed in a charming, old-fashioned building at the end of an alleyway. An invaluable haven of Kurdish thinking under exiled Turkish Kurd scholar Kendal Nezan, it is one of the few institutions to remain comparatively free of domination by the PKK. But, his face deeply lined, Nezan could only lament the record of a Turkish state that had brutalized Kurdish society, had decapitated generations of its élite and had gaoled or exiled anyone who showed a capacity for communal leadership. Worst of all, he feared that a new generation of Kurdish exiles was emerging who nursed a visceral, rather than simply a political hatred for the Turks.

In many ways, the words written earlier by Nezan about Europe's flirtation with the Kurds of Iraq and Turkey in the 1920s remained valid for the European position in the 1990s.

> The Great Powers continued to foster the myth that the civilized West might help the Kurds; what this really meant, of course, was that the Western powers would be able to use their influence on Kurdish leaders as a bargaining counter in any eventual negotiation [with the Turks].[27]

The Kurdish problem has always been only a small and easily sacrificed part of the West's overall relationship with Turkey. New facets of its strategic importance in its legendarily rough neighbourhood are always being rediscovered. None of these, however, could match the significance that became attached to the major and genuinely new policy initiative of the Turkish republic in the era following the Second World War: its grand offensive to embrace the Turkic republics of the former Soviet Union.

16

The Wolf and the Bear

O Muslim brother in Azerbaijan
Don't weep, in your steps I will follow
The day is coming when the spilled blood will rise
    Don't forget that, O oppressor Moscow!

Cemal Bayat, Turkish border poet, 1990

THE DEEP VOICE was rough and emotional as it took over Turkey's state-run television news in January 1990. The words were indistinct but still comprehensible to most. For up to fifteen minutes at a time, evening after evening, Turks concentrated on a man they had not heard of, who spoke a language few even knew existed: Azeri Turkish. It was both mysterious and arousing. So was the news given over the telephone by the owner of the voice, in hiding in the Azerbaijani capital, Baku. Abulfez Elchibey told of a new war against the Armenians, of a Turkish nationalist uprising, of its suppression by the tanks of the Red Army, of the many Azeri Turks who had died.

These events of Baku's 'Black January' were not just a rediscovery of long-lost cousins, but a rude political awakening for both the Turks and the Turkish government. They triggered a nationalist ferment in the provinces on the borders of the Caucasus, where Turkey's large ethnic Azeri community is concentrated. Some officials tried to calm the atmosphere. But other Turks did not hide their new ambitions, presaging the consequences of the fall of the Soviet Union eighteen months later. Articles in the Turkish press looked forward to the possibility of a new union of Turkic states for the world's 110–130 million speakers of the Turkic family of languages. Right-wingers in the Motherland Party competed for space on the new nationalist platform. One declared that the twenty-first century would be an Islamic-Turkish age. State Minister Ercument Konukman declared that 'in the years to come, Turks in surrounding states will form independent states under the Turkish flag. The nineteenth century's sick old Ottoman Turk will regain his former strength.' The Turkish prime minister even talked of those in the Azerbaijani uprising as 'our citizens'.

Many Turks were also confused. Their awareness of the Turkish east had been deliberately suppressed by republican ideologues. When Mustafa Kemal beat his rival Enver Pasha to supreme power in 1920s Turkey, the republic had rejected Enver's pan-Turkism as decisively as Sultan Abdülhamit's pan-Islamism. Instead, Atatürk chose Ziya Gökalp's idea of a Westernizing nation state with a single, reformed, 'Turkish' culture. Preaching the doctrine of the Central Asian Turks' take-over of Anatolia centuries ago to school-children was one thing. Dealing with the real Turkic peoples who remained in Central Asia was quite another. They could drag Ankara into unwanted conflict with Moscow, and the very variety of the Turkic peoples posed too many questions about the real nature of the monolithic Turkish ethnicity central to Kemalist doctrines.

The Turks had also got used to the isolated position of their self-made cultural island in the world. The inward-looking policies of the early republic had partly been an expression of that. Which-ever way the Turks looked they saw hostility: a hall of mirrors of Persian arrogance, Arab distrust, Greek hatred, Slavic suspicion or European imperiousness. Turkish diplomats ploughed a lonely furrow, Turkish students on holiday would conceal their origin when meeting their peers and Turkish business travellers were humiliated in foreign consulates. Not surprisingly, the Turks usu-ally felt unloved and unwanted.

Yet as the bonds tying the Turkic peoples to Moscow weakened, a group of peoples suddenly arrived on Turkey's doorstep who openly expressed a love for the Turks. Visiting Turkic ministers would kiss Turkish soil on stepping off their plane. Even Islam Karimov, the unsmiling and authoritarian President of Uzbekistan, wept on arrival in Ankara and presented his old foreign ministry building to Turkey for use as its embassy in Tashkent. The outburst of feeling was enough to turn anyone's head.

The Turks of Anatolia had in fact only gradually lost contact with their Central Asian cousins who stayed in the greater geographical area still often called Turkestan. Rulers of the Seljuk empire of the eleventh to thirteenth centuries still had a foot in both worlds. When the Turko-Mongol Tamerlane campaigned against Ottoman Sultan 'Thunderbolt' Beyazıt in Anatolia to restore the former suzerainty of the Mongols, he won the key battle of Ankara in 1402 partly by appealing to anti-Ottoman Türkmen marcher lords to take his side. In the sixteenth century, the Ottomans made a brief attempt to dig a Volga–Don canal in order to form a link with Sunni Muslims in Turkestan against the rising Shia Safavids in Iran. In the eighteenth century, one Ottoman Black Sea governor raised an army of 10,000 to settle and intermarry in the Caucasus to help implant a Sunni Islam loyal to Istanbul, a religious outreach that was to be a major part of Turkey's efforts in the 1990s as well.

In the nineteenth century, it was in fact the Tartars of Russia who first developed the idea of pan-Turkism, feeling the need to arm themselves against the rising nationalism of the Slavs. This movement spread to Turkish intellectuals and officers like Enver Pasha in the Ottoman domain, who felt threatened by growing Armenian, Greek and other Christian nationalisms. Enver Pasha's attempt to march east – partly a bid to unite the Turkic world – may have failed in 1914. But the collapse in 1917 of the Tsarist Russian empire, like the dissolution of the Soviet Union nearly eight decades later, provided an opportunity for local Turkic and Muslim populations to bid for self-determination.

In the Caucasus, Ottoman forces briefly captured Baku. The episode was to have many parallels with the 1990s. For two years from May 1918, the pro-Turkish, independent-minded Musavat Party managed to rule independently of Moscow, but in April 1920 Bolshevik forces took the city. In Central Asia, the medieval court of the Emir of Bukhara held out until September 1920. A year later, Enver Pasha found his last role in Turkish history. After fleeing the coming Allied occupation of Istanbul in 1918, he had travelled first to Berlin and then to Moscow, where he cut a dashing figure briefly entertained by the Soviets as a possible alternative to the increasingly successful Mustafa Kemal in Anatolia. In 1921, Moscow redirected him to help suppress the last anti-Soviet Muslim rebels of Turkestan. It was a strange misreading of Enver on the Soviets' part, and within days of his arrival in Bukhara in November 1921, Enver Pasha put himself at the head of the anti-Bolshevik Basmachi forces. But they lacked a unifying ideology, lost the legitimacy of support by traditional leaders and were undermined by the airs and incompetence of Enver himself. The Turkish general was mowed down by Bolshevik machine-gun fire on the Tajik-Afghan border in August 1922, his body only to be returned to Turkey in 1996. His blood-stained uniform was taken off for display in a Moscow military museum. The Soviet Union embarked on a thorough destructuring and rebuilding of Turkestan and the Caucasus, aiming to prevent it from being able to unite economically, ethnically or politically ever again.

First, the Bolshevik authorities drew up a new set of borders. However honourable may have been the intentions of the Communist revolutionaries in the 1920s, their eyes on the construction of a great new Soviet state rather than minor administrative divisions, the map that resulted made it certain in the 1990s that the southern republics would always be at each others' throats. The future Soviet leader Joseph Stalin was also in charge of much of the process, and, coming himself from an ethnic minority in Georgia, he must have known what he was doing. In the Caucasus, Georgia became a fragile mini-empire, Armenia was left landlocked and Azerbaijan was awarded sovereignty over the self-contained Armenian-majority enclave of Nagorny-Karabagh. In Central Asia, only finally conquered by the Tsarist empire during the preceding half-century, the biggest ethnic group, the Uzbeks, were left tightly landlocked. The Tajiks lost their two main cities, Samarkand and Bukhara, to Uzbekistan, and instead were given the small market town of Dushanbe to be their capital. To complicate things further, the fertile, self-contained, Uzbek-populated and potentially rebellious Fergana valley was divided between Uzbekistan, Tajikistan and the Kyrgyz Republic. Kazakstan was drawn enormous and left the Kazaks a minority in their own country. Only the Türkmens had anything like a coherent entity, but were too poor and ill-educated to put up much competition with the Slav settlers who soon arrived to graft new Soviet cities and Soviet civilization on to the Central Asian steppe.

Under the Soviet Union, central planning made all the economies of the republics extraordinarily interdependent. The borders of the 1920s were still serving Russia's purpose in the 1990s. No single republic, with the qualified exception of Turkmenistan, was able to survive alone. Nor were any regional groupings to prove able to act collectively. Just as importantly from Moscow's point of view, no outside power was in a position to challenge Russia's dominance. Iran was perhaps best placed to do so, but was exhausted by its eight-year war with Iraq and lacked the resources to project much power. It also had to tread carefully because of its own Türkmen and especially Azeri minorities, who, though thoroughly integrated into Iranian society, constituted more than a third of Iran's population. China also had borders with three Central Asian states. But, while encouraging trade, Peking had reason to be nervous about too much cross-border contact. Authorities in China's westernmost province of Xinjiang were busy repressing their own Turkic minority, the Uygurs. Uygur separatist organizations congregated in Kazakstan, although their main leader, Isa Beg, having briefly represented his people in the 1940s, lived out his last days in Istanbul, in a modest flat overlooking the railway line once used by the Orient Express.

Turkey's only direct contact with the Turkic east was a marshy seven-kilometre stretch along the Araxes river that bordered Nakhichevan, the result of another gesture of goodwill from Lenin to Atatürk. This small exclave of Azerbaijan was cut off from the rest of the republic by a flange of Armenia that joined the Iranian border, a flange that was extensively widened during a series of offensives by the Nagorny-Karabagh Armenians in late 1993. This lack of a geographic connection was to prove hugely frustrating both to Turkish traders needing to find safe through-roads for their trucks and to planners of pipeline routes intended to carry oil from Turkic states to Turkey and the Mediterranean.

Even before the collapse of the Soviet Union, however, Turkish contractors were working hard on a new road bridge over the Araxes into Nakhichevan. Locals called it the 'Bridge of Longing' for renewed contact with their kinsmen on the other side. Indeed, Turkey and the Communist governments of Turkic republics in the Caucasus and Central Asia had been putting out feelers to each other for years, although always with a carefully articulated determination not to provoke jealousy in Moscow. Even after a small flock of sheep were sacrificed for Süleyman Demirel to open the Araxes crossing in 1992, the then prime minister felt obliged to underline the old Turkish folk saying that Turks should 'keep calling the bear uncle until you are over the bridge'.

As part of these messages of reassurance to the Russian bear, Turkey proposed the formation of a trading group, the Black Sea Economic Co-operation (BSEC), that would bring together all the rivals and friends of the Caucasus and the Balkans. Russian President Boris Yeltsin showed Moscow's early indulgence by attending the inaugural summit in June 1992. Turkey also urged the creation of a similar grouping as a forum for stabilizing the Balkans following the end of the Cold War. Increasing Turkish-Russian and other rivalries later put paid to serious co-operation under the umbrella of the BSEC, but summits were regularly held, and its institutions kept ready for use should the atmosphere improve.

Ironically, it was the flourishing of Turkish trade with the Soviet Union in the late 1980s on the back of the huge gas pipeline that opened many doors for Turkish businessmen. In 1988, the opening of a first border gate between Turkey and Georgia at the town of Sarp also transformed the economy of Turkey's north-east. Turkish businessmen went on to dominate a first business conference in Azerbaijan in 1990, at which time the then Communist Azerbaijani prime minister, stealing the nationalist opposition's thunder, happily talked of Azerbaijan's individual pro-Turkish identity and its wish for independence. On the other hand, private Turkish associations of immigrants from these countries had many influential contacts with the Turkish nationalist movements in the east. The pressures of these fringe Turkish domestic lobby groups, which more than once had a hand in plotting coups, were sometimes to cause considerable embarrassment to the Turkish government of the day.

All in all, when the time for everyone to declare their interests came with the collapse of the Soviet Union in late 1991, Turkey was the country prepared to bid highest for a stake in the Caucasus and Central Asia. It was not a meeting of complete strangers when leaders of the five countries to become known as 'Turkic' first came together at the World Economic Forum in Davos in February 1992. Turkey moved as fast as it could, often being the first country to recognize and open an embassy in each state, even when this meant transporting an ambassador with a broken leg to Baku to beat the Iranians to the honour.

Uncertainty over the intentions of Iran's Islamic Republic likewise persuaded the United States to support Turkey's efforts. Even Russia, in the grip of overwhelming problems of readjustment in 1992, at first welcomed Turkey's initiative as a least-bad guarantee against its fears of Islamic instability to the south. 'We actively support the development of these relationships, within civilized degrees,' said the outgoing Soviet ambassador to Turkey, Albert Chernishev, in September 1991. Flying to the Central Asian republics, Demirel also made sure that he visited Moscow as well.

Washington underlined its support for Turkey even as the Turkic leaders met in Davos. An airlift called 'Operation Provide Hope' was deliberately routed through airbases in Turkey as the planes headed east to Central Asia in a gesture of support to celebrate the end of the Cold War and the birth of a family of newly independent states. One such freezing night flight to Tajikistan on a Vietnam-vintage C-41 Starlifter brought just 26 tons of supplies, including crates of medicine from Japan, raisins, sugar and cigarettes from Turkey and ex-Gulf War American military canteen supplies of cookies, pasta and vanilla puddings. Perhaps more significantly, sophisticated-looking radio equipment was also passed to the American military mission awaiting the plane. The few Tajiks on hand to voice an opinion thought it all shockingly superficial. But of such materials was built the dam against the feared Islamic take-over of Central Asia. Such gestures helped lay the foundation of a much-talked of 'Turkish model' and a Turkish sphere of influence in a region that stretched from the Adriatic coast to the Great Wall of China.

At first, the auguries appeared good for Turkey. Turkey's star rose highest over the new Azerbaijan. The victory of the pro-Turkish Popular Front in the June 1992 election brought to power Abulfez Elchibey, a man so pro-Turkish that he kept a picture of Atatürk in his office. On the streets, shop signs proclaimed the Azeris' choice of Turkey's Latin script over Cyrillic or the Arabic letters used by Iran. Stencilled on the canvas tops of the Popular Front's interior ministry jeeps, a wolf howled up to a Turkish crescent moon. The interior minister even kept a stuffed grey wolf by his desk. 'It's the sign of freedom for all the Turks. We are all grey wolves now, and Elchibey is the leader of a greater Turkish world,' said a policeman in one of the jeeps, packing a great pistol on his hip in case there was anyone who wished to argue the point.

Elchibey always insisted that this pro-Turkishness did not mean pan-Turkishness, but his neighbours were not so sure. He granted asylum to pro-Turkish refugees from the Turkic republics to the east, mostly run by ex-Communists for whom any such gesture was little less than a declaration of war. He made wild claims on 'southern Azerbaijan', that is, north-western Iran. He was implacable in his hostility to Russia. A former translator in the Soviet embassy in Egypt, he was also completely unprepared for leading a country run by Soviet-educated bureaucrats, which, at the same time, was losing a war in Nagorny-Karabagh. In short, he was riding for a fall, even if this was not immediately obvious at the time.

Pushed by President Özal, Turkey tried to maximize its advantage. The Turkish state offered to take 10,000 students from the Turkic republics each year. A billion dollars' worth of loans from Turkey's Eximbank were made available, even if suitable projects to use the money turned out to be in short supply. A number of Turkish state schools were set up. Ankara offered to train bureaucrats, diplomats, imams and officers in countries which, thanks to the subtle ethnic discrimination of the Soviet system, had few such functionaries. Turkish Airlines was the pioneer in opening up air routes from Istanbul. Turkish state banks set up a branch or two in each republic, and each new government was advanced a new telephone exchange. A new television channel, Avrasya, or Eurasia, was set up for viewing in all the republics at the same time, although this project never fully overcame the cultural differences between the various states. Turkish satellites with footprints stretching from western Europe to eastern Kazakstan were sent into space.

The Turkish state's rapid incursion into the Caucasus and Central Asia was arguably heavy-handed. But it established Turkey as a friend who cared. Many of the hurried bilateral agreements may have fallen by the wayside, but a significant number took root. The Turks knew they lacked financial resources, but felt they could hold out a helping hand to the élites of the new republics. Turkey delivered introductions for membership of all the Western clubs that it could. An example of the process was described by Gün Kut, a Bosphorus University academic who worked with Prime Minister Süleyman Demirel during those critical months and witnessed his first working meetings with President Nursultan Nazarbayev of Kazakstan in the spring of 1992.

At first, Nazarbayev seemed to be making light of Demirel's visit and was not planning to join him on a tour of the Kazak provinces. He hinted politely that Turkey's promises were all very well, but he knew that Turkey had problems of its own. Demirel proved difficult to shake off. 'Have you got a constitution?' he asked. On receiving a negative reply, Demirel handed one over. 'Do you have a banking system?' No. Demirel pointed to a group of Turkish banking specialists he had brought with him. And so it went on. Nazarbayev did an about-turn, started paying attention and accompanied Demirel throughout his whole visit. Their conversations would stretch into the early hours.[1]

The Turks understandably felt flattered when they heard of the extraordinary initial enthusiasm of other Turkic leaders. Uzbekistan's President Karimov, for instance, announced in December 1991: 'I declare to the whole world that my country will go by the Turkish route. We have chosen this road and will not turn back.' Even the proud President Nazarbayev of Kazakstan was to say publicly at the same time: 'We want to implement a free-market economy. The only model we have is Turkey. I want firmly to underline that Turkey is our economic hope.' In private, he may have preferred more authoritarian South-east Asian models like Korea; his views were also tinged with a sense of rivalry with Turkey, which he saw as a threat to his own ambitions to serve as a bridge between Europe and Asia.

However, an edge of arrogance crept into the Turkish side of these relationships, a big-brotherliness much resented by peoples newly escaped from the clutches of the Soviet Union. Demirel was once asked to introduce briefly the Uzbek and Türkmen presidents to a group of high-powered businessmen meeting in Istanbul: like a primary school teacher giving a geography lesson, he rambled on for more than an hour about their countries while they shifted uncomfortably in their seats beside him. A new agency was also set up in Ankara to co-ordinate aid to the newly independent republics run by diplomat Umut Arık, off whose lips rolled crusty phrases belittling 'Johnny Slav' and 'this gentleman Boris'. For him, the Turkish entrepreneurs then heading east were going to be the Rhodes and Mellons of the next century. The map on the wall of Arık's sumptuously fitted office showed that although the agency aimed to cover all the republics, the flags of the Turkic states got priority. Arık publicly claimed the region as Turkey's 'near-abroad', not the Russians'.

'It is not true that the Russians had a civilizing influence. We are reviving the presence of these peoples, whose identities had been cleansed,' he would say, noting the colonial nature of Tsarist Russian interests and the damage done to ecosystems like the Aral Sea by Soviet agricultural practices.

Even so, Arık was not propounding a form of pan-Turkism. His desire, along with that of most Turkish policy-makers, was to support the Central Asians in their goal of setting up independent nation states for the Turkic nationalities that had grown up under Soviet rule. The energy- and resource-rich nature of these Central Asian republics made a good fit with Turkey's more consumer-oriented manufacturers. All shared a wariness of and a need to get along with their powerful northern neighbour, Russia. Even after the euphoria of the initial meetings had died down, there seemed to be a natural pool of shared cultural, religious and geographic norms sufficient to form the basis of an international platform.

When official voices in Central Asia rose to deny any special links with Turkey, many Turks preferred to believe that this was simply the result of Russian pressure forcing them to hide their true selves. Interestingly, this contrasted with Turks' scepticism of the rare European statements of goodwill, which Turks generally perceived as expressions of false friendship intended to soften their resistance to a dirty or difficult task in the region, such as helping to bomb Baghdad or to stand up to Iran. At the peak of Turkey's Turkic enthusiasm in November 1992, this basic solidarity seemed to be proved by a United States Information Agency poll which showed that more Turks favoured building close relations with Central Asia than favoured close relations with the West.[2] The Turkic courtship, however, did not result in any marriage, even though all concerned did promise to stay good friends.

The unravelling started when President Turgut Özal staged a grand Turkic summit in October 1992. For a start, the only common language of the 'Turkic' delegations in those days was Russian. Kazakstan's Nursultan Nazarbayev dug in his heels when Azerbaijan's new Turkish nationalist administration sought an outright condemnation of Armenian aggression. Turkey also underestimated the different agendas and personalities of the new states themselves. Doubts began to arise among the Central Asians as they heard Özal formulate plans for a free trade zone, customs harmonization, joint banks – in short, as some Turkish diplomats hinted, for a kind of Turkic commonwealth.

'I can't hide my pleasure at the progress made in the past year. We have come a long way. Our relationships are becoming closer and closer. We must not betray the great hopes of our nation,' Özal told them. 'We must integrate. Maybe we could have a secretariat, dealing first with the economy, then with regional co-operation. We are from the same root, we are a large family. If we make no mistakes, the twenty-first century will be ours.'

Özal appealed indirectly to Russia and others not to misunderstand him and promised that they would lose nothing. A journalist from China's Uygur Turkic community in the wings was in no doubt about what Özal meant, and whispered excitedly, 'You wait, we'll be here too in ten years' time.' Moscow heard the same message. It had already signalled severe misgivings about Turkey's motives in summoning the conference, and speeches like Özal's confirmed their suspicions. Strings started to be pulled. The Ankara Summit declaration fell far short of Özal's hopes.

The Central Asians did however start to meet together in Tashkent in January 1993. They changed the joint name of their region to Central Asia, instead of the former 'Kazakstan and Middle Asia'. But they too got no further than vague talk of common roots and customs tariffs. Any attempt to raise the question of Turkestan's division among the various states immediately stumbled on the leaders' reluctance to concede any of their new-won authority to a joint entity.

The origins of this push for a new Turkic region in a crescent

across south-west Asia are interesting to examine. Although the
concept of a Turkic region was quickly adopted by Turkish policy-
makers – and in Uzbekistan, ideologues would even talk of a strategic Turkic buffer zone between Russia and China – the phrase
was first prominently uttered by Henry Kissinger in a speech he
made at Davos in February 1992. The idea was then popularized
in the United States by Turkophile strategists.[3] In April 1992, as
a joint American-Turkish business delegation set off for a tour
of Central Asia, US ambassador Richard Barkley found himself
lecturing Turkish businessmen on the riches awaiting them in the
Turkic east.

'You have to be overawed by the virgin territories for capitalists.
We will all benefit from stable, Western-oriented republics,' he
told them. At one table, a Turkish businessman, Güngör Aras,
pushed his dessert around his plate. 'We're bored with this subject.
What we really want to know is how to develop ties with the US,'
Aras complained. From a business point of view, Aras was to prove
short-sighted; but strategically he was correct. Turkey was being
manipulated. When the international configuration changed in
1993, talk of a 'Turkish model' disappeared from the geopolitical
scene as fast as it had arrived.

The new 'Great Game' between Turkey and Iran for influence in
the Turkic republics, much vaunted by American and other
writers, turned out initially to be something of a no-contest. In
Azerbaijan, a small pro-Iranian mob shouting '*Allah-u Akbar*' (God
is Great) and other religious slogans in May 1992 never had much
chance of heading off the pro-Turkish Abulfez Elchibey and rein-
stating the potentially pro-Iranian regime of Azerbaijani President
Ayaz Mutalibov. Further east, the Uzbek regime of Islam Karimov
stamped hard on any sign of Islamic fundamentalist organization.
The only pro-Islamic movement that came close to pleasing Tehran's radical ideologues lasted just ten weeks in power in the
mainly Tajik Persian-speaking republic of Tajikistan in the autumn
of 1992. After that a Russian- and Uzbek-supported counter-attack
forced the Islamists to withdraw to the mountains on the Afghan
border, and, although Tehran remained an important intermedi-
ary as the fighting dragged on, Iranian foreign policy as a whole
reverted to a more old-fashioned regional strategy in which the
Islamic Republic was often better friends with Christian Armenia
than with its Turkic co-religionists in Azerbaijan.

The new Great Game turned out to be between Turkey and

Russia, even if Tehran proved an occasional adjunct to Moscow's efforts. On the delicate question of the division of the Caspian Sea's oil wealth Russia and Iran were agreed: it should be split up under the international laws applying to lakes that would give everyone a share. The other littoral powers, however, argued that the law governing open seas should apply: a result which would mainly benefit those with offshore oil close by, like Azerbaijan, Turkmenistan and Kazakstan. This Great Game was hard for Turkey to win against the well-entrenched Russians. Some of Turkey's more grandiose projects collapsed under their own weight and the country's perennial lack of cash. Another problem for Ankara was lack of support for its projects from the West, due to events over which, as usual, it had virtually no control.

Domestic events in Russia had concentrated Western minds and distracted what little attention had been paid to the Caucasus and Central Asia, especially after Kazakstan let go of its nuclear weapons in May 1992. An idea became fixed that Russia's future depended on one man, Boris Yeltsin. Everything had to be sacrificed to ensure his political survival. For Yeltsin, that meant turning a blind eye to the activities of Russian generals spear-heading efforts to re-establish Russian control of the Caucasus. Yeltsin also had to respond to Russian domestic concern that national interests were being damaged as foreigners became players in the republics of the old Soviet Union, and that something had to be done for the 25 million Russians living in what became known as Russia's 'near abroad'.

'Just as the model suggested by Turkey was about to be put into practice, Turkey was left without support. For the sake of a project that it thought would be of help to everyone, Turkey became the target of Russia,' lamented Demirel's prime ministerial adviser Gün Kut.

When in December 1992 Demirel broke a trip back from Tokyo to meet Russian officials, he was served notice that Moscow was not going to let go of the Caucasus. Soon afterwards, Russia informed NATO that it wanted to renegotiate upwards troop ceilings agreed in the Treaty on Conventional Forces in Europe. Turkey objected to seeing more Russian troops concentrated close to its borders, but found itself with little clout compared to larger players anxious to preserve the overall arms-reduction deal. A series of events confirmed Turkey's fears for the future independence of Turkic and other Caucasus states, an independence that was vital if Turkey was to enjoy the full benefits of trade and pipeline routes over its eastern border.

An early conundrum was the question of Armenia. Turkey had been quick to recognize independent Armenia in 1991, but decided not to open an embassy there. Both sides proved unable to transcend the still unburied history of the Turks' First World War deportations and massacres of Armenians. Given the historic conflict, perhaps Turkey never had a chance to secure a new friend and a geographically ideal route for its oil pipelines. Openings for co-operation existed, but they were never backed up, and the Armenian diaspora in the United States and the Azeri lobby in Turkey were always ready to ambush them. With strong, forward-looking leadership, much more could have been made of the opportunities offered by the Soviet collapse. But it was not to be.

The new parliament in Yerevan could not bring itself to drop territorial claims on Turkey, even if these were more apparent than real. For its part, Ankara proved unable to draw a distinction between Armenia proper and the Armenians in the exclave of Nagorny-Karabagh, who led the fight against Turkey's new allies in Azerbaijan. While the tough Karabagh Armenians were led by the uncompromising diaspora-backed descendants of the same Dashnak party that had challenged the late Ottoman empire, Armenian President Levon Ter-Petrossian was in fact a natural rival of the Dashnaks, whom he eventually banished from his realm. But when Ter-Petrossian turned up at Süleyman Demirel's hotel in Davos in February 1992 with only two bodyguards, pleading to be allowed a few minutes with him, he was coldly turned away. Hard-liners in the Turkish system and the foreign ministry – which had lost thirty of its own officials to Armenian assassins – believed the ambitions of Nagorny-Karabagh could be reduced by force.

Under American pressure, some supplies of European wheat and sales of electricity were made to Armenia in 1992 and later the cross-border air corridor to Yerevan was opened up. But in the end these half-hearted measures did little more than antagonize the Azerbaijanis, while the Armenian lobby in the United States, claiming that the continued closure of the Turkish-Armenian border was a 'blockade', continued to pillory Turkey and encourage the US Senate to cut back Turkey's aid money. Soon the Turkish bet on Elchibey and a military solution was also proved mistaken, amid laments from the more martial Turks that 'these Azeris are just useless poets'. Armenia had already been forced to compromise with Moscow to obtain more wheat in 1992. Lack of alternatives gradually forced Ter-Petrossian back into the arms of Russia and an intimate relationship of military co-operation.

There was probably never anything that Turkey could do about the chaotic slide back to Russian strategic dominance of its other main ex-Soviet neighbour, Georgia. Yet Turkey faced strange dilemmas here too. A remarkable number of people in Turkey's republican élite have at least one grandparent who was a Muslim refugee from the Caucasus (or from the Balkans, a fact that has strongly coloured Turkish policies towards Bosnia too). So when an ethnic Muslim rebellion broke out in the lush Black Sea resort republic of Abkhazia, Turkey's head told it to back the Georgian leader Eduard Shevardnadze in his efforts to suppress it. But a strong ethnically Caucasian lobby in Turkey was busy backing the Abkhaz with supplies and some 200 youthful fighters. The Turkish government expressed its dilemma by sending emergency relief to the Abkhaz, but allowing Georgian officials to inspect it first. In the end, Shevardnadze never had a real chance, and, simply to end the fighting, was forced – temporarily at least – to accept garrisons of Russian troops on the Turkish border, to rejoin the Moscow-dominated Commonwealth of Independent States and undoubtedly to make other strategic concessions to Moscow.

Turkey's biggest setback was in Azerbaijan. Abulfez Elchibey's government had been unable to overcome the challenges it faced, and in 1993 his men began to lose control. Elchibey's wolf-loving interior minister stormed on to a live television programme to shout insults at his opponents and pistol-whipped the editor of an opposition newspaper. Elchibey's death knell sounded when Armenian forces captured the Azerbaijani town of Kelbadzhar in April 1993, greatly widening the corridor of land that had linked Nagorny-Karabagh to Armenia proper since the capture of the access route through Lachin in June 1992. All Turkey could do was to send warplanes up and down the Armenian border; even a desperate request by Elchibey for Turkish helicopters to evacuate trapped civilians was turned down for fear Russia would see it as intervention.

The Armenians' Kelbadzhar offensive also came in the middle of a peace initiative that Turkey believed it was sponsoring mutually with Russia. 'We have been made fools of. It took us two days even to get the Russian foreign minister to return our calls. We now realize that ultimately they are only interested in discrediting any initiative that does not leave Russia as the sole power broker,' protested one angry Turkish official engaged in the process.

That was not all. Within two months, the pro-Turkish Elchibey had fallen from power, finished off by a series of amateurish attacks by Surat Husseinov, an apparently Russian-backed Azerbaijani provincial drugs and mafia baron. The casual walk into Baku by his mixed rebel force bore a bizarre resemblance to the first Ottoman Turkish attempt to capture the city in 1918. Husseinov's moment of glory was similarly brief. In June 1993, the reins of power fell into the hands of Heidar Aliyev, 70 years old, tall, cunning and ruthless, a man whose whole previous career had been in the service of Moscow.

Turkey had been closely identified with Elchibey and his Popular Front. Failure to stand by their ally in his hour of need did little good to Turkey's general standing, even if there had been some anguished debate in the Turkish military about what more they could do than train, advise and secretly supply. However, Ankara had taken out an insurance policy by protecting Heidar Aliyev in Nakhichevan from any purge by Elchibey's men. So the new Aliyev era neither left Turkey out in the cold, nor resulted in complete capitulation to Russia. Taking his time, Aliyev allowed parliament to approve Azerbaijan's entry into the Commonwealth of Independent States in September. But he put off Russian demands to reposition troops in his republic. After a particularly public rebuff to Moscow in October 1993, the Nagorny-Karabagh Armenians attacked again and linked their territory up to the Iranian border. Once more, as the Azerbaijanis never tired of pointing out, an Armenian offensive had followed an Azerbaijani dispute with Russia.

A lasting cease-fire was eventually established in May 1994. The Azerbaijanis had no further power to resist. They had lost 20 per cent of their territory, and nearly one million of their seven million people had been displaced. But there was still one major question to settle, a question that had always lurked in the background and did not concern just Azerbaijan. It was the multi-billion dollar question of the future of the Turkic republics' bountiful reserves of oil.

Nobody knows quite how much oil lies under the Caspian Sea and adjacent areas. Since time immemorial, it has simply oozed out of the rocks around Baku, which in the late nineteenth century was the mother of all oil boom towns. Oil executives believe there is still plenty left. Under the waters of the Caspian alone, estimated reserves range from 40 to 200 billion tons of oil. That is a prize of which the Russian establishment, however confused the politics in Moscow, has been determined not to let go.

Even before the collapse of the Soviet Union, British Petroleum was leading a Western consortium keen to exploit deep sea fields off Azerbaijan. In rough figures, an investment of eight billion dollars by the dozen companies that in September 1994 signed up to form the BP-led Azerbaijan International Operating Company (AIOC) aimed to extract more than 600 million tons of oil. Even at a sale price of about fifteen dollars a barrel, and after deducting investment and pipeline costs, a net profit of 50 billion dollars could be predicted over a period of twenty to thirty years; if the oil price rose, so would the profit. More than half of that profit was due to be paid to the republic of Azerbaijan.

Initially, Turkey was in with a small share and Russia was excluded. As part of his package to mollify Russia on coming to power in June 1994, Heidar Aliyev had allocated 10 per cent from the Azerbaijani oil company's share to the Russian company LUKoil. Russia, however, was still not satisfied, especially when it came to the question of which route to Western markets would be taken by the consortium's estimated exports of 500,000 barrels per day (about 25 million tons per year). Initially, Turkey, Azerbaijan and the United States, whose companies at one stage made up nearly half the consortium, entertained the idea of a 2-billion-dollar, 1,650-kilometre pipeline through the Caucasus to Turkey's Mediterranean coast, probably transiting Georgia. This route, Turkey maintained, would keep the Bosphorus safe, was a more marketable lifting point and kept Azerbaijan's strategic options open. Russia, however, wanted the oil to pass through its territory to the Black Sea port of Novorossisk, thus taking the prize of the oil transit fees and keeping a strategic monopoly on the Caucasus.

Forces supporting the Moscow line were prepared to play as rough in this game as they had in bringing other Caucasian republics to heel. Five days after Georgian President Eduard Shevardnadze had agreed to a plan for one of the oil pipelines to pass through his republic in August 1995, a big car bomb nearly killed him. The Georgian leader strongly hinted that oil politics were responsible. And in the thirteen months leading up to the consortium decision of October 1995 on oil pipeline routes, Heidar Aliyev in Azerbaijan faced two attempted coups, blamed squarely on pro-Russian forces by his aides in his marble-clad palace overlooking the Caspian. Conflicting forces in Moscow vied for dominance of Russian policy – the main oil contract was signed in September 1994 by the minister of energy even while the foreign ministry was criticizing it – but there were basic shared attitudes. The then Russian intelligence chief Yevgeny Primakov saw the Western-dominated AIOC in Baku as a threat to national security. Prime Minister Viktor Chernomyrdin spoke of foreign states and oil companies trying to dominate the former Soviet Union and to undermine its energy security. The foreign minister threatened sanctions.[4]

'Not a drop of oil will flow until the legal status of the Caspian Sea is settled. Everyone talks about Azerbaijani oil but forgets that it belongs equally to the Caspian littoral states, Russia, Kazakstan, Turkmenistan and Iran,' said Albert Chernishev, then the Russian deputy foreign minister, in June 1996.[5]

In fact, a virtual Russian blockade of Azerbaijan had already been in progress since the outbreak of the Chechen crisis in December 1994. The Russian drive against separatist Chechnya was also in part an attempt to reassert control of a republic that lay astride the existing Russian pipeline route for Azeri oil. Occasionally Russia would accuse Turkish agents of lending support to the Chechen rebels, while Turkish officials would level the same accusations against Russia and the Kurds. The Turkish oil route lay through troubled Kurdish areas, and at oil conferences in Moscow, Kurdish rebel representatives were permitted to distribute threatening leaflets to rub in the point. To counter Turkey's protests about oil tanker overload on the Bosphorus Strait, Russia alternated threats about the Montreux Convention with plans for a by-pass pipeline through its traditional Balkan friends Bulgaria and Greece.

Ankara was forced on to the defensive. Its hopes for a pipeline through Turkey revived faintly in early 1995 after Washington decided to back the Turkish route. Partly as a result of twenty-five minutes of telephone diplomacy between US President Bill Clinton and Heidar Aliyev, the AIOC announced in October 1995 that the first oil would be exported equally through Russia and Georgia, where Turkey was ready to finance a pipeline to the Black Sea. But in May 1996, Ankara withdrew the offer when the AIOC refused to commit itself to building the main pipeline to the Mediterranean through Turkey.

At around the same time, it was agreed that the pipeline from the great Tengiz oilfield being developed by the American company Chevron just east of the Caspian Sea in Kazakstan should go to the Russian port of Novorossisk as well. This appeared to be another setback for Turkey, since in mid-1995 Kazakstan had signed a protocol showing interest in the Turkish pipeline route. Due to produce a similar quantity of oil to the AIOC consortium – about 700,000 barrels per day, or 36 million tons per year – Kazakstan had suffered an equally bruising series of bouts with Russia. At first, Russia had objected to pumping more than a minimal amount of Tengiz oil polluted with mercaptans, a foul-smelling sulphur compound, through its leaky old Soviet pipelines. Chevron duly installed a plant to clean up the crude, but Russia still would not pump more. The problem was only put on the road to a solution in early 1996 by the signing over to Russia and Russian companies of a 44 per cent equity stake in the pipeline. Chevron also seemed likely to have to cede part of its equity stake in the Tengiz field to Russia's LUKoil.

A survey by the Turkish ministry of transport estimated that the flow of new oil from Azerbaijan, Kazakstan and Russia's own fields would amount to an extra 35 million tons of oil per year by early in the next century. This, it said, would increase the number of tankers and effectively close the Bosphorus to other traffic for an unacceptable average time of three to four hours more per day. About 30–32 million tons of crude oil and oil products already pass through the Bosphorus each year, and Turkish foreign ministry officials have stated that, whatever the Montreux Convention says, it will not allow that figure to grow by more than 20 per cent or so.

Everyone in Istanbul remembers the catastrophe caused by the terrible burning oil slick from the Romanian tanker *Independenta* in 1979, which turned day into night. The problem is not going to go away: the number of accidents seems unlikely to decrease, Istanbul's population of 12 million is likely to grow, the super-tankers get no smaller and ordinary ship traffic will increase. In 1936, when the Montreux Convention was signed, only a few ships of up to 18,000 deadweight tons would use the Strait each month. Now about 50,000 ships use it each year carrying more than 100 million tons of cargo; tankers more than 200 metres long are the norm. Coasters crash into the bedrooms of wooden seaside villas known as *yalıs*. Freighters mount the coast road beside fish restaurants. So many ships ram the coast road at the trickiest of fourteen bends on the 31-kilometre strait that the municipality seems to have given up repairing it. In March 1994, a midnight collision between a tanker and a freighter killed thirteen seamen, spilled oil and started a frightening blaze. It also provided the pretext Turkey needed to act.

'Oil companies obviously favour the non-investment solution – to load up a boat and send it through the Straits. But it is not possible for large amounts of oil to pass through the Bosphorus. You'd have to shut the Bosphorus down for 300 days a year,' explained Ahmet Banguoğlu, the Turkish foreign ministry's expert on the matter. 'The European Union is talking about a 15-mile exclusion zone for tankers from uninhabited places like the Shetlands. In the Bosphorus tankers can come as close as 50 metres. This is asking Turkey for too much of a sacrifice.'

On 1 July 1994, Turkey brought in new regulations. From then on, ships carrying oil and dangerous cargo had to give notice of their intentions. They were forbidden to travel at the same time. New visibility minimums were to apply to ships more than 150 metres long: that is, tankers. They were strongly advised to take pilots, a precaution not necessary under Montreux; but Turkey knows that only one per cent of accidents take place when there are pilots on both ships' bridges. While not directly contravening the right of free passage enshrined in Montreux, Bosphorus traffic controllers could and did make tanker captains wait expensively for hours if they did not take a pilot.

Russia and Black Sea states cried foul, saying better radar and monitoring systems would solve the problem. But Turkey seemed determined to go even further. From his eyrie on a prettily situated state-sponsored institute overlooking the Bosphorus, semi-retired diplomat Ismail Soysal keeps a beady eye on the never-ending criss-crossings of fishing boats, ferries, flat Danube–Rhine ferries, Baltic trading ships, cruiser liners, and especially the big, silent, potentially deadly tankers. In 1994, an average of three tankers a day slipped past the lovely skyline of domes and minarets. Soysal has now made it his life's mission to divert them somewhere else. He believes that, if no other solution is found, one day Turkey will simply unilaterally abrogate the Montreux Convention.

As nationalist Russian politicians, ex-Communist *apparatchiks*, ambitious Russian generals, local militia lords and international oil executives acted out their parts on the chessboard of the post-Soviet Caucasus and Central Asia, Ankara seemed to cast an ever-shorter shadow. But that was only part of the picture of Turkey's involvement with the Turkic republics and the rest of that intermediate region which some like to call Eurasia.

The first Turkish business delegation to fly east to Azerbaijan from Istanbul in 1990 was a motley Noah's Ark of all the forces at work in Turkey. There were Turkish nationalist revolutionaries, shady traders from the Istanbul bazaar and some outright conmen. But it included some genuine businessmen seeking a new market easier to penetrate than the saturated and competitive countries of Europe. Six years later, their energetic efforts had achieved remarkable results. Importantly, their Turkic involvement usually came as part of an overall expansion into the whole Eurasian region north and east of Turkey that included southern Russia and the Balkans as well.

The change was graphically illustrated in April 1996 when an up-and-coming Turkish businessman was able to hire a Turkish Airlines airbus to take his friends to Kazakstan and the Kyrgyz Republic to show off two new Coca-Cola bottling plants that he had financed and built. Modest enough, but, in the case of the Kyrgyz Republic, it was the first modern factory to be constructed there. It symbolized all that the Turks had shown they could do best in the east: to supply contract builders, to act as vehicles for outside investors, to supply seed capital and, an important consideration, to finish projects on time in decidedly uncertain business climates. The company's strategy also included plants in Rostov in southern Russia and in Romania.

This kind of project was only the top end of what amounted to a huge and largely undocumented network of thousands of small businesses that had found a foothold in the young republics. Typically, an individual Turk would invest in a Turkish bread oven, truck it east and set up shop with a local partner. Others would set up restaurants, and still more had small trading concerns. The majority of new hotels in the region were built by Turks; some were owned by them. In the smallest and poorest capital, Bishkek in the Kyrgyz Republic, 4,000 kilometres from Istanbul, there were 400 Turks active in business. In Almaty there were 2,000 Turks. In Turkmenistan, Turkish cotton ginning and even textile factories cropped up on the Karakum Desert landscape at almost every major town on the country's main east–west road. Both Turks and Turkic officials felt at ease doing business with each other. Just as Europeans felt most comfortable doing business in Eastern Europe, so Turks felt comfortable in the Turkic republics. 'We even try to cheat each other in the same way,' joked the Turkish chief of the company operating the Coca-Cola bottling plants.

Putting a figure on the volume of business was notoriously hard, although it was clear that Turkish trade with Russia and the Ukraine was far higher. Officially, Turks invested just 161 million dollars between 1992 and 1995 in the five Turkic republics. The real figure was probably more than one billion dollars. Much of this investment has been in areas of rapid potential growth. The Russian relationship is still much more important to the newly independent republics, but it tends to be dominated by bruising horse-trading sessions that exchange trading debts for the impoverished republics' rusting prime assets.

Another feature of Turkey's outreach was the growth of Turkish schools in the Caucasus and Central Asia. By 1996, their number had reached 300, the great majority of them private enterprises aimed at fee-paying students wanting to learn in English. Ironically, considering the West's early stress on promoting Turkey as a model of secular development, many of these schools were sponsored by various kinds of Islamic brotherhood in Turkey. The Directorate of Religious Affairs was also highly active, supporting the development of what Ankara strategist Seyfi Taşhan liked to call the Turks' 'protestant' Islam. Turkey spent millions of dollars building mosques from Daghestan to Mazar-i Sharif in northern Afghanistan, where local warlord General Dostum, being an Uzbek, was sent funds as a natural friend of Turkey. Little of this activity could be described as radically Islamic. Among the Turkish salesmen, Western oilmen and diplomats celebrating their departure from Central Asia on board Turkish planes could also be found the odd bearded Turkish fundamentalist missionary. 'The Muslims in the republics are no use to us. Sold-out heathens, the lot of them,' one confided in 1993. 'But we are having lots of success with the Muslims inside Russia.'

Academics found it as hard as the missionary to develop deep relationships, even though official support kept them at it. 'There is a big obstacle to researching the history of the influence of Turkish culture today – that is, the fact that we don't share the Russian language,' said Büsra Ersanlı Bahar in the first post-Soviet survey of the region by Turkish academics in 1994. 'We came to realize that the Turkish language that we were glad to think we shared at the start was insufficient as our relations became more varied and richer. But our studies will certainly be encouraged by the colourful harmony of differences between us – the poetic freedom of the Azeris, the pride of the tight-lipped Uzbeks, the unguarded frankness of the Türkmens, the democratic decency of the Kyrgyz and the cautious determination of the Kazaks.'[6]

Despite this wide network of relationships, nowhere in the Turkic republics could Turkey be said to dominate: indeed, the Kazak and Uzbek presidents rated Turkey well below almost all their neighbours in importance. But some convergence could be detected. A lack of shared language was apparent at the tense first Turkic summit in 1992, where only the Turks were not doing business in Russian. But by the time the next summit was held in Istanbul in 1994, many Central Asian officials had spent a few weeks in Turkey and could communicate easily in Turkish and were more secure in their respective identities. In Uzbekistan,

Communism's worship of Lenin had been replaced with hero-legends of Timur (Tamerlane). In Kazakstan, Marx's place on the old banknotes had been replaced by wispy-bearded descendants of Genghis Khan. Everybody was more relaxed at the 1994 get-together, despite Russia's hasty organization of a rival summit immediately afterwards in Moscow. Russia had already tried and failed to force the Central Asians to choose between the Moscow-dominated Commonwealth of Independent States and the non-Arab regional Muslim organization ECO, the Economic Co-operation Organization led by Iran, Turkey and Pakistan. Meetings of ECO showed how much less lonely Turkey had become, sharing with the Turkic leaders a pragmatic, secular and generally pro-Western suit-and-tie approach to their place in the world.

'Of course the Russians are very unhappy. We now think of ourselves as coming from Turkestan,' said the Uzbek president's spokesman at the Istanbul summit. Nazarbayev was cautious in public, but in his hotel corridor he underlined his belief that 'the old Union was born of force and violence. Attempts to go backwards will not succeed.'

Even so, while businessmen, schoolteachers and diplomats were slowly bringing the various Turkic nations closer together, a Turkic commonwealth still seemed a long way off. Only the late Turgut Özal had ever pushed the idea hard. After his death Turkey became too wrapped up in its domestic political and economic agenda to pursue a truly pioneering role. When the dust settled after Özal's death in April 1993, the more cautious Süleyman Demirel took over the presidency. A completely new kind of person was to sweep into office as Turkey's prime minister, a woman who, whatever her qualities of courage and determination, came to power not knowing where many places in eastern Turkey were, let alone understanding the complex geopolitics of the Turkic east.

17

The Çiller Phenomenon

He who does not beat his daughter into obedience will later beat his knee in regret.

Turkish proverb

THE ATMOSPHERE WAS electric in the hot and smoky sports stadium in Ankara where, on 13 June 1993, 1,150 delegates of the True Path Party – the Doğru Yol Partisi or DYP – had gathered to elect a successor to right-wing veteran Süleyman Demirel. Finding a replacement for the populist leader would not be easy. For thirty years, the rotund Demirel had dominated the conservative right. The True Path Party's roots were deeply embedded in rural Anatolia, being the direct heir of the Justice Party closed down by the generals after 1980 and, through the Justice Party, the successor of Adnan Menderes' popular Democrat Party, closed down by the 1960 coup.

President Turgut Özal's death, on 17 April 1993, had given Süleyman Demirel a chance to fulfil his lifelong ambition to become head of state. Never mind that his sudden departure would leave his party in the lurch: Demirel left the leadership without looking back. Even so, a few days before the party congress, he had let it be known, indirectly, that his old friend Ismet Sezgin, who had been an unexciting minister of interior in the coalition, was his preferred choice for the succession.

Lending excitement to the proceedings was the surprising candidacy of Tansu Çiller, the glamorous minister of state for the economy. An academic by training, best known for reports scathingly critical of Turgut Özal's economic policies, the ambitious Çiller was still wet behind the ears as a politician. She had only joined the party shortly before the 1991 elections when Demirel had brought her in to brighten up his party's rather dusty and conservative image.

The single child of a prosperous family – her father rose through municipal government to become governor of Muğla province – Tansu Çiller married when she was still a high school student at Istanbul's famous Robert College. Her school friends remember her as an ambitious student whose success was due to assiduous rote-learning from books. Özer Uçuran, of more modest extraction, chose her as his 'queen' when he was elected the traditional 'king' of the senior year. Tansu's father, who wanted the family name to be carried on, demanded that his son-in-law adopt his bride's last name, a highly unusual and perhaps unique event in Turkey's male-dominated society of the time.

The two young people, then 'so poor they could not afford a can of Coca-Cola', as Tansu later claimed, flew to America where she graduated in economics from a series of East Coast colleges. When she returned to Turkey, she became one of the youngest candidates to win an appointment as professor at the prestigious Bosphorus University. Her burning ambition marked her out from many of her academic colleagues; more disturbing was her role in selling land at extravagant prices to a house-building co-operative that left the Çillers much richer, and later, the subject of a protracted lawsuit. A state bank managed by Özer Çiller collapsed with spectacular losses in the 1980s. The couple's extraordinary wealth now includes many properties in Turkey and in the United States.

Tansu Çiller's performance as minister in charge of the economy had generally been thought to be undistinguished. Nobody could understand her computer-aided concept for solving Turkey's ills. When she snatched time to give interviews in a small room behind her office, it was hard to follow her arguments. But her self-confidence never slipped. An abrupt and autocratic style brought her into conflict with the bureaucracy and with her colleagues on more than one occasion. Despite her professorship and her doctorate, she had little feel for the real dynamics of the economy, tending to focus to the exclusion of everything else on the minute details of the subject in hand.

Demirel himself had grown wary of his protégée. For a start, with her glowing smile, good looks and dynamic image, she made too much of an impression on foreign visitors, who were less inclined to be attracted to the cautious, uninspiring Demirel. As president, Demirel had given her a less-than-encouraging response when she approached him to seek his approval to enter the race for the succession. Even so, she went ahead and put her name forward. No one in Turkey seriously thought she could win.

Editorials in the newspapers prior to the congress explained at length how unlikely it was that this young and wealthy woman, with a cosmopolitan image and virtually no experience of politics, would appeal to Anatolian peasants used to a populist arm-around-the-shoulder political style.

Before the voting had even begun, however, it became obvious that a small miracle was taking place in a congress hall rendered almost opaque by cigarette smoke. A defeated-looking Ismet Sezgin, sensing the trend, charged around the back rooms to lobby the waverers with a small group of the party's old faithful in his train. But it was no use. He ended up sitting amid the debris and television vans at the back of the hall, grimly fanning himself with a sheaf of papers.

Those who believed that Tansu Çiller would only attract the votes of city delegates and that conservative Anatolians would not accept a woman leader were proved wrong. Many of Çiller's strongest supporters came in fact from deepest Anatolia, regions thought to be Turkey's most reactionary. 'My wife told me I could not come home unless I voted for Çiller,' joked one delegate from the eastern district of Gümüşhane. Others, not necessarily under pressure from their spouses, said they would also support this novel candidate. They wanted modernity and change. The party also needed a younger leader to compete with its centre-right rival, the Motherland Party, which had already in 1991 appointed a younger man, Mesut Yılmaz, to carry on the job started by Turgut Özal.

Perhaps the 'Baba' (Father), as Demirel is affectionately known in Turkey, had felt that taking on Tansu Çiller in 1991 to freshen up his image was a stroke of political wizardry. But she proved a true sorcerer's apprentice. Many were taken by surprise when the blonde politician, resplendent in her trade-mark white suit, won the first round by a sufficient margin to force the other two contenders out of the race. Turkey now had a woman party leader, and, because the DYP was the dominant partner in the ruling coalition, for the first time it was to be led by a woman prime minister.

Tansu Çiller unwittingly assumed a pioneering role as a woman in Turkish politics, but she can in no way be described as a feminist. Like Margaret Thatcher, who was said to have encouraged her to run for the party leadership during a dinner in London in the spring of 1993, she had made her own way in a man's world and saw no reason why others should not fight the same battle. In fact, intellectuals and members of the élite despise her for attempting to court the 'backward' Anatolians with religious and nationalist slogans about her love for the Turkish flag and the *ezan*, the Muslim call to prayer. Feminists say she has done little to advance the cause of women, yet her presence at the head of the government was in itself a sign that the domination of society by conservative males was crumbling. And she became a role model for many Turkish women, particularly in rural areas.

Çiller was younger and more attractive than Thatcher, and used her feminine charm to great effect. A caressing arm and a dazzling smile could go a long way to melt the resistance of a fierce opponent. Abroad too, her charisma was initially effective. This young prime minister charmed heads of states with her sober elegance and an image that contrasted sharply with the traditional perception of the woman's role in a conservative Muslim country struggling with the rising forces of political Islam.

It would be wrong to say that Çiller did it all on her own. By the time she was elected, women had already made substantial inroads into the world of business and the professions. Enter any bank in Turkey: most of the clerks are women, and there is a good chance that the manager is too. Ayfer Yılmaz, who became a deputy in Çiller's DYP, was head of the Turkish treasury. The percentage of women lawyers, doctors and stockbrokers is higher than in many Western countries.

Atatürk gave Turkish women equal status, in theory at least, but society took a long time to digest the change. The first parliaments included several female deputies, but this novelty did not take root and the proportion they represented decreased over subsequent decades. While women could do well in most walks of life, the old boys' club of politics was notoriously reluctant to admit them in any great numbers. In big cities like Istanbul, young women of the élite can now live as they choose, like their Western counterparts. But society as a whole is still very conservative. If they cannot afford hired help, many successful female professionals have to assume a traditional role at home. Schoolbooks still reinforce the attitude that 'the father is the head of the family, and the wife, who does the cooking and looks after the children, is his assistant and companion'.

Anatolian girls are often married off at a very young age to men they have seldom or never seen. Legally they could object but the price would be rejection by their community. In many rural families, girls are considered little better than cattle to change hands at the proper price. Once married, the girl 'belongs' to the husband's family and can expect very little help from her parents if the marriage turns sour.

Domestic violence is commonplace: according to one survey 49 per cent of women believed a man might have legitimate reasons to beat his wife, 41 per cent admitted to having been victims of such violence and 28 per cent thought they deserved it.[1] (Outraged by a judicial ruling that domestic violence did not constitute sufficient grounds for divorce, feminists founded a shelter for battered wives in Istanbul.) While the Kemalist élite accepts divorce, in villages a divorced woman is still considered damaged goods. Living on her own is not socially acceptable, whilst her own family may not take her back. Few women are aware of the rights given to them by law, and even if they knew, they would not dare confront a hostile society. Newspapers are regularly filled with heart-rending stories of silent women snapping after years of abuse and killing their husbands. Even worse are crimes of honour, committed by male members of a family against a girl who is believed, rightly or wrongly, to have sinned.

Virginity, for girls, is still a major issue in rural Turkey. Young brides talk of the humiliation of having to display publicly a bloody sheet after their wedding night. Failure to do so may result in the girl being sent back to her family, beaten black and blue by her irate husband. She can then expect a second thrashing at the hands of her own relatives, although she may be totally 'innocent'.

Even the state, despite its proud assertion of equal rights for women, still routinely carries out virginity tests on women detainees in police custody, or on schoolgirls suspected of improper behaviour. The ministry of education was taken to task in 1995, when it condoned the actions of a school headmaster who had sent some pupils for virginity tests. A young student committed suicide rather than face such a humiliating ordeal but when, on her father's orders, the test was carried out on her corpse, it turned out that her hymen was intact.

When a girl or a woman sins, the honour of the whole family is sullied. The extended group of relatives, in some cases, meets and decides on her fate. Supposed crimes can range from leaving a husband for another man to simply being seen talking to another man in the street. In the spring of 1996, an 11-year-old boy obeyed his father's order and shot dead his mother while she slept. In Urfa, a brother slit the throat of his 16-year-old sister in broad daylight. Such murderers usually get lenient gaol sentences and very seldom express regret. In their eyes, a woman is not an individual but part of a family or community. In the province of Adıyaman in June 1996, a weeping father bid goodbye to his 16-year-old daughter who had secretly borne a child out of wedlock before handing her over to his youngest son to do his duty and shoot her. The murder was not only considered normal, it was deemed necessary by the local people. Moral integrity has to be maintained so that other girls are not set a bad example.

Greater access to education, urbanization and the power of television are beginning to erode these gruesome traditions. Urban society has begun to value girls more highly, since the number of children per family has fallen and educated girls stand a better chance of finding well-paid employment. Women are slowly becoming more conscious of their power. A landmark decision has freed women from the obligation to seek their husbands' permission to work or travel abroad. Single women are increasingly able to live on their own, even though traditional society still frowns on such displays of independence.

The arrival of Tansu Çiller as prime minister probably encouraged the trend. The lack of women candidates was for the first time a real issue during the December 1995 electoral campaign. Parties were criticized for not accommodating more women, and the Islamic Welfare Party was castigated for not having a single one on its electoral lists, even though its huge task force of women activists was the key to its election victory. Only thirteen women were elected to the national assembly in 1995 – not an encouraging figure when compared with the eighteen women given seats in the first republican parliament. But when the Islamists formed a coalition with Tansu Çiller's True Path Party, they were forced to compromise on their radical ideas. Their joint cabinet included three women ministers.

Tansu Çiller's promises of reforms and her Westernized outlook raised hopes of major changes in Turkey. But, as the day-to-day running of the government began to take its toll, Tansu Çiller, with no real power base in the leadership of her own party, disappointed all these hopes by seeking strength from the army and abandoning many of her more progressive ideas.

Çiller also bore the burden of taking over the coalition formed after Süleyman Demirel's party came first in the October 1991 elections. The poll results had allowed the conservative DYP to overthrow its centre-right rival ANAP, but had not given it enough seats in parliament to rule on its own. The Turks had at first extended much goodwill and support to the alliance formed by Prime Minister Demirel with Erdal Inönü's Social Democrats. There was a feeling that both parties had mellowed with time and moved closer to the centre. This alliance of left and right seemed to have a good chance of pushing through much-needed reforms, epitomized by one of Turkey's more daring government programmes. But in practice, the coalition proved unable to take radical decisions.

During the election campaign, Demirel – already six times prime minister, twice overthrown by military coups after his governments had led to political gridlock – had somehow managed, partly by appearing everywhere with the modern-looking Tansu Çiller, to convince the electorate that he was a new man. He did his best to shake off his image of Özal's taunting title of *statukocu*, a man bent on maintaining the *status quo*. He promised change, democratization, police stations with 'walls made of glass' – a reference to the mounting allegations of human rights abuses. Always a man of political flexibility, he quietly shelved all these ideas within a few months of coming to power.

Nobody was more desperate for a change of heart by the state than the Kurds in the south-east of Turkey, devastated by the conflict between rebel guerrillas and government forces. Soon after coming to power in 1991, the new prime minister and his deputy Inönü had toured the region and had been given a triumphal reception by local Kurds exhausted by the war and praying that government policy would change. 'We recognize the Kurdish reality,' Demirel told them.

This was indeed a historic opportunity to solve the conflict most Turks coyly refer to as the 'south-eastern problem'. There had always been a number of Turkish Kurd deputies in the Turkish parliament, but for the first time twenty-two openly nationalist Kurds had taken seats in the national assembly. They had been elected on the party lists of Inönü's Social Democrat People's Party (the Sosyaldemokrat Halk Partisi or SHP), because their party, HEP, for purely procedural reasons, could not take part in the poll.

Elected by the south-eastern Turkish Kurds as their representatives, with a foothold now in Turkey's political establishment, these parliamentarians were in a unique position to bridge the gap between the two communities. A forum to reach a negotiated end to the conflict seemed to be in place. The youngest among the newly chosen Turkish Kurd representatives even included the radical Leyla Zana, a beautiful, raven-haired 30-year-old mother of two teenage children. A traditional Kurdish village girl, she had been married at 14, according to local custom, to a distant relative. When her husband, Mehdi Zana, then mayor of the Turkish Kurd city of Diyarbakır, was arrested after the 1980 coup and sentenced to thirty-six years' imprisonment – of which he served eleven years in the notorious Diyarbakır gaol – his young wife took up his struggle and found unlikely fame by becoming the Pasionaria of the Kurds.

It rapidly turned out that neither side had enough political maturity to make good use of the opportunity offered. The Kurdish deputies, instead of gradually gaining the confidence of their wary colleagues, chose shock tactics instead. On the day of the official swearing-in, the two most fiery nationalists, Leyla Zana and Hatip Dicle, delivered a speech in Kurdish from the assembly's rostrum. Its content spoke of good intentions – 'Long live the brotherhood of Turks and Kurds,' said Leyla Zana – but its form was provocative. In the nationalist atmosphere of Turkey's Grand National Assembly, they knew they were pouring oil on the fire. While the shouts and strong reactions of their audience demonstrated the irrational anger of Turkish nationalists, it also raised doubts about some of the Kurdish deputies' commitment to finding a compromise solution.

From then on, the Kurdish deputies were barely tolerated in parliament. Any hope they had had of making a useful contribution was crushed. In January 1992, Leyla Zana and Hatip Dicle were forced out of Inönü's SHP. Two months later, fourteen more of their colleagues followed them. The experiment was over almost before it had started. The violent clashes between security forces and demonstrators during the Kurdish Nowruz celebrations in 1992 marked the end of the honeymoon period for the DYP–SHP coalition.

Tansu Çiller's initial pledge to approach the Kurdish issue 'with a mother's love' had briefly rekindled hopes of a change in policy. But they were short-lived. Çiller's haste in removing Demirel's old supporters from key positions led to opposition within her own party. In the bureaucracy, she had few friends: her stubbornness and her tendency to make her own decisions, while evading responsibility when things went wrong, had alienated most senior officials. Nor could she claim to command the population's support. She had come to power through the party, but had not yet faced the electorate as prime minister.

Rather than swim against the current and adhere to the liberal views she had expressed, she sought the army's protection and support, in exchange for which she let the security forces have a free hand in attacking the Turkish Kurd insurgency. A military solution, however, proved difficult to find. Despite over-optimistic statements from the chief of staff, Doğan Güreş, that 'the PKK will be finished by the end of the summer' – later moved to the 'end of the year' – the rebellion showed little signs of abating.

To show willing, Çiller visited the south-east a number of times. On her first tour through the mountains by helicopter, the army carefully prepared and controlled everything she saw. Wearing hiking boots which she claimed belonged to her son Mert – she had in fact bought them the day before – she toured an army camp close to the point where the Turkish, Iranian and Iraqi borders meet. Inspecting a tiny one-soldier mountain tent with Chief of Staff Güreş, she blithely remarked that she 'liked camping holidays'. Meanwhile, an artillery battalion noisily shelled a mountain peak just below the Iranian border for her benefit. Still, Çiller told reporters that she wanted 'equal rights for all ethnic groups, as in the United States'.

Until late 1993, Çiller's contribution to the government's Kurdish policy had remained essentially passive: all she did was tolerate and openly support in her speeches a repressive policy that had been devised before her time. But there was no escaping the consequences of the economic disaster that struck the republic within months of her taking over. She tried to avoid her share of the blame, insisting that her period as minister in charge of the economy did not count since Demirel 'was too scared to do anything'. But it was she who had to face the flight of international capital and the crash that followed years in which the Turkish government had borrowed heavily to finance its deficits.

It was in January 1994 that the American rating agencies chose to exercise their power. Worried by Turkey's increasing debts and its overvalued currency, Moody's lowered the country's rating a notch in January. This decision punctured the economic balloon, puffed up since the Özal era. Overnight, international confidence in Turkey's ability to surmount its difficulties evaporated. The lira tumbled and lost 50 per cent of its value within three months. Çiller, pulling the strings at the Central Bank, was blamed for adding to the problem by mishandling the crisis with constant interventions and changes of direction.

With local elections due in March – her first electoral test since coming to power – the prime minister had to distract the voters with a new issue. Under pressure from the army, she chose to deal with the Kurdish nationalist MPs from DEP who, despite being ostracized by their colleagues, were still active, clamouring for cultural rights and denouncing Turkey's brutal official policy towards the Kurds. Zealous prosecutors from the state security courts had opened cases against them for their pro-Kurdish statements, but parliamentary immunity protected them from prosecution. When Kurdish deputy Hatip Dicle justified a PKK bomb attack on the platform of a train station that killed five cadets by declaring it 'normal' given the conflict that raged in south-eastern Turkey, Çiller, under intense pressure from the army, moved rapidly. Within days, the national assembly had voted to have the immunity of the Turkish Kurd deputies lifted. Some were picked up as they left the Grand National Assembly and bundled, with indecent haste, into police cars to be put behind bars.

Çiller won the municipal elections by a small margin, although the Islamic Welfare Party's victory in Istanbul and Ankara and a string of other towns overshadowed her dubious success. Her decision to have the Kurdish nationalist MPs tried came back to haunt her a year later, when their imprisonment, and the heavy sentences they had received – fifteen years each for Leyla Zana and Hatip Dicle – became a major obstacle to the Customs Union agreement between Turkey and Europe.

Turkey's European destiny was one element of her policy in which Tansu Çiller believed. She had ducked and made U-turns on almost every other issue, but she fought hard to get the free trade agreement accepted, proving that when she tackled a topic single-mindedly, she could give it all her energy until her aim was achieved. The Customs Union, part of a process of rapprochement that started in 1963, was signed in March 1995 by European ministers, but the European parliament then decided to flex the new muscles given to it by the Maastricht Treaty. Customs Union would have to be approved by European parliamentarians who, unlike their governments, were more concerned about public opinion than lucrative contracts. And European opinion, heavily influenced by human rights organizations and often by the PKK under different guises, was not favourable to Turkey.

The Europeans demanded substantial changes to the infamous Article 8 of the April 1991 anti-terrorism law, which had been used to imprison journalists and any person speaking out publicly in favour of a softer approach to Kurdish insurgency. They also wanted the Kurdish nationalist MPs released immediately. Much work also had to be done to make Turkey's commercial and patent laws conform with international standards.

Outside Turkey, Çiller, using all her charm, launched a counter-offensive to persuade the Europeans that unless they allowed Turkey in, the country would be washed away by a tidal wave of Muslim fundamentalism. Inside Turkey, she fought tooth and nail to get parliament – in particular, reluctant deputies within her own party – to approve the reform of Article 8. It took months and the end result was disappointing: the minor changes were essentially cosmetic. Courts were no longer able simply to condemn people on the basis of their words, but had to prove an intent to harm the Turkish republic. Although Çiller looked into the possibility of an amnesty for the Kurdish deputies, the process she had set in motion when helping to remove their parliamentary immunity was now out of her control. The court of appeal released two deputies, whose trial had to start anew. But although Leyla Zana received the European Parliament's Sakharov Prize for freedom of speech, the Turkish Supreme Court confirmed the 15-year sentences that had been handed down to her, Hatip Dicle, Orhan Doğan, Selim Sadak and Ahmet Türk on 8 December 1994, for membership of the PKK.

Even so, the release of a few prisoners after the revision of Article 8 proved sufficient for Turkey to obtain approval of a Customs Union from a reluctant European parliament. Çiller had achieved the goal she had set herself. She hoped the successful completion of her mission would mean victory at the polls, but the 1995 general election results showed a fall in the True Path Party's following from 27 per cent in 1991 to 19 per cent.

There are many reasons for Tansu Çiller's failure as Turkey's first woman prime minister. Close associates believe she wanted serious reforms but that she found herself battling against a system too deeply embedded to be easily moved. She also lacked a proper vision and plan of action. Rapidly resorting to short-term measures intended to guarantee her political survival for a few more days or weeks, she was sometimes obliged to contradict statements made the day before to the assembled media, or even to reverse whole policies. One newspaper caricaturist portrays her without a face, a visual pun on the Turkish word for a shameless liar.

Çiller also committed a dangerous sin in threatening a political establishment entrenched for thirty years. Opponents claimed that Tansu Çiller was naïve and understood little about the world of politics, but diplomats believed her to be a quick learner. Beginning as a hesitant, if ambitious, politician with a squeaky voice, she rapidly developed a commanding presence, despite her short size. She could still be prone to awkward statements. 'We have come a long way, baby, in human rights,' she said in answer to a question about the government's harsh methods in dealing with the Kurdish problem.[2]

Her ruthlessness and tenacity in the face of vigorous opposition singled her out among political leaders too often ready to accept the inertia of the state system. One of her first successes, in 1993, had been the lifting of a ban on private radio stations. Ushering in a different political style, she seized rapidly on the opportunity that dozens of new private television stations provided to enter into the sitting-rooms of millions of viewers, regularly speaking to the nation in American-style addresses from the prime minister's desk. Discarding the horse-trading style of traditional politicians, she introduced into the DYP newcomers who were familiar to television audiences as businessmen or top-level bureaucrats.

As a result of this policy, she fought the 1995 elections with a motley crew dominated by hard-line security force members: the ex-chief of general staff Doğan Güreş, the former governor of the state-of-emergency region Ünal Erkan, ex-chief of police Mehmet Ağar, all well known to the public as major figures in the fight against PKK 'terrorists', as they were called by the authorities. But it also included businessmen like Sedat Aloğlu, who led the campaign for Customs Union at the head of the Economic Development Foundation, and top economic bureaucrats such as Ayfer Yılmaz and Ufuk Söylemez, who briefly led the privatization office.

The old-time DYP members were angered by the arrival of these famous faces, parachuted into the party at the whim of their leader. Dissidents, such as Hüsamettin Çindoruk, the influential parliamentary speaker as well as one of the DYP's founders and a key supporter of Çiller's leadership campaign in 1993, was summarily expelled when he rebelled against her.

Çiller's tarnished star began to wane. She was no longer the miraculous leader who was to take Turkey into the twenty-first century, but just one of many public figures struggling in the murky world of politics. Çiller had hoped to win a sufficient majority to rule alone in the 1995 elections. In fact, her party only came third, behind the Welfare Party and Mesut Yılmaz's Motherland Party.

The great battle between Çiller and Yılmaz had resulted in a draw. Yet state institutions, the army and public opinion were clearly not ready for an Islamic-led government. After long negotiations, the two rival conservative parties were forced into a coalition which neither leader really wanted. Mesut Yılmaz, who has an almost allergic dislike of Tansu Çiller, was to be prime minister until the end of the year and Çiller was to take over for two years after that. But the 'Anayol' (Motherpath) coalition – a contraction of the names of the two parties – did not turn out to be the miracle medicine that business circles expected. Putting two conservative parties with similar outlooks together should in time have led to the formation of a strong centre-right group, but the Islamists of the Welfare Party, intensely frustrated at having been kept out of power, made sure that this fusion could not happen.

The strong personal rivalry between Yılmaz and Çiller gave them an easy target. During the election campaign, television viewers were treated to the sight of the two leaders side by side during special television debates, clearly loathing each other. Tongue-tied on policy, with few ready answers to sharp questions, Çiller did not come across as being in command of the issues. But she never lost her calm and goaded Mesut Yılmaz who, although better prepared, was criticized for his unchivalrous behaviour as he ranted and raved against 'that woman', on one memorable occasion spitting out the crumbs of the biscuits on which he was inelegantly munching at the time.

The Islamists played on the unfinished business between the two leaders who, despite having publicly put aside their differences, were still both hoping one day to take control of a united right. When the Welfare Party tabled two motions in parliament, demanding the opening of corruption enquiries against Tansu Çiller, Mesut Yılmaz and ANAP were only too pleased to support them. If Çiller could be sent to the Supreme Court, it would effectively prevent her from taking over from Mesut Yılmaz as prime minister when her time came. The Supreme Court could be expected to take up to two years to come to any decision, and by Turkish law a politician who is under investigation cannot be prime minister. ANAP also hoped that dissenters in the DYP would raise their voice and overthrow a party leader now tainted in the eyes of the voters.

Çiller's reputation was buffeted by the disclosure that she had withdrawn more than six million dollars from a secret prime minister's fund shortly before leaving office. But she refused to reveal how it was spent or to go down without a fight. Her party brought down the coalition after only three months, having achieved little apart from convincing the Turkish public that their politicians were selfish and useless.

Cornered, Çiller, who had promoted herself as a guarantor of Turkish secularism against the rise of Islam, took the biggest gamble of her political life by forming a coalition with the people she had accused of wanting to divide Turkey: the Islamists of the Welfare Party. Her betrayal of election promises and her alliance with the party that had brought accusations of corruption against her shocked many of her supporters. Inside the party she faced open rebellion. 'The country urgently needs a government, it needs stability,' she said to justify her move. In fact, despite her apparently weak position, she had managed to negotiate a favourable agreement that left her party in charge of major ministries and would allow her to return to office after two years under a power-sharing deal. Nothing in the protocol she signed with the Welfare Party could be seen as being contrary to the secular ideals of the republic. Realizing that she had to keep a high profile to survive politically, she also added the job of foreign minister to her responsibilities as deputy prime minister.

Her influence as head of the Turkish diplomatic corps was limited, however. Foreign governments no longer trusted the woman who had initially promised to keep the Islamists out of government and then made an alliance with them. Inside the ministry she was also mistrusted by her own diplomats, who resented her constant interference and her tendency to speak out of turn. The political necessity of preventing corruption charges against her from being investigated by parliament made her a virtual hostage in the coalition. Although foreign minister, she was unable to persuade Prime Minister Erbakan to abandon his plans to visit controversial destinations such as Iran and Libya.

In return for Çiller's support in the coalition, the Welfare Party switched position and voted to clear her of wrongdoing in parliamentary investigations it had itself brought against her. Çiller's single-mindedness and lack of scruples had allowed her to survive many plots hatched against her by frustrated opponents. But she would need to harness all her political skills to survive a partnership with one of Turkey's most cunning politicians, Necmettin Erbakan, who, thanks to her, became the first pro-Islamic prime minister of the republic in July 1996.

18

A Turkish-Islamic Synthesis

> The national spirit has risen up again to give
> life to the National Order Party, the same
> spirit that a thousand years ago confronted the
> Crusader armies, that five hundred years ago
> pulled boats overland [to conquer Constanti-
> nople], that four hundred years ago laid siege
> to the gates of Vienna and that half a century
> ago worked the masterpieces of Çanakkale
> [Gallipoli] and the War of Independence.
>
> National Order Party, founding manifesto, 1970

NECMETTIN ERBAKAN IS probably Turkey's most single-minded
politician, the man who led his pro-Islamic faithful from the political wilderness in the 1960s to become Turkey's biggest and best-
disciplined party of the 1990s. With his round face, his chubby
cheeks and his dashing Italian ties, Erbakan looks more like a
prosperous merchant than an Islamic fundamentalist. Add a white
beard, and he could make a kindly Father Christmas. Yet in the
eyes of many Turks, Erbakan is little short of the Devil incarnate,
bent on destroying the very basis of the secular modern republic
envisaged by Atatürk.

Islam is the most controversial issue to divide the Turkish republic since it was founded in 1923, deeper even than the ethnic
Kurdish question. Kemalist Turks known as the *aydınlar*, or enlightened ones, people who have totally embraced the secularist agenda
of the Kemalist republic, have often despised the rural tradition-
alists who kept their Muslim faith and who declined to identify
with the non-Islamic aspects of the Westernizing trend. In the eyes
of the *aydınlar*, to be religious is automatically to be backward.
Thus the political conflict between secularism and Islam is often

described as a struggle between modernity and reaction, between enlightenment and obscurantism.

Of all the radical reforms introduced by Atatürk, the abolition of the caliphate and the introduction of the concept of *laiklik*, or secularism, encountered the most serious opposition. But dissent from the official republican line was viewed as an attack by the forces of reaction and immediately crushed. It was partly in the name of this Westernizing secularism that Atatürk ordered the crackdown on the first major Kurdish rebellion in 1925, led by the Muslim rebel Sheikh Said. In December 1930, a young officer named Kubilay was captured and beheaded by an angry mob in the Aegean town of Menemen when he attempted to break up a demonstration in favour of the return of the veil and the old Ottoman Arabic script. The new state's response was crushingly swift.

But just how secular is the modern Turkish republic? The Kemalist establishment would say that thanks to republican reforms, religion has been kept firmly excluded from affairs of state. Yet, as the late scholar and writer Jean-Pierre Thieck noted, 'far from being the equivalent of a separation between Church and State, [the secularist republic] extended even further the traditional control of the latter over the men of religion, who all became civil servants.'[1]

A country cannot really be called secular when it pays, every month, the salaries of 60,000 imams and dictates the contents of their weekly sermons at Friday prayers, sometimes down to the last word. This curious paradox is reflected in society, where defenders of secularism insist on maintaining state control over religion, believing the 1,300-year-old laws and social dictates of Islam to be incompatible with modern pluralist democracy. The Islamists, on the other hand, have been in favour of a more liberal attitude that would make religion truly separate from the state. 'All we want is the same freedom for religion that is current in Britain or Switzerland,' Erbakan often says.

Although the recent rise of political Islam has fuelled the West's fear of a fundamentalist Turkey – along the lines of Iran or Algeria – Muslim activism is neither a new phenomenon, nor is it necessarily threatening. Many interpretations of Islam coexist in Turkey. The Welfare Party in fact represents only one strand of this. Even then it shows no sign of being able to choose between its fundamentalist fringe and those who enjoin the Koranic phrase 'there is no forcing in religion' to justify a moderate approach.

The rise of political Islam may be more apparent than real, reflecting the arrival in major cities of a previously uncounted rural population. While the urban élite of the early republic quickly adopted Atatürk's brand of secularism, they were relatively few in numbers and secularism was not uniformly applied throughout the country. Rural areas on the whole escaped its strictures. Even in the cities, it was only successfully imposed in the period of the iron-fisted one-party regime.

As soon as Turkey converted to a multi-party system, religion became a political tool. With the founding of the Democrat Party in 1946, Ismet Inönü himself, although a somewhat rigid enforcer of the republican reforms, was compelled to compromise to stem the haemorrhage of voters. In 1949, he appointed a prime minister, Şemsettin Günaltay, who, inside the Republican People's Party, was considered almost an Islamist. Optional classes on religion were reintroduced as part of the school curriculum at the primary level. These measures did not prevent his party's electoral defeat in 1950. When the Democrats came to power they went further along the Islamic path, allowing the call to prayer to be made in Arabic again, despite the fact that Atatürk had wanted it in Turkish, and funding the creation of *imam hatip* schools to train religious officials. These schools have multiplied over the past four decades, but only a small proportion of those they train actually join the ranks of the Muslim clergy. Instead, with time, graduates have come to infiltrate all levels of the bureaucracy, much to the horror of the secular establishment.

On three occasions since 1960 the army has stepped in to put the country back on the tracks of Mustafa Kemal's reforms, yet even the staunchly secular military were not above using religion when it suited their purposes. After the 1980 coup, the junta made religious study lessons compulsory in schools in an attempt to depoliticize a population deeply scarred and polarized by the left–right conflict that had dominated the late 1970s.

Throughout the 1980s, political Islam discreetly spread through the political establishment. Özal's Motherland Party had a strong Muslim component, among them conservative ministers such as Cemil Çiçek, who once said that 'to flirt was like prostitution'. The faction was counterbalanced by the pro-Western liberals in the party. Özal, who could claim to have a foot in both camps, managed to maintain the delicate balance. But when his more liberal successors pushed aside the Muslim faction of the party, the broad church that was ANAP lost many of its more religious voters to the Welfare Party, which stepped into the breach with the claim that it alone was the standard-bearer of Muslim conservatism.

*

The Welfare Party was essentially the brainchild of one man, Necmettin Erbakan, who, since the 1960s, has steered and dominated this political formation through its various reincarnations. Erbakan, a German-trained specialist in diesel engine ignition systems, had tried initially to join Demirel's Justice Party. But despite the fact that the two men had been classmates at Istanbul Technical University, the party rejected the candidacy of this pious Muslim, son of an Ottoman judge and the descendant of a line of minor south Anatolian aristocrats.

Erbakan reacted to this rebuff by founding his own National Order Party, which only survived from 1969 until the 1971 military intervention. A year later, the ambitious politician was back on the offensive, this time forming the National Salvation Party. Although his party won only forty-eight seats in the 1973 elections, Erbakan was suddenly propelled to the front of the political stage when he formed a coalition government with Bülent Ecevit, then the leader of the Republican People's Party. The shaky alliance tried unsuccessfully to join the two extremes of society, Atatürk's staunchly secular old party and the newly self-confident Islamists. What little the two men had in common was a strong Turkish nationalism, which in 1974 led them to order troops into northern Cyprus to protect the Turkish Cypriots.

But Erbakan went further than Ecevit: he wanted to take the whole island. The lack of trust between the two men eventually caused the downfall of their government. Ecevit had been invited to visit Scandinavia, a tour that would have kept him out of the country for two weeks. 'I could not allow him to deputize for me at this sensitive, critical period. There was no such condition in our coalition agreement,' Ecevit explained more than two decades later. 'Erbakan objected to that and said his party would not sign the decree allowing me to leave the country. That was the practical reason why I had to resign.'[2]

This ended Erbakan's first taste of real power. He and his party later joined two right-wing coalition governments as the decade went on. By the end he had been deputy prime minister for more than three years, with another eleven months in which Demirel's minority government relied on his support. This added up to a formidable period of patronage, one of the main prizes of Turkish politics. The National Salvation Party packed its faithful into the ministries of justice, interior, labour, agriculture and industry, the parts of government it judged vital to serve its main base of support, the *esnaf* class of old-fashioned small businessmen. Twenty years later, many of those appointed had reached senior positions.

When the military took power in 1980, they dissolved the existing political parties and imposed a political ban on their leaders, including Necmettin Erbakan and his National Salvation Party. It was not long, however, until his supporters began to reorganize. In 1983, the Welfare Party was born. It started modestly, but slowly and steadily increased its share of the votes during the 1980s. By 1987, when the old political leaders were again allowed to enter politics, Erbakan, who until then had guided the party by remote control, could finally reclaim its leadership.

Charismatic, using humour to great effect in his lengthy speeches, Erbakan has kept an iron grip on his followers. Extremely wealthy – he lists among his assets 150 kilos of gold and several properties, while his brother has acquired pieces of land so large they are counted in square kilometres – he hardly fits the image of an ascetic religious extremist. Unlike younger elements in his party, who have taken over the mission of the Turkish left, working actively in the slums to help poor immigrants, Erbakan is very much a man of the conservative right. Although a sincere believer, he is also a wily and opportunistic politician, devoured by a burning ambition.

There is no mistaking the religious tone of his party's message, but Erbakan gives only sparing details of its programme. Its central concept of 'a just order' is extremely vague, allowing it to be understood by the radical elements as referring to Islamic *sharia* law or, in the case of more moderate supporters, simply to a less corrupt society and political system. Fiery electoral rhetoric promising the abolition of interest rates as contrary to the rules of Islam, forming an Islamic common market and introducing an Islamic dinar in Turkey was quietly forgotten when a more statesmanlike and circumspect attitude was called for. Thus when the Welfare Party actually came to power in July 1996, Necmettin *Hoca*, or 'teacher' as he is often called, suddenly abandoned his earlier opposition on such issues as Customs Union with Europe, Turkey's membership of NATO and military co-operation with Israel.

Despite repeated assurances of his party's commitment to democracy and tolerance, Erbakan is a despotic leader. While he has undoubtedly been the glue that has kept together the Welfare Party's many tendencies – radical and moderate, reformist and orthodox, left and right – his rhetorical excesses have at times antagonized cautious voters. When Israel launched its bloody offensive into southern Lebanon in May 1996, Erbakan condemned the attack in a speech that targeted the Jews rather than the state of Israel. 'Did the Jews not bomb our Muslim brothers in Lebanon?' he told party supporters. 'Given these truths, if you give a vote to anyone outside the Welfare Party, you will give a vote to the Jews. Martyrs and saints will strike down such people.' A deeply held belief in a 'Jewish conspiracy' that rules the world revealed his surprising naïvety, as did his refusal to see any threat to Turkey in hard-line regimes such as those that hold sway in Libya, Iran, Saudi Arabia or Syria. Erbakan's folly became evident in his first months in office. A trip to Iran had little immediate effect on Tehran's tolerance of Turkey's rebel Kurds; feelers to Syria brought no warm embrace, and a highly publicized visit to Libya ended in an outright insult from Libyan leader Muammar Gaddafi.

Some Welfare officials of the younger generation, such as Istanbul mayor Recep Tayyıp Erdoğan, appeared more in tune with the times, but their reticence disguised a more ideological approach to Islam. Erbakan also promoted his foreign affairs specialist Abdüllah Gül, a moderate who was able to forge links with Turkey's traditional Western partners. But Erbakan retains total control over his organization. Compared to other parties, constantly weakened by discontent, internal plots and disloyalty, the Welfare Party is run with a military discipline. Women form the infantry, canvassing households, street by street, all over the country. The network they have built up is remarkable. For the year 1994, in the province of Istanbul alone, 69,000 members of the women's wing of the party, organized in 600 neighbourhoods, had contacted 2.6 million people.

The various factions within the organization are carefully held together by Erbakan's imam-like charisma. His negotiations with Tansu Çiller on the formation of a coalition, in June 1996, were a rare occasion when the party did not act with its usual cohesion. Having successfully demolished the previous government by targeting Tansu Çiller with allegations of corruption, Necmettin Erbakan encountered unusually stiff opposition from his parliamentary group when, to ease the way for a potential alliance with her DYP, Erbakan asked his colleagues to reject one of their own investigations into her alleged misuse of the six million dollars she had suddenly withdrawn shortly before resigning as prime minister. The motion against the former head of government was rejected as Erbakan desired, but several Welfare deputies broke ranks with their leader and voted in favour of the inquiry.

They were not the only ones surprised by Necmettin Erbakan's turnabout. It came from a man whose whole political platform was based on the fight against corruption and who claimed to have launched the movement against Mrs Çiller for the sake of a 'clean Turkey'. The U-turn showed that Necmettin Erbakan was, above all, a politician hungry for power and not a terrifying ideologue, or, as some of his supporters might have believed, a miracle man imbued with a divine mission.

Each year in August thousands of Turks flock to a little town in Central Anatolia near Cappadocia, where magical valleys of rock-carved churches, underground cities and mushroom-shaped rock formations attract tourists from all over the world. The Turks, however, are heading for the mausoleum of Haci Bektaş in the town of the same name. Here at an annual gathering they pay their respects at the tomb of the saint, the carefully groomed drapes on his sarcophagus still surrounded by the gleaming standards of the Janissary battalions. The scene is living proof of the enduring tradition of the *tarikats* in Turkey, a tradition that has little to do with political Islam.

The cult of Haci Bektaş is just one sign that the Welfare Party has no monopoly on Turkish Islam, despite the party's spectacular rise and Islamist stance. Indeed, the Turkish understanding of religion has taken diverse forms over the centuries. *Tarikats* or Muslim brotherhoods traditionally played an important role in the Ottoman empire – notable among them the Nakshibendis, a widespread movement that began in Bukhara in Central Asia, and the Mevlevis, better known as the whirling dervishes. Offering a mystic closeness to God and a like-mind network of pious contacts, they have continued to flourish under the republic, despite a Kemalist order to disband that forced them underground for several decades. They gradually re-emerged and have been active in their support for various conservative political parties such as the Motherland and True Path parties. Turgut Özal pushed through a cabinet decision to bury his mother next to the grave of a famous twentieth-century Nakshibendi sheikh, Said Kotku, himself buried near the *türbe*, or tomb, of Süleyman the Magnificent.

As the Welfare Party continued to gain ground, other prominent figures such as Fethullah Gülen, a powerful moderate *tarikat* leader, who openly supported the separation of mosque and state, came to the fore. He had supporters in both the secular media and among politicians such as Tansu Çiller keen to show that religious alternatives to the Welfare Party can exist. Gülen is a leader of the Nurcu sect, whose congregations unite in following the teachings of Said-i Nursi, a sheikh who emerged in the 1920s and whose life's work was to reconcile Islam with Western modernity.

Other *tarikats* are less benign, among them the Aczimendiler, who dress up in long robes, cover their long and straggly hair with black turbans and seem to support fundamentalism wherever they find it, rallying in front of Ayasofya and staging noisy demonstrations in the grand mosque in Ankara.

The main religious divide in Turkey is however not to be found within the Sunni community, which comprises a majority of Turkish Muslims, but between the Sunnis and the substantial Alevi minority, a sect of Shia origin but strongly attached to the secularist system.

Mystery surrounds the exact number of Alevis in Turkey. The figures bandied around vary enormously, but they are believed to number between ten and fifteen million, that is between 15 and 25 per cent of the population, including both ethnic Turks and Kurds.[3] Sometimes known as the *kızılbaş* or 'red heads', after turbans they once wore, the Alevis have been in conflict with Sunni orthodoxy for centuries. Unlike the more austere Sunnis, the Alevis celebrate their humanist religion with songs, the music of the *saz* (a kind of lute) and dances that at times resemble the whirling movements of the dervishes. Most shocking in the eyes of religious Sunnis, these dances are performed by men and women together during intense ceremonies known as *cem* that can last for hours. The combination of music, men and women dancing together in a kind of trance, the worship of Imam Ali and his son Hussein – Shia heroes killed at Kerbala on 10 October 680 – all conspires to give the Alevis a bad name among Sunnis. Popular Sunni prejudices abound, most outrageously that the *kızılbaş* organize incestuous group orgies at the moment a candle is snuffed out during their religious ceremonies.

The Alevis, by contrast, believe theirs to be a true form of Turkish Islam. Unlike Sunni orthodoxy, borrowed from the Arabs, their religion, they say, evolved from the shamanism of the early Turks in Central Asia and gradually acquired new dimensions as it came under various influences, among them that of Shia Muslim missionaries from Safavid Iran. Unlike their Sunni and Shia cousins, the Alevis do not believe that prophets or prayer leaders are necessary for man to communicate with God. Thus they have no real clergy, only a *dede*, a 'wise old man' – a title often passed on from father to son in well-respected families – who advises and leads in local communities.

Sunni suspicions of Alevis are deep-rooted. The Safavid Shah Ismail did not send his missionaries from Iran in the early sixteenth century for purely religious reasons. He was seeking popular support and territorial aggrandizement at the expense of the Sunni Ottomans. The Alevis suffered greatly in the subsequent war, still remembered in Alevi folk poetry. Sultan Selim (1512–20) earned his nickname 'the Grim' when he took revenge on those judged disloyal by slaughtering the Alevi 'red heads' at will.

Added to the religious conflict is a political dimension that has brought the Sunnis and Alevis into open conflict on several occasions in recent history. The Alevis, staunch defenders of Atatürk's reforms since the birth of the republic, have often supported leftist parties, from the Republican People's Party to the more radical extremist parties that fuelled the left–right struggle in the 1970s. Earlier massacres of Alevis in Sivas, Kahramanmaraş and Çorum in the 1970s showed how volatile the mixing of religion and politics could become.

In the 1990s, the Alevis suffered new tragedies, the most shocking being the Sivas massacre in July 1993. Intellectuals had gathered in this ancient Anatolian town for a festival in honour of the medieval Alevi poet Pir Sultan Abdal. Among the guests was the famous Turkish satirist, Aziz Nesin, who had made his name with caustic novels and plays illustrating the absurdities of Turkish life and government. Nesin, a supporter of the left, was also a staunch defender of secularism. He had often openly condemned the 'stupidity' of Turks and spoken out against religious bigots. As a writer he had sponsored the publication in the leftist newspaper *Aydınlık* of a translation of Salman Rushdie's *Satanic Verses*, a book that is officially banned in Turkey. Nesin, a man who delighted in provoking, admitted he had never read the book and had no interest in its literary merit. But its publication, which was meant mainly to highlight state censorship, was like a red rag to a bull for the Islamists.

On arrival in Sivas, Nesin made a rousing speech with strong anti-Islamic overtones that was published the next day in the local press. By the time the crowds came out of traditional Friday prayers, they had worked themselves into a frenzy. Gathering in front of the hotel where the Alevis and intellectuals had taken refuge, they demonstrated for hours. Despite calls for help to Ankara from the beleaguered Alevis and intellectuals stuck inside the hotel, the security forces held back. Then someone in the crowd set fire to the building and huge shouts of '*Allah-u Akbar*',

God is Great, rose as flames licked up the side of the building. Thirty-seven people died from burns and suffocation, sending shock waves through the country. Aziz Nesin, brought shakily down a fire-engine ladder, said he was only saved because the firemen thought they were rescuing the police chief. When they realized their mistake, they kicked the 78-year-old writer all the way to the police car that eventually took him away.

The wound left by this tragedy in Turkish society has never successfully healed. Islamists, who hated Aziz Nesin, refused to condemn the attack. The trial of various people thought to be responsible failed to resolve the conflict. Some fundamentalists were condemned to gaol sentences, but the court decided to open a case against Aziz Nesin as well for provoking the incident. In the end, neither the Islamists nor the shocked defenders of secularism and Alevism felt vindicated.

The growing community activism that this engendered among the Alevis was shown in their reaction to an ill-advised joke by a popular television broadcaster in January 1995, which reflected prejudiced Sunni ideas about the supposed Alevi practice of group sex. Huge crowds of Alevi protestors gathered in front of the television station in an Istanbul suburb. Alevi concerns were further brought to the attention of the Turkish public in March 1995, during the Gaziosmanpaşa riots, which started when unknown gunmen opened fire on a café frequented by Alevis in a poor suburb of Istanbul, killing three people. The outrage felt by local Alevis at this provocation turned into a violent confrontation with police brought in to control the crowd. Using their usual brutal methods, the police only succeeded in aggravating the situation. The demonstrations were rapidly taken over by radical youths from illegal extreme-leftist groups, who fought with the state forces for several days. At least sixteen people died in these riots.

Orthodox Sunnis and Alevis have few religious beliefs in common – the reason why, unlike Turks and Kurds, they rarely intermarry. There are similarities, however. As they settled into urban life, Alevis began to build public community centres known as *cemevis* for their prayer meetings, just as the Sunni communities built mosques. They also began to institutionalize their religion and their politics, a far cry from the formerly secretive, scattered rural communities of Alevis loyal to individual *dedes*. Both Alevi and Sunni activists share a dislike of the state stranglehold on religion. Like some Islamists, the Alevis would like the Directorate of Religious Affairs, the state body that effectively controls official Islam in Turkey, to be abolished. At the very least, they lay claim to a share of the funds the state distributes for the construction of mosques and the salaries of the imams.

But their differences outweigh their common complaints. The Alevis fear the rise of political Islam and a Sunni majority that often shows little tolerance to their approach to life and religious beliefs. They are therefore among the most ardent defenders of the secular system, even if the republic has not repaid their loyalty with much support.

The violent attacks against Alevis in Sivas raised the spectre of Islamic terrorism. Too often, secularists associate political Islam with fundamentalism, a label that immediately brings to mind images of bomb explosions in Algeria or executions in Iran. Most supporters of the Welfare Party are law-abiding citizens who would not think of imposing their views by force. But the fact of the matter is that a more violent interpretation of religion does exist in Turkey, as throughout the Middle East.

The early 1990s saw a spate of fundamentalist-inspired attacks in which several well-known secular figures were killed, including writer Turan Dursun, secularist academic Bahriye Uçok, Atatürk Thought Association leader Muammer Aksoy and journalist Çetin Emeç, apparently for their open and sometimes fiercely stated opposition to Islamic forces. When Uğur Mumcu, the well-known leader writer on the newspaper *Cumhuriyet*, a publication that has for decades been the voice of secular Turkey, was blown up by a car bomb in 1993, the whole country rose in protest. For days, an outpouring of grief and anger shook the nation. In many cities, demonstrations of support for the secularists were organized. Tens of thousands shouting 'Turkey will not be a second Iran' marched in Istanbul and Ankara to demonstrate against Islamic terrorism.

The murders remained unsolved for several years, until the arrest in 1996 of Irfan Çağırıcı, the gunman who allegedly organized several of the killings. Among his accomplices he named several Iranian diplomats who, he claimed, had provided him with weapons, training in Iran and the expertise to carry out the assassinations. The role allegedly played by Tehran caused a new coolness between the two states, who once again found themselves accusing each other of harbouring spies and plotters. Rogue Turkish state operatives later seemed more likely suspects in the murder of Mumcu.

In the seventies, angry young men turned to leftist extremism or fascist violence. In the 1990s they were joined by Islamists aiming to spread their radical ideology and to impose a theocratic regime. The desolate concrete suburbs of the big cities provide a fertile breeding-ground for violent action. In the turbulent politics of the Middle East, such opportunities are easily exploited by rival powers. Turkish officials have accused both Iran and Syria of stirring up trouble. Others are more discreet. In its heyday in the 1980s, even Saudi Arabia was rumoured to have financed the education of young girls willing to wear the Islamic headscarf.

South-eastern Turkey, already divided by the Kurdish conflict, had to contend briefly with the added burden of a conflict between Iranian-inspired organizations like Hezbollah and the Marxist PKK. Both wanted an independent Kurdistan, but the Islamists wanted theirs to be an Islamic republic. For a while, the Turkish state tolerated this Islamic movement, with whom it shared a common enemy. But when links between violent actions in the south-east and Istanbul appeared, the government realized it had to act. Whole networks were dismantled before the situation got out of control.

Would a government dominated by mainstream Islamists be willing to crack down on more radical elements, seeking similar goals through violent means? The question has weighed on the mind of many defenders of secularism, among them the Alevis, who remember that the Welfare Party and their supporters never condemned the appalling mob violence in Sivas. Other members of society who had good reason to view the Welfare Party with suspicion were Turkey's up-and-coming women.

Western-educated women, particularly those of the old Kemalist school, have been among the most active campaigners against the Welfare Party. Statements of party officials do nothing to reassure them. Women are described as 'flowers' that need to be protected, which generally means they should stay at home. Even younger party figures, such as Istanbul mayor Recep Tayyıp Erdoğan, at times said to be the heir apparent of Welfare Party leader Necmettin Erbakan, seldom takes his wife, who wears a headscarf, to official functions. He also advocates high birth rates. People who have worked with him and admire his dynamism and efficiency say he privately believes women should try first to find fulfilment in family life, and, failing that, should confine themselves to voluntary work for the party.

It may seem contradictory, but while the men in the party are clearly not in favour of women's rights, contact with the party's grass roots is mostly managed by women, who are often as modern and intellectually advanced as their secular sisters. Contrary to perceptions in the West, these women, who often wear a long Islamic coat as well as a headscarf, are not always uneducated peasants submitting to tradition. Some are well-educated professional women, who have made a conscious choice to embrace religion.

Sibel Eraslan is typical of these modern young activists. Like many Western women, she juggles family and work. The daughter of secular parents and a lawyer by training, she came to Islam while a student. She and others like her learned their activism when challenging the establishment's strong opposition to those militant Muslim students who wanted to wear the *türban*, the tightly pinned headscarf that distinguishes the politically conscious Islamic woman, as compared with the normal *başörtü* of rural women, which is loosely knotted under the chin. Expelled from law school for wearing a headscarf, Sibel managed eventually to finish her studies. But strict rules against lawyers wearing Islamic headgear in court prevented her from registering at the Istanbul Bar Association. In order to practise her profession, she had to team up with her husband, himself a lawyer, who would plead in her place using the files she had prepared. Like many other Muslim women who insisted on wearing the *türban*, and thus were expelled from nursing schools, dismissed from jobs or barred from universities, she was attracted to the Welfare Party by the intransigence of the official republican system. The party thus benefited from Sibel's energy. At the head of the Welfare Party's formidable female wing in Istanbul province, she organized the election campaign that resulted in the victory of Recep Tayyıp Erdoğan, elected mayor of Istanbul in March 1994.

Sibel's outspokenness and her dynamism must have unnerved some old party officials. A year after Erdoğan's election victory, she and other members of her team were removed from their posts. An edge of bitterness crept into her voice as she explained that she had been considered too left-wing in the eyes of the party leadership. Wanting to attract more middle-class voters, they had replaced her with a well-to-do lady clad in a silk headscarf.[4] Sibel did not turn her back on the party, however, and continued to campaign all over the country. Welfare Party women such as Sibel Eraslan could almost be likened to feminists with social-democrat tendencies, perceiving Islam as a religious form of social work. She believes her place is in the slums of Istanbul, where she teaches, helps the poor to cope with the difficulties of life and encourages women to educate their daughters. By the same token, her modest neighbourhood of the Istanbul suburb of Ümraniye, now dominated by Welfare Party supporters, was in the 1970s a bastion of the extreme left known as the 'First of May District'.

Women may well prove to be an Achilles heel for the old guard of the Welfare Party. How long will these militants, who turn up at rallies in their hundreds, loyally waving the party flag, agree to work for the party without any public reward? Several Welfare women put their name forward during the election campaign in 1995, but party leaders decided not to include any female candidates on their lists. To be fair, other, secular, parties had little more than a token sprinkling of women in theirs, but the Welfare Party was the only one with no women at all.

The Welfare Party leadership came up with two excuses. The first was that Turkish society was not yet ready to see women in headscarves in parliament and that the party wanted to avoid confrontation. An antiquated republican law prohibits women from covering their heads in public buildings, which is why Muslim female lawyers cannot plead in court. The leadership also argued, rather lamely, that the Welfare Party's female candidates were still too inexperienced. It is true that the most militant of them were often in their early twenties, and would therefore not qualify for election since Turkish law requires deputies to be at least 30 years old. In the female wing of the party, there was clear disappointment. For the sake of unity, Sibel Eraslan and others expressed any complaints behind closed doors, if at all. But the issue may well come back to haunt the party later.

At meetings, most women are covered. Only a few choose the black ankle-length *çarşaf* that closely resembles the Iranian chador. Many are dressed with elegance, using silk headscarves creatively, and fashion shows for Muslim women can in their way be very glamorous affairs. To prove its modernity the party also proudly displays some unveiled women. A young blonde dentist was briefly promoted by the party as its answer to Tansu Çiller, but allegations of adultery spread by the media tarnished her image and she slipped from view. The contrast between the young and dynamic women, and the older, grey, bearded and obviously staunchly conservative men who still lead the party is so striking that it is at times hard to understand why these women allow themselves to be patronized in this way. One explanation given is that working for the Welfare Party is sometimes the only way a woman can have an active, independent and socially acceptable life outside a conservative Muslim home.

While these strong women are clearly capable of fending for themselves, feminists worry about a more vulnerable category, uneducated immigrants, often young girls who are easily influenced and have little to defend themselves with. Young Semra is a perfect example. At first her mother Zeynep, coming from a traditional Anatolian village, was a pious Muslim of the pragmatic, tolerant kind usual in Turkey. She would fast during Ramadan, wear a headscarf because women in her village always did, rather than specifically for religious reasons, and would occasionally go to the mosque. When she moved to Istanbul, she and many of her neighbours fell under the spell of a fundamentalist *hoca* preaching on the Asian side of Istanbul. He threatened them all with everlasting hellfire if they did not change their ways. Television and music were outlawed as *günah*, or 'sinful'. They had to go to the mosque five times a day to pray. Zeynep drank it all in unquestioningly, outdoing her family with her new religious zeal. Her teenaged children were reluctantly dragged out of bed at dawn to go and pray. Zeynep would argue with her more moderate sisters, trying to persuade them not to watch the traditional New Year's Eve shows on television when the country is entertained by famous singers and belly dancers. For her two daughters, life changed drastically. Barely in their teens, they were packed off to a Koranic boarding school, the modern equivalent of the most repressive convents of Europe. After several years in these establishments, they emerged with virtually no formal education, other than an extensive knowledge of the Arabic language and the Koran. They rejected the simple headscarf and long coat worn by their mother, preferring to hide completely behind a black *çarşaf* that shows only their eyes. They will not appear in the presence of men, other than their father and brothers, refusing in the name of religion to speak even to their favourite uncle.

This tragic situation – although the two young girls did not see it as such – was a source of great anxiety to other members of the extended family who believe in respecting religion, but fear, rightly, that such an upbringing could prove a grievous handicap for young girls living in a metropolis like Istanbul. Lacking an education, never able to work, the two young sisters will always be totally dependent on their father, or the husband who will be chosen for them by their parents.

The municipal elections held on 27 March 1994 were an important test for Turkish democracy. Despite polls claiming that the

Islamists could not win in major centres, the Welfare Party succeeded in winning 327 mayoralties, including those of twenty-eight
cities. More important still, they conquered the republican capital,
Ankara, and the historic commercial, cultural and financial centre
of Istanbul.

Welfare's success was received with shocked disbelief. For days,
the national pro-secularist newspapers filled their columns with
horror stories. They reprinted rumours claiming that women were
being forced to wear headscarves on Istiklal Street, the main pedestrian thoroughfare in what had once been the old European
quarter of the Ottoman capital. A large mosque would soon be
built in the middle of Taksim Square, they said. These sen-
sationalist reports turned out to have been vastly exaggerated,
although it was true that in the evenings immediately following
the poll some people were harassed by young Islamists celebrating
what they saw as a first step to power.

The political establishment was equally shocked. Both the
centre-left and centre-right had failed to catch the mood of the
population and their power was crumbling in consequence. Yet
the older parties refused to heed the warning. Instead of analysing
the reasons behind the Welfare Party's success, they continued
irresponsibly down the path to self-destruction, devoting more
energy to their attempts to topple their rivals rather than to the
needs of the nation. The result was that, two and a half years later,
Refah came first in the general elections in December 1995 with
21.3 per cent of the vote.

While traditional parties have never been able to shake off a
certain disdain for the peasant population of Anatolia, the Welfare
Party, in appearance at least, has tried to give dignity to those left
behind by Turkey's economic boom. The fact that there is little
democracy within the party does not seem to affect their support.
The Turkish public is, unfortunately, used to being dictated to.
Yet 'people's parliaments', set up in many districts controlled by
the party, have at least given ordinary people an opportunity to
air their complaints in front of municipal officials. Whether these
grievances are acted upon is another question, but the signs are
that the Welfare Party will still be working hard to prove itself for
some time to come.

In the suburbs, efficient teams of women had built up a network
that allowed them to keep track of local events. 'We want to grieve
with people when a relation dies, celebrate with them if a baby is
born, and help them if they are in difficulties,' explained Sibel
Eraslan. There is no doubt that there was a measure of electoral

bribery too, which took the form mostly of small presents of food or household necessities. Some claim that recipients of material assistance were asked to swear on the Koran that they would vote for the Welfare Party. In any case, the party organization was not ready to take chances. Supporters were often bussed in to polling stations to make sure they would vote.

By staking a claim to the country's Ottoman past, the Welfare Party also restored a sense of identity to those in the populace who had never understood or accepted Atatürk's revolution. They seized on nostalgia for the glories of empire. Under the new Welfare Party mayor, the 31 May anniversary of the conquest of Istanbul by Mehmet the Conqueror in 1453 became a major event. Life-size copies of Ottoman ships were dragged through modern city streets by volunteers dressed up in Janissary costumes and stiff felt hats. Leading them were the raucous reed-pipes and booming drums of the Ottoman-style *mehter* band that had so frightened the last Byzantine defenders of the city. A stadium was filled with cheering crowds to celebrate the occasion. Even so, the Islamists did not have a monopoly of the Ottoman heritage. Previous municipal authorities had long re-enacted the victorious last push through the thick Byzantine walls that still stand outside the old city.

This nationalist tendency could also be seen in the development of the Welfare Party's approach to the Kurdish problem. In 1991, the party was openly promising to enact wide Kurdish cultural freedoms in election campaign manifestos distributed in the southeast. In the eyes of the Islamists then, Kurds and Turks could reunite under the banner of Islam. There was little hint of this cultural liberalism, however, during the 1995 election campaign as Erbakan sought to reassure state institutions and secure his home base of voters, knowing that the Turkish majority had become more nationalistic as a result of the long conflict with the PKK. When the party's local administration in Diyarbakır, the capital of the mainly Kurdish region, protested at the omission from the electoral lists of several of their Kurdish colleagues, Erbakan dismissed them overnight.

Nationalism and religion are often intricately linked in Turkey, as indeed they were in Ottoman times, when the sultan represented not only Islam but also, first and foremost, the state. An extensive survey published in 1993 by the newspaper *Milliyet* showed that 4 per cent of those questioned in Istanbul still defined themselves simply as Muslims, not wanting the addition of a Turkish or other ethnic label. Another 21 per cent were unwilling to choose between nationalism and religion and preferred to be called Muslim Turks. Two-thirds perceived themselves as being Turks above all else, although doubtless many had differing ideas of what that meant.

Islamists are often described by Kemalists as reactionaries, people turned towards the past, and some of their older members show little willingness to look ahead to the future. But Turkey's Islamic movement as a whole had embraced science and progress with great gusto. Extensive lists of members and sympathizers are all computerized and the Welfare Party mayors brought in experts to head executive branches of their municipalities. Among the party's supporters are many businessmen and industrialists who deal with goods such as cars, computers and hospital equipment that are at the cutting edge of technology.

The municipalities, on the whole, have been successful. In Istanbul and Ankara, even the more ardent defenders of secularism have been forced to admit that their dire predictions have not materialized. A few early incidents were quickly resolved. In Istanbul, the Beyoğlu municipality sought to force the restaurateurs to remove the tables they had laid on the pavements and take them indoors, but public outcry forced the officials to retreat. For a while, newspapers harried the municipality over petty details such as the colour of warning marks on the pavements: the municipality briefly used green paint – the colour of Islam – to replace the former yellow. The secular press at times accused the new city leaders unfairly. Photographs of the mayor of Istanbul's new secretaries, with their headscarves and modest clothes, left out the two remaining employees in Erdoğan's office, two women who, despite not wearing the headscarf, had been kept on from the previous administration.

Many people praised the mayors for bringing in better management, and, unusually in Turkey, even Istanbul's biased and scandal-hungry media was unable to track down any of the gross financial irregularities that featured in previous administrations. Rubbish is collected regularly, trees have been planted and better coal has been introduced to replace the foul lignite responsible for the Istanbul winter smog: the last no mean achievement, involving as it did a confrontation with powerful and sometimes violent vested interests.

The cultural policy of the municipalities has come under attack. It started in Ankara where the mayor Melih Gökçek decided to remove a naked statue, which he thought to be indecent, from a public park. The Welfare Party municipalities also showed themselves keener to finance endless seminars on aspects of Islamic life than to encourage ballet – a 'degenerate' form of art – or classical music. They have however revived traditional Turkish customs, such as the ancient horseback game of *cirit*, a spectacular sport that re-creates all the excitement of cavalry at war.

While organizing Islamic symposia that reflect their world view, the Welfare Party municipalities, perhaps appreciating the strength of civil society more than the established parties, refrained from interfering with others. Nothing was done to touch the main cycle of Istanbul's music, jazz, theatre, film and art festivals, which feature everything from Islamic fundamentalist films to erotica. 'The new municipality is almost better than the previous ones. They give us free billboards and venues and are very co-operative,' said Nilgün Mirze, one of the festival directors and herself a fervent secularist dressed in billowing white skirts. 'We are not censored at all and in fact we no longer rely much on any public institutions. They give just 8–10 per cent of our budget, if we're lucky. The government cannot change anything, and people would not accept it anyway. We try to bring everything together. We are all looking for a new synthesis, part of being a bridge between Europe and Asia.'

The mayors' successes in Istanbul and Ankara have made them strong contenders for Erbakan's succession. Recep Tayyıp Erdoğan runs his municipality like an election campaign. All his achievements, however small, are celebrated with big posters stuck on billboards across Istanbul. Having shown the doubters that Welfare Party municipalities could perform, more than adequately, the job that was given to them, Erdoğan obviously feels that greater power is within reach.

After the municipalities, the next step was national government. The Welfare Party moved closer to that goal with its 21.3 per cent victory in the 24 December 1995 general elections. Negotiations to form a government took weeks, and Necmettin Erbakan and Mesut Yılmaz came within an ace of signing a deal. A coalition was about to be formed that would, for the first time, have given a majority stake to an Islamic party in secular Turkey.

It was not to be, at least not immediately. The would-be alliance was blocked after heavy pressure from business circles frightened by Necmettin Erbakan's eccentric rhetoric about the economy, from the secular media with all its vested interests in the old political set-up and, last but not least, from the army, which discreetly twisted the arms of the bickering secularist politicians behind the scenes. They pressured Mesut Yılmaz to join forces with True Path Party leader Tansu Çiller. But these two rivals for the leadership of Turkey's secular centre-right completely failed to overcome an antipathy that verged on mutual hatred. Their coalition never gelled and collapsed after three months, when the country found itself, yet again, faced with the same problem: the Islamists controlled only 158 seats in the 550-seat parliament, but the establishment parties could not agree on a coalition that would exclude them.

Now it was Tansu Çiller who sat down for talks with the Welfare Party – a surprising move, since she had campaigned principally on the platform that she would never deal with the Islamists, let alone form a government with them. But the self-proclaimed guardian of Turkish secularism was now fighting for political survival, having been pushed into a corner by Erbakan's and Mesut Yılmaz's cunning allegations of corruption during her period as prime minister. To save her skin, she had little choice but to risk doing a deal with the Welfare Party.

This time, the country had no more energy to resist Erbakan's embrace. Çiller's minister of health, Yıldırım Aktuna, joked that 'When you have such a fervent suitor, a lady can only say no for so long.'[5] Disgusted at the failure of the Yılmaz–Çiller government, the army and big business folded their hands but let it be known that they would be keeping a strict eye on things. The government was formed on 28 June 1996, a historic turning point for the Kemalist republic. It narrowly won a vote of confidence in parliament in July after huge pressure had been applied to waverers on both sides. The tension overflowed into shouting and fisticuffs. 'My rival could not keep the bird he had in his hand,' a delighted Erbakan joked at Yılmaz's expense from the rostrum, looking, as he was to put it later, as happy 'as a butterfly'.

Again and again, Erbakan insisted that the Welfare Party remained bound by the constitution and democratic principles. But secular Turks remain convinced that the Welfare Party's softly-softly approach hides an underlying fundamentalist agenda that has nothing to do with democracy, and instead aims to overthrow the secularist establishment. Prisoners of their fervent belief that Islamists could have a catastrophic influence on democracy, they appear blind to the idea that democracy may also influence the Welfare Party.

Unlike many Islamic movements in the Middle East, which have emerged as underground, illegal opposition groups, even in countries like Saudi Arabia where strict Islamic law has long been in force, the Welfare Party has played by the rules as much as any other political party in Turkey. The vagueness of its programme reflects the fact that it cannot claim to represent a universally approved form of Islam, since Alevis and the *tarikat* brotherhoods all have very different views. Even among its Sunni voters it has to take into account a wide range of opinions. Necmettin Erbakan, the man who led a demonstration in 1980 during which cries went up demanding the introduction of Islamic *sharia* law, thus helping to trigger the 1980 coup, has become more cautious in articulating his position on this subject. Apart from the legal difficulties he would no doubt incur if he espoused it, his party would probably lose much of its new-found support if it openly advocated the introduction of *sharia*; but his party's more radical elements would probably look elsewhere, perhaps go underground, if he ruled it out.

These differing views are evidence that, as a political party, Welfare is not immune to the wishes of the general public – perhaps even more so than other parties who have remained aloof from proper organization in the provinces and *gecekondu* districts. Dozens of Islamic newspapers and magazines published in Turkey prove that a wide debate is going on, arguably the freest in any Muslim country. There are Islamists far more hard-line than the Welfare Party who would not shy at using ruthless means to overthrow the regime; there are also moderates who believe that Islam has to adapt to modern life, that it has to continue to pursue a special Turkish process of Islamic reformation.

Erbakan showed that his party was ready to compromise when he announced the programme of his coalition government with Tansu Çiller's True Path Party in July 1996. Not only did he agree to bring a record number of three women into the cabinet, but there was little sign of his idealistic rhetoric about an Islamic dinar or a commonwealth of Islamic states. The coalition protocol was a direct continuation of the programmes introduced by previous right-wing governments. Indeed, Erbakan repeatedly underlined his desire for the Welfare Party to resurrect the Democrat Party's 'spirit of 1946' and the Motherland Party's 'spirit of 1983' – that is, to become the mainstream party of Turkey's centre-right.

There are few signs that the Welfare Party has any plans for armed underground resistance, unlike some right-wing Islamic nationalist groups which are far more radical in their approach. Although some secularists still reject it, the Welfare Party has become an integral part of the Turkish political system. Questions as old as the republic itself will always remain: Can the country integrate the traditionalist views of Islam into its modernizing, Westernizing project, or will secularists and Islamists remain forever locked in an 'us and them' situation? Can Turkey make peace with its traditions and its culture, and formally and universally adopt a pragmatic form of Islam? And could this Turkish-Islamic synthesis become a model for other Muslim states?

These questions may never find definitive answers, but Turkey's long-term stability depends on everyone working at them peacefully. Some social, political and religious gulfs have yet to be comfortably bridged. One of the most charming sights in Turkey is that of two women walking arm in arm in the street, laughing, one in a headscarf and one without. Yet there are radicals on both sides who disapprove. Their intolerance risks worsening a possible Islamic-secular polarization of Turkish society. Luckily, thanks to rapid economic and social development, the growth of provincial cities, of non-governmental organizations, of independent media, or private business, and, in a word, of Turkey's civil society, it seems unlikely that this country can ever again be conquered by any single ideology.

Conclusion

Soul here sails the what-has-been
its contrast and complexity
shifting images that correspond
to starlit domes of hierarchs,
to tankers in the churning sea.

Sidney Wade, from *Byzantium*, 1994

FEW TURKS FIND it easy to judge in which direction Kemal Atatürk's republic will head in the next millennium. Turgut Özal's promises of a 'Turkish century' in league with the newly emerging Turkic states now sound hollow. Necmettin Erbakan's visions of a Turkey-led Islamic commonwealth look dubious. As usual in recent Turkish history, the main challenge is domestic reform. And yet, if the Kemalist establishment does not learn to relax its brittle conservatism, something seems sure to break.

The country is 99 per cent Muslim, but the state is far from making peace with its Islamic identity. Turks cannot count on automatic economic progress, the cement that has helped keep the structure of society together since 1980. Commercialization has brought much higher expectations of material comforts, just as greater exposure to the outside world has made ethnicity a more difficult problem to manage. It is no longer simply a question of satisfying the aspirations of 12 million ethnic Kurds. There are also many Turks who have inherited powerful connections with the Caucasus and the Balkans from grandparents who fled the disintegrating provinces of the Ottoman empire, some of whom are ready to stage international hijacks, coup attempts and clandestine arms shipments to prove it.

Dangerous fault-lines have appeared inside the Turkish state. Its institutions, their roots deep in the Ottoman past, have responded to the inadequacy of politicians by trying to take matters into their own hands. Above all, the state is failing to hold the keystone of justice in place. Court cases drag on for years and witnesses are easily intimidated. Poorly paid judges, especially in commercial and political cases, bend easily to the strongest wind. The police force operates as a state within a state with its own brutal methods; some policemen are hand in hand with the mafias whose gunmen learned their trade in the right-wing gangs that plagued the 1970s. Turks are learning to overcome their age-old belief that anything not specifically permitted by the state is illegal. But with no legal framework to take its place, people feel that the pendulum is once again swinging away from strong government towards a kind of anarchy in which only the rich, big business and Turkey's many mafias hold sway.

The Turkish Armed Forces has survived as the single institution most trusted by the Turk in the street. Many innovations in the Ottoman empire can be associated with the military: modern schools, medical colleges, revolutionary movements for reform and, as Turkish schoolbooks proudly point out, Western skills like landscape painting. Even the oppressed Turkish Kurds in the south-east distinguish clearly between the often scandalous behaviour of the police and disciplined units of soldiers. But the military is blind to its one great weakness. It is an institution as ideologically trained and puritanical as the Islamic Revolutionary Guards in Iran. The only difference is that in the case of the Turkish military the ideology is a fierce secularism that is identified exclusively with what it calls democracy. Any officer who thinks differently can expect to be cashiered without appeal.

The general staff have been scared by the collapse of twentieth-century political orders nearby, including the Iranian monarchy, the Soviet Union and the Yugoslav federation. They feel strongly that Atatürk's state faces the same threat. Negotiating with ethnic Kurdish rebels is out of the question, they say, pointing at the break-up of their socialist neighbours once the ethnic genie was out of the bottle. They tell and retell the stories of the Iranian military commanders who took refuge in Turkey in 1979, and who bewailed the fact that they had left the fight against resurgent Islam too late.

As the Turkish chief of general staff, Ismail Hakki Karadayı, said to a reporter at a 1996 reception commemorating the 74th anniversary of Victory Day over Greece, 'If you lose Atatürk and his principles, you will lose the country, the regime, democracy, in short everything. That's why you have to hold tighter to them than ever.'[1]

Holding tight has so far been relatively easy, since the constitution drawn up under military rule in 1982 gave the armed forces a constant right of oversight. Civilian governments have never directly tried to challenge the recommendations emanating from their monthly meetings with the armed forces commanders in the National Security Council decreed by the constitution. The military apparently have never considered that one reason why politicians have become so irresponsible is because the army commanders, like overbearing parents, have refused to allow them ultimate responsibility for their actions. The same is true in Turkish families; the uncles may feud, but there is little tradition of children rebelling or plotting lives truly independent of their elders.

By the late 1990s, all sense of principle and moral standards had left Turkish politics. The president would condemn closer relations with Europe on one day, and say he was the guardian of them the next. On the campaign trail, the prime minister had promised Islamic *jihad* to liberate Grozny, Sarajevo and Jerusalem, but quietly swallowed his words after being sworn in. His coalition partner had stood on a platform that vowed to keep out the Islamists, but then brought them to office. And with no trace of compunction, opposition parties voted against measures they had ardently defended when in power.

The effects of this long-term political irresponsibility have been most visible in the economy. Fear of the army, still the second biggest in NATO, allows it apparently infinite credit, the one line of the budget that members of the Turkish parliament vote through unanimously. Their continued war against Kurdish rebels in the south-east – to which the army high command rules out any political solution – remains a serious drain on the economy.

Then there are the fertile political grazing grounds of the public sector. Turkey's public sector played a key role in getting the republic on its feet in the 1920s and 1930s, when commercial life had been winded by the sudden loss of the capital and know-how of the Greek and Armenian minorities. But by the 1990s their ageing, overstaffed factories were a drag on the rest of the country. Huge buildings were still being erected in Ankara to house clerks who did little to disguise their underemployment. Turks did not mind paying for causes they believed in – time and again donating money to army charity appeals, for example – but a growing resentment was felt at the way salaried workers were forced to shoulder the main tax burden while the state wasted money.

The reforms of the early 1980s nearly broke the vicious circle in which the republican economy had become trapped. Western lenders no longer accepted the *status quo*, and for a brief moment at the end of the 1970s Turkish leaders realized that something had to be done. But when Turgut Özal began to lose popularity in the late 1980s, he went back to the short-term populism that has condemned the Turks to an inflation rate that has hovered at over 50 per cent a year for more than a decade. Özal's red-tape cutting did rouse the people to commercial activity, but now perhaps only a bout of serious hyperinflation can shake the establishment awake. The Turkish state, designed to rule a population of just over thirteen million people in 1927 – most of them illiterate peasants – is now unable to cope with the far more numerous, and articulate, population of the 1990s. Whereas less than one-quarter of the early republican population lived in towns, now two-thirds of the people live in cities.

The state's inability to cope is vividly obvious to any Turkish parent sending a child to school. Inner city colleges often have to run two shifts a day to cope with the numbers. Even then, parents are obliged to pay large sums under the school desks to register at state schools. On top of that, if they want their child to succeed, they are forced to spend a small fortune on private tuition.

Non-governmental organizations (NGOs) have sprung up to fill in the gaps. One Istanbul group backed by powerful private businessmen started a major overhaul of the deeply old-fashioned education system. Such efforts were part of a broader development of civil society, which surprised even itself when all the Turkish NGOs first came under one roof during the United Nations' Habitat II meetings in Istanbul in 1996. The NGOs represented many social concerns. Among the more active groups were the Islamic charities, whose constituencies always felt neglected by the secularist republic. By the mid-1990s private citizens were organizing a women's library, refuges for battered wives, orphanages, music festivals, religious schools, Western universities and even efforts to limit the runaway erosion of Turkey's topsoil.

The first shock of the pro-Islamic Welfare Party's success in the 1994 municipal elections also prompted a political reaction. Some in the secularist bourgeoisie decided to take matters into their own hands and to experiment with their own grass-roots political organization and popular seminars on democracy. Of a dozen groups that appeared around the country, the biggest impact was made by the New Democracy Movement (Yeni Demokrasi Hareketi, or YDH), which turned itself into a party to contest the 1995 general election. In some ways the movement seemed to stand for the kind of post-Kemalist state the pro-Western, modernizing élite wanted. Its leader Cem Boyner was handsome, young and athletic, the millionaire son of a business tycoon whose family interests ranged from textile mills that led Turkey's 1980s export success to the gleaming new breed of shopping malls that sprang up in Turkish cities in the 1990s. Boyner articulated the new spirit of the middle classes seeking a way forward from Kemalism that would accommodate Islam and the Kurds. But Boyner failed, a victim of his own high-mindedness. Only 133,889 people chose his New Democracy Movement in the 1995 general election, handing him 0.48 per cent of the vote.

Perhaps Boyner was right to describe himself as the mule that Kurdish smugglers send ahead of them through mountain passes to be sure that they themselves are not killed by mines. His ideas on the separation of mosque and state and cultural rights for the Kurds were sometimes not very different from those of the pro-Islamic Welfare Party; even leading civil servants privately agreed with his views. But the Welfare Party benefited even more from popular anger with established centre-right parties, owing to its excellent party organization and a relatively scandal-free reputation in municipal government.

There are many schools of thought about the likely fate of the Welfare Party-led coalition that came to power in July 1996. Die-hard republicans are convinced that the party is pursuing a gradualist approach aimed at changing Turkey into an Islamic republic. The Welfare Party's organ, *Milli Gazete*, sometimes encourages such thinking. 'It has been almost a century that the foes of Islam have governed Turkey. Now a new period begins, the period of the believers . . . Now Turkey will accelerate its run towards Islam,' it proclaimed soon after Erbakan took office.

Any run towards Islam is unlikely to follow the fundamentalist course that the army seems to fear. It is not simply a question of Turkey's religious diversity. The Turkish economy is also far more broadly based than any of the scare-models of Iran, Algeria or Saudi Arabia, with their vast unchecked oil incomes that can easily finance authoritarian Islamic rule. Any Turkish government has to raise taxes, to borrow domestically, and to sell bonds internationally. Its room for fiscal manoeuvre is limited, as Erbakan has discovered, as is its power to dictate to a society that is less and less reliant on the state.

More experienced politicians believe that holding office is a mixed blessing in Turkey. Turks are fickle voters and jealous rivals are always laying traps for the party in power. This school of thought holds that even though the Welfare Party's popularity initially grew, its populist promises will prove unworkable. They also expect the party to split between its pro-Islamic and reformist wings when its leader, Necmettin Erbakan, departs the scene.

A third group believes that the reformation of Islam left half finished by Atatürk has in practice been fully digested now by Turkish society, and that the Welfare Party may evolve into the new mainstream centre-right party. The religion of the ever-pragmatic Turks could evolve into a kind of Euro-Islam. 'If Islam one day plays the role in Turkey that the Catholic Church plays in Italy, I will be very happy,' the late President Turgut Özal used to say.

One of the greatest challenges Turkey faces is to resolve the Kurdish rebellion, in progress since 1984. The Welfare Party's instinct is to buy Kurdish popularity with the granting of cultural rights under the umbrella of Islamic brotherhood; but at the same time, it has to avoid confrontation with the army, who are resolutely against concessions which its officers believe are the first step down a slippery slope to the break-up of the country.

The Kurdish rebels remain powerful among Kurdish communities in Europe and will always be used by Turkey's rivals in Syria, Greece, Iran and even Russia. But an organization run by exiles that has lost its main hopes of a permanent foothold in Turkey itself always runs the risk of losing touch with the Kurds of Turkey, especially if Turkey's economy continues to grow and continues to attract Turkish Kurds westwards into the orbit of mainstream society.

Atatürk's heirs have clearly failed to deal with the Turkish Kurd problem in a civilized way. Racism has started to mix with nationalism on both sides of a conflict already often marred by murder and terrorism. But the story is not all of failure. Atatürk wanted to forge a new nationality for all the diverse Muslim peoples gathered in Turkey after the end of the war of independence against Greece and the Allies. In many ways, he did. In 1993, a groundbreaking newspaper poll found that 90 per cent of the population felt in some way Turkish, and that 65 per cent of those questioned felt themselves without qualification to be Turks.[2]

Turkey still lays claim to be a bridge between east and west. One day, perhaps, this may become true. For the moment, however, republican Turkey remains something of a whipping boy for both east and west. Turkey's weak governments and bad human rights record have not inspired much Western respect. Islamic neighbours view with intense suspicion Turkey's European ambitions and its close friendship with the United States. Its relations with its many difficult neighbours are often tense, sometimes verging on war. Nothing is going to change that in the immediate future.

Turkey's influence, moreover, is far less than the sum of its parts; it fails to project the power of an economy whose production, despite the lack of oil, is more than half that of all the Arab states combined. At times, even Turkish Kurd rebels run a more impressive press service from a desktop computer in Germany than anything put together with the millions of dollars the Turkish government spends on trying to burnish its image. The reasons are familiar: one part of the state does not know what the other is doing, more intelligent Turkish officials clash with the blinkered attitudes of old-fashioned colleagues, departmental responsibilities overlap and nobody wants to take the risk of stepping out of line.

Some Turkish intellectuals go so far as to say that common values have been eradicated by the militaristic Atatürk and his successors. In their place have come competing beliefs and ideologies, some ossified and bizarre. 'Turkey is like a dinosaur park for old ideologies. Since military discipline replaced personal standards, there is no morality left. Society lacks a social project for the future. Individuals only have private projects,' left-wing writer Murat Belge would say with a weary smile.

The influential pro-Islamic politician Korkut Özal, the younger brother of Turgut, also believes that the Kemalist revolution destroyed a great deal that was good in the Ottoman system and that the wounds are only now beginning to heal. 'This did not happen overnight. The changes had to be forced through. As the Turkish army says, "Orders cut iron." Objectors were crushed,' Korkut Özal explained. 'We used to have a collective consciousness. We lost it in the Kemalist revolution. The revolution smashed all the established institutions. Only now are we learning to live without Ankara, to develop a new collective culture.'

Some voters may have hoped that the Islamic-based government of the Welfare Party would provide a welcome return to moral values. Their municipal government certainly seemed more efficient and scandal-free. But the people will probably be let down again: Erbakan has shown every sign of being as dictatorial and intolerant of opposition as other Turkish party leaders.

Islamic or secular, however, ordinary people in Turkey are increasingly taking matters into their own hands. As people have despaired of the state, there has been a blossoming of private associations devoted to improving education and the environment. Cities have changed beyond recognition: after the rapid spread of traffic-lights in the past decade came pedestrian zones, proper pavements, parking meters and well-planned building developments. People have started to take care of the appearance of homes and streets, to plant trees and flowers.

Some Turkish intellectuals now aspire to bypass multi-ethnicity and to re-create the cosmopolitan ethos associated with the Ottoman empire. There is a sense, too, that Turkey has gone beyond an obsession with being accepted as a full member of Europe. Turks are now more self-confident as they search for their place in the world, less reliant on foreign aid and more willing to risk experiments.

Perhaps this ambivalence was reflected in the foreign policy of the coalition government which brought together the pro-Islamic Welfare Party and Tansu Çiller's pro-Western True Path Party. As economic growth slowed in Europe, Turkey, which learned to expand its markets in the 1980s, shifted its attention to the former Soviet Union and the Middle East. As early as 1991, Turgut Özal was confiding to a Turkish journalist: 'Our competitors have multiplied. This has made it difficult or even impossible for us to join the EC. We must develop ties with Turkic republics, Black Sea countries and the Balkans.'[3]

This evolving picture is graphically illustrated by the way pre-First World War bustle has returned to the ancient quays of Galata by the Bosphorus in Istanbul. White-painted coasters, cruise liners and former research ships named after long-forgotten Soviet academicians can be seen tied up in pursuit of the more mundane gains of Black Sea trade. Decks and holds are piled up with all manner of Turkish cargoes for a trade unimaginable a few years before: fruit, tomatoes, crates of beer, new rubbish bins, plastic jerry cans, sacks of Turkish leather coats, bundles of jeans and whole suites of bedroom furniture.

Likewise, Istanbul airport's departures board, once easily able to hold a whole day's worth of flights, can now only fit in a couple of hours' worth of destinations. The last restrictions on travel abroad have been lifted, and the number of foreigners visiting the country is rising rapidly. A new business élite educated in the best American schools is internationally competitive. Even the bureaucracy can still attract high-calibre recruits.

The following example is simplified but instructive. The sudden rise in oil prices in 1973, devastating to Turkey's state-planned economy, elicited no real change of economic course for a whole six years. In 1983, reaction time had improved, but it still took the government more than six months to respond to a major financial crisis. By 1987, it only took six weeks to respond to a foreign exchange crisis. In 1990, the Gulf crisis provoked reaction within six days. Today's Turkey is probably flexible enough to react to any external shock within six hours.[4]

A new generation of Turks has a wide general knowledge of English; vivacious Turkish television shows have found audiences throughout the Middle East. Millions of Turks now work abroad, mostly in Europe, but tens of thousands also in Israel, Arab countries, Russia and the Turkic republics. Many people from these countries come to Istanbul for business and pleasure. There has been a multiplication of speakers of Turkish languages in diplomatic get-togethers, sharing the same taste in square-shouldered suits and Turkic politics at regional groupings of Muslim countries like the Economic Co-operation Organization.[5]

Whatever reactionary outrages the politicians, the police and the military may inflict on Turkey – including the ever-present possibility of further military interventions – there is little they can do to stop the people's convergence with the rest of the world. It is rare now to come across the once common signs of ignorance that betrayed the country's introverted isolationism like the black Scottie dog that used to be kept as a marvel of the West to be viewed in a labelled cage in the Gülhane park zoo behind Istanbul's Topkapı palace.

'He died,' said an ageing keeper, resting on his broom. 'We didn't think it worth replacing him. There's no call for such things any more. Nowadays, everybody seems to have one.'

Chronology

552 AD	Chinese chronicles mention the founding of an empire in Central Asia by the *T'u-küe*, the first people known to call themselves Turks
674	Governor of Basra hires 2,000 Turkish archers. First recorded Turkish mercenaries in Islamic world
730	Orkhon inscriptions carved on stone memorials in what is now Mongolia. First known written Turkish from first self-consciously Turkish state
751	Chinese Buddhists driven out of Central Asia in the battle of Talas with Arab Muslim armies, opening the way for Turks' conversion to Islam
861	Turkish slave soldiers kill the Muslim caliph al-Mutawakkil. Turks become arbiters of the caliphate
1071	Seljuk Turkish sultan Alparslan Beg defeats Byzantine emperor Romanus Diogenes IV at Malizgert (Manzikert) near Lake Van. Anatolia open for settlement by Turkish tribes
1097	The First Crusade ravages Seljuk domains and allows Byzantines to retake control of some of Anatolia
1206–27	Mongols unite under Genghis Khan, conquer Central Asia and much of China with help of Turkic soldiers
1243	The Konya-based Seljuk Turks of Rum are defeated by Mongol armies at Koşe Dağ near Erzincan
1290s	First reports of the emergence near Söğüt of the house of Osman, future rulers of the Ottoman empire
1453	Ottoman armies conquer Constantinople
1789	Selim III, first Westernizing sultan, ascends the throne
1826	Selim's successor, Mahmut II, defeats the Janissaries
1839	Gülhane Rescript ushers in major period of Ottoman reform known as the *tanzimat*
1854–6	Crimean War. Turks fight on side of British and French against Russia, contract first foreign debt, are briefly offered place in Concert of Europe
1876	First Constitution briefly encourages Turkish reformers, but Abdülhamit II soon dashes their hopes
1908	Revolt backed by Young Turk army officers in the Balkans ends rule of Abdülhamit II and brings second constitutional period

1913   Young Turk coup brings era of triumvirate of Enver, Cemal and Talaat

1915   British, French and Allies land on Gallipoli peninsula in April. Forced to withdraw in January 1916

1918–22   Allied occupation of Constantinople after Young Turk leaders flee

1919   Greek forces, encouraged by the British and others, land in Smyrna in May and start to occupy Anatolia

        19 May Mustafa Kemal lands in Samsun and the Turkish War of Independence starts

        21 June Kemal issues Amasya declaration against the sultan's policy of submission to the Allies

1920   *23 April* The Turkish Grand National Assembly meets for the first time in Ankara as representatives of the new Turkish nation

        20 August Allies force the sultan's government to sign the Treaty of Sèvres, aiming to split Anatolia between British, French, Italian, Greek, Armenian and possibly Kurdish regions with international control of the Straits. The treaty is never ratified

1922   *August* After 22-day battle with Greeks at Sakarya, the war turns in the Turks' favour

        9 September The Turkish army enters Izmir (Smyrna) and the city centre burns

        1 November Mustafa Kemal abolishes the sultanate

1923   *30 January* Turkish-Greek treaty exchanges nearly one million ethnic Greek Christians from Anatolia with about 400,000 Turkish Muslims in Greece

        24 July The signing of the Lausanne Treaty provides the basis of international legitimacy for the new Turkey

        29 October The Turkish Republic is proclaimed. Mustafa Kemal is its president, Ankara its capital

1924   *3 March* Parliament abolishes the Islamic caliphate. Kurdish associations and newspapers are shut down the same day

1925   *February* Kurds rise up in the eastern provinces under the leadership of Sheikh Said. The rebellion is brutally suppressed by June

        The Kemalist revolution starts. Religious orders and brotherhoods are suppressed, the fez is abolished, the Western calendar adopted

1926   *February* Swiss civil code and Italian penal code enacted

        June Plot uncovered in Izmir against Kemal, followed by trials and purges of his opponents

1928   Introduction of the Latin alphabet; secularism replaces Islam as official ethos of the state

1930   *December* Religious riots in Menemen, near Izmir, are followed by trials and executions

1931   Metric system adopted

1934	Turks ordered to take family names; parliament grants Mustafa Kemal the surname Atatürk; women given the right to vote
1936	*July* Signing of the Montreux Convention gives Turkey sovereignty over the Straits but requires free passage for merchant shipping and some warships
1937	Kurdish revolt in Dersim (now Tunceli) brutally suppressed
1938–9	Turkey gains control of province of Hatay from Syria with support of France
1938	*10 November* Atatürk dies. Ismet Inönü succeeds him as president
1945	*23 February* Turkey finally joins the Allied camp and declares war on Japan and Germany
1946	To counter growing Soviet influence, the US Administration develops the 'Truman Doctrine', pledging support for Greece and Turkey
	21 July The republic holds its first multi-party elections, but results are disputed
1950	*14 May* Democrat Party sweeps general elections. Adnan Menderes becomes prime minister. President Inönü resigns and is replaced by Celal Bayar
1952	*18 February* Turkey and Greece join NATO
1955	*September* Riots in Istanbul as tension rises over Cyprus. Many ethnic Greeks leave
1960	*27 May* A military coup overthrows prime minister Adnan Menderes
	Cyprus wins independence, with Britain, Turkey and Greece as guarantors
1961	*17 September* Ex-premier Adnan Menderes is hanged, a day after his foreign and finance ministers, Zorlu and Polatkan
1962	*July* Parliamentary vote of confidence in a new broad coalition formed by Inönü
1964	Turkey concerned by renewed ethnic violence in Cyprus. US President Johnson intervenes to prevent a Turkish military operation on the island
1965	*November* Süleyman Demirel starts first premiership
1971	Heading off action by young left-wing officers, general staff sends warning letter to government
	12 March Demirel forced to resign in new military intervention
1974	*15 July* Cyprus coup backed by Athens attempts to unite island with Greece. Britain refuses to act on appeals from Turkey to intervene
	20 July The Turkish armed forces invade Cyprus. By September, they control the northern third of the island and have resettled the 17 per cent ethnic Turk minority there
1975	*February* US freezes all aid to Turkey and embargoes military supplies because of Ankara's actions in Cyprus

1977   *1 May*   Gunfire and stampede kill 39 during a May Day demonstration by 200,000 workers in Istanbul's Taksim Square

1978   *September*   Riots pitting rightists and Sunni Muslims against leftists and Alevis kill 12 in Sivas

December   107 killed in similar bloodshed in Kahramanmaraş

25 December   Martial law declared in 13 provinces

1980   *24 January*   Measures launching the first major attempt to turn Turkey into a free market. The value of the Turkish lira is halved and many goods double in price

12 September   General Kenan Evren leads a military coup after nearly 5,000 people had been killed in 1970s political violence. Turgut Özal becomes deputy prime minister

1981   *October*   Military abolishes all political parties

1982   *6 November*   Referendum approves the republic's longest and most restrictive constitution, enshrines a strong role for the military, applies strict rules against leftists and Kurdish nationalists and envisages a powerful presidency

1983   *6 November*   Turgut Özal's Motherland Party wins general elections with 45 per cent of the vote

December   Military hands back power

1987   *February*   Özal has triple heart bypass operation in Houston

14 April   Özal government applies for full membership of European Community

6 September   Pre-1980 politicians return to politics after narrow victory in referendum

29 November   Özal's Motherland Party share of vote slips to 36 per cent in general election but gets two-thirds of seats in parliament

1989   *May–July*   Crisis with Bulgaria over ethnic Turks. More than 330,000 flood into Turkey before Ankara closes border

October   Motherland deputies in parliament elect Özal president

1990   *2 August*   Özal seizes on Iraqi invasion of Kuwait to restore his influence as a statesman with the West

1991   *April*   More than 500,000 Iraqi Kurd refugees mass on Turkish border after Gulf War; Özal promotes idea of a safe haven inside Iraq

October   Süleyman Demirel's conservative True Path Party tops general elections, promises reforms in new coalition with Social Democrats

1992   *21 March*   Clashes during Turkish Kurd New Year kill 92

1993   *17 April*   Özal dies of heart attack. Parliament elects Süleyman Demirel in his place as president

13 June   True Path Party chooses Tansu Çiller to become Turkey's first woman prime minister

July   Islamist mob burns hotel during Alevi festival in Sivas; 37 die

1994   *March*   Pro-Islamic Welfare Party tops municipal elections, taking city halls in Istanbul and Ankara

1995   *March*   Turkey sends 35,000 troops into northern Iraq to flush out Turkish Kurd rebels; forced to pull back by world criticism

     20 September   Coalition government collapses when Social Democrats pull out

1995   *25 December*   Pro-Islamic Welfare Party tops general elections with 21.3 per cent of the vote

1996   *March–June*   Motherland Party's Mesut Yılmaz leads short-lived coalition government before constitutional court annuls its parliamentary vote of confidence

     8 July   Welfare Party coalition with True Path Party receives a parliamentary vote of confidence

Notes

Publication details of all works cited below may be found in the Bibliography on pages 363–6.

CHAPTER 1: TANGLED ROOTS

1. Cemal Granda, *Atatürk'ün Uşağı Idim* (I was Atatürk's Manservant).
2. Ahmet Mumcu *et al.*, *Liseler Için Tarih*.
3. Mahmud of Ghazna is said to have given Firdausi a paltry recompense for his years of work on the masterpiece that became Iran's classic work of epic poetry. Some say that Mahmud the Sunni Muslim had not liked the epic because of Firdausi's Shia beliefs; others that, even though Mahmud was like other early Islamic rulers of Turkish origin and did not dwell on his Turkishness, he was nevertheless displeased that the Turks often came off worse in the *Shahnameh*'s theme of perennial conflict between Iran and Turan, that is, between the Persians and the Turks. Firdausi had been so disgusted by his patron's first payment that he divided it between a brewer and a hammam attendant. When Mahmud repented his meanness and sent a caravan of camels laden with indigo to Firdausi, it was too late: the great poet died before they reached him.
4. Though it is impossible to give precise figures for Turkish immigration to Anatolia, Claude Cahen suggests a figure of two to three hundred thousand nomads and warriors (*Pre-Ottoman Turkey*). He quotes the noted medieval traveller William of Rubruck in the thirteenth century as saying that the native population outnumbered Turks by ten to one. Cahen concludes: 'it is certain that the majority of the population was not Turkish, it was not even Muslim, and it was not unified. And yet it is equally certain that a country, Turkey, was in the process of creation.'

CHAPTER 2: OTTOMAN GLORY AND DECLINE

1. A. Bryer and H. Lowry (eds.), *Continuity and Change in Late Byzantine and Early Ottoman Society*.
2. Heath W. Lowry Jr, *Studies in Defterology: Ottoman Society in the Fifteenth and Sixteenth centuries*.
3. Kenan Evren, *Kenan Evren'in Anıları*, vol. 3.
4. Edmondo de Amicis, *Constantinople*.
5. Otto Liman von Sanders, *Cinq Ans de Turquie*.

CHAPTER 3: TURKEY FOR THE TURKS

1. Steven Runciman was speaking in *Crusades*, by the History Channel, BBC-MCM-XTV, 1995.
2. Christopher J. Walker, *Armenia*.
3. Mükerrem Su and Ahmet Mumcu, *Türkiye Cumhuriyeti Inkilap Tarihi ve Atatürküçülük*.
4. All figures relating to the number of people killed in what Armenians argue is the first genocide of the century should be viewed with caution; as retired Turkish diplomat Kamuran Gürün points out, however, the minimum figure is 300,000

Armenian dead. The first task is to arrive at a starting figure for the Armenian population prior to the First World War. Kamuran Gürün in *Le Dossier arménien* uses Ottoman official census figures of Armenians, including Armenian Catholics and Protestants, to reach a figure of 1.294 million. Armenian nationalist historian Richard Hovanassian in *Armenia on the Road to Independence* offers a figure of 1.5 million to two million, whilst contemporary European sources prefer a figure around 1.5 million. Other Armenian historians claim that there were nearer three million Armenians. From this pre-war population must be subtracted the figure for Armenians surviving after the First World War. Gürün calculates that in Russia there were 400,000–420,000 Armenian refugees, according to the League of Nations report by Dr Fridtjob Nansen, and 625,000 in the Ottoman empire, the official number given by the Armenian patriarchate to the British Embassy at the time; that is, 1.045 million survivors. Gürün reaches a similar figure for survivors by adding up census figures for Armenians in all countries later in the 1920s. Gürün's figures have been challenged by dissident Turkish historian Taner Akçam (*Türk Ulusal Kimliği ve Ermeni Sorunu*), who could count only 800,000 Armenian survivors: 250,000 survivors found in Russia, about 150,000–200,000 in Turkey, 200,000 in exile, and 200,000 'adopted' in Turkish and Kurdish homes. Christopher Walker in *Armenia* suggested the figure of 600,000 survivors, but, unlike Akçam, did not count as survivors the many Armenians who changed religion or were taken into Turkish Muslim families.

5. According to tables provided by the Turkish Armed Forces General Staff to the authors in February 1996, Turkish military casualties in the First World War totalled over 850,000 dead or missing (225,000 killed in the field of battle, 22,763 dead of wounds, 330,796 dead of disease, 373,237 wounded and 275,000 missing or taken prisoner, presumed dead). The figures include more than 88,500 Ottoman officers and men killed or missing, presumed dead, during the Gallipoli campaign. The total of Allied dead at Gallipoli was 46,000.

6. See Taner Akçam, op. cit.

7. See Kenan Evren, *Kenan Evren'in Anıları*, vol. 2. He denied that Turkey was so 'amateur' that it would resort to blowing up Armenian churches in revenge. But he implied that a reaction was inevitable. 'The Turkish nation is very patient, but when its fury breaks it knows no bounds. They should know this well . . . some people are suggesting that we kill Armenians living in Turkey and some people are trying to get organized to do that. We are working to stop it.'

8. 'The fact that the records of the Teşkilat-i Mahsusa (Special Organization) have been destroyed and those of the CUP lost makes it hard, if not impossible, to prove their involvement beyond doubt, but this author at least is of the opinion that there was a centrally controlled policy of extermination, instigated by the CUP': Erik J. Zürcher, *Modern Turkey*.

CHAPTER 4: ATATURK, IMMORTAL LEADER

1. Halide Edib, *The Turkish Ordeal*.
2. 'I must confess that Mustafa Kemal's name conveyed nothing to me when Damad Ferid spoke to me, in April 1919, about the scheme for inspectorates. I instinctively mistrusted the scheme . . . He reassured me, saying that he had had Mustafa Kemal to dinner and received from him satisfactory assurances of his loyalty': Sir Andrew Ryan, *The Last of the Dragomans*.
3. Hümeyra Özbaş, interview with the authors, July 1995.
4. Cemal Kutay, interview with the authors, June 1995.
5. Falih Rıfkı Atay, *The Atatürk I Knew*.
6. Berthe George-Gaulis, *La Nouvelle Turquie*.

7. Falih Rıfkı Atay, op. cit.
8. Official figures supplied by the Turkish General Staff, February 1996.
9. For Lloyd George's comments in November 1914, see Selim Deringil, *Turkish Foreign Policy during the Second World War*, citing D. Werder, *The Chanak Affair*.
10. André Mandelstam, *Le Sort de l'Empire ottoman*.
11. Quoted in Selim Deringil, op. cit.
12. James W. Gerard, quoted in Comité national d'études sociales et politiques, séance du 13 janvier 1919, in N. Politis, *Les Aspirations sociales de la Grèce*, Paris, 1919.
13. Cited by Afet Inan in *Medeni Bilgiler ve Mustafa Kemal Atatürk'ün El Yazıları* (Ankara: Türk Tarih Kurum Basımevi, 1969).
14. Falih Rıfkı Atay, op. cit.
15. Halide Edib, op. cit.
16. Erdal İnönü, *Anılar ve Düşünceler*.
17. Falih Rıfkı Atay, op. cit.
18. Berthe George-Gaulis, op. cit.
19. Vamik D. Volkan and Norman Itzkowitz, *The Immortal Ataturk: A Psychobiography*.
20. Only in November 1953 were Atatürk's mortal remains moved to their current place of honour in Ankara's *Anıtkabir*, or great mausoleum.

CHAPTER 5: WALKING THE TIGHTROPE

1. Halide Edib, *The Turkish Ordeal*.
2. Kenan Evren, *Kenan Evren'in Anıları*.
3. Selim Deringil, *Turkish Foreign Policy during the Second World War: An Active Neutrality*.
4. Harry N. Howard, *Turkey, the Straits and US Policy*.
5. Erdal İnönü, *Anılar ve Düşünceler*.
6. Selim Deringil, op. cit.
7. Barry Rubin, *Istanbul Intrigues: Espionage, Sabotage and Diplomatic Treachery in the Spy Capital of World War II*.
8. ibid.
9. ibid.
10. Selim Deringil, op. cit.
11. Berthe George-Gaulis, *La Nouvelle Turquie*.
12. Barry Rubin, op. cit.
13. Bruce R. Kuniholm, *The Origins of the Cold War in the Near East: Great Power Conflict and Diplomacy in Iran, Turkey and Greece*.

CHAPTER 6: A NEW BEGINNING

1. Bernard Lewis, *The Emergence of Modern Turkey*.
2. Yaşar Kemal, interview with the authors, March 1996.
3. Metin Heper, *The State Tradition in Turkey*.
4. ibid.
5. Kenan Evren, *Kenan Evren'in Anıları*.
6. Alparslan Türkeş, interview with the authors, June 1995.
7. Kenan Evren, op. cit.
8. Stanford and Ezel Shaw, *History of the Ottoman Empire and Modern Turkey*.
9. Mükerrem Sarol, interview with the authors, May 1995.

CHAPTER 7: THE ARMY SHOWS ITS HAND

1. Alparslan Türkeş, interview with the authors, June 1995.
2. Interview published in Mehmet Ali Birand, Can Dündar and Bülent Çaplı, *Demirkırat*.

Notes

3. Mehmet Ali Birand, *The Generals' Coup in Turkey: An Inside Story of 12 September.*
4. Mehmet Ali Birand, Can Dündar and Bülent Çaplı, *12 Mart.*
5. Cited in Feroz Ahmad, *The Turkish Experiment in Democracy, 1950–1975.*
6. ibid.

CHAPTER 8: THE CYPRUS DISASTER

1. Most recently at the UN on 17 April 1996, Reuters reported that the five permanent members of the Council 'exchanged views on the present situation on the island and reaffirmed that the *status quo* is unacceptable'.
2. *Les Rapports gréco-turcs: Mythes et réalités,* Cahiers d'Études sur la Méditerranée Orientale et le Monde Turco-Iranien, 1986.
3. Renée Hirschon, *Heirs of the Great Catastrophe: The Social Life of Asia Minor Refugees in Piraeus.*
4. Renée Hirschon, ibid., gives figures of 350,000 Turks and 1.25 million Greeks; Erik J. Zürcher (*Modern Turkey*) gives figures of 400,000 Turks and 900,000 Greeks; Shaw and Shaw (*History of the Ottoman Empire and Modern Turkey*) give a figure of 500,000 Turks and 1.3 million Greeks.
5. Hülya Demir and Rıdvan Akar, *Istanbul'un Son Sürgünleri.*
6. Series in *Milliyet,* 13 June 1995.
7. Kenan Evren, *Kenan Evren'Anıları,* vol. 1.

CHAPTER 9: WILDERNESS YEARS

1. Bülent Ecevit, interview with the authors, June 1995.
2. Kenan Evren, *Kenan Evren'in Anıları,* vol. 1.
3. Daniel Cohn-Bendit, interview with the authors, 1996.
4. Kenan Evren, op. cit. Information given by Interior Minister Gülcügil to Martial Law Co-ordination Meeting, 17 March 1979.
5. Interior Minister Ülkü Güney, statement to reporters, 2 May 1996.
6. Mehmet Ali Birand, *The Generals' Coup in Turkey: An Inside Story of 12 September.*

CHAPTER 10: THE GENERALS TAKE CHARGE

1. Apparently surprised by Turkish outrage at *Midnight Express,* Alan Parker later said he should not have left unchallenged a statement in the film that the Turks were a 'nation of pigs'. He is quoted as saying, 'I was shocked when people said it was anti-Turk . . . We hadn't meant it to be racist. We thought we were making a film about injustice. There are things I would change now, things to do with an intellectual and political maturity that I don't think I had then.' David Puttnam, the film's producer, added his belief that the film was based on a 'dishonest book': author Billy Hayes maintains his innocence throughout, a dubious claim, and asserts that he escaped, whereas he was released under an amnesty agreement. For details see Derviş Zaimağaoğlu, *Representation of the Turkish People in 'Midnight Express'* (World Wide Web, 1994).
2. Mehmet Ali Birand, *The Generals' Coup in Turkey: An Inside Story of 12 September.*
3. Bülent Ecevit, interview with the authors, June 1995.

CHAPTER 11: THE OZAL REVOLUTION

1. Information on the Özals' family background is from Korkut Özal, interview with the authors, May 1996.
2. Hasan Cemal, *Özal'ın Hikayesi.*

3. Turgut Özal, *La Turquie en Europe*.
4. Yavuz Canevi, *The Political Economy of Policy Reform*.

CHAPTER 12: A BRIDGE TOO FAR

1. Orhan Pamuk, interview with the authors, 1996.
2. Kenan Evren, *Kenan Evren'in Anıları*, vol. 4.
3. Cited in J.C. Hurewitz, *The Middle East and North Africa in World Politics: A Documentary Record*, vol. 1, *European Expansion 1535–1914*.
4. For instance, the Press and Information Department of the Prime Minister's Office reacted this way in faxes to foreign media organizations following the conviction of the ex-parliamentarians of the pro-Kurdish Democracy Party (DEP) in December 1994. Also, Özdem Sanberk, Turkey's ambassador to London, reacting to Amnesty International condemnations of torture in Turkey, told the *Today* programme on Radio 4 on 22 May 1996: 'I think there is a means to redress because Turkey is open to international mechanisms. Turkey is party to the convention on the prevention of torture ... Turkey accepts judicial supranationality ... which makes the biggest difference.'
5. Manuel Marin, the European commissioner responsible for Mediterranean issues, outlined this priority in May 1995: 'When NATO linked security to religion it made an enormous mistake. We must not repeat it ... Normal religious practice for whatever religion must be treated differently from fundamentalism. We have to develop levels of economic and political co-operation with real, continuous contact with civil society ... a dynamic co-operation at all levels.'
6. General Doğan Güreş, interview with the authors, February 1992.
7. Süleyman Demirel, interview with the authors, December 1991.
8. 'It is hard not to believe that given the client state politics that it conducts in this part of the world, Washington did not maintain, at a tolerable level, the local tension between Greece and Turkey, in order to increase its arms sales, which, according to Western strategists, would nevertheless not serve to save the two armies from a worrying obsolescence. In any event, such tension, even if it was not created by Washington artificially, did not go without serving its economic interests:' Semih Vaner, *Le Différend gréco-turc*, Colloque des 29–30 mai 1986, Centre d'Études et de Recherches Internationales, Paris.
9. Özedmir Kalpakçıoğlu, *Yunan'dan Dost Olmaz*.
10. Semih Vaner, op. cit.

CHAPTER 13: OZAL STUMBLES

1. Korkut Özal, interview with the authors, May 1996.
2. Hasan Cemal, *Özal'ın Hikayesi*.
3. Turgut Özal, interview with the authors, October 1989.
4. Korkut Özal, interview with the authors, May 1996.
5. Turgut Özal, interview with the authors, March 1990.
6. Hasan Cemal, *Özal'ın Hikayesi*.
7. Understanding the volumes of figures put out by Turkey's State Institute of Statistics is an art in itself. They are best for comparing like with like. In this case, between 1986 and 1992, the number of state sector enterprises in manufacturing industry employing more than 25 people rose from 398 to 419 and the number of their employees fell 16.5 per cent from 270,594 to 226,000. In the same period, private sector firms employing 25 or more rose in number from 4,666 to 5,557, and the number of employees rose 12.2 per cent from 606,319 to 680,157: State Institute of Statistics, 1995 yearbook.

8. *Yeni Yüzyıl* newspaper, 18 June 1996.
9. Bülent Şemiler, interview with the authors, 1989.
10. Interview with *Günaydin* newspaper, 26 November 1990.
11. According to Erdal Inönü, the apartment buildings were put up to finance and support a museum and charitable foundation in his father's honour.

CHAPTER 14: A PLACE AT THE FEAST

1. *Milliyet* newspaper, 6 March 1991.
2. Figures on water flow vary according to sources. The average flow of the Euphrates river is between 900 and 1,000 cubic metres per second at the Turkish exit; its annual flow is reckoned to be between 26 and 28 cubic kilometres, about 93 per cent of which comes from Turkish territory. The Tigris river has a flow of over 1,200 cubic metres per second at Baghdad, or about 38 cubic kilometres per year, but it takes less than half of its flow from Turkey. Usage before most Turkish projects came on stream in the mid-1990s was Iraq 13–15 km^3, Syria 4.47–5.9 km^3, Turkey 1.8 km^3. The best study of the technical data is to be found in Nurit Kliot, *Water Resources and Conflict in the Middle East.*
3. A detailed study can be found in Philip Robins, *Turkey and the Middle East* – the best summary of republican Turkey's relations with the Arabs.
4. Anecdote from former World Bank official John Golden, who sat in on the meeting. Interview with the authors, September 1995.
5. *Yeni Yüzyıl* newspaper, 9 June 1996.
6. Speech to an anti-war meeting in Istanbul, 9 January 1991.
7. The Moudros armistice of 30 October 1918 left Mosul in Ottoman Turkish hands. Britain started moving up six weeks later on the pretext that it had the right under Article 7 to occupy areas that were a strategic threat. Turkey wanted the area back at Lausanne. Britain refused. The League of Nations intervened. Turkey wanted a plebiscite, since although Turks were in a minority, Turkey believed Kurds, as Muslims, would vote for Turkey; Britain wanted to keep Mosul as part of Iraq for strategic reasons and for its oil. A commission of the League of Nations declared that 'the majority of people would have preferred Turkish to Arab sovereignty'. But that was ignored, according to George Gruen of Columbia University, 'in effect ratifying secret wartime deals made by the victorious Western powers'. Some in Ankara wanted war. In 1926, Atatürk reluctantly accepted an agreement to leave Mosul to British-controlled Iraq in return for 10 per cent of oil revenues for twenty-five years.
8. Speech to the Young Businessmen's Association, quoted in the English-language *Turkish Daily News,* 6 March 1992.
9. Eight nations eventually took part: the United States, the United Kingdom, the Netherlands, France, Germany, Canada, Spain and Italy.
10. Colonel Richard Nabb, interview with the authors, May 1992.
11. Masoud Barzani, interview with the authors, November 1995.
12. Hoshyar Zibari, interview with the authors, August 1990.
13. Sami Abdul-Rahman, interview with the authors, September 1991.
14. Report by Robert Fisk, *Independent,* 30 April 1991.
15. According to British diplomats, the Yeşilova incident started after Turkish soldiers took a set of wooden pallets on which aid shipments had arrived, wanting to use them as flooring for their tents. British soldiers had tried to reclaim the pallets for shipment back home, considering them valuable British government property. The confrontation between about 15 men on both sides lasted about 10 minutes before being resolved locally by the respective platoon lieutenants. Turkish soldiers did not appropriate unusual or substantial amounts of aid meant

for the refugees, the diplomats said later. The Yeşilova incident remained the only direct physical confrontation of its kind between Turks and Allied troops during the emergency.

16. Interview with then prime minister Hasan Cemal, January 1993.
17. Interestingly enough, the first Turkish 'hot pursuit' cross-border raids against Kurdish rebel camps in the northern Iraqi mountains were routinely conducted with the approval of the regime in Baghdad. The first three-day operation went ahead in May 1983.
18. Jalal Talabani, interview with the authors, December 1992.
19. The influx of weapons to Turkey was the result not of gratitude for its support during the Gulf War but of the West's scaling down of its armaments following the end of the Cold War. According to *Süddeutsche Zeitung* (1 April 1994), armaments delivered by Germany since 1990 were worth more than DM 1 billion and included 240 Leopard tanks, 13 F-4 Phantom fighters along with 300 armoured personnel carriers with 60 million rounds of ammunition, 256,000 AK-47 assault rifles with 100 million rounds of ammunition, 5,000 light and heavy machine-guns and 100,000 hand-held anti-tank weapons from NVA (East German) stocks. Quoted by Human Rights Watch/Helsinki, Vol. 6, No. 12, October 1994.
20. See William Hale, 'Turkey, the Middle East and the Gulf Crisis', in *International Affairs* 68, 4 (1992), pp. 679–92 for the best and most comprehensive analysis of Turkey's role in the Gulf War.

CHAPTER 15: THE KURDISH REALITY

1. *Yeni Yüzyıl* newspaper, 17 September 1995.
2. Doğu Perinçek (ed.), *Mustafa Kemal'ın Eskişehir-Izmir Konuşmaları 1923*.
3. Kendal Nezan in G. Chaliand (ed.), *People Without a Country: The Kurds and Kurdistan*.
4. The report in *Ikibin-e Doğru* magazine (Towards 2000) included a section for remarks by provincial officials who would make personal judgements on each tribe such as 'their moral standards do not conform to our Turkish traditions', 'their attachment to the state is not to be trusted', 'they have a tendency to be thieves and pickpockets' or 'their women work in the brothels of Mosul and Baghdad'.
5. Kendal Nezan, in G. Chaliand (ed.), op. cit.
6. History related by Abdülmelik Fırat, member of parliament and grandson of Sheikh Said, *Yeni Demokrasi* newspaper, 11 March 1996.
7. Abdülmelik Fırat, interview with the authors.
8. 1992 Konda poll published in *Milliyet*, 16 August 1995.
9. Statistical Yearbook of Turkey, 1995.
10. Interview with Yalçın Küçük, *Yeni Ülke* newspaper, 17 January 1993.
11. PKK statement faxed to the authors, November 1991.
12. Abdüllah Öcalan, interview with *Hürriyet* newspaper, March 1993.
13. Michael Ignatieff, *Independent on Sunday*, Review, 31 October 1993.
14. Jalal Talabani, interview with the authors, October 1992.
15. The translator was Jean-Pierre Thieck. Interview with the authors, May 1989.
16. Speech reported by most Turkish newspapers, 31 July 1990.
17. *Milliyet*, 4 April 1990.
18. Turgut Özal, interview with the authors, 3 April 1990.
19. *Sabah* newspaper listed the names of all 139 teachers killed in the preceding seven years in a report on 23 November 1994.
20. 30 September 1992.
21. Chief of General Staff Doğan Güreş to *Hürriyet* newspaper, October 1991.

22. Press conference in Vienna, reported by the English-language newspaper, the *Turkish Daily News*, 21 June 1995.
23. Information from an interview by the authors with agents of the US Drugs Enforcement Agency, 1989.
24. Masoud Barzani and Jalal Talabani tried to put the record straight with a joint statement on 25 June 1993: 'The Kurdish movement in general has adhered to honourable means of struggle in the domains of both political activity as well as armed resistance. We have always stayed away from terrorism, indiscriminate violence and immature extremist activities.'
25. The European section of the ERNK, the political wing of the PKK, said on 6 June 1994: 'The present German Government's insistent and unjust enmity towards the Kurdish people is seen most clearly in the Kohl, Kindel and Kanther trio, with the direct support of the genocide of the Kurdish people.'
26. Statement carried by Reuters news agency, 2 February 1996.
27. Gérard Chaliand (ed.), *People Without a Country: The Kurds and Kurdistan.*

CHAPTER 16: THE WOLF AND THE BEAR

1. Gün Kut, interview with the authors, June 1996.
2. Morton Abramowitz, 'Dateline Ankara: Turkey after Özal', in *Foreign Policy*, Summer 1993, p. 169.
3. Gün Kut in Ersanlı Behar (ed.), *Bağımsızlığın İlk Yılları.*
4. *Washington Post*, 1 October 1995.
5. *Milliyet*, 1 July 1996.
6. Ersanlı Behar (ed.), op. cit.

CHAPTER 17: THE ÇILLER PHENOMENON

1. Şirin Tekeli, 'Les femmes, vecteur de la modernisation', in Stéphane Yerasimos (ed.), *Les Turcs.*
2. Tansu Çiller, interview with the authors, January 1994.

CHAPTER 18: A TURKISH-ISLAMIC SYNTHESIS

1. Jean-Pierre Thieck (alias Michel Farrère), *Le Monde*, 13 April 1989.
2. Bülent Ecevit, interview with the authors, June 1995.
3. Altan Gökalp, 'Les Alévi', in Stéphane Yerasimos (ed.), *Les Turcs.*
4. Sibel Eraslan, interview with the authors, December 1995.
5. Yıldırım Aktuna, interview with the authors, June 1996.

CONCLUSION

1. *Sabah* newspaper, 1 September 1996.
2. In answer to the question, 'What is your ethnic origin?', 65 per cent said they felt themselves to be Turks, 21 per cent Muslim Turks, 4 per cent Turkish but with Kurdish parents, 4 per cent Kurdish or Zaza, and 4 per cent said they felt they were Muslims. Konda poll published in *Milliyet* newspaper, 1 March 1993.
3. *Milliyet*, 10 December 1991.
4. Dani Rodrik, cited by Yavuz Canevi, *The Political Economy of Policy Reform.*
5. By 1996, the Economic Co-operation Organization had grown to include Turkey, Iran, Pakistan, Azerbaijan, Turkmenistan, Uzbekistan, the Kyrgyz Republic, Kazakstan, Tajikistan and Afghanistan.

Bibliography

The place of publication, unless otherwise indicated, is London, for English titles; Paris, for French titles; and Istanbul, for Turkish titles.

Ağaoğlu, Adalet *et al.*, *Yine Düşünce Özgürlüğü, Yine Türkiye* (Can, 1995)

Ahmad, Feroz, *The Turkish Experiment in Democracy 1950–1975* (C. Hurst & Co., 1977)

Akçam, Taner, *Türk Ulusal Kimliği ve Ermeni Sorunu* (İletişim, 1994)

Akin, Doğan, *Uçuran Holding* (Bilgi Yayınevi, 1995)

Amicis, Edmondo de, *Constantinople* (Hachette, 1878)

Amnesty International, *Turkey: No Security without Human Rights* (Amnesty International Publications, 1996)

Arcayürek, Cüneyt, *Ku-de-ta* (Bilgi Yayınevi, 1985)

Armstrong, Harold, *Grey Wolf: An Intimate Study of a Dictator* (Arthur Barker, 1932)

Atay, Falih Rıfkı, *The Atatürk I Knew*, trans. Geoffrey Lewis (Istanbul: Isis, 1981)

Aydemir, Şevket Sürreya, *Tek Adam, Mustafa Kemal 1881–1919* (Remzi, 1976)

Barchard, David, *Turkey and the West* (Routledge & Kegan Paul, 1985)

Bardakçı, Murat, *Son Osmanlılar* (Gri Yayın, 1991)

Barlas, Mehmet, *Turgut Özal'in Anıları* (Sabah Kitapları, 1994)

Başgil, Ali Fuat, *La Révolution militaire de 1960 en Turquie* (1963)

Behar, Ersanlı (ed.), *Bağımsızlığın İlk Yılları* (Ankara: T.C. Kültür Bakanlığı, 1994)

Benoist-Méchin, Jacques, *Mustapha Kémal: ou la mort d'un empire* (Albin Michel, 1954)

Beşikçi, İsmail, *Doğu Anadolunun Düzeni* (E. Yayınları, 1969)

Birand, Mehmet Ali, *The Generals' Coup in Turkey: An Inside Story of 12 September* (Brassey's Defence Publishers, 1987)

—— *Shirts of Steel: An Anatomy of the Turkish Armed Forces* (I.B. Tauris, 1991)

—— *Apo ve PKK* (Milliyet Yayınları, 1992)

Birand, Mehmet Ali, Dündar, Can, and Çaplı, Bülent, *12 Mart* (Imge Yayınevi, 1994)

—— *Demirkırat* (Milliyet Yayınları, 1995)

Borak, S., *Atatürk'un Özel Mektupları* (Varlık Yayınevi, 1970)

Bryer, A., and Lowry, H. (eds.), *Continuity and Change in Late Byzantine and Early Ottoman Society* (University of Birmingham and Dumbarton Oaks, 1986)

Cahen, Claude, *Pre-Ottoman Turkey* (Sidgwick & Jackson, 1968)

Çakir, Rüşen, *Ayet ve Slogan* (Metis Yayınları, 1990)

—— *Ne Şeriat ne Demokrasi* (Siyah Beyaz, 1994)

Canevi, Yavuz, *The Political Economy of Policy Reform* (YASED Publication No. 50, 1994)

Cemal, Hasan, *Tank Sesiyle Uyanmak* (Bilgi Yayınları, 1986)

—— *Özal'in Hikayesi* (Bilgi Yayınevi, 1989)

Chaliand, Gérard, *Le Malheur kurde* (Seuil, 1992)

—— (ed.), *People Without a Country: The Kurds and Kurdistan* (Zed Press, 1980)

Çiller, Tansu, *Türkiyem* (Ankara: Prime Minister's Office, 1995)

Çölaşan, Emin, *Turgut Nereden Koşuyor?* (Tekin Yayınevi, 1989)

Davison, Roderic H., *Turkey: A Short History* (Huntingdon, England: Eothen Press, 1981)

Deleon, Jak, *Beyoğlu'nda Beyaz Ruslar 1920–1990* (Istanbul Kütüphanesi, 1990)

Demir, Hülya, and Akar, Rıdvan, *Istanbul'un Son Sürgünleri* (Iletişim, 1994)

Denktaş, Rauf, *Documents and Comments on the Cyprus Dispute* (Presidency of the Turkish Republic of North Cyprus, 1996)

Deringil, Selim, *Turkish Foreign Policy during the Second World War: An Active Neutrality* (Cambridge University Press, 1989)

Devrim, Shirin, *A Turkish Tapestry: The Shakirs of Istanbul* (Quartet Books, 1994)

Dodd, Clement, *The Crisis of Turkish Democracy* (Huntingdon, England: Eothen Press, 1983)

Dündar, Can, *Sarı Zeybek: Atatürk'ün Son 300 Günü* (Milliyet Yayınları, 1995)

Düzgören, Koray, *Kürt Çıkmazı* (Verso, 1994)

Edib, Halide, *Memoirs* (John Murray, 1926)

—— *The Turkish Ordeal* (John Murray, 1928)

Ellison, Grace, *An Englishwoman in Angora* (Hutchinson, 1923)

Erel, Nursun, and Bilge, Ali, *Tansu Çiller'in Siyaset Romanı* (Bilgi Yayınevi, 1994)

Evren, Kenan, *Kenan Evren'in Anıları*, vols. 1–5 (Milliyet Yayınları, 1991)

Fromkin, David, *A Peace to End All Peace: Creating the Modern Middle East 1914–1922* (André Deutsch, 1989)

George-Gaulis, Berthe, *La Nouvelle Turquie* (Librairie Armand Colin, 1924)

Granda, Cemal, *Atatürk'ün Uşaği Idim* (Hürriyet Yayınları, 1973)

Guest, John S., *The Yezidis* (KPI/Routledge, 1987)

Gürsel, Kadri, *Dağdakiler – Bagok'tan Gabar'a 26 Gün* (Metis Yayınları, 1996)

Gürün, Kamuran, *Le Dossier arménien* (Istanbul: Triangle, 1983)

Hale, William, *Turkish Politics and the Military* (Routledge, 1994)

Heper, Metin, *The State Tradition in Turkey* (Beverley, North Humberside: Eothen Press, 1985)

Hirschon, Renée, *Heirs of the Greek Catastrophe: The Social Life of Asia Minor Refugees in Piraeus* (Oxford University Press, 1989)

Hopkirk, Peter, *On Secret Service East of Constantinople* (John Murray, 1994)

Howard, Harry N., *Turkey, the Straits and US Policy* (Johns Hopkins University Press, published in co-operation with the Middle East Institute, Baltimore, 1974)

Hurewitz, J.C., *The Middle East and North Africa in World Politics: A Documentary Record*, Vol. I, *European Expansion 1535–1914* (Yale University Press, New Haven, 1975)

Imset, Ismet, *The PKK* (Ankara: Turkish Daily News Publications, 1992)

Inalcık, Halil, *The Ottoman Empire: The Classical Age 1300–1600* (Weidenfeld & Nicolson, 1973)

Inönü, Erdal, *Anılar ve Düşünceler* (Idea Iletişim, 1996)

Jevakhoff, Alexandre, *Kemal Atatürk, les chemins de l'Occident* (Tallandier, 1989)

Kalpakçıoğlu, Özdemir, *Yunan'dan Dost Olmaz* (Dizgi Matbaacılık, 1994)

Karpat, K.H., *Turkey's Politics: The Transition to a Multi-Party System* (Princeton, N.J.: Princeton University Press, 1959)

Kazançgil, Ali, and Özbudun, Ergün (eds.), *Ataturk: Founder of a Modern State* (C. Hurst & Co., 1981)

Kemal, Yaşar, *Memet my Hawk* (Collins & Harvill Press, 1961)

Kemal, Yachar, *Entretiens avec Alain Bosquet* (Gallimard, 1992)

Keyder, Çaglar, *The Definition of a Peripheral Economy: Turkey 1923–1929* (Cambridge University Press, 1981)

—— *State and Class in Turkey: A Study in Capitalist Development* (London and New York: Verso, 1987)

Kinross, Lord (Patrick Balfour), *Atatürk: The Rebirth of a Nation* (Weidenfeld & Nicolson, 1964)

Kliot, Nurit, *Water Resources and Conflict in the Middle East* (Routledge, 1994)

Koçak, Cemil, *Türkiye'de Milli Şef Dönemi, 1938–1945* (Ankara: Yurt Yayınları, 1986)

Kuniholm, Bruce R., *The Origins of the Cold War in the Near East: Great Power Conflict and Diplomacy in Iran, Turkey and Greece* (Princeton University Press, 1980)

Kunt, Metin, and Woodhead, Christine (eds.), *Süleyman the Magnificent and His Age* (Longman, 1995)

Landau, Jacob M., *Pan-Turkism in Turkey: A Study of Irredentism* (C. Hurst & Co., 1981)

Lewis, Bernard, *The Emergence of Modern Turkey* (Oxford University Press, 1961)

Liman von Sanders, Otto, *Cinq Ans de Turquie* (Payot, 1923)

Loti, Pierre, *Constantinople, or Aziyadé* (T. Werner Laurie, 1927)

Lowry, Jr, Heath W., *The Story behind Ambassador Morgenthau's Story* (Istanbul: Isis Press, 1990)

——— *Studies in Defterology: Ottoman Society in the Fifteenth and Sixteenth Centuries* (Istanbul: Isis, 1992)

Mandelstam, André, *Le Sort de l'Empire ottoman* (Librairie Payot, 1917)

Mango, Andrew, *Turkey: The Challenge of a New Role* (New York: Praeger, 1994)

Mansel, Philip, *Constantinople: City of the World's Desire, 1453–1924* (John Murray, 1995)

McDowall, David, *A Modern History of the Kurds* (I.B. Tauris, 1996)

Montagu, Mary Wortley, *The Turkish Embassy Letters* (Virago, 1994)

Morgan, David, *The Mongols* (Oxford: Blackwell, 1986)

Mourad, Kenizé, *De la part de la Princesse morte* (Robert Laffont, 1987)

Mumcu, Ahmet, Güneş, Ihsan, and Bilim, Cahit, *Liseler için Tarih*, vols. 1–3 (Inkilap Kitabevi, 1995)

Mumcu, Uğur, *Kürt-Islam Ayaklanması* (Tekin Yayınevi, 1991)

Öcalan, Abdüllah, *PKK 5. Kongresi'ne sunulan Politik Rapor* (Güneş Ülkesi Yayıncılık, 1995)

Oranlı, Z., *Hitherto unpublished recollections of Atatürk by Ali Metin, his orderly* (Alkan Matbaası, 1967)

Orga, Irfan, *Portrait of a Turkish Family* (Michael Joseph, 1950)

Orga, Irfan and Margerete, *Atatürk* (Michael Joseph, 1962)

Özal, Turgut, *La Turquie en Europe* (Plon, 1988)

Palmer, Alan, *The Decline and Fall of the Ottoman Empire* (John Murray, 1992)

Perinçek, Dogu (ed.), *Mustafa Kemal'in Eskişehir-Izmir Konuşmaları 1923* (Kaynak Yayınları, 1993)

Picard, Elizabeth, *La Question kurde* (Editions Complexe, 1991)

Robins, Philip, *Turkey and the Middle East* (Royal Institute of International Affairs, 1991)

Roux, Jean-Paul, *Histoire des Turcs* (Fayard, 1972)

Rubin, Barry, *Istanbul Intrigues: Espionage, Sabotage and Diplomatic Treachery in the Spy Capital of World War II* (New York: Pharas Books, 1992)

Rugman, Jonathan, *Atatürk's Children* (Cassell, 1996)

Ryan, Sir Andrew, *The Last of the Dragomans* (Geoffrey Bles, 1951)

Sabancı, Sakip, *This is my Life* (Istanbul: World of Information, 1985)

Savant, Jean, *La Turquie d'Ismet Inönü* (Fernand Soriot, 1944)

Shaw, Stanford J., and Ezel Kural, *History of the Ottoman Empire and Modern Turkey*, Vol. I, *Empire of the Gazis* (Cambridge University Press, 1976)

——— *History of the Ottoman Empire and Modern Turkey*, Vol. II, *Reform, Revolution and Republic* (Cambridge University Press, 1977)

Soysal, Ismail, *Les Relations politiques turco-françaises* (Istanbul: Isis, 1985)

——— (ed.), *Turkish Straits: New Problems, New Solutions* (Istanbul: Isis, 1995)

Su, Mükerrem K., and Mumcu, Ahmet, *Türkiye Cumhuriyeti Inkilap Tarihi ve Atatürkçülük* (Milli Eğitim Basımevi, 1995)

Thieck, Jean-Pierre (Michel Farrère), ed. Gilles Kepel, *Passion d'Orient* (Karthala, 1992)

Toprak, Binnaz, *Islam and Political Development in Turkey* (Leiden: E.J. Brill, 1981)

Torumtay, Necip, *Orgeneral Torumtay'in Anıları* (Milliyet Yayınları, 1994)

Turgut, Hulusi, *Şahinlerin Dansı: Türkeş'in Anıları* (ABC, 1995)

Ulugay, Osman, *Kim Kazandı, Kim Kaybetti* (Bilgi Yayınevi, 1987)

Van Bruinessen, Martin, *Agha, Shaikh and State: The Social and Political Structures of Kurdistan* (Zed Press, 1982)

Vaner, Semih (ed.), *Istanbul, gloire et dérives* (Editions Autrement, 1993)

Volkan, Vamik D., and Itzkowitz, Norman, *The Immortal Atatürk: A Psychobiography* (University of Chicago Press, 1984)

Walker, Christopher, *Armenia: The Survival of a Nation* (Croom Helm, 1980)

Weiker, Walter F., *The Turkish Revolution 1960–1961: Aspects of Military Politics* (Brookings Institution, Washington, 1963)

Wheatcroft, Andrew, *The Ottomans* (Viking, 1993)

Winrow, Gareth, *Turkey in post-Soviet Central Asia* (Royal Institute of International Affairs)

Yalçin, Soner, *Hangi Erbakan* (Basak Yayınları, 1993)

Yerasimos, Stéphane (ed.), *Istanbul 1914–1923, Capitale d'un monde illusoire ou l'agonie des vieux empires* (Editions Autrement, 1992)

—— *Les Turcs* (Editions Autrement, 1994)

Zana, Mehdi, *La Prison no. 5: Onze ans dans les geôles turques* (Arléa, 1995)

Zürcher, Erik J., *The Unionist Faction: The Role of the Committee of Union and Progress in the Turkish National Movement* (Leiden: E.J. Brill, 1984)

—— *Modern Turkey* (I.B. Tauris, 1995)

Index